NEGOTIATING RELIEF

MICHELE ACUTO

(*editor*)

Negotiating Relief

The Politics of Humanitarian Space

HURST & COMPANY, LONDON

First published in the United Kingdom in 2014 by
C. Hurst & Co. (Publishers) Ltd.,
41 Great Russell Street, London, WC1B 3PL
© Michele Acuto and the Contributors, 2014
All rights reserved.

Distributed in the United States, Canada and Latin America by
Oxford University Press, 198 Madison Avenue, New York, NY 10016,
United States of America.

Printed in India

The right of Michele Acuto and the Contributors to be identified as the
authors of this publication is asserted by them in accordance with the
Copyright, Designs and Patents Act, 1988.

A Cataloguing-in-Publication data record for this book
is available from the British Library.

ISBNs: 9781849042383 (hardback)
9781849042666 (paperback)

www.hurstpublishers.com

This book is printed using paper from registered sustainable
and managed sources.

CONTENTS

CONTENTS

CONTENTS

NOTES ON THE CONTRIBUTORS

Michele Acuto is Senior Lecturer in the Department of Science, Technology, Engineering and Public Policy (STEaPP) at University College London, and Stephen Barter Research Fellow in the Institute of Science, Innovation and Society at the University of Oxford. He was previously Fellow of the Center on Public Diplomacy at the University of Southern California, contributing editor for the *Diplomatic Courier*, independent consultant on the Kimberley Process and JPO at the International Campaign to Ban Landmines. He taught at the University of Canberra and the Australian National University, where most of the work for this volume was undertaken at the Asia-Pacific College of Diplomacy. He is the author of *The Urban Link* (2013) and editor of *Global City Challenges* (2013).

Alex J. Bellamy is Professor of International Security at the Griffith Asia Institute/Centre for Governance and Public Policy, Griffith University, and co-editor of the journal *Global Responsibility to Protect*. From 2002–2010 he was Lecturer and then Professor of International Relations and Executive Director of the Asia-Pacific Centre for the Responsibility to Protect at the University of Queensland. He was previously Lecturer in Defence Studies at King's College London. He has also served as co-chair of the CSCAP Study Group on the Responsibility to Protect, a member of a readers group for the UNDP and as a member of the UN Emergency Peace Service Working Group.

Roland Bleiker is Professor of International Relations at the University of Queensland. His publications include *Popular Dissent, Human Agency* *and Global Politics* (2000); *Divided Korea: Toward a Culture of Reconciliation* (2005); and *Aesthetics and World Politics* (2009). He is currently working with Emma Hutchinson and David Campbell on an ARC-funded project that examines how images shape responses to humanitarian crises.

Cynthia Brassard-Boudreau is the Program Coordinator of the Center for International Policy Studies at the University of Ottawa. She has worked for the Department of Foreign Affairs and International Trade Canada as a junior advisor in the West and Central Africa division and in the Canadian Embassy in Thailand, as well as a research assistant in the Democracy division. She holds a Master's degree from the Graduate School of Public and International Affairs, University of Ottawa. Her major research paper focused on the security of aid workers in Afghanistan.

David Campbell is a scholar, photography consultant and multimedia producer affiliated with Durham University and the University of Queensland, where he is Honorary Professor. Campbell has authored/edited six books and some fifty academic articles/essays that examine how atrocity, famine, war and "Africa" are represented, how photographs function to visualise the global landscape, and how US foreign policy and wars in Bosnia and Iraq have been produced. He runs a blog on photography, multimedia and politics: http://www.david-campbell.org/.

David Chandler is Professor of International Relations at the Centre for the Study of Democracy, University of Westminster, a founding editor of the *Journal of Intervention and Statebuilding* and a regular media commentator. His research focus is on new forms of international intervention and regulation, particularly those projected in the therapeutic language of ethical foreign policy, the rule of law, human security, empowerment, democratisation, state capacity-building, human rights, civil society development, anti-corruption and transparency, country "ownership," post-conditionality, and "pro-poor" development. He is the author of a number of monographs, including *Empire in Denial: The Politics of State-Building* (2006); *Constructing Global Civil Society* (2004, 2005); *From Kosovo to Kabul (and Beyond): Human Rights and International Intervention* (2002, 2006); and *Bosnia: Faking Democracy after Dayton* (1999, 2000).

NOTES ON THE CONTRIBUTORS

Sarah Collinson is Research Associate and former Research Fellow of the Humanitarian Policy Group at the Overseas Development Institute. Her current research is focused on the challenges of humanitarian action in difficult political and security environments. It includes work on trends affecting humanitarian space and a joint project with Professor Mark Duffield on risk management and aid culture in Sudan and Afghanistan. She has previously held senior research and policy positions at Chatham House and ActionAid.

Mathew J. Davies is Senior Tutor and Lecturer in the Graduate Studies in International Affairs Programme of the Department of International Relations, School of International, Political and Strategic Studies, Australian National University. He also collaborates with the ANU Asia-Pacific College of Diplomacy, coordinating a professional training program for African diplomats. His research focuses on the way in which human rights are socialised in international politics, with a particular interest in regional organisations and in the relationship between humanitarianism and International Relations theory. He has published on the UN Human Rights system as well as the nature of human rights socialisation patterns displayed by the European Union.

Antonio Donini is Senior Researcher at the Feinstein International Center, Tufts University. From 2002 to 2004 he was a Visiting Senior Fellow at the Watson Institute for International Studies at Brown University. He has worked for twenty-six years in the United Nations in research, evaluation and humanitarian capacities. His last post was as Director of the UN Office for the Coordination of Humanitarian Assistance to Afghanistan (1999–2002), and previously as chief of the Lessons Learned Unit at OCHA. He has published widely on evaluation, humanitarian and UN reform issues. He co-edited the volume *Nation-Building Unraveled? Aid, Peace, and Justice in Afghanistan* (2004) as well as several articles exploring the implications of the crises in Afghanistan and Iraq for the future of humanitarian action.

Conor Foley is a columnist for *The Guardian*, and research fellow at the Human Rights Law Centre at the University of Nottingham. He worked for many years as a humanitarian worker, serving for a variety of aid organisations, including Liberty, Amnesty International and the UN

High Commissioner for Refugees (UNHCR), in Kosovo, Afghanistan, Colombia, Sri Lanka, Indonesia and Bosnia-Herzegovina. Conor's books include *Combating Torture* (2003), which was published by the Human Rights Centre at the University of Essex and the UK Foreign and Commonwealth Office, and *A Guide to Property Law in Afghanistan* (2005), which was published by the Norwegian Refugee Council and UNHCR. He currently lives and works in Brazil.

Don Hubert is Associate Professor at the Graduate School of Public and International Affairs, University of Ottawa. For nearly a decade, he led policy development on Canada's human security agenda within the Department of Foreign Affairs. More recently he was Director of the Human Security Division, with previous positions in Policy Planning, as Coordinator of Humanitarian Affairs, and as Deputy to the Chair of the Kimberley Process. He has held post-doctoral positions at the Centre for Foreign Policy Studies at Dalhousie University and the Humanitarianism and War Project at Brown University, was a consultant for the International Commission on Intervention and State Sovereignty, and has taught at the School of International Affairs at Carleton University.

Emma Hutchinson is a Postdoctoral Research Fellow in the School of Political Science and International Studies at the University of Queensland. During 2010 she was the Australian European University Institute Postdoctoral Fellow at the European University Institute, Florence. Her current research questions the role that trauma and emotions play in constituting world politics. Her work has appeared in *International Relations, Review of International Studies, European Journal of Social Theory, Global Society* and other outlets.

Jennifer Hyndman is Professor in the Departments of Social Science and Geography, and is Associate Director for Research in the Centre for Refugee Studies, at York University. Her research focuses on conflict and related human displacement, humanitarian emergencies, as well as refugee resettlement in Canada. She was previously Associate Professor at Simon Fraser University, where she received the President's Award for Teaching Excellence in 2006, Professor at Syracuse University, adjunct Professor at the Norwegian University of Science & Technology, as well as Assistant Professor at Arizona State University and SSHRC Postdoctoral Fellow at York University. She has also worked for United Nations High Commissioner for Refugees in Somalia as well as for CARE International in northern Kenya.

Janaka Jayawickrama is a Senior Lecturer at Northumbria University. Trained in India, the United States and the United Kingdom, Janaka draws his strength from the tradition of anthropology as well as ancient Eastern philosophies. Since 1994, he has been conducting research, education and evaluation activities in Asia, Africa, Europe and the Middle East. Widely published in the areas of disaster and conflict mental health, Janaka closely works with the United Nations system, national governments and community-based organisations. Janaka has conducted projects on mental health in disasters and conflicts, HIV/AIDS, refugee care and protection, damage assessment of disasters, displacement, applied peace building, post-conflict rehabilitation and humanitarian assistance.

Marie Juul Petersen is a postdoctoral researcher at the Danish Institute for Human Rights in Copenhagen. She was previously postdoctoral researcher at the Danish Institute for International Studies, and PhD Scholar at the University of Copenhagen. She also served as Project Coordinator for the Danish Institute for Human Rights and as Associate Programme Officer for Save the Children Denmark in Guatemala. She is the author of *For Humanity or for the Umma? Aid and Islam in International Muslim NGOs*, forthcoming for Hurst & Co.

William Maley is Professor and Director of the Asia-Pacific College of Diplomacy at the Australian National University. He is a Member of the Order of Australia (AM), and a Fellow of the Academy of the Social Sciences in Australia (FASSA) and previously taught for many years in the School of Politics, University College, University of New South Wales, Australian Defence Force Academy. He is author of *Rescuing Afghanistan* (2006), and *The Afghanistan Wars* (2002, 2nd edn 2009); edited *Fundamentalism Reborn? Afghanistan and the Taliban* (1998, 2nd edn 2001); and co-edited *From Civil Strife to Civil Society: Civil and Military Responsibilities in Disrupted States* (2003) and *Global Governance and Diplomacy: Worlds Apart?* (2008).

Ken Menkhaus is Professor of Political Science at Davidson College, where he has taught since 1991. He received his PhD in International

Studies as Fulbright Scholar in 1989 from the University of South Carolina. In 1993–1994, he served as special political advisor in the UN Operation in Somalia, and in 2010–2011 was visiting scholar at the US Army Strategic Studies Institute. He regularly serves as a consultant for the UN, US government, NGOs and policy research institutes, and has provided expert testimony on five occasions before US Congressional subcommittees. He is author of over fifty articles, book chapters and monographs, including *Somalia: State Collapse and the Threat of Terrorism* (2004). He has been interviewed on BBC, CNN, FOX, NPR, the Voice of America and several other media on the crisis in Somalia.

Kurt Mills is Senior Lecturer in Politics in the School of Social and Political Sciences at the University of Glasgow, which he joined in 2004. He received his BA from Hampshire College (1988), and MA (1990) and PhD (1995) from the University of Notre Dame, and previously taught at The American University in Cairo, Mount Holyoke College, James Madison University, and Gettysburg College, and served as the Assistant Director of the Five College Program in Peace and World Security Studies at Hampshire College. His main teaching and research interests are in the areas of international organizations, human rights, refugees, and humanitarianism.

Geoff O'Brien is a Senior Lecturer in environmental management, disaster management and sustainable development at Northumbria University. His research interests are focused on resilient communities and climate adaptation. Geoff was involved in the Netherlands Climate Assistance Programme (NCAP) that worked with fifteen countries to develop climate change adaptation strategies. He is involved in public life and serves as a city councillor for Newcastle-upon-Tyne. He was a Director of New Deal for Communities, a ten-year programme that worked with disadvantaged communities within the city. He currently serves as a trustee of Centre West, a charity that is continuing the work of the New Deal.

Phil O'Keefe is Professor of Economic Development and Environmental Management at Northumbria University. Phil's research interests focus on the political economy of environmental issues with particular reference to Eastern and Southern Africa. He has written extensively on environmental risk and hazard which, over the last fifteen years, has increasingly focused on the delivery of humanitarian assistance after natural disasters and in complex emergencies. He is actively involved in broader debates about the production of nature, sustainability, vulnerability and poverty alleviation, contributing to major global policy documents as well as polemically challenging what this policy means in practice.

Heather M. Roff is Visiting Assistant Professor at the Josef Korbel School of International Studies at the University of Denver and a Research Associate at the Eisenhower Center for Space and Defense Studies at the United States Air Force Academy. She specialises in political theory and international relations, specifically international ethics. She has held positions at the University of Waterloo, the United States Air Force Academy and the University of Colorado at Boulder. Her research interests include Kant's moral and political philosophy, humanitarian intervention, the Responsibility to Protect, global governance and justice and the ethics of cyber and robotic warfare.

Mark Schuller is Assistant Professor of African-American Studies and Anthropology at York College, the City University of New York. His insights have appeared in public media, including the *Huffington Post, Counterpunch, Common Dreams* and the Center for International Policy, and media interviews, including the BBC, Al Jazeera and Democracy Now! He has published a half dozen peer-reviewed articles and two book chapters about Haiti, in addition to several online articles. He co-edited *Capitalizing on Catastrophe: Neoliberal Strategies in Disaster Reconstruction* (2008) and co-directed/co-produced the documentary *Poto Mitan: Haitian Women, Pillars of the Global Economy* (2009). He also co-edited *Homing Devices: the Poor as Targets of Public Housing Policy and Practice* (2006). He chairs the Society for Applied Anthropology's Human Rights and Social Justice Committee and is active in many grassroots efforts, including earthquake response.

Fiona Terry is an independent researcher who recently completed studies for the International Committee of the Red Cross in Sudan and Afghanistan, and was previously Director of Research at Doctors Without Borders/Médecins Sans Frontières (MSF) in Paris. She holds a doctorate in international relations from the Australian National University, and is the author of *Condemned to Repeat? The Paradox of Humanitarian Action* (2002), which won the 2006 Grawemeyer Award for Ideas Improving World Order.

Andrea Edoardo Varisco is a PhD researcher at the Post-War Reconstruction and Development Unit of the University of York, currently involved in the ESRC/DFID project "The influence of DFID-Sponsored State Building-Oriented Research on British Policy in Fragile, Post-Conflict Environments." He holds a Master in International Affairs from the Australian National University, a specialisation in Peace and Conflict Studies from the International Peace Research Institute, Oslo and a Master's Degree in Politics and Comparative Institutions from the University of Milan. He previously worked for the United Nations Department for Disarmament Affairs, as well as at the Flemish Peace Institute, the Italian Observatory on Arms Trade and the European Foundation for Democracy.

Thomas G. Weiss is Presidential Professor of Political Science at the Graduate Center and Director of the Ralph Bunche Institute for International Studies at the City University of New York. Past President of the International Studies Association (2009–2010) and Past Chair of the Academic Council on the UN System (2006–2009), he was the Research Director of the International Commission on Intervention and State Sovereignty. He has written or edited some forty books and 175 articles and book chapters. His latest volumes are *What's Wrong with the United Nations and How to Fix It* (2009); *UN Ideas That Changed the World* (2009 with Richard Jolly and Louis Emmerij); *Global Governance and the UN: An Unfinished Journey* (2010 with Ramesh Thakur); *Humanitarianism Contested* (2011 with Michael Barnett); and *Thinking about Global Governance: Why People and Ideas Matter* (2011).

Fabrice Weissman is the Director of the Centre de Réflexions sur l'Action et les Savoirs Humanitaires (CRASH) hosted by the Médecins Sans Frontières Foundation (Paris). Since 1995, he has been alternating field missions and research work on humanitarian action. He has published several articles and books, including *Humanitarian Negotiations Revealed. The Experience of MSF* (with Claire Magone and Michaël Neuman, 2011).

NOTES ON THE CONTRIBUTORS

Paul Zeccola works as humanitarian officer at AusAID, and has recently completed a PhD in the Department of Political and Social Change of the Australian National University. His research interests are on community resilience and the impact of local and foreign humanitarian assistance in Aceh, Indonesia. He obtained his BA from La Trobe University (2000) and the University of Sydney (2004), and has previously worked extensively in Aceh including as a delegate for Peace Brigades International (2001–2002 and 2005) and as Protection Advisor for the International Rescue Committee (2005–2006).

EDITOR'S ACKNOWLEDGEMENTS

This project began a few years ago in the classrooms of the Australian National University's Graduate Studies in International Affairs programme, and in particular in my interaction with two years of extremely qualified, challenging and convivial students that partook in a course, then called International Humanitarian Assistance, which sought to problematise the contemporary bases of humanitarianism. It was from the delightful partnership with the somewhat unconventional, eccentric and critical take of its core convenor, Raymond Apthorpe, that this collection's "think plural" rationale sprang. Some reflections from that course, as the chapters by Matt Davies and Andrea Varisco demonstrate, made it into this final version. Yet, as I would like to think, the collaborative, critical and experience-based spirit of those seminars hovers through the pages of *Negotiating Relief*. My thanks to those whom I had the pleasure to work with in that adventure, as well as more recently to Bill Maley, Pauline Kerr, Fiona Terry, Antonio Donini and Hugo Slim for exchanging ideas, opinions and suggestions on how to best stir this eclectic group in a productive direction. Likewise, this project would never have seen the light of day without the trust of Hurst's managing director Michael Dwyer. A necessary acknowledgement should also be paid to the *Journal of Humanitarian Assistance* and its editors, where the chapters by Weissman as well as Hubert and Brassard-Boudreau first appeared. Finally, the collection would have not taken the prolific path it found without the charitable, some would say "humanitarian" availability and patience of all of the authors who decided to contribute their extensive expertise in this field through a snippet of their work. To all, my appreciation.

Michele Acuto   October 2011

PREFACE

THE POLITICS OF HUMANITARIAN SPACE

Thomas G. Weiss

This collection permits me to look back on the last two decades. The operational space within which humanitarians manoeuvre is a helpful way to examine the evolving tactics of aid agencies that seek to rescue strangers caught in the cross-hairs of violence and war. I define "humanitarian space" as the physical arena within which relief and protection can be effectively and safely provided to victims of armed conflict. Humanitarian action (both succour and protection) is not a modern phenomenon. Kith and kin have long sought to extend helping hands, symbolised by the Biblical tale of the Good Samaritan, but Michael Barnett's "the empire of humanity," or the institutionalisation of such action, is a creation in the last century and a half.[1] Elsewhere I have argued for a longer historical perspective, but this essay assesses "space" in the post-Cold War era and more specifically the pluses and minuses of the expanded area within which aid personnel operate, as well as their second thoughts about doing so. In particular, it confronts the frustrations of those pursuing the humanitarian imperative—trying to satisfy humanitarian needs, whenever and wherever they arise, a territory where sometimes even "angels fear to tread." The contradictions between principles and politics, between rhetoric and reality, explain "humanitarianism contested."[2]

Creating "humanitarian space"

The International Committee of the Red Cross (ICRC) is the oldest humanitarian agency and often considered the gold standard of even-handed assistance and protection.[3] In his *desiderata*, Jean Pictet identified seven defining principles, with four as the core:[4] humanity, impartiality, neutrality and independence. The ICRC derived them from decades of experience about which principles best facilitated its work—that is, which created the most space within which they could help war victims with consent from political authorities. Many humanitarians look upon principles as a sacrosanct part of their identity, but the origin is not ideological but practical—guidance about how best to reach people in need. If aid agencies were perceived by combatants as partial, allied with the opposing side, or having a vested interest in outcomes, they had difficulties in finding the necessary room to operate. When principles were respected, a sanctuary opened for victims and aid workers within which assistance and protection were available.

The ICRC and like-minded organisations go so far as to excommunicate those who depart from their principles and claim to be "humanitarians." As a consequentialist, I am agnostic and calculate the value of traditional principles—championing them when they work, setting them aside when they do not. An essential element in this approach is abandoning the fool's errand that humanitarian organisations can operate independently of political agendas.[5] In fact, most aid agencies do not act according to black-and-white distinctions. Otherwise, there would be few actors in humanitarian space.

During the Cold War, the humanitarian United Nations was essentially missing in action in civil wars. The UN system—with the exception of UNICEF because the welfare of women and children was supposedly apolitical—avoided non-state actors (armed opposition and belligerents) because interacting with them would have implied legal recognition, anathema to many member states. A handful of non-governmental organisations (NGOs) deployed cross-border operations, but their resources were limited. Among other things, the Cold War's end meant that the United Nations could call upon its members to authorise military force to create space for humanitarian action and to protect civilians. Between international efforts in 1991 on behalf of the Kurds and in 2011 to create a no-fly zone in Libya, a notable development in world politics was "the responsibility to protect" (R2P), the title of the 2001 report from the International Commission on Intervention and State Sovereignty (ICISS).[6] With the exception of Raphael Lemkin's efforts and the 1948 Genocide Convention, no idea moved faster or further in the international normative arena, including R2P's adoption at the UN's 2005 World Summit.[7] Other chapters detail contingent sovereignty—after centuries of largely looking the other way, it no longer provides a licence for mass atrocities. Here I stress that military force expanded dramatically the space for civilian humanitarians. Traditionally they had operated with consent from political authorities, but that was no longer a *sine qua non*. As a result, many NGO and UN agencies engaged in activities to protect and succour populations in war zones where earlier the ICRC had a virtual monopoly. The fact that few if any war zones today are off-limits is evidence of expanding not shrinking space for humanitarians.

Implications for the humanitarian enterprise

The last two decades have witnessed an increase in the scope, scale and danger of humanitarian enterprise.[8] The use of military force to open space for human protection purposes also has politicised civilian-military interactions.[9] The crux of controversy among humanitarians is the extent to which, reverting to my definition, relief and protection have been effectively and safely provided to victims of armed conflict.

To start, the sheer growth in organisational numbers is striking.[10] There are at least 2,500 NGOs in the business, with about 260 being serious players.[11] Already by 2001 the half-a-dozen or so largest NGOs controlled between $2.5 billion and $3 billion, about half of global humanitarian assistance.[12] Global longitudinal data are lacking,[13] but a detailed survey of US-based private voluntary agencies suggests considerable growth over the last seventy-five years. Shortly after the start of the Second World War, the number of US-based organisations rose to 387 (from 240), but the numbers dropped to 103 in 1946 and sixty in 1948. They rose steadily thereafter and reached 543 in 2005. The growth was especially dramatic from 1986 to 1994 when the number increased from 178 to 506.[14]

Not only has the total number increased but so too have the funds and market share of the largest. Specific emergencies account for spikes, and the numbers of people working in the NGO sector grew by 91 per cent from 1997 to 2005. Overall the international humanitarian system (including the UN system and the ICRC) experienced a 77 per cent surge in personnel.[15]

The Office of the UN High Commissioner for Refugees (UNHCR) was created to help displaced persons, but the bulk of UN agencies were to foster development.[16] However, they too are increasingly involved in relief, including the United Nations Development Programme and the World Bank, both of which have steadily enlarged programming for disasters. Until recently other UN specialised agencies had virtually non-existent disaster programmes but also have decided to pursue available funding. Organisations that were once dedicated to relief expanded into other domains, moving "upstream" (helping in the midst of war) and "downstream" (post-conflict peace-building and ultimately development). As a result, few UN organisations or NGOs are indifferent about creating more humanitarian space or the "scramble" for funds and turf.[17]

Another indicator of growth is the number of international and regional organisations whose primary responsibility is coordination, including the European Community Humanitarian Aid Office, the UN's Inter-Agency Standing Committee (IASC) and the Office for the Coordination of Humanitarian Affairs. The same phenomenon exists for NGOs in the United States and Europe, including InterAction in Washington, DC, the International Council for Voluntary Action and Emergency Committee for Humanitarian Response in Geneva and Voluntary Organisations in Cooperation in Emergencies in Brussels.

States, for-profit disaster firms, businesses and foundations are also increasingly prominent contributors to humanitarian action. More and more governments are responding to disasters of all sorts. Whereas sixteen states pledged their support to Bosnia in the mid-1990s, most from the West, a more diverse group of seventy-three attended the 2003 pledging conference in Madrid for Iraq, and ninety-two responded to the December 2004 tsunami. One overview summarised, "From as few as a dozen government financiers just over a decade ago, it is now commonplace to see 50 or 60 donor governments supporting a humanitarian response."[18]

Such non-Western donors as China, Saudi Arabia and India have accounted for up to 12 per cent of official humanitarian assistance in a given year; and their influence in certain crises—for example, Afghanistan or Palestine—is significant. Most countries not members of the Organization for Economic Co-operation and Development's Development Assistance Committee (OECD/DAC) concentrate on immediate neighbours; and the bulk of such assistance (over 90 per cent or almost $1 billion in 2008) emanates from the Gulf states. In fact, Saudi Arabia accounted for three-quarters of the non-OECD/DAC sum and was the third largest humanitarian donor that year.[19] Along with the United Arab Emirates and Kuwait, these states now contribute larger humanitarian resources than some of the smaller Western countries. We know little about whether non-traditional donors follow the major Western states in their rationales for aid disbursements, their priorities and policy options or their choices for response channels.[20] But they resemble their OECD counterparts in preferring bilateral aid to increase influence. Moreover, NGOs are now major players—for instance, expenditures by Médecins Sans Frontières (MSF) in 2007 were larger than Saudi Arabia's while those by World Vision and Caritas outstripped all but four DAC donor countries.[21]

Nonetheless, the international humanitarian system remains essentially a North American and Western European enterprise, accounting for about $11 billion of the total of just over $12 billion of official humanitarian assistance in 2008.[22] In short, "It works wherever it can in international society but is not really owned by all of international society."[23] Private contributions have increased, but the growth in official (governmental) assistance has been most impressive. Between 1990 and 2000 aid levels rose nearly threefold, from $2.1 billion to $5.9 billion—and in 2005–2006 amounted to over $10 billion.[24] In the last year for which data are available, 2008, the best "guesstimate" was a total of some $18 billion, up about $3 billion from the previous year.[25]

How many humanitarian aid workers are there? Observers hazard a guess of 200,000 worldwide. But Peter Walker and Catherine Russ humbly confess: "We have no idea what size this population is." Extrapolating from solid Oxfam data, they estimate some 30,000 humanitarian professionals (both local and expatriate).[26] The large increase in the size, scope and number of participants demonstrates the extent to which such space has grown not contracted; but simultaneously aid workers have been exposed to more life-threatening attacks, which some believe indicates shrinking space.[27] In the last decade alone over 200 civilian UN staff (that is, not including military peacekeepers whose fatalities have been fewer) died in almost fifty countries, and another 300 were taken hostage. The ICRC has lost some fifty staff. One study of the impact of firearms on aid workers notes that "between July 2003 and July 2004 at least 100 civilian UN and NGO personnel died due to targeted violence."[28] Afghanistan and Iraq are in a category by themselves for fatalities. In Afghanistan, at least twenty-six aid-agency staff died in 2004.[29] The intrepid MSF decided that enough was enough and withdrew after the murder of five staff. Afterwards, three insurgents dressed as police scaled a fence at a guesthouse in northern Afghanistan and killed five UN staff in a two-hour gun battle. August 2010 witnessed the grisly execution of ten medical personnel, seven years after the cowardly assaults in Iraq that shook humanitarians to the core: the attack on UN headquarters in Baghdad with twenty-two fatalities, including the charismatic head of the mission, Sergio Vieira de Mello; and six weeks later, a car bomb delivered in a white ambulance painted with a red-crescent symbol killed fifteen at the ICRC's country headquarters.

And the list goes on. After the death of seventeen staff in a 2007 attack on headquarters in Algiers, the former Algerian foreign minister and veteran UN handyman Lakhdar Brahimi chaired the Independent Panel on Safety and Security of United Nations Personnel and Premises with a leitmotif: the UN blue flag no longer provides safety within humanitarian space,[30] especially in war-torn societies with Muslim majorities where the UN is viewed as serving the interests of the major powers while doing little to enforce long-standing resolutions in favour of Palestinians against Israel.

The "new wars" label is overused and misleading in some ways[31]— especially the suggestion that civilians fared better in earlier wars—but the vulnerability of aid workers suggests some relevance.[32] The doubling of attacks and fatalities between 1997 and 2005 also reflected the presence of more aid workers than ever in the additional humanitarian space—further evidence of expansion that contradicts conventional wisdom.[33] Specifically, "the annual number of victims per 10,000 aid workers in the field averaged five in the first half of the period and six in the second." It seems that NGOs were most likely to be targeted, but with considerable variation. A 2009 update of these statistics found that attacks had increased sharply over 2006–2008—almost a doubling in deaths and kidnappings from the previous three years—with rates being especially bad for NGO expatriate staff and UN local contractors. Three conflicts (Darfur, Afghanistan and Somalia) accounted for some 60 per cent of the violence and victims.[34] Moreover, a growing percentage of personnel operating within humanitarian space are local recruits. To the extent that Western aid workers remove or distance themselves, the distribution of risk might be shifting towards local hires. The "performance" value of violent attacks on humanitarians has a currency over and above any practical pay-off.[35] In any case, aid personnel can no longer assume (if they ever could) that their good intentions shield them.[36]

Two reactions

Weighing the costs and benefits of more room in which to operate has led humanitarians to one of two stances: either to acknowledge the politicisation of humanitarian action, become consequentialists and make the best of it (my preference); or to long for the "golden years" of humanitarianism. Although human beings are not becoming less cruel, there is evidence of running greater risks to help others. There are more expectations, more promises and more possibilities to protect lives at risk. There is a growing acceptance of the legitimacy of humanitarian action and its prominence on the global agenda. Funding has skyrocketed. There are an increasing number of organisations, states and agencies dedicated to the idea of relieving the needless suffering of afflicted peoples. There exists a global positioning system that allows relief to be unleashed when and if summoned. However, a drearier worldview imagines humanitarianism as entering a new dark ages, singling out the kinds of dilemmas and dangers confronted by those who help afflicted populations. Again the meaning of "effectively and safely provided" enters the conversation. Some humanitarians believe that being accompanied by or working alongside states and other interested parties compromises their ability to act. They nostalgically covet their former humanitarian space, a pocket that supposedly provided breathing room in an otherwise suffocating environment. Should humanitarians give aid purely on the basis of need and not worry about the effects? Should they provide aid unconditionally? What if doing so means feeding the armies, militias and killers who clearly benefit from terrorising civilian populations? At what point should aid workers withdraw either to exert pressure or because conditions were too dangerous? What if aid is no more than a band-aid? Should humanitarianism address the causes of the suffering?

Even stalwart defenders of traditional humanitarianism concede that the moral necessity of their action is no longer self-evident. David Rieff, for one, has pivoted 180 degrees and recommends a return to the "good old days," when the standard operating procedures reflected the principles of the ICRC and its offshoot, MSF.[37] However, it is worth repeating Ian Smillie's view that respect for such principles has always been "patchy, weak or simply non-existent,"[38] and Hugo Slim's denial "that things used to be much better. Even a brief glance at humanitarian history shows this to be a rather eccentric view."[39] Since the so-called golden years, humanitarians have benefited from additional resources and been freer to help, with the United Nations able to act sometimes as its founders had intended in creating the space for humanitarians to do what they do—help the helpless. Humanitarians can't have it both ways. They have more resources and staff working in more arenas than previously, along with heightened politicisation and danger. There is no alternative to humanitarians entering the political fray.

Conclusion

If I were unkind, I would argue that those uncomfortable with the contemporary political temperature should stay out of the humanitarian kitchen. It is not going to get cooler or easier. Politics—including double standards and inconsistencies—are a fact of humanitarian or any other life. Modesty is a virtue for both aid workers and social scientists. Many would have us believe in the humanitarian "imperative," the obligation to treat affected populations similarly and react to crises consistently; but such a notion flies in the face of politics, which consists of drawing lines as well as weighing options and available resources in order to make tough decisions about doing the greatest good or the least harm. A more accurate description of likely efforts to save strangers is the humanitarian "impulse"—sometimes we can act and sometimes we cannot.[40] Humanitarian action is desirable, not obligatory. The humanitarian impulse is permissive; the humanitarian imperative would be peremptory. Whatever the morality and law affecting humanitarian space, politics and military capacity ultimately are more important in determining when, where, why and how to protect and assist affected populations.[41] The

PREFACE

2011 international action in Libya was unusual in that moral, legal, political and military dimensions came together under the R2P rubric.[42] However shocking to the conscience a particular emergency and however hard or soft the applicable public international law, when political will and a military capacity exist, humanitarian space will open in which war victims will receive relief and protection.

INTRODUCTION

HUMANITARIAN PUZZLES

Michele Acuto

Humanitarianism is no doubt a fast emerging magnet of academic discussion and practitioner engagement. In the past few decades both scholarly analysis and media attention concerned with aid have grown in extent and popularity. These have thrived on the upsizing international efforts and worldwide echoes of several crises of the most disparate types, ranging from civil wars to natural disasters, pandemics and protracted human security emergencies. However, as Alex de Waal argued more than a decade ago conscious of the complexities brought about by the post-Cold War world politics of the 1990s, the humanitarian system has thus far demonstrated "an extraordinary capacity to absorb criticism, not reform itself, and yet emerge strengthened."[1] The so-called "humanitarian enterprise" has surfaced in the popular imagination as a ubiquitous eminence tasked with providing aid to those in need, and often capable of overcoming crises and limitations to deliver salvation at large. Humanitarianism has become an ever-present constant in international affairs as if it constituted a single omnipresent "empire of humanity."[2] Contra this simplification, de Waal also pointed out more recently, the "intellectual work of humanitarian scholars" has

1

become crucial today to reconcile the operation of this enterprise, its modalities and its claims "with the strong political, military and economic forces that determine the lives of poor and vulnerable people across the world," because this burgeoning enterprise "has been acquired in a fit of absence of analysis."[3]

It is in spirit that we begin here with a perhaps more modest, but no less critical, task: rather than putting forward alternatives to the worldwide provision of relief, this collection seeks to generate more attention for the socio-political dynamics inherent in the negotiation of aid. The core contention setting the course for this inquiry is that, precisely because of both this mounting interest and capacity for self-perpetration, we need to move to more critical and crosscutting understandings of humanitarianism. This is paramount today because its manifold socio-political dynamics are too easily subsumed under the dangerous dichotomy of relief-givers and aid-takers. By highlighting the dialectical relationship between international actors and local agents, as well as between situated spaces for relief and globalised political processes, we aim to render the depth of the humanitarian enterprise not just as a relief delivery mechanism, but as a socialisation experience, where all ends of the humanitarian "conversation" are forced to adapt their strategies (and, recurrently, nature) to each other's features.[4] From this perspective, we attempt here to take a step back from the specialist literature, often too wedded into the policy operationalisation of the field, as well as from the broader international academia, often too concerned with generalisable meta-speculations. Humanitarianism, on the contrary, is inherently in dialogue with both its localised contexts and its globalised politics. To highlight the negotiated essence of these relationships, the book focuses on the dynamics of humanitarian space and on the geopolitics (both "local" and "global") that sustain it. In this chapter I attempt to draw up some of the common ground on which the collection's authors have provided their contributions. I begin with a short note on the book's focus, "humanitarian space," and with a bird's eye overview of the changing humanitarian scenarios that constitute the political landscapes' humanitarianism, to then offer a short account of the limited analytical engagement with the negotiated nature of this context.

INTRODUCTION: HUMANITARIAN PUZZLES

"Humanitarian" spaces

The focus on the "spaces" of humanitarianism prompts us to investigate the embeddedness of these practices in everyday relations in the field— as Terry for instance shows us is her chapter with a poignant example of face-to-face negotiation in Rwanda in 1994—as much as in the echoes that these operations have worldwide—as in Bleiker, Hutchinson and Campbell's emotional responses to "humanitarian" portraits from crises such as the Boxing Day Tsunami, all the way into the halls and fora of international relations like the UN, which many contributors bring us back to. Here we meet another key puzzle of the book. As the introductory chapter by Hubert and Brassard-Boudreau will argue more extensively, there remains little agreement on what "humanitarian space" actually represents, and what its fate might be in the twenty-first century. From the "sanctuary" descriptions of the First and Fourth Geneva Conventions (1949 and 1977) that presented them as "hospital and safety zones and localities to protect from the effects of war," to more vague and management-oriented ideas of an "operating environment" for humanitarian operations presented by OCHA, almost every key actor in the field has today provided its understanding of humanitarian spaces.[5] Without delving into a specific definition of the term—a task that is here left to the various takes offered by the collection's contributors to better illustrate the variety of humanitarian viewpoints—it is fundamental to highlight how, despite this divergence of views and operationalisations and the continuous search for coherence in the field, the study of humanitarian negotiation and of the relations between relief agencies and the spaces in which they act is surprisingly underdeveloped. At present there is a paucity of studies and policy recommendations that are readily accessible to both scholars and practitioners in the sector, and almost no systematic attention has been paid to the dynamics underpinning the development of humanitarian spaces. The background literature accessible for those interested in this subject matter is therefore particularly limited when it comes to practical, policy-oriented and comprehensive studies of the framework of humanitarian negotiation, where texts such as Larry Minear and Hazel Smith's *Humanitarian Diplomacy* or the now dated *Towards a Humanitarian Diplomacy* by Tom Farer are rare, if not unique, primers.[6] Moreover, both studies remain tied to a "traditional" view of diplomacy that is state-based and exclusionary, and which is perhaps less and less representative of the multitude of entities that populate international humanitarian systems and, as highlighted thus far, that present us with the greatest challenges.[7] Responding to this lacuna, the collection therefore seeks to establish the ground on which further research should be developed, and provide initial suggestions for governmental and private actors involved in delivering humanitarian aid to such complex environments.

In particular, we attempt here to provide a set of critical responses to several common limits of the scholarly and practitioner discussions on humanitarian spaces. First, the small literature that tackles this theme tends to have a somewhat implicit eulogistic notion of what such spaces stand for: seen as the places (or "operating environment") for relief-givers, humanitarian spaces tend to be represented in a "positive" light as desirable and necessary.[8] Far from denying the utility of such contexts, several of this collection's critical insights also remind us that these spaces can also, and fortunately in a minority of cases, become contexts for subjugation, one-way exchanges and violence. Consequently, the purpose and orientation of these spaces tends to be met by a lack of analytical criticism. In the field, as much as in academia, it is perhaps much more common to encounter discussion on what to do with these spaces than on what they are. Besides, attempts at self-criticism and re-examination of the spatial positioning of agencies remain at times pin-pointed on an assumed clarity on basic terms like "humanitarian space" or "operating environment" which in turn remain dangerously unscru-tinised.[9] This limitation, in turn, also prompts a third crucial problem we try to address throughout the book: the production of humanitarian spaces is often seen from either a case-study particularistic or cookie-cutter generalised viewpoint dissociated from what we might call the "human geography" of humanitarianism.[10] As I highlight more extensively in my concluding chapter, the task of unpacking the negotiation dynamics that constitute such spaces demands a more holistic understanding of their underlying geopolitics: much of the discussion on the limits and shrinking of humanitarian spaces tends, in fact, to represent these in a mostly materialist fashion, underscoring their physical and logistic dynamics and therefore forgetting their inherent social construction. The workings of humanitarian diplomacy, and the spaces for relief it creates, tends to be divorced from both the situated practices they not only shape, but are also shaped by, as well as the globalised contexts it is both reliant on and representative of. The need for critical reassessment of the negotiating dynamics of humanitarianism stems, in fact, from the contemporary revolutions that are defining the shape of humanitarian spaces in particular, as well as of world politics in general. The post-Cold War international shifts and the impact of 9/11 on world affairs, along with the pervasive echoes that major humanitarian crises of the 1990s have had on political relations worldwide, beg for a renewed understanding of the realm of relief and aid. In order to do this, however, we must first understand what transformations this political landscape is currently undergoing.

Aidland: a contested terrain

Finding the thread of the contemporary revolutions in the world of "aidland" is no easy undertaking.[11] "Humanitarianism" remains indeed an in inherently contested concept, carrying (as for instance the chapters by Donini and Roff remind us) a baggage of ethical dilemmas in itself. In the first place, one could not easily speak today of "humanitarianism" but rather of a multitude of "humanitarianisms" because the practice both in the field and in academia has, in the past few decades, seen the evolution of alternative understandings of its principles and boundaries.

This is for instance represented in the widespread notion that the idea of assistance in emergency situations is rooted in the so-called "old" humanitarianism, and is currently witnessing the emergence of somewhat "new" forms of humanitarianism more self-consciously entrepreneurial.[12] As suggested by Michael Barnett, the idea of an independent, neutral and impartial assistance that Henri Dunant avowed in the early days of the ICRC has been weakened by Wilsonian understandings promoting tighter relationships between humanitarianism and overt political agendas.[13] This means that some frames of action have also changed: many relief workers are no longer making do with "quick fix" solutions, but rather trying to radically change the context they are dealing with.[14] By engaging with international politics, many "humanitarians" had to sacrifice their professed neutrality, which was originally not only a means but also a moral standpoint, and "take sides" in the changing contexts of humanitarianism. With decreasing inter-state conflict and more and more intra-state guerrillas as the most common scenario of contemporary humanitarianism, many authors have gone as far as describing neutrality as a "sin" that contravenes that moral duty that the international community has to "save strangers."[15] Yet this partial evolution of humanitarianism has had to deal with the inevitable political biases that, as famously pointed out by Fiona Terry (who reiterates this problem in her chapter here), make this field a "second-best world" to which we can only "adjust accordingly."[16] All of this accounts for an expanding (or at least more visible) political, economic, cultural and even religious complexity of an already precarious field.

Moreover, it is not just the context of humanitarianism that has been expanding; the sheer number of actors involved in the business of aid has also seen a progressive multiplication which brought more and more voices to crowd the humanitarian enterprise. On August 1870, when the Franco-Prussian war was at its harshest, the Red Cross was almost the sole humanitarian agency on the battlefields, and it had clear goals: provide medical assistance, delivering messages to those separated by war and channel relief to conflict victims. Some 124 years after, in Rwanda, NGOs and IGOs dealing with the refugee crisis numbered in the hundreds. Nowadays, in Iraq and Haiti, the total amount of aid agencies is ten times more than in the African emergency, and the humanitarian enterprise is a $10 billion a year industry.[17] In the chaos of today's crises more than ever, as Haitian and Iraqi situations testify, international actors should rely on well-conceived strategies, and understand that relief begins with the comprehension of the framework were it has to be delivered. Nonetheless, reports of uncoordinated aid efforts, lack of basic goods and a surplus of "aid packs" of scarce usage, as well as poor response to the local demands are a daily litany echoing from the screens of BBC, CNN and the like broadcasting live from Baghdad or Port-au-Prince.

As we will see in detail in Hyndman's and Schuller's chapters, this does not just amount to an expansion in the genus of "humanitarians." The present world political landscape has also seen a rising popularity of "complex humanitarian emergencies" (CHEs), contexts that have been for instance defined by the UN Office for the Coordination of Humanitarian Affairs (OCHA) as representing a "humanitarian crisis in a country, region or society where there is total or considerable breakdown of authority, resulting from internal or external conflict and which requires an international response that goes beyond the mandate or capacity of any single agency."[18] Typically, such conditions become destabilising not only for the area "affected" by the CHE, but for the surrounding neighbourhood as well, upsetting delicate balances often pinpointed on fragile diplomatic relations and scarce development rates. Factors that contribute to the spill-over of these localised events into the realm of world politics are issues of refugee flows, resource scarcity, health hazards and prospects of "conflict contagion" as well as illegal traffics and "backchannel" governmental ties, which all play a key role in the internationalisation of the emergency.[19] However, these "inside-out" factors are also coupled, as many chapters in this collection will more explicitly illustrate, by broader geopolitical dynamics.

The collection

Providing some critical insight into these challenges, the collection is therefore focused on the politics underpinning the establishment, transformation and limitations of humanitarian spaces in contemporary scenarios. The project brings together the analysis of political and international relations and the study of humanitarian relief, bridging between the two fields through particular attention to the political bases that link them. By looking at the dynamics of engagement of humanitarianism and its negotiations the book seeks to highlight "local" modalities to engage with external "humanitarian" actors, as well as strategies that NGOs, IGOs and governmental aid agencies put in place to secure "humanitarian spaces" in the vast array of political settings they are presently faced with. In particular, the authors have focused on those contexts where external actors need to develop spaces in order to provide humanitarian assistance, and thus where collaborative and pre-established political channels for such activities might not be present or functioning. Complex humanitarian crises, war-torn areas, authoritarian states, repressive regimes as well as areas controlled by insurgent groups represent the scenarios of the collection, in an attempt to scrutinise the diversity of negotiation mechanisms underpinning humanitarian action.

To this extent, the book does not rest on case studies only, nor does it rely on pure theoretical speculation. On the contrary, it seeks to develop a collection that encompasses practical experience, scholarly perspectives and real-world insights on the practices of humanitarian negotiation, in order to set the path in this discipline, and bring together the study of international relief and negotiation. For this reason, the heterogenous composition of the contributors' list is based essentially on experts of the humanitarian system, anthropology, politics or the particular case studies gathered here. Yet this might require here a necessary caveat underpinning this collection's rationale. Rather than forcing the authors under an artificial definition of "space" or "negotiation" set out at the beginning of the book, the collection seeks to gain further insight on what these terms mean in academia and practice by allowing contributors to set up their own spatial and political boundaries This, in practice, means that we will encounter not only a multiplicity of styles, from more journalistic takes to classical scholarly analyses, or reports from wider researches in the field, but also a plurality of understandings of what "humanitarian space" and "humanitarian diplomacy" mean. This orientation stems from an attempt to balance out academia and practice, experience and innovative inquiry, context-specific and generalist assumptions, to better unpack the critical diversity that underscores both phrases. Yet, this multiplicity also allows the collection to rest on a set of three shared problématiques stemming from the engagement puzzles described above:

– What is 'humanitarian space'?
– How is humanitarianism "negotiated?"
– What geopolitical dynamics underpin the relations between the two?

Presenting a multidisciplinary response to these questions, the book is therefore divided into four main parts. These are respectively aimed at providing a series of insights on the core theoretical background, some up-to-date cases, and the "inner" dilemmas and the wider geopolitical dynamics of humanitarianism. First, an introductory part provides a theoretical umbrella for the collection, and sets up a key practical problem: how is humanitarian space changing and what diplomatic, ethical and international questions underpin this evolution? This section does not only set the scene for the book. It pushes us beyond the comfortable boundaries of traditionalist international analyses, in equal measure, to take into account the emotional, legal, economic or religious geographies of present-day humanitarian action. Subsequently, a number of cases (Darfur, Kosovo, Aceh, Haiti and Somalia) take us "into the field" to scrutinise the embeddedness of humanitarian diplomacy in those contexts where humanitarianism primarily operates. This allows us to take into account, in each case, the main factors underpinning the dialectics between humanitarian spaces and their negotiated practices, observing these not just between humanitarian actors and local contexts, but also between humanitarianism and world politics at large. Then, the book steps beyond the traditional "cases" of humanitarianism in order to underscore how humanitarian diplomacy is both broader and broadening beyond the traditionalist interpretations of relief. Part III thus presents us with some of the emerging concerns around the issue of humanitarian intervention and the complexities surrounding the ethics of humanitarianism. These changes are not free from socio-political quandaries. Therefore, the book turns in this section to some of the most commonly voiced concerns and paradoxes of the construction of political spaces in which to carry out "humanitarian" initiatives, looking for example at the difficult relation between humanitarianism and military intervention, the problems of establishing the "enemy" for contexts directly affecting relief mechanisms or the challenging questions arising from the blurred practices of humanitarianism by faith-based initiatives. As such, this part challenges us to further promote a more balanced understanding of what humanitarian negotiations are and entail. Finally, the book is rounded off by concluding reflections on the expanding geopolitical complexity of the spaces of humanitarianism.

PART I

QUESTIONING HUMANITARIAN SPACES

1

IS HUMANITARIAN SPACE SHRINKING?

Don Hubert and Cynthia Brassard-Boudreau

The notion of "shrinking humanitarian space" is commonly used to describe the situation where the changing nature of armed conflict and the geopolitical shifts, particularly since 9/11, have combined to limit or restrict the capacity of humanitarian organisations to safely and effectively provide material relief to populations suffering the ravages of war. Most analyses of humanitarian space accept uncritically the notion that it is indeed shrinking and seek to assess the dynamics behind the seemingly growing challenges facing humanitarian operations. The debate has therefore focused on issues such as the proliferation of non-state actors, the growth of asymmetrical warfare and increase in the targeting of civilian populations, deliberate attacks on humanitarian workers, the co-optation of humanitarian response within counter-insurgency operations, the push for coherence within integrated UN missions and the ever-increasing overlap with longer-term development programming.[1]

The focus on the causes of shrinking humanitarian space has diverted attention from a robust analysis of the actual trends and has contributed to an unnecessarily gloomy outlook on the prospects for future humanitarian operations. This chapter begins with a review of the varying definitions associated with the concept of humanitarian space. It then breaks the concept down into three constituent parts—respect for humanitarian law, attacks on humanitarian workers and access to populations at risk—and assesses each against the longer-term evidence currently available. The conclusion contests the widely held view that humanitarian space is shrinking. An examination of broad trends rather than anecdotal evidence from the worst of this decade's crises suggests that the trends are far more promising than the conventional wisdom would imply.[2]

Defining "humanitarian space"

There is no common definition for the term "humanitarian space." The phrase was first used to describe the limitations imposed on the "operating environment" of humanitarian agencies operating in the highly politicised context of Cold War conflicts in Central America.[3] Its broader usage by humanitarian organisations seems to have begun in the 1990s when the former president of Médécins Sans Frontières (MSF), Rony Brauman, used the phrase *"espace humanitaire"* to refer to an environment in which humanitarian agencies could operate independently of external political agendas. By the late 1990s the term was in widespread use by the International Committee of the Red Cross (ICRC) and other humanitarian organisations. While there are some common elements in the use of the term across the range of humanitarian organisations, there are also important differences of emphasis.

The ICRC has been vocal over the last two decades in deploring the erosion of humanitarian space and the resulting difficulty in delivering humanitarian assistance. For the ICRC, the concept of humanitarian space is rooted in International Humanitarian Law (IHL). The mandate of the ICRC requires adherence to the principles of impartiality, neutrality and independence that enable the organisation to "remain active and assist victims of conflict throughout the world."[4] According to IHL, states have the primary responsibility to facilitate humanitarian action. The ICRC acknowledges that the "humanitarian space" involves a range of actors, many of whom are not bound by humanitarian principles. Ultimately, the creation and maintenance of humanitarian space requires proactive efforts by humanitarian actors themselves.[5]

MSF calls for a "space for humanitarian action" in which aid agencies are "free to evaluate needs, free to monitor the delivery and use of assistance, free to have a dialogue with the people."[6] In their view, political actors are responsible for creating and maintaining the humanitarian space in which humanitarian organisations undertake relief activities in accordance with humanitarian principles. As Von Pilar, former executive director of MSF Germany, makes clear, their notion of humanitarian space should focus on the suffering and needs of people in danger and MSF therefore does not give priority to neutrality.[7]

Oxfam's use of the concept of humanitarian space places greater emphasis on the rights of beneficiary populations. For Oxfam International, humanitarian space refers to "an operating environment in which the right of populations to receive protection and assistance is upheld, and aid agencies can carry out effective humanitarian action by responding to their needs in an impartial and independent way."[8] The organisation adds that such space "allows humanitarian agencies to work independently and impartially to assist populations in need, without fear of attack or obstruction by political or physical barriers to their work. For this to be the case, humanitarian agencies need to be free to make their own choices, based solely on the criteria of need."[9]

The United Nations adopts a more instrumental view. The UN Office of the Coordination of Humanitarian Affairs (OCHA), refers to humanitarian space as an "operating environment" for relief organisations and recognises that the "perception of adherence to the key operating principles of neutrality and impartiality [...] represents the critical means by which the prime objective of ensuring that suffering must be met wherever it is found, can be achieved."[10] They claim that "maintaining a clear distinction between the role and function of humanitarian actors and that of the military is the determining factor in creating an operating environment in which humanitarian organisations can discharge their responsibilities both effectively and safely."[11] But as a state-based organisation pursuing multiple objectives, the United Nations's definition explicitly omits the principle of independence as a condition for maintaining humanitarian space.

From these and other uses of the term, it is possible to identify three distinct dimensions.[12] First, humanitarian space can be understood as synonymous with respect for IHL.[13] The notion of humanitarian space is not explicitly specified in the Geneva Conventions. But states party to the Geneva Conventions, when involved in conflict, are obligated to provide for the basic needs of civilian populations affected by conflict or to allow and facilitate relief action that is "humanitarian and impartial in nature." A second variation focuses on the existence of a practical, even physical, space within which humanitarian action—saving lives by providing relief to victims of armed conflicts—can be undertaken safely and effectively. This can be conceived narrowly in opposition to "military" or "political" space with a focus on humanitarian corridors, refugee camps, demilitarised zones and "safe areas." More commonly, however, it is synonymous with acceptance of the role and activities of humanitarian actors by both the parties to a conflict and by beneficiaries.[14] Third, there are times when humanitarian space seems synonymous with humanitarian action writ large. In analysing the situation in Somalia, for example, one humanitarian organisation lists the following phenomenon as limiting humanitarian space:

general insecurity, administrative delays, restrictions or delays in movement of goods, targeting of humanitarian workers and assets including the looting of aid and car-jackings, piracy, negative perception of humanitarian workers, targeting civil society and media, localised disputes/competition over resources, lack of will and/or ability by authorities to address security incidents within their control.[15]

Overall, the review above of various understandings of humanitarian space identifies three main criteria against which to assess the claim that humanitarian space is shrinking: general respect for the provisions of IHL, the relative safety and security of humanitarian workers, and the degree of access to populations at risk.

Respect for International Humanitarian Law

For at least three decades, it has been commonplace to lament a declining respect for IHL.[16] This conclusion fits neatly with the commonly held view that the number of armed conflicts is increasing and that the vast majority of the victims of contemporary conflicts are civilians. Conventional wisdom, however, can be misleading. There is near consensus among empirical researchers that the number of armed conflicts has been in decline since the mid-1990s.[17] Furthermore, there is an erroneous "perception that violence in old civil wars is limited, disciplined, or understandable and the view that violence in new civil wars is senseless, gratuitous, and uncontrolled."[18] Those who have looked at the claim systematically conclude that it simply "fails to find support in the available evidence".[19] Adam Roberts, a leading researcher on armed conflict and humanitarian law agrees: "The suggestion that there was a much better era for civilians in earlier wars, based on agreed standards encoded in the laws of war, is misleading."[20]

And what of the widely held notion that the vast majority—as many as 90 per cent—of the casualties of contemporary armed conflict are civilians? The original sources for these claims, made in the early 1990s, had neither reliable data nor methodology.[21] That these figures have been widely cited since that time by researchers, international organisations and governments does not increase their reliability. Trend analysis of the human costs of armed conflict also rejects the myth that contemporary wars are more savage. On average, armed conflicts in the 1990s and 2000s kill fewer soldiers and fewer civilians than in previous decades.[22] A recent overview on whether conflicts after the Cold War are more "atrocious" concludes as follows:

What we find is that the human impact of civil conflict has diminished in the post-Cold War period. Battle severity, measured as battle deaths, has significantly declined. The magnitude of direct violence against civilians in civil conflict has also decreased.[23]

Contemporary civil wars do involve horrific levels of violence against civilian populations. Contemporary conflicts where IHL is violated with impunity are easy to identify. But this does not necessarily demonstrate a broader trend. Claims of declining respect for international humanitarian law imply that there was greater respect in the past. When assessing trends, it is important to note that the decades immediately following the Second World War were far more violent, and resulted in far more civilian casualties, than is commonly imagined.

Finally, claims about the declining respect for IHL commonly focus on the proliferation of non-state armed groups. But it is not clear that non-state armed groups are in fact proliferating. The majority of armed conflicts since the Second World War have been internal conflicts in which at least one of the warring factions was a non-state armed group.[24] In many of these civil wars, there were multiple and competing armed groups. Whether more or less, the real question is the degree to which non-state armed groups respect IHL. Once again, there is no systematic evidence to support the notion that armed groups in the past were more respectful of humanitarian law or the immunity of civilians in war. Ultimately, the residual category of "non-state armed group" says nothing about the objectives of any specific group or the military tactics that they might employ, and therefore reveals little about the likelihood of respect for IHL. One factor that seems to be important in assessing the prospects for future respect for IHL is the motivations of armed groups. In some cases, groups that seek to acquire statehood seem to be more willing to place constraints on their behaviour. Furthermore, organisational coherence and internal discipline are also important factors—a fragmented chain of command makes it difficult to distinguish political targeting from common banditry.

Safety of humanitarian workers

According to the UN's Interagency Standing Committee, one of the most prominent manifestations of shrinking humanitarian space is the insecurity of humanitarian staff.[25] Again, perspective is important. It is commonly acknowledged that efforts to more consistently respond to humanitarian crises have led to aid workers operating in more dangerous situations. International humanitarian workers did not operate in many of the greatest crises of the Cold War. In contrast, few of today's conflicts are entirely off limits to humanitarian actors. Insecurity for aid workers was indisputably high in Iraq following the US-led invasion, but it is worth noting that there were no substantial humanitarian operations at all during the Iran/Iraq war in the 1980s, the deadliest conflict in the world during that decade.

The Overseas Development Institute reports that "260 humanitarian aid workers were killed, kidnapped or seriously injured in violent attacks" in 2008, the highest total in the twelve years for which these incidents have been tracked.[26] The report goes on to note however that, "there is a concentration of incidents in a few high violence contexts. Three-quarters of all aid worker attacks over the past three years took place in just six countries."[27] And "the spike over the past three years was driven by violence in just three contexts: Sudan (Darfur), Afghanistan and Somalia."[28] Reviewing the same data, one analyst concludes that, excluding Afghanistan, Sudan and Somalia, major attacks on aid workers are decreasing.[29]

In line with the shrinking humanitarian space rhetoric, there is a growing tendency to attribute the bulk of attacks against aid workers to the militarisation or politicisation of humanitarian action. Yet for more than half of the security incidents tallied in the ODI report, the motives behind the attacks remain unknown. Among the attacks that can be categorised, only half during 2007–2008 were attributable specifically to armed opposition groups. For the riskiest environment, Sudan/ Darfur, the bulk of the attacks were attributed to "common banditry" while "in Afghanistan and Somalia criminality has colluded with political forces pursuing national (and in the case of al-Qaeda, global) aims," making it hard to identify the nature of insecurity.[30]

With evidence linking only one-in-four security incidents to warring factions acting with political motives, perhaps something else accounts for the increase in numbers. The former head of the ICRC office in Baghdad concludes bluntly, "More often than not, the security incidents suffered by aid agencies are due to foolish mistakes by ill-prepared individuals, and to faulty appraisals of local conditions."[31] He goes on to point out that "Most agencies admit that they have insufficient knowledge of the contexts in which they operate, that they lack local networks and information sources and that most of their international staff are not familiar with local customs, language and culture."[32] In a recent study on humanitarian space commissioned by UNHCR, aid workers admitted that negative perceptions of humanitarian organisations "were likely to arise primarily from insensitive or inappropriate conduct."[33] Yet the very concept of shrinking humanitarian space largely omits this part of responsibility of humanitarians for their own security.[34]

Humanitarian access

There is a direct correlation between the findings noted above on the security of humanitarian workers and the ability of those workers to access populations at risk. "Of the 380 incidents in the Aid Worker Security Database (AWSD) for 2006–2008, eighty-two resulted in suspension, withdrawal or relocation, in fifteen countries."[35] The evidence is compelling that access has been severely restricted in high-profile conflicts including Afghanistan, Iraq, Somalia and the DRC, but this is far from a complete picture.

Although difficult to measure, sweeping claims about a decline in humanitarian access seem inconsistent with a reduction in the number of civil wars combined with a continued expansion of humanitarian operations. Budgets for humanitarian operations continue to increase over time: $800 million in 1989, $4.4 billion in 1999, $10 billion in 2004 and $11.2 billion in 2008.[36] And so too have the numbers of personnel employed in these operations: "Global estimates of the number of field-based aid workers employed by UN humanitarian agencies, the ICRC and international NGOs indicate an increase from 136,204 to 241,654 (77 per cent) over the period 1997 to 2005."[37] These figures translate into a 54 per cent increase for the UN, a 74 per cent increase for the ICRC and a 91 per cent increase for international NGOs.[38] In Afghanistan, one of the most dangerous places for humanitarian workers, humanitarian action has expanded greatly over the last several years. In 2009 the Red Cross has opened new offices in five provinces. Save the Children UK states that they expanded their programme considerably in 2008, reaching 238,843 children, compared with 57,293 in 2007.

Once again, analyses of broader trends require a historical perspective. It is clear that some of the challenges facing contemporary humanitarian operations arise from the willingness and capacity of humanitarian organisations to operate in more risky environments than they did in the past.[39] This alone suggests that on balance, access for humanitarian organisations has been increasing rather than decreasing. In seeking to respond to crises on the basis of humanitarian need, there are two main barriers to consider: denial of access by a sovereign government and outright physical insecurity. There are some civil wars—Kashmir, Burma, Colombia—where the consent of the sovereign government is the principle barrier to broad humanitarian access. But focusing on the hard cases diverts attention from numerous examples such as Chechnya and Aceh where governments allow humanitarian organisations to operate even where this seems contrary to their political and military interests. Darfur provides an even starker example. The expulsion of aid workers following the ICC indictment of President Bashir has been widely cited as an example of declining humanitarian space. But the fact that there were massive humanitarian operations taking place within the sovereign territory of an Islamic state in the midst of the US-led war on terror is an indication of how far the normative goal posts have shifted in favour of humanitarian access. Physical insecurity remains a barrier to access in crises like Somalia and the Eastern Congo. But these highly insecure areas have existed in the past and are probably becoming less rather than more common.

IS HUMANITARIAN SPACE SHRINKING?

An expanding space?

The concept of humanitarian space does far more than define physical or theoretical arenas within which humanitarian operations are conducted. It also embodies a series of assumptions that together imply a seemingly inexorable decline in the ability to provide material assistance to populations affected by armed conflict. By misreading long-term trends and conflating disconnected phenomena under this single heading, humanitarian organisations have generated an unnecessarily gloomy outlook on the prospects for effective humanitarian operations. Far more effort has been devoted to providing a diagnosis for the shrinking of humanitarian space than in examining the available evidence to determine whether this shrinking is actually taking place. Across all three empirical measures of humanitarian space—respect for IHL, safety of aid workers and access to populations at risk—the data is incomplete or unreliable. Careful analysts draw differing conclusions about what the trends really are. At the very least, it is clear that there is no conclusive evidence to support the claim that humanitarian space is shrinking over time.

Given the evidence at hand, it is at least plausible that a counter claim could be sustained. By almost any measure—size of budgets, number of personnel—there continues to be decade upon decade growth in humanitarian operations even as the number of armed conflicts and their severity declines. Violations of IHL are indeed widespread but macro-trends suggest that there are fewer violations today than in the past. The recent increase in attacks on humanitarian workers is confined to a few high-risk conflicts; and even here only one-quarter of attacks can be attributed to "political targeting." Finally, barriers to access in a few high-profile conflicts have diverted attention away from the increasingly robust and formalised norm of humanitarian access in zones of armed conflict. More important, perhaps, than the recent debate over the causes of shrinking humanitarian space is the forward looking research agenda to account for its expansion.

2

THE HUMANITARIAN SYSTEM

HOW DOES IT AFFECT HUMANITARIAN SPACE?

Sarah Collinson

Whether approached primarily from the viewpoint of humanitarian agencies and their operational preoccupations, or from a broader concern with civilians" protection and access to assistance, "humanitarian space' is essentially about context—the context of humanitarian action and the context of needs to which humanitarian actors are seeking to respond. As noted by Hubert and Brassard-Boudreau, although concerns with humanitarian space sometimes evoke a delimited practical, even physical space within which humanitarian action can be undertaken, humanitarian space often seems synonymous with humanitarian action writ large, covering everything from general insecurity to administrative delays.[1] Humanitarian space is therefore an unavoidably wide and subjective concept, since different actors with varying priorities, interests and viewpoints will inevitably focus on different aspects and attributes of any particular context and reach different understandings of what they see or experience across space and time. The variation between different definitions reflects the essentially arbitrary and often quite narrow basis upon which particular problems affecting humanitarian action or affected populations are selected or prioritised by agencies at particular points in time. To the extent that definitions or discussions of humanitarian space have included consideration of aid actors themselves, the focus of attention has been overwhelmingly on how external factors affect agencies' ability to adhere to humanitarian principles. This is generally seen as being under assault and in decline due to a range of external pressures associated with shrinking humanitarian space, such as the politicisation of humanitarian assistance by donor governments. Yet, as a complex and dynamic political, military and legal arena of civilian protection and assistance, "humanitarian space" and its perceived contraction is also very much influenced by the nature of the international aid presence in these contexts and the way that humanitarian agencies themselves operate and engage—and how these have changed over time and vary across different operational environments.

Many of the difficulties faced today in delivering relief or providing protection in these complex environments can be seen as a consequence of a rapid expansion of the reach and ambitions of the international humanitarian sector into the types of conflict and crisis situations that, in the past, were politically off-limits and operationally way beyond what could be conceived of in terms of the overall resources and capabilities available. This chapter explores how the humanitarian sector's own evolution as a system over the past two decades has affected and been affected by agencies' engagement in conflict-affected countries, and what the implications of this might be for the dynamics of humanitarian space in complex and contested political and security environments.

This chapter traces some key attributes of the international humanitarian aid presence in fragile and conflict-affected countries that in many respects appear contradictory to one another, but all have profound implications for how the humanitarian sector engages in these contexts and hence for what the implications and outcomes of this engagement might be. First, it explores the extent to which the aid industry seems to operate as a separate, independent and relatively powerful economic, social and political actor in many poor and crisis-affected countries where indigenous sovereignty and indigenous economies are often relatively weak. Second, and despite this, the discussion examines inherent weaknesses in the structure and governance of the humanitarian "system" that result from the relatively unregulated and networks-based nature of the sector. Third, and related to the lack of top-down normative authority and regulation within the system, it highlights powerful competitive market dynamics between agencies within the sector that appear to generate simultaneous and contradictory tendencies towards cohesion and fragmentation among different actors across the system. Taken together, these combine into highly complex institutional dynamics and relationships across the sector that, as discussed in the final section, have important implications for how the sector performs and engages in situations of conflict and other challenging operating environments. Often, they fundamentally hamper humanitarian agencies' collective capacity to function strategically and effectively in difficult arenas of contested "humanitarian space" where civilian protection and assistance needs are often most acute.

The humanitarian system's occupation of "umanitarian space"

As discussed in the following section, the humanitarian system can be seen as relatively weak in terms of structure and leadership compared with many other international or transnational regimes.[2] This is reflected, for instance, in the limited respect or adherence to IHL by belligerents in most contemporary conflicts, or the fact that, among aid actors themselves, supposedly common foundational humanitarian "principles" are incorporated, interpreted and applied very differently. This, in turn, is a reflection of the extent to which the humanitarian system as a whole has developed through the expansion and proliferation of essentially private self-mandated and self-regulating organisations. Yet the relative weakness of the overall "system" as a coherent or structured international regime does not mean that humanitarian aid actors are necessarily lacking in power and resources, at least in certain operational contexts. In countries with the weakest states that fundamentally lack empirical sovereignty, particularly in Africa, the aid system can be seen as exercising a kind of separate and exclusive non-state or "petty" sovereignty, with aid agencies representing a relatively powerful and well-resourced group of inter-connected international actors who are able to operate to a large extent separately from, and sometimes in opposition to, the (weak) empirical sovereignty of the state and other national organisations and power-holders.[3]

Jeff Crisp and Amy Slaughter, for example, have observed how the "care and maintenance" model to refugee and IDP assistance in situations of protracted displacement "endowed UNHCR with responsibility for the establishment of systems and services for refugees that were parallel to, separate from, and in many cases better resourced than those available to the local population." This "created a widespread perception that the organisation was a surrogate state, complete with its own territory (refugee camps), citizens (refugees), public services (education, health care, water, sanitation, etc.) and even ideology (community participation, gender equality)."[4] For Duffield, the petty sovereignty of aid actors—often in competition with or contradiction to the sovereignty of state or other national actors—is reflected physically in the form of fortified aid compounds in many countries. These graphically mark out the boundaries of aid as an archipelago of international flows and simultaneously reflect and create a separation of the international aid elite from the populations and societies that they are supposed to be engaged with.[5]

Humanitarian organisations, therefore, cannot credibly claim that they lack power, least of all the largest agencies that are positioned most centrally within the sector.[6] Indeed, a number of humanitarian organisations not only now have annual budgets that match some of the states in which they are intervening, but, whether intentionally or not, they also represent an important part of international governance structures that are purposefully intended to transform many of these states and their societies.[7] A 2004 review by the Feinstein International Center highlighted the extent to which a disproportionate share of international humanitarian funding and other resources have become concentrated in the hands of just a few "mega-NGOs."[8] A 2004 assessment of NGO engagement in Sierra Leone reported that, while there were hundreds of NGOs operational in that context, around three-quarters of their humanitarian spending was handled by fewer than fifteen large transnationals.[9]

The dominance of the biggest UN and NGO agencies in the financing flows and governance of the system suggests that the nature of the "system" corresponds broadly with an oligopoly of organisations that, despite some differences in specific missions and mandates, operates as a relatively closed group with interrelated histories and limited scope for entry.[10] At the international level, career paths often span these few dominant organisations, effectively creating an "international relief elite" or a "humanitarian establishment."[11] This establishment creates and maintains a dominant international humanitarian discourse that powerfully shapes the collective "memory" of past humanitarian action and defines and legitimises the role of key agencies and the wider humanitarian system based on "a way of knowledge, a background of assumptions and agreements about how reality is to be interpreted and expressed."[12] Through this shared narrative and discourse, the most established organisations and institutions are able to strongly determine the dominant terms of reference and rules of the game that define the system, despite the proliferation of self-organising actors across the system.[13]

The consequent boundaries defined by and for the system have been reinforced by the creation of institutional structures and a sequence of inter-organisational initiatives and reforms that have been intended to strengthen or improve the institutional and operational effectiveness of the sector. These include the Inter-Agency Standing Committee (IASC) and its various sub-networks, the Sphere Humanitarian Charter and Minimum Standards in Disaster Response, and the Clusters and Humanitarian Country Team structures. While undoubtedly helping to strengthen the industry in terms of supporting and improving its performance and professionalism, these institutional developments also risk marginalising, excluding or obscuring numerous other types of actors and networks that, in practice, are involved in humanitarian action but are not explicitly recognised as established, legitimate or equal humanitarian actors by the international humanitarian establishment. At risk are local and national government and civil society organisations, small Western-based and national NGOs originating and acting independently of the mainstream system, religious and diaspora networks and organisations, international for-profit contractors, local private sector actors, and peacekeeping and other international military actors. A 2007 meta-evaluation of international humanitarian responses to natural disasters reports the key role played by local actors and institutions, but also the frequently problematic relationship of local with international aid actors: once the international agencies move in, local structures are typically marginalised in decision-making processes and implementation, key personnel in local organisations are recruited by international organisations, or local organisations are simply sub-contracted by the bigger international players, with these relationships often undermining rather than developing the capacities of local actors.[14] Similarly, a recent comprehensive evaluation of the cluster approach found that while the cluster framework seems to have supported better led coordination and stronger partnerships between UN actors and other international humanitarian actors and strengthened the humanitarian identity of cluster members, the cluster system also tends to exclude national and local actors and frequently fails to link in with, build on or support existing coordination and response mechanisms, with insufficient analysis of local or national structures and capacities.

In certain situations, the resulting barriers—both concrete and perceived—may reinforce impressions (if not the reality) of the sector's predominantly Western identity, and as such, as a system representing interests, values and modes of behaviour that may be strongly distrusted, contested or rejected by local populations.[15] The conclusions of a recent high-level roundtable on humanitarian space in Sri Lanka, for example, noted that inter-agency meetings were "generally dominated by international organisations, with very few Sri Lankan organisations represented;" the small club of foreigners who met in the so-called "Coffee Club was easily portrayed in the Sinhala media as a neo-colonial group conspiring against the government and Sri Lanka's interests;" the sector "remained isolated from civil society and presided over by expatriates, with engagement with local actors limited to narrow funding and subcontracting relationships."[16] This contributed to the flourishing growth of anti-NGO sentiment. In South Sudan, Duffield observes how aid compounds have come to represent a highly visible and separated island of modernity where vehicles, diesel, electricity, medical supplies, safe water and telecommunications are concentrated, exposing the exclusivity of the international space and its unequal relationship with the surrounding environment.[17] As such, it risks inciting the hostility and envy that it claims to protect against, with potentially profound implications for the relationships between aid workers and beneficiaries.[18] A wide-ranging study of local perceptions of humanitarian action carried out by the Feinstein Center found that:

The system is viewed as inflexible, arrogant, and culturally insensitive. This is sometimes exacerbated by inappropriate personal behavior, conspicuous consumption, and other manifestations of the "white car syndrome". Never far from the surface are perceptions that the aid system does not deliver on expectations, is expat-heavy and "corrupted" by the long chain of intermediaries between distant capitals and would-be beneficiaries.[19]

THE HUMANITARIAN SYSTEM

*Networks-based governance within the humanitarian sector
and the implications for humanitarian space*

The concentration of humanitarian aid flows through a core group of UN agencies and NGOs and the shared discourse and relationships linking these organisations might make it appear that the system is relatively centralised globally. Yet, in reality, there is little in the way of any formalised or centralised structure of authority supporting the system. Functional interdependence among key operational actors and between them and their donors, and the existence of an international humanitarian establishment with a broadly-shared discourse of humanitarianism, creates the sense of a defined system, at least for those actors firmly positioned within it, but in practice the "system," such as it is, is relatively loosely configured compared with many other international policy communities: it lacks any explicit or overarching rules-based regime and the actors within it are mostly self-regulating.[20] A number of intersecting international and regional rule-based regimes have created certain structures and legal constraints that govern particular aspects of humanitarian action—notably those relating to refugee protection, IHL, human rights, peacekeeping and specific policy regimes established by certain regional organisations (European Union, African Union, and others)—but these do not establish a distinct or coherent normative framework for the sector as a whole.

Dobusch and Quack document how, in self-regulating transnational communities of this kind, "various private and public actors concerned with a particular type of transnational activity come together," often in "non-structured and rather unformalised settings, to elaborate and agree on collective rules of the game."[21] The process is one of "voluntary and relatively informal negotiation; the emerging structural arrangements are relatively amorphous, fluid, and multifocal in nature" with a high degree of reliance on "voluntary compliance and socialisation of the members into a common cognitive and normative framework."[22] With the sector's very wide geographical and sectoral scope, the upshot is a complex and relatively dispersed form of networks-based governance within the sector that leaves considerable room for autonomous or semi-autonomous actors with varying priorities to jostle for leverage across all levels and areas of policy and action—or, alternatively, to ignore or dissociate from any normative or joint operational frameworks. While, to a large extent, "money always talks" power to determine and implement policies at the system-wide level is distributed relatively horizontally among UN specialised agencies, the bigger INGOs and donors.[23]

A variety of established and ad hoc networks have succeeded in developing and agreeing joint standards and codes of conduct for various different levels, sectors and contexts of humanitarian policy and operations, including, at country or field level, operational codes of conduct such as the OLS Ground Rules in Sudan and, at global level, the Good Humanitarian Donorship Principles, the Humanitarian Accountability Partnership (HAP) principles and various guidelines developed by the IASC.[24] Although ubiquitous across the sector as a form of mutual standard-setting and regulation, these various codes and guidelines typically lack any monitoring or enforcement mechanisms and compliance is almost always weak and uneven in practice. In Somalia, Hammond and Vaughan-Lee report, for instance, how the Joint Operating Principles (JOPs) for Somalia developed in 2007/2008 aimed at ensuring principled humanitarian action and a "do no harm" approach were never formally operationalised due, in part, to the inability of NGOs and UN actors to agree on the principles without compromises that might undermine their purpose.[25] The Negotiation Ground Rules introduced through the IASC in March 2009, the NGO Position Paper on Operating Principles and Red Lines and the UN Country Team's Policy on Humanitarian Engagement, both issued in late 2009, were not applied consistently, if at all, in practice. On the ground, agencies have pursued individual approaches to operational challenges and risk management, with competitive relationships prevailing among multilateral agencies and between international and national NGOs and limited collaboration, coordination or information sharing.

The international humanitarian "marketplace" and the commercialisation of agency space

The essentially fluid and unsettled nature of the system's supporting normative and institutional frameworks both contributes to, and is amplified by, powerful competitive market incentives and imperatives that operate between key actors within and beyond the mainstream system—for funds, for public profile, for market share or for niche expansion. On the basis of detailed analysis of what they term an "NGO scramble," Cooley and Ron conclude that non-profit INGOs respond to contractual incentives and organisational pressures much like firms do in markets, pointing to high levels of organisational insecurity, competitive pressures and fiscal uncertainty among agencies as they compete to raise money and secure donor contracts. These contracts are often performance-based, renewable and short term, creating counterproductive incentives that encourage opportunism and that often lead to dysfunctional outcomes.[26]

These market dynamics simultaneously encourage contradictory tendencies towards cohesion and fragmentation across the system. Thus, while the global INGO relief market is dominated by a small number of large agencies, each of their country offices is forced to compete heavily for individual contracts in particular conflict settings.[27] At the same time donors—themselves signed up to Good Humanitarian Donorship Principles aimed to synchronise international humanitarian financing priorities and arrangements across the donor community—require contracted agencies to operate within joint systems of operational cooperation and coordination, such as the Clusters, and to adhere to commonly recognised norms or standards, such as the Sphere standards. As the biggest organisations have grown and their coverage has expanded internationally, they have evolved increasingly into funding institutionally for numerous smaller sub-contracted operational providers while still exercising dominance as the main contractors in the system. Meanwhile, as Cooley and Ron note, "hundreds of smaller INGOs are seeking entry to the aid and relief market, hoping to raise funds for future work by raising their flag in media-saturated humanitarian hot spots."[28]

The fact that the mainstream humanitarian system is in direct and growing competition with other types of actors exploiting other forms of assistance and other sectoral markets connected with the wider aid industry creates incentives for the lead humanitarian actors to club together and seek to define themselves as distinctive from other spheres of international engagement and other types of actors, including military and for-profit contractors. The common rhetoric of humanitarian principles plays an important part in humanitarian actors' efforts to mark out and protect for themselves a distinctive market niche—as well as a distinctive political and operational (security) space—in the wider marketplaces of international aid and intervention. Yet, in practice, different humanitarian agencies take very different positions and pursue highly variable strategies towards these competing sectors and actors, with some, for instance, willing to engage directly with peace-building or state-building activities and the associated funding while others insist on a more purist and isolationist approach to humanitarian engagement.

Marketised relationships and processes within the mainstream humanitarian system itself are, in turn, nested within the competitive and increasingly privatised marketplace of much broader international aid and intervention environments. In some contexts, the official donors and their lead operational partners—particularly "humanitarian" donors and agencies—are only bit-players in the broader picture of international aid engagement. Indeed, in the highest-profile situations of international intervention, the resources controlled and managed by the humanitarian aid sector are dwarfed by other forms of aid, and in major sudden-onset disasters they are easily overtaken by private donations channelled through a diverse array of networks and organisations, many of which are more or less entirely off the established international humanitarian map. In Afghanistan, for instance, with the US as the dominant donor and operating with an aid model that favours implementation of aid programmes through large US contracting companies, this funding environment has created a highly lucrative marketplace for a wide variety of private, non-governmental and multilateral organisations, and one in which the dividing lines between the many different types of contractors and service providers is often blurred, sometimes purposefully so. DynCorp International Inc., for example—listed as twelfth in a recent ranking of US government contractors and partners—describes itself on its main home page as providing "[r]apid response capabilities in emergencies, world-class post-conflict and transition programs, and sustainable solutions for long-term development, with an emphasis on building local capacity;" its subsidiary, DI Development, is described as having the capability "to assess, plan and execute the creation of major population support facilities in times of distress and emergency."[29]

While competition for limited international humanitarian funds in many contexts would be expected to encourage rivalry and fragmentation among agencies at country level, a surge or surplus of international aid funding into a particular crisis can also generate intense competitive and fragmentary dynamics. This has been seen in a number of higher-profile contexts of international humanitarian action or response, including Iraq, Afghanistan, the Indian Ocean tsunami response and the 2010 Haiti earthquake. This competition is often perceived by humanitarian agencies as impeding their agency space. Hillhorst and Jansen report, for instance, how severe competition among humanitarian agencies in the tsunami response in Sri Lanka meant that, rather than competing over funds, they had to compete over territory, programmes, people and staff: Sri Lankan NGOs were displaced by international agencies, and humanitarian organisations found themselves competing for "assistance" space with a huge variety of private humanitarian initiatives.[30]

The implications for humanitarian space

The fluid, dynamic and relatively weak governance frameworks and the fragmenting influence of internal and external market imperatives and dynamics suggest that the humanitarian system's institutional "architecture" is perhaps not as robust, defended or defined by clear boundaries as its physical footprint might sometimes indicate. Indeed, despite all its outward manifestations of institutional and material power, there is a clear tendency for systemic weakness in the face of the often intense and highly complex pressures and risks of supporting or implementing humanitarian action in difficult and insecure operating environments. In these contexts, "humanitarian principles" have not only served in recent years as a central and purposefully binding rhetorical narrative or discourse for the system's key actors, but also, paradoxically, as a focus of controversy, frustration and splintering among them as these actors interpret and apply them in contrasting ways or sidestep them altogether. Whilst jointly claiming to uphold shared principles, agencies usually have other competing priorities and imperatives that drive their actions in practice, such as maintaining their operations, institutional presence and funding in a particular context, or aligning with a particular party to a conflict in an effort to address the structural causes of conflict. The humanitarian principles agenda has therefore itself become a political battleground among aid actors as they compete with one another to maintain or expand their presence and activities in a variety of highly volatile and contested environments. This is reflected in competing and contradictory narratives of relative legitimacy among different aid actors ("humanitarian," "multi-mandate," civilian, military, for-profit), as witnessed in the distancing and, at times, open critique that MSF and ICRC have targeted at multi-mandate INGOs, in the propensity of INGOs to criticise the UN, and the hostility and distrust that humanitarian NGOs and UN agencies collectively exhibit towards military and for-profit aid providers.[31]

It is not altogether surprising, therefore, that the rapid expansion of the aid industry—in terms of the numbers of agencies and the range of sectors and activities that they are engaged in—has frequently generated negative and sometimes perverse dynamics of interacting or competing institutional interests which undermine principled humanitarian action or negatively impact on the negotiation or protection of humanitarian (civilian) space. Cooley and Ron report, for instance, how in DRC following the Rwandan genocide in the mid-1990s an extreme marketisation of NGO activities produced powerful disincentives to protest aid diversion in the notorious Goma refugee camps. Securing funding became a core priority of many INGOs, "pushing other concerns—such as ethics, project efficacy or self-criticism—to the margins;" competition between INGOs, they conclude, critically undercut the collective action necessary to protest misuse of refugee aid.[32] Clearly agencies wanted to provide relief and help the refugees, but, "[n]ormative considerations aside, the material stakes were also high [… as] [n]o major organisation concerned about self-preservation could risk losing such an important source of funding."[33]

A key question for understanding trends affecting humanitarian space is what happens to the norms, rules and institutions of the international humanitarian system in the most challenging political and security conditions? Do they have a tendency to collapse, adapt or fragment? Lack of relative influence, independence and "agency space" enjoyed by humanitarian agencies is most obvious in the most politically challenging environments where, in practice, the system is subject to the influences and constraints of all sorts of more powerful actors and interests. This is particularly obvious in situations where the international civilian aid regime's assumed autonomy and authority to operate is rejected by states or powerful non-state actors who exercise substantive empirical sovereignty, such as Burma and Sri Lanka; or where it is in direct competition with other competing regimes, such as those more unambiguously connected with Western stabilisation agendas that are more powerful in political, financial and institutional terms due to better resourcing, stronger governance structures and closer or more explicit alignment with the primary interests of the major powers. "Hard" defensive security measures and bunkerised material installations in the higher-risk operating environments can be seen from one vantage point as a manifestation of the system's weak or limited control and authority, reflecting all too starkly the degree to which the aid presence is challenged or rejected by national and local actors and institutions.

In the most contested environments, the humanitarian aid industry has shown itself to be liable to be co-opted or captured by more powerful political and economic actors, or pulled into competing and potentially contradictory agendas or regimes—for example government-led military or political campaigns, or counter-insurgency and state-building led by the great powers, and/or local agendas of violence and power-play. In Pakistan following the 2010 floods, for example, the IASC-commissioned inter-agency real-time evaluation of the response found that "[t]he selection of beneficiaries was, at times, not done independently but was subordinated to political interference [... and] unknown quantities of assistance have reportedly reached those that were the least vulnerable, close to feudal landlords or connected through certain political affiliations."[34] In Somalia, humanitarian programming has for decades interacted in highly complex ways with national and local political and conflict dynamics, often benefiting more powerful community members; at the local level, gatekeepers, known locally known as "black cats"—including businessmen, political actors, senior members of the community or clan or other powerful individuals—often decide who should receive aid or insist that recipients should hand over a portion of the relief they receive.[35]

It is therefore no accident that the aid industry's expanded engagement and involvement in contexts of highly partisan international political and military intervention in situations of continuing violence has gone hand-in-hand with a growing concern across the humanitarian sector with its own politicisation. The very fact that such a high proportion of today's humanitarian aid and the key actors delivering it are concentrated in the highest-profile contexts of international intervention where humanitarian needs are not the greatest reflects the extent to which it (and they) are, indeed, fundamentally politicised at a global level. The politicisation of agencies and their assistance—and their politicising impacts on the contexts in which aid is concentrated—is partly driven by institutional interests, where agency presence and access, and hence agency space, is supported by high levels of donor funding for humanitarian action, and/ or where their presence and operations are contingent upon agencies accommodating to certain international, national or local political or military agendas. A Feinstein Center consultation on the implications of Iraq, for instance, found that agencies were split within and among themselves as they struggled with the contending pressures of humanitarian principles versus institutional survival in seeking to operate in a highly contested, politicised and competitive aid context. The prioritisation of institutional presence and access over principle was reflected in the observation that "practically no-one in the global humanitarian assistance community was prepared to express the view openly that 'we should not be in Iraq'." Meanwhile, it noted that the view taken by some that "we have no choice but to be there" obscured a wider range of options that did exist and deserved consideration:

There was no consensus among discussants on the nature of the crisis. The starting point was that humanitarian agencies would respond only to humanitarian need. When it became clear that there was no major food or displacement crisis and only pockets of vulnerability among civilians, the issue was fudged for reasons of institutional survival. [...] The stark choice was between cooption and irrelevance: for fear of losing funds and contracts, many agencies found reasons to stay on, regardless of their particular mandate. [...] The murkiness of the situation is also compounded by two additional factors for which humanitarians themselves are responsible. The first is the lack of a clear understanding of the nature of the situation on the ground which was arbitrarily defined as "humanitarian" in order to justify the presence of the UN and NGOs in the absence of a UN mandate. This simple act immediately politicized subsequent perceptions of humanitarianism. The second factor is the conflation of humanitarian, development, and advocacy agendas to suit agency survival imperatives.[36]

Similarly, the conclusions of the recent high-level roundtable on humanitarian space in Sri Lanka noted how, during the final phases of the war in 2008 and 2009 and in the context of the ensuing IDP crisis, institutional and bureaucratic interests and imperatives skewed agency's judgements about the appropriate balance between advocacy and access. The concessions and silences that appeared to serve the imperative of securing access only emboldened the Sri Lankan government in its efforts to progressively and systematically shrink humanitarian space, and neither access nor staff security were enhanced as a consequence. Operational security risks were purposefully reduced and so made acceptable through various compromises agreed with national and local military and political actors, and through the direct transfer of risk from international personnel to local staff and the civilian population.[37]

During the 1990s—and particularly in the shadow of Goma and the realisation that aid agencies had played a direct role in aiding Rwanda's *genocidaires*—concern across the sector was very much with how humanitarian relief itself risks politicising conflict-affected environments with scrutiny of the negative effects of relief in war, and how relief can affect the violence around it by fuelling war economies, facilitating forced displacement, undermining coping strategies, and legitimising warlords and other non-state armed actors. This was reflected in the emergence in the late 1990s of the "do no harm" agenda as a new orthodoxy to guide humanitarian action.[38] By contrast, the dominant discourse today appears much more internally preoccupied with how the sector has itself become politicised by its association with or instrumentalisation by the international political agendas of its primary paymasters, and consequently, with how this politicisation might affect agencies' own access, security and acceptance on the ground. Reflecting this, the dominant narrative around humanitarian space appears increasingly limited to a problem of operational space, rather than a problem of how war, violence and malign political forces affect vulnerable populations' safety and welfare, or of how relief agencies' own activities might play into these dynamics. In Somalia, for instance, Hammond and Vaughan-Lee note how civilian protection concerns are all but absent from discussion around humanitarian space, with attention instead focused on the reduction in and constraints to agencies' operating space.[39]

The overwhelming response among aid practitioners has been to call for a renewed commitment to the traditional principles of humanitarian action in order to resist or reverse its adverse politicisation and the perceived assault on operational/agency space. Yet the potential disconnect between, on the one hand, these internally-focused preoccupations with politicisation, and on the other, attention to the external political and other impacts and implications of agencies' engagement in complex environments risks accentuating a gulf between the rhetorical narrative of principled humanitarianism—resting on an assumed or hoped-for separation from political imperatives—and real-life, unavoidably, political challenges on the ground. Indeed, paradoxically, by sweeping many of the critical dilemmas and challenges of their engagement under a collective rug of ill-defined humanitarian principles, humanitarian actors are perhaps making themselves even less equipped to live up to these principles in practice.

3

HUMANITARIANISM, PERCEPTIONS AND POWER

Antonio Donini

The good news...

Universality was one of the key themes of a major research project conducted at the Feinstein International Center under the rubric Humanitarian Agenda 2015: Principles, Power and Perceptions. The research involved thirteen country case studies of local perceptions of the work of humanitarian agencies in conflict and non-conflict environments.[1] Qualitative information was collected from several thousand respondents—beneficiaries and non beneficiaries—via interviews and focus groups at the community level. The research yielded a wealth of information on how local people viewed the work, attitudes and behaviours of aid workers and their agencies with a focus on what was meaningful to those interviewed, that is "judgements" rather than "facts." It also said a lot about how humanitarians see themselves, but more on that later. The importance of universality in the conduct of the humanitarian enterprise emerged clearly from all the case studies, as it does from other similar research.[2] Humanitarianism—and the values of compassion and alleviation of suffering that underpin it—is a global good,

39

broadly recognised the world over. A common core of humanitarian values emerges from the country studies, although these values may be interpreted differently from place to place reflecting the experiences of particular conflicts and crises.

It seems that only al-Qaeda and some extremist militant groups it inspires maintains an outright rejectionist stance.[3] Many belligerent groups, of course, want to manipulate humanitarian action to their advantage or, as with the Liberation Tigers of Tamil Eelam (LTTE) in Sri Lanka, to accept the provision of relief only on their own terms. Even the Taliban, which has often targeted aid workers, has developed a more nuanced position. They are able to distinguish between the International Committee of the Red Cross (ICRC), and other "Dunantist" actors, with whose principles they have no quarrel, and the "corrupt agencies" that have taken the side of the government and the US-led coalition forces. Similarly in Iraq, despite the toxic political and security environment, we found a strong resonance between the core elements of the humanitarian ethos and Islamic and Iraqi understandings of what "good charity" entails. Neutrality and impartiality, the studies showed, are not theoretical concepts or pie-in-the-sky constructs; they are essential ingredients of effective humanitarian action. "Neutrality is not an abstract notion in Iraq," our country study concluded, "but is regarded by communities and most remaining humanitarian organisations as an essential protection against targeted attack."

There are of course a number of variations on the basic theme of universality. There is no situation where humanitarian action is totally principled and allowed to operate as such. Nor do all humanitarians strive to insulate their activities from partisan politics, advocacy or expressions of solidarity. From the perspective of the affected communities, such nuances and the affiliations of agencies to the political agendas of donor governments do not appear to be a cause of major concern, except to the extent that political baggage directly affects the quality of the assistance and protection provided. In life-and-death situations, assistance will generally be accepted whether it comes in a Wilsonian, Dunantist or even military truck. But over time, the nature of the giver begins to matter. This was most evident in Iraq and Afghanistan—where the animosity vis-à-vis agencies seen as linked to "the occupier" was palpable—as well as in Palestine and Darfur, where the UN aid agencies and NGOs are widely seen as "guilty by association" with donor-promoted political frameworks and where the anti-terrorist legislation of donor countries directly affects the conduct of humanitarian action. In Afghanistan, except for the ICRC and MSF, the contract of acceptability between aid agencies and communities has broken down in large swaths of the country. Not only is it too dangerous for NGOs (let alone the UN) to access communities where they have sometimes worked for decades, communities themselves often refuse assistance, not because they don't need it, but because of the associations it carries. In sum, humanitarianism emerged from the research as a universal value that resonates in all cultures and societies. The specificities may differ from place to place, as does the actual respect for norms and values, but the universal substratum is solid—perhaps surprisingly so. In all cultures people recognise themselves in largely similar precepts of what is admissible and not admissible when conflict or disaster strikes. We all seem to share this fundamental aspect of our common humanity. But this is where the good news ends.

and the bad news....

Universal ethos, Western apparatus: humanitarian ideals have the potential to unite but humanitarian practice very often divides. Our findings showed that the universality issue underscores a real and often damaging clash between the value systems of "locals" and "outsiders." The humanitarian enterprise affirms that the core values of humanitarianism have universal resonance, but this is not the same as saying that such values have universal articulation and application. Our case studies documented many instances of friction at an operational level, reflecting general cultural insensitivity, poor accountability and bad technique among humanitarian agencies. Cultural insensitivity affects the humanitarian relationship on both sides, though the onus for dealing with complex and delicate cultural issues in an appropriate manner falls primarily on aid workers and their organisations. The other two negatives—poor accountability to beneficiaries and bad programming or technique—are the sole preserve of aid workers. The consequence is that the "otherness" of the humanitarian enterprise undermines the effectiveness of assistance and protection activities. The prevalence of questions about the motivation, agenda, *modus operandi* and cultural baggage of Western aid agencies is clearly troubling and presents major challenges.

"Why do these young people come to our country?"—people ask—"Is it because they can't find work at home?" or "They want to help, but they tell us what to do without asking us."

Our case studies, as well as more recent work undertaken in Nepal, Somalia and Pakistan, reconfirm the seriousness of this tension between insiders and outsiders arising from the cultural and political "baggage" that aid agencies bring to the communities they serve.[4] The nuances are different, but the message is the same: humanitarian action is a top-down, externally driven and relatively rigid process that allows little space for local participation beyond formalistic consultation. Much of what happens escapes local scrutiny and control. The system is viewed as inflexible, arrogant and culturally insensitive. This is sometimes exacerbated by inappropriate personal behaviour, conspicuous consumption and other manifestations of the "white car syndrome." Never far from the surface are perceptions that the aid system does not deliver on expectations and is "corrupted" by the long chain of intermediaries between distant capitals and would-be beneficiaries. In other words, seen from below, the enterprise is self-referential and reflects the expectation that humanitarian theatres should adapt to it, rather than the reverse.[5] It thrives on isomorphism (you can join us, but only on our terms) and deploys its network power through the imposition of management practices and standards that act as barriers to entry for local initiatives or non-like minded national players or community groups.[6]

What this tells us about ourselves

As with other aspects of globalisation, the nature of the processes of humanitarian action and the standards that guide them are decided by outsiders and imposed through network power.[7] Moreover, the top down nature of the enterprise affects not only the response but also, and perhaps more importantly, the conceptualisation of crises: as humanitarians we address those vulnerabilities that we recognise and fit our schemas, we speak to those who speak our same language and who have copied our institutions, we impose our mental models, we tend to shape reality in our image rather than trying to see it from the ground up. While agencies and academics have sharpened their tools to analyse local perceptions—and this in itself may well be a positive thing—has this actually made any difference in our relationships with communities on the ground? Paradoxically, not much.

We cannot see ourselves. We may hear the feedback, but it is very difficult for us to listen to it and to see how we really look. And the growing cottage industry of perception studies may well just be a fig leaf to justify what we do and how we do it. The perception gap is wide because we hear what we want to hear and people often tell us what they think we want to hear. The perception issue is a minor aspect of a much more serious problem: the essentially lop-sided nature of the relationship between outsiders and insiders that breeds disempowerment, and sometimes victimisation. Like it or not, the discourse is a dominant one where "we" control the terms of the relationship and the volume button. The point here is that "humanitarian action" can mean very different things to the aid worker in her big white vehicle and to the "helpless recipient" or to the extremist who negates the value of humanitarian action. What "we" experience is not what "they" experience. In other words: "The experience of receiving humanitarian action is not the experience of being a humanitarian."[8] For the well-meaning compassion-driven international aid worker the baggage and trappings that come with the job and the dust they kick up are not problematic. They may be critical or feel ambivalent about their work but the big white vehicles, antennas, satphones, food aid, water pipes, expertise, competence and swashbuckling Sphere handbook-waving are integral parts of what they do. They may or may not see that the arrogance and the technology combine to create distance. For the people on the ground, the perceptions and the meanings of these same objects and activities may be quite different. As Hugo Slim puts it: "The same warm metal of Toyotas and water pipes may feel physically the same but might be mentally shaped by ideas of imposition, conquest, colonialism, arrogance and outrage."[9] Some extremist fringes will reject assistance altogether as an intolerable humiliation and will try to capitalise politically on the imposition. Most will accept the food aid and the new school even if it is not what they asked for. Many will wonder about the patronising attitude of the outsiders who are here one day and gone the next.

The bigger picture

Humanitarian action works as a powerful vector for western ideas and modes of behaviour. It is a powerful mechanism for shaping the relationships between the "modernised" outsiders and the multitude of the insiders. Technical knowledge and expertise—the nutritionist, the camp manager, the protection officer—are never neutral. Try as they may, aid workers carry baggage, practice and ideology that shape the relationship. And power.

This is somewhat paradoxical because, like its human rights cousin, humanitarianism emerged largely in confrontation with power. We were on the side of the vulnerable and powerless, but in the process we have become strong. Humanitarianism started off as a powerful discourse; now it is a discourse of power, both at the international and at the community level. The humanitarian establishment mobilises and moves huge resources, it interacts with politics (and business) at the highest level. It has become part of governance.[10] Some would even say that it is part of government. The Northern/Western humanitarian enterprise has positioned itself as the central vehicle for relief and protection in crisis. It has lost the aura of voluntariness and the sense of mission it had when it was at the margins. It is now central to the conceptualisation and management of the relations between the citadels of the north and the borderlands of the vast Third World periphery. It has crossed the threshold of power, even if most humanitarians—with a lack of self-awareness that borders on the schizophrenic—are loathe to admit it.

At the local level, it is deceitfully participatory. Despite much rhetoric about consultation and accountability to beneficiaries, it imposes pre-designed terms of engagement. Humanitarianism imposes Western forms of organisation, concepts of management, technical standards, and the like. It brings the values, food, clothing and music of the North to the last corners of the earth. The encounter between MTV-generation humanitarian outsiders and vulnerable groups in the periphery is not always easy or effective. Even when the outcome is positive, however, the encounter takes place on the terms and power relationships of the outsiders. The network power of the system acts as a barrier for different or alternative approaches.

Why this matters

"There is nothing so ethnocentric, so particularistic, as the claim of universalism."[11] The challenge for those who recognise themselves in the values inherent in humanitarianism is to determine whether or not it is feasible, intellectually and practically, to devise a more culturally grounded approach to providing assistance and protection to people *in extremis*, that is, an approach that is based on truly universal values—a sort of "universal universalism"—rather than on the currently dominant Western universalism. So far, there is no consensus, no clear picture of what such a framework might look like. Is it a big picture ethical framework applicable across all cultures? Or perhaps a coalition of compatible universalisms? Should an open debate where "we" do not determine "their" agenda conclude that some new and more acceptable synthesis is indeed possible, this would go a long way in re-establishing the bona fides of a humanitarian apparatus that is currently seen as blind-sided and compromised. This would imply addressing the question of whether the relationship between the "giver" and the "receiver" is inherently a disempowering one or whether it could tend towards equality.[12] It would also imply turning on its head the top-down nature of the current enterprise. A tall order given the drive to isomorphism and the power dynamics that are pushing in the opposite direction.

A glimmer of hope is to be found, perhaps, in the fact that humanitarianism in its different manifestations—as an ideology, a movement, a profession and a political economy—remains a fundamentally ethical endeavour. The question, then, is to explore whether the humanitarian ethos can become a rallying point around which a more balanced, culturally sensitive and grounded enterprise could be rebuilt. Humanitarians often find themselves in the uncomfortable situation of being "condemned to repeat."[13] It is neither practical nor useful for Northern humanitarians to claim a monopoly in holding up a Sisyphean boulder that may well end up crushing them. It is essential that they reach out to others. To be successful, however, any such attempt would have to be grounded in an approach that allows perspectives other than the dominant Western universalist discourse to emerge and be heard.

4

IMAGINING CATASTROPHE

THE POLITICS OF REPRESENTING
HUMANITARIAN CRISES

Roland Bleiker, Emma Hutchinson and David Campbell

"Like people around the world I've been watching the images on our TV screens. They are truly shocking. This is a major disaster..."

Australian prime minister Julia Gillard[1]

Images play an important role in conveying the meaning of humanitarian crises to distant audiences. By drawing attention to catastrophe and human suffering, images can also mobilise political action. So much is this the case that when crises emerge, commentators commonly urge photojournalists to produce more images, particularly of those atrocities that seem to exist in silence and demand urgent action, such as the genocide in Darfur or the systematic rape of women in the Congo.[2] A common refrain among humanitarian activists is thus the urgent need to visualise the unspeakable, to diffuse it through various media outlets and to rally the global community in a way that generates political action. Scholars largely confirm these patterns. They speak of a visual iconography of humanitarian crises and point out that images are essential for audiences to feel for and subsequently respond to those in need.[3]

The key question then is: how exactly do images influence our moral and political obligation to assist people in need? The purpose of our chapter is to address this question. We do not pretend that we are able to come up with definitive answers to the complex issues at stake. But we highlight two points that are important for understanding the linkages between images of humanitarian crises and the subsequent practice of providing humanitarian aid. First, we draw attention to the pivotal role played by the intensely emotional nature of photographs of humanitarian crises. Understanding emotions is all the more important since they have largely been sidelined in political debates and policy analyses. Prevailing approaches tend to view emotions as irrational and private phenomena, and thus of little relevance to political deliberations. Second, we show how the increasingly global circulation of images leads to changes in humanitarian space. If a crisis becomes visualised in media networks then there is also a chance for a humanitarian response to gain momentum. We thus agree with Don Hubert and Cynthia Brassard-Boudreau that humanitarian space is—contrary to widely held pessimistic opinions—not necessarily shrinking.[4] There is, for instance, little evidence that the so-called compassion fatigue syndrome is as widespread as commonly assumed. People often give generously when asked for help, as was amply demonstrated in the aftermath of the Boxing Day tsunami, for instance. But there is always power, interest and politics in all visualisations of humanitarian crises. We draw attention to the need to be aware of the ensuing ethical dilemmas.

The power of images

We live in a visual age. Images shape our understanding of the world. This phenomenon is so persuasive that influential scholars speak of a "pictorial turn," stressing that people often perceive and remember key events more through images than through factual accounts.[5] We illustrate the issues at stake by focusing on photographs. They are, of course, not the only visual sources. Moving images on television and in new media outlets are probably more influential. But photographs offer unique insights. At a time when we are saturated with information stemming from multiple media sources, photographs remain influential for their ability to capture social and political issues in succinct and mesmerising ways. They serve as "visual quotations."[6] As opposed to moving images, photographs can also be shared easily across a range of different media and for a range of different purposes—from print and online news to humanitarian ad campaigns and informal networks.

Photographs are powerful because they seem to authentically reflect what they depict.[7] More than other mediums, photographs appear to give us a genuine glimpse of "reality," a snapshot of the world as it really is. They provide us with the seductive belief that what is revealed correlates exactly with what was happening at a particular moment in time. Barbie Zelizer speaks of a kind of "eyewitness authority."[8] This is why it was long-assumed that a documentary photographer, observing the world from a distance, is an "objective witness" to political phenomena, providing accurate representations of, say, war or poverty.[9]

Few if any scholars today still believe that photographs objectively represent the world. Representation is meanwhile recognised as an inevitable aspect of politics. Photographs depict the world from a certain angle and are inevitably part of a range of political processes. But it is precisely the illusion of authenticity that makes photographs such powerful tools to convey the meaning of crises to distant audiences. Jonathon Friday writes of photographs as generating a near-compulsive draw to view the horror and spectacle of a crisis: a kind of "demonic curiosity."[10] Spectators view and re-view a humanitarian crisis through various media sources until the enormity of the event seems graspable. In doing so, photographs not only shape an individual's perception but also larger, collective forms of consciousness.

Some scholars go as far as stressing that images are so effective in recalling political events that they often become "primary markers" themselves.[11] This is to say that over time an event is recognised publicly not primarily by its political content but by its photographic representation. The representation then becomes content itself. Consider two well known examples of iconic photographs that have come to stand for the humanitarian crises they depict. First is Nick Ut's Pulitzer Prize-winning Vietnam War image of 1972. It depicts nine-year-old Kim Phuc, naked, badly burned and fleeing from her South Vietnam village after it was napalmed. At the time this photograph directed public gaze to the atrocities committed against innocent civilians. It transformed public and political perceptions of the war, so much so that it contributed to further eroding the war's legitimacy.[12] We do not represent the photograph here precisely because it is so well known. In fact, four decades later the image still stands as a metaphorical representation of the Vietnam War and the suffering it brought. The second well known example is another Pulitzer Prize-winning photograph, taken in 1993 in the famine-stricken Sudan, by Kevin Carter. Carter's photograph depicts a starving child in an unfathomable manner: kneeling helplessly on the ground, her head in her hands, while a vulture watches over. It was an image that "made the world weep" and stood—as it continues to do so—as a powerful marker of the problem of poverty in the developing world.[13]

Hardly a day goes by without photographs depicting some type of humanitarian crisis to audiences worldwide. A recent example is how, in March 2011, an earthquake and tsunami devastated large parts of Japan's northern pacific coast. Here is a photograph that appeared in the Australian newspaper the *Sydney Morning Herald* and was subsequently featured in a special website devoted to visual representations of the catastrophe:[14]

Image 1: March 2011, The Earthquake/Tsunami in Japan in the *Sydney Morning Herald*

IMAGINING CATASTROPHE

This particular photograph symbolises the tsunami's physical destruction—here in Ofunato, Iwate Prefecture—more so than any text possibly could. It provides viewers with a sense of how terrible the disaster must have been for those who faced it and, most likely, did not live to tell their trauma. This image is one of many—still and moving—that captured the world's attention. And here too, it is not just individuals who are being influenced by these visual representations: they shape both public debates and the political leaders who address them. The Australian prime minister, Julia Gillard, noted that she received the news of the disaster, like everybody else around the world, through images. And she adds, in several separate statements, how much she was "truly shocked by what I have seen."[15] It is inevitable that she, just as other leaders around the world, was influenced by the images she saw and by the politics that was inevitably associated with them: media networks and newspapers trying to capture the moment and attract viewers or readers with the most spectacular images. These images, in turn, are part of a long history of representing humanitarian catastrophes. They are also part of a long history in which governments, humanitarian agencies and other organisations rely on images—either explicitly or implicitly—to gain public support and attract donations that are meant to save those in need.[16] We now try to shed light on some aspects that shape this form of humanitarian engagement.

The emotional nature of communicating catastrophe through photographs

Photographs of crises are inherently emotional in nature and impact. They represent some of the most horrendous situations: war, genocide, famine, natural disaster. They often depict individuals in an utter state of need and despair. Emotions are in this way central to the communication of catastrophe. Indeed, crisis photographs are powerful not only because of the surreal manner in which they bring distant catastrophes into the homes of people far away, but also because they have an uncanny ability to capture that which is difficult to say: the intimately emotional nature of suffering.[17] Photographs may, as such, capture crisis in ways that words cannot. Words may be used to speak of crisis, but unlike a photograph words cannot capture the visceral and strangely visual nature of catastrophe.[18] Photographs thus provide a poignant medium through which to represent the suffering and trauma ensuing from humanitarian crises.

Vividly depicting pain, shock and horror, photographs can influence public, political perceptions and procure humanitarian sentiments precisely because they resonate emotionally with viewers.[19] Underpinning this argument is the idea that emotions pervade ways of seeing. Emotions are inseparable from both the representational and interpretative processes used to communicate and make sense of crises. They must therefore be seen as central to how photographs can (and can also fail to) elicit particular humanitarian meanings consonant with an impetus to provide aid. Consider, as an example, a photograph of another recent humanitarian natural disaster: the Boxing Day tsunami of December 2004. It was featured on the *New York Times* front page just two days after the wave struck. Set against the unprecedented natural catastrophe, which claimed the lives of more than 275,000 people, the photograph shows the trauma of one mother upon finding her dead children. It is a confronting depiction of the loss of life and corresponding grief.[20]

There is little doubt that the photograph is emotive, and it is emotive in two interrelated ways. It depicts a highly emotional situation: a

Image 2: December 2004, The Boxing Day Tsunami in the *New York Times*

woman in a state of utter of despair. But the image is also very likely to generate an emotional response from viewers. Indeed, the photograph challenges audiences with the reality and tragedy of so many young lives lost. A number of powerful techniques are employed to bring the tsunami's tragic human toll into a viewer's focus. The depiction of a mother, distraught and powerless, amidst so many tiny and now lifeless children, presents not only an arresting picture but also invokes a well-recognised symbol of sympathy and humanitarianism. Representing the scope of death in such a manner is key to the photograph's emotional appeal. Indeed, not only does it communicate the tremendous sorrow and loss but also, crucially, it helps to produce the idea that the tsunami is an unprecedented catastrophe for which viewers should feel compassion and be drawn into some form of humanitarian response. David Perlmutter suggests that photographs are politically persuasive because of their ability to incite "outrage"—an emotional response he defines as loosely based on anger, agitation, sympathy and fear.[21]

Photographs that are circulated and viewed around the world give meaning to a humanitarian crisis. The emotions involved in viewing and remembering images are not just individual, but inevitably collective: they create emotional bonds between immediate victims and distant viewers. Some commentators believe that emotions have a negative impact on humanitarian operations. For instance, proponents of the "compassion fatigue" argument maintain that emotions will inevitably err on the side of apathy and inaction rather than those associated with a genuine concern and corresponding will to help those in need. The main point such scholars make is that an overexposure to images of suffering eventually renders the viewer numb and indifferent.[22] We believe that there is no evidence to support such a gloomy view. Humanitarian space is not necessarily shrinking. While individuals and societies often block out or even deny images of human suffering,[23] there is ample evidence that the public reacts generously when charity organisations appeal for help.[24] If images of a humanitarian crisis circulate in global media networks then they can reach a worldwide audience, thus creating the potential for a significant humanitarian response. But even scholars who recognise the importance of this expanding humanitarian space acknowledge that crises photographs pose "troubling options" for viewers: they generate compassion and even a sense of shared suffering while, at the same time, also eliciting "cynicism and despair."[25] There is, then, a need to investigate the precise politics involved in visually representing humanitarian crises—a task we will now take up during the remaining part of this chapter.

The politics of representing humanitarian crises

One thing is clear, then: politics and human interest are an essential element in how images, and the emotions they engender, shape our understanding and responses to humanitarian crises.[26] We would like to illustrate some of the key issues at stake through a concrete example of a humanitarian crisis image: a widely circulated, iconic HIV/AIDS photograph, taken in 1986 by Ed Hooper.[27] It depicts a Ugandan woman, Florence, and her child, Ssengabi, sitting outside their home in Gwanda, Uganda.[28] When the photograph was taken both Florence and Ssengabi were visibly ill.

Taken during the early period of Western public awareness about HIV/AIDS, this photograph provided a "face" that could symbolise the crisis in Africa. It was subsequently published widely in the international media, including *Newsweek* and two years later in the *Washington Post*. The Hooper photograph illustrates how an image can have a tremendous impact on raising global awareness of a pressing humanitarian issue. But the very prominence—and success—of this photograph also illustrates the deeply political aspects involved in crisis photography. Four issues stand out.

First: the image illustrates the use of a persistent aesthetic style in crisis photography: the use of individual subjects to "put a face" to a larger catastrophic event, thereby encouraging viewers to identify with and feel for the distant suffering being depicted. Michael Shapiro has called this technique a "personal code:" a representational strategy designed not only to centre the viewer's attention but also to capture an overall issue or crisis.[29] While humanitarian emergencies tend to be complex in origin and nature, such a "personal code" compresses the complexities into a schematic, readily identifiable picture. It simplifies—and supposedly humanises—the situation for distant audiences. The objective here is to simultaneously convey the personal details of an individual life and in so doing provide enough context to allow viewers to generalise widely about the nature and impact of the crisis. The plight of Florence and her child thus comes to stand for the far more complex

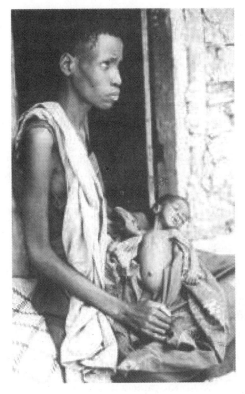

Image 3: 1986, Ed Hooper's Ugandan portrait in *Newsweek* (later also in the *Washington Post*)

and far more political "HIV/AIDS crisis in Africa." The result is inevitably inadequate, perhaps even dehumanising. Look at the Hooper photograph: it depicts a dying mother and child, sitting alone in an open doorway somewhere in Africa. No other people are visible, nor are there any features that can be recognised as part of a particular society or culture. Hooper displays Florence and Ssengabi passively, as if they were unable to do anything but wait for death. They are seen in one function only, as sufferers. Indeed, Florence and Ssengabi are entirely defined by their suffering. But this was, of course, not their only identity, even though they were facing imminent death. One could have just as well presented them in different ways, as being integrated in their surroundings, or as pursuing an activity.

Second: the image employs a powerful humanitarian icon, namely the image of mother and child. Numerous scholars argue that women and children are commonly used as international "symbols of distress."[30] For some, images of mothers and child call to mind the pieta: the Madonna mourning the loss of her child, a universally recognised icon of compassion and grief. Lisa Malkki goes further to suggest that there is an "international expectation of a certain kind of helplessness" associated with images of women and children. So much is this the case that they have become a "conventionalised" mechanism for the representation of tragic humanitarian situations. Women and children—like this picture of Florence and Ssengabi, presented as helpless and vulnerable—can call to mind a pressing humanitarian message: that victims not only need (your) help but they need it fast. It is thus not surprising that photojournalists often employ particular recognised icons to represent humanitarian hardship and distress. These are the representations viewers are most accustomed to: images of passive and powerless mothers and children, usually staring big-eyed into cameras, of destitute refugees represented en masse, and of the spectacular devastation that both natural and human-made crises can reap.

Third: Hooper's image of Florence and Ssengabi's displays a deeply "colonial" perspective, invoking stereotypical perceptions of life in the developing world.[31] With the camera tilted down and Florence and Ssengabi sitting silent, the image voids Florence and Ssengabi of independence and agency. It stresses the misery, vulnerability and seemingly inactive nature of their situation—and by extension of the developing world more generally. In this way the image taps into existing assumptions about Third World dependency, effectively communicating that victims are desperately reliant upon outside aid. Survivors are depicted as victims; the helpless and needy recipients of aid. The audience, by contrast, is the humanitarian provider. This is why photographs do not stand alone but, rather, are part of a "system of representation."[32] The meanings attained by crisis photographs are inevitably intertwined with the context in which they are viewed. Simply put, the understandings and the knowledge produced by photographs are at least partially contingent upon the particular historically-developed cultural, aesthetic and affective sensibilities of those who view them. Photographs are in this way part of a much wider set of representational practices that bestow often distant humanitarian crises with social, political and humanitarian meanings.

Fourth: the very fact that Hooper's shocking image shows Florence and Ssengabi close to death means that any kind of humanitarian help will come too late, at least for them. This is, indeed, one of the key dilemmas of crises photography: the media is, as David Campbell points out, often a "late indicator of distress, not an early warning agency."[33] The challenge for humanitarian organisations and the media then is to actively engage the politics of representation and to find a way of visualising crises before they escalate. This is also why Campbell believes the problem is not compassion fatigue but "official indifference and the media's entrapment in that indifference until it is too late."[34]

Conclusion

We cannot take the politics out of pictures. Any form of representation involves making choices. It is a form of power and thus inevitably political. But the issues at stake are particularly vexing when it comes to political responses to humanitarian crises. Dominant forms of crisis photography often focus on the horror, desperation and neediness of distant others. And although they often come late, at a time when a crisis is already in its final stage, such images also provide those viewing them from a distance with the motivation to help.[35] There are mixed motives in these media representations: commercial interests as well as seemingly more noble humanitarian intentions. Robert Hariman and John Lewis Lucaites have demonstrated that these types of crisis images lie at the heart of a particularly troubling conundrum: while the dominant iconography of crisis is in many ways problematic, it also seems to be the most powerful in procuring international aid. Dominant images are blatant in their humanitarian appeals. They tap directly into to established meanings of charity and goodwill, particularly in the liberal West.[36]

As scholars we need to understand and critique how images of crises use shock, horror and cultural stereotypes. We need to deconstruct the politics involved in this process: the moment when a crisis is visualised, the simplifying mechanisms involved in it and the manner in which iconic images often hark back to and feed into highly problematic and often colonial power relations. But as human beings we also need to recognise that such images, problematic as they might be, can be a powerful tool to mobilise humanitarian relief. Finding the fragile balance between these two poles—and searching for alternatives to them—is as difficult as it is imperative. Our chapter has sought to make a small contribution to addressing this inevitably political humanitarian challenge.

PART II

FIVE SPACES FOR
HUMANITARIAN POLITICS

5

HUMANITARIAN SPACE IN DARFUR

CAUGHT BETWEEN THE LOCAL AND THE GLOBAL

Kurt Mills

Since the start of the conflict in Darfur in February 2003, humanitarian action has been a complex affair. Like many situations today, humanitarian actors find themselves in a difficult and complex operating environment, caught between competing actors. Darfur is emblematic of a changing global environment, which, while at least partially characterised by positive developments in human rights, norms and practices, nonetheless creates more uncertainty for humanitarians. As such, it raises very significant questions about notions of humanitarian space. In this chapter I will first briefly describe this evolving global normative environment which may dramatically affect humanitarian action on the ground. I will then briefly discuss the contested concept of humanitarian space. Following this, I will look at the specific case of Darfur and analyse how evolving global and local dynamics have affected humanitarian action in Darfur.

NEGOTIATING RELIEF

Old, new and emerging responsibilities and responses

Since the late 1990s, the global human rights and humanitarian discourse has undergone significant shifts which, on the one hand would appear to strengthen the hand of those wanting to protect civilians in the midst of conflict but which, in reality, sometimes makes their job more difficult. The move from notions of absolute sovereignty to those which put the human rights of the individual at the centre of state—and international—responsibility, particularly in the midst of conflict and mass atrocity situations, is founded to a large extent on state responsibilities found in international human rights law and international humanitarian law (IHL), on which humanitarian action is based. From these developments we can identify three human rights-related responsibilities of states and the international community writ large in the context of violent conflict. These three responsibilities—named elsewhere as the responsibilities to protect, to prosecute and to feed—correspond to three interrelated sets of norms and practices which form the main responses to mass atrocities and associated humanitarian crises, and which constitute and constrain humanitarian action. They thus, as we shall see, help to define humanitarian space.[1] Although they have similar roots, the nature and political context of the responsibilities means that while we might expect them to be mutually supportive, at times the existence of these norms and practices may create dilemmas and difficulties for those responding to such situations—particularly for humanitarians.

Taking these three in reverse order, we begin with the responsibility to feed, or classic humanitarian action—providing food, water, shelter, medical and other assistance to victims of conflict. Given its conceptual, normative and legal pedigree dating back to the mid-nineteenth century running through the 1949 Geneva Conventions and beyond, this is the most firmly rooted and accepted responsibility.[2] In one way or another it forms the basis for the mandates of all humanitarian actors—whether legally endowed or self-ascribed. It is, in one sense, the most basic of actions one can take to help people in conflict. Of the three main international responses to violent conflict it is—conceptually anyway—the least political and the least reliant on formal political actors, although, regardless of rhetoric, most humanitarians would accept that their actions are in many—perhaps fundamental—ways, political. This is especially the case with regard to the move towards rights-based humanitarianism, where humanitarian actors look at the political context in which the violations are occurring and potentially try to alter that political context—that is to try to stop the violations rather than just treating the symptoms of the violations. While conceptually humanitarian action is less dependent on the other actions I will discuss, humanitarians are frequently dependent upon political actors—states, but also other non-state actors—for resources and, frequently, access to those they are trying to help. For many of these political actors, especially Western donor states, supporting humanitarian action is frequently the least costly—at least in the short term—of their options in dealing with conflict and widespread gross violations of human rights. And once international actors make such a determination to support humanitarian actors, such action is politicised. Humanitarian action, even though legally non-political, is also politicised by actors on the ground as both governments and rebel groups try to use humanitarian aid for their own ends.[3] This has obvious implications for humanitarian space, as will be elaborated below.

The second responsibility of states and the international community, while also founded in IHL and post-Second World War war crimes trials, has much more recent legal foundations. Building upon the International Tribunals for the Former Yugoslavia and Rwanda, the International Criminal Court is a global institutional manifestation of the fight against impunity.[4] After it formally came into being in 2002, it theoretically became much harder for leaders and others to escape punishment for war crimes, crimes against humanity and genocide. With an independent prosecutor it was, as all justice systems are supposed to be, theoretically non-political. However, given that it was created through a political process, to prosecute political actors, and with a direct connection to the UN Security Council, which was given power to refer situations to the ICC and temporarily defer ICC proceedings, it obviously has the potential to be a tool for states. And given that it can be—and has been—invoked during ongoing conflicts, the mere existence of the ICC can make the work of humanitarian actors more complicated as they may be perceived by various actors on the ground as potential sources of information for the prosecutor. While the potentially overtly political nature of the ICC, and the sovereignty costs associated with the ICC as an international institution, make recourse to the ICC on the part of the international community more problematic, it can still be an attractive option, particularly when the other alternative—the responsibility to protect—is also on the table. Thus, humanitarian actors may be affected by domestic political calculations in Washington, DC, London, Paris and elsewhere.

The responsibility to protect (R2P) is, in one sense, nothing new.[5] It is founded, conceptually, on international human rights law and IHL, which define state responsibilities towards their citizens—and others—during times of peace and conflict. Examples of R2P-like international action can be found in the early 1990s as the UN Security Council started using human rights and humanitarian crises as a basis for Chapter VII military action.[6] It was given a name in 2001 and formally endorsed by the World Summit in 2005.[7] Yet the fact that the entire international community stated, for the first time, that the UN could sanction military action to stop mass atrocities was new. While not a legally binding norm—the World Summit Outcome Document includes many caveats, and in any case did not create new international law—R2P has changed global discourse and, as a result, has changed conflict dynamics in a variety of situations. The invocation and application of R2P has the possibility for both enhancing and problematising action by humanitarian actors.

Humanitarian space

As will be seen, the application of these three responsibilities can have a significant effect on humanitarian space. However, before analysing this situation, we need to understand what we mean by humanitarian space in both conceptual and practical senses. In one of the opening chapters, Don Hubert and Cynthia Brassard-Boudreau provide a number of definitions from various humanitarian actors. These definitions are all very conceptual. But if we are to apply an understanding of humanitarian space in practice, we need to think in more concrete and practical terms. Hubert and Brassard-Boudreau identify three dimensions of humanitarian space, focusing on the actual physical area in which humanitarians deliver assistance. While generally agreeing with the approach taken, I would like to address the issue from a slightly different—and broader—perspective. The first element of the concept—"humanitarian"—is perhaps the easiest in concretise. We are talking about people's ability to be safe and protected and have at least the bare minimum of resources necessary to live. So they need to be free from threats like being killed by governmental or non-governmental entities. They also need food, water, shelter and clothing. The displaced, and many other war-affected victims, will likely—although perhaps not always—need to rely on others to provide the latter, particularly if they find themselves in camps, or in other situations where they do not have access to normal support systems. Regarding the former, such individuals might gain safety by fleeing to another part of their country or to another country—although this is certainly not always a route to real safety. They may find safety in camps. Many international humanitarian organisations (IHOs) talk about assistance as protection, including the supposition that just being on the ground in conflict situations can deter potential attackers.[8] While this may be the case at times, history is replete with situations where displaced camps and other situations where IHOs are located are not safe for the simple reasons that they are no match to people with guns. Thus, there may be situations where other people with guns—frequently in the form of UN peacekeeping and peace enforcement missions—are needed on the ground to physically protect people. Even this is not always a guarantee of protection, however, if the peacekeepers do not have the mandate or the resources to stand up to the other people with guns.

"Space" is a more difficult concept to operationalise. It can mean the immediate environment in which the displaced are located and IHOs are operating. We can ask who controls the physical space—the government? Rebel groups? Do the displaced have the ability to move to places they consider to be safe either within or outside their country? Do IHOs have the ability to move as they please, gain access to affected populations to both consult with them and provide assistance? If not, is this because of the physical environment in which they are operating—for example how are the roads—or is it because they are restricted in their access by one or more parties to the conflict?

More broadly, however, humanitarian space can be conceptualised as the broader ideational and political environment in which humanitarian actors operate, and in which the displaced are frequently moved about as pawns on a geopolitical chessboard. Humanitarian actors are not only subject to those on the ground in the midst of a conflict. Ideas, laws and norms, states, intergovernmental organisations and other actors all serve to constitute the environment in which they operate and can either enable or constrain their action. Such global actors provide funds for

IHOs. They can make the immediate physical operating environment for IHOs either more secure or less secure by their actions. They can support individuals' access to protection through robust peacekeeping and opening borders, or they can close borders, prevent people from reaching safety and engage in military activities which put them in harm's way. They can also act in other ways which may have an influence on IHOs' ability to operate effectively.

Thus, for purposes of this chapter, I will define humanitarian space as the local and global physical, ideational, political and strategic environment in which individuals attempt to claim their right to assistance and protection, and in which humanitarian actors operate. However, given the focus of this book, this chapter will concentrate on the perspective of humanitarian actors, while recognising that individuals are the ultimate starting point, and also play a significant role in creating their own humanitarian space.[9] As will be demonstrated, taking into account both the local and global aspects of humanitarian space, humanitarian actors had their freedom of movement and action severely curtailed in Darfur.

The locality and globality of humanitarian action in Darfur

The three responsibilities outlined above have all been implemented in varying ways in Darfur. The practice and interaction of these responsibilities has created a complex operating environment for humanitarian actors. The conflict began in February 2003 when a group of Darfuris started a rebellion against the government in Khartoum in response to decades of maldevelopment on the part of the government.[10] The government responded with a vengeance by, among other things, arming local militias. These militias—and government troops—not only fought the rebel groups, but also went on widespread killing sprees, razing villages and displacing many hundreds of thousands of Darfuris. Humanitarian actors, as is usually the case, were on the scene in Darfur long before the international community began to take notice. The African Union (AU) deployed a small peacekeeping force, AMIS, which was ineffectual—as a result both of a lack of resources and also a lack of a mandate to challenge the regime in Khartoum.[11] Thus, where there was insecurity for individuals and humanitarian actors, they could not count on AMIS to protect them. Initially, this insecurity stemmed from the actions of the government and Janjaweed militias, although as rebel groups splintered they became another source of insecurity.

It was not until 2004 that the international community beyond the AU began to take notice of the situation. As the term genocide began to be bandied about, there was great pressure on the UN—and especially Western powers—to do something to stop the violence. Although the something was frequently not specified, it was understood to mean military intervention. For a great variety of reasons, this was not on the cards. Instead, at the end of March 2005, the UN Security Council decided to refer the situation in Darfur to the ICC. As we shall see, it was not until 2009 that this had a significant effect on the operations of humanitarian actors, although it will be interesting to note that one of the first people to have an arrest warrant issued against them was Ahmed Haroun, who was then the Sudanese minister for humanitarian affairs— the individual responsible for interacting with humanitarian actors and facilitating the provision of assistance.[12] The arrest warrant indicated that he had been doing the exact opposite.

The humanitarian situation got better in the first part of 2005. While there was still fighting and insecurity, the level of killing dropped significantly for a few months. Humanitarian actors were better able to access the affected populations. This changed in September when the fighting erupted again. Civilians were attacked and because of insecurity, particularly in West Darfur, NGOs were forced to withdraw, and humanitarian organisations were able to reach less than half of the population.[13] Yet, because there was still significant fighting and insecurity, the UN deployed the hybrid AU-UN Mission in Darfur (UNAMID) at the end of 2007, although with only around one-third of the planned troop-strength of 26,000 initially. This was essentially a "re-hatting" of AMIS, but also represented a significant expansion of the force with expanded resources. However, it was still constrained by resources and mandate. In terms of resources, it lacked simple things like helicopters which were needed to ferry troops around the vast area of Darfur and respond rapidly to situations of insecurity and killing. Excuses given by those countries which might have contributed helicopters were that there was a global shortage of military grade helicopters because they were in use elsewhere—particularly Afghanistan and Iraq. Thus the so-called "global war on terror" undermined security—and humanitarian space—in Darfur. UNAMID finally received the first five helicopters in February 2010, more than two years after its deployment.[14] Just three months later, the government banned helicopter flights by UNAMID for a couple of weeks.[15] This was part of a broader pattern whereby the government placed significant restrictions on when the UN could fly its aircraft, particularly at night. Even though UNAMID was deployed under Chapter VII of the UN Charter, which allows the Security Council to authorise missions against the wishes of governments, UNAMID did not have the mandate to defy the wishes of Khartoum, but rather had to negotiate over issues like when it could fly its planes or, indeed, where it troops could go.[16]

The humanitarian space constricted significantly in 2009. On 4 March 2009 the ICC issued an arrest warrant for Sudanese president Omar al Bashir. Almost immediately Bashir ejected thirteen international humanitarian organisations from Darfur, claiming that they had given false information to the ICC. They thus became pawns in a much broader geopolitical game. When this happened, there was very significant worry that this could lead to extremely dire consequences for the people on the ground. The thirteen aid agencies represented 40 per cent of aid agency staff and were responsible for feeding more than one million people.[17] The World Food Programme had used two expelled agencies for 80 per cent of their food distribution.[18] While this did have significant negative effects on civilians in Darfur, the impact was not as severe as many had feared, as organisations still on the ground worked hard to fill the gap.[19] Further, some of the NGOs had been "re-hatted" and come back into Darfur under different guises. In particular, different chapters of the same global federations moved in. For example, while Oxfam UK was kicked out of Darfur, Oxfam US, which was already operating in other parts of Sudan, was able to move into Darfur.[20] In addition, Mercy Corps Scotland registered to work in Darfur after US-based Mercy Corps was expelled. CARE International Foundation (Switzerland) did the same after CARE USA was expelled.[21] All these expelled organisations reiterated that those going back into Darfur were separate entities. This was not part of an international strategy on the part of Oxfam International, for example, and as a matter of policy, Oxfam as a global movement/organisation would not try to get around such restrictions merely by substituting one element for the other.[22] However, the fact that other elements of the same global organisation with the same humanitarian ideology are sometimes able to fill a void does highlight complex interactions within humanitarian space of various elements of the humanitarian international community. Other organisations expelled, such as the International Rescue Committee, do not have such a federal structure; nor do its operating principles allow it to pursue such strategies.[23]

During this same period there was an ongoing debate about the necessity and wisdom of more robust military action in Darfur. On the one side were those who argued that the killing was continuing unabated and, invoking R2P, called for much stronger action to protect civilians.[24] On the other side were those who argued that the violence was not nearly as bad as it was in 2003–2004, and/or that such military action would imperil the humanitarian aid efforts.[25] While UNAMID expanded, it had not enhanced it capabilities nearly as fast as many hoped. It is still lacking helicopters necessary to cover the very large area of Darfur and is still at the mercy of various factions—government, militia and rebel—which have attacked and killed dozens of peacekeepers.[26]

Complex humanitarian space in Darfur

This very brief review of the situation in Darfur reveals very complex dynamics which affect humanitarian action and the "space" in which humanitarians operate. In this final section I will highlight the complexities of humanitarian space as revealed in Darfur by identifying the various axes and planes which constitute the space in which humanitarian actors operate. If we imagine a three-sided pyramid, with IHOs at the top, and armed groups (both governmental and non-governmental), peacekeepers and the ICC at the three base points, we make concrete the planes and axes of the space in which IHOs operate (see Figure 1).[27] There is the military environment/plane, defined by the IHOs, armed groups and peacekeeping points. This plane has the IHO-armed groups axis, where IHOs must negotiate with various armed groups to get access to affected populations. IHOs must also deal with peacekeepers, both as potential sources of security and insecurity. In Darfur, IHOs have been attacked by various military actors, and otherwise have been prevented from gaining access to affected populations. While there have been efforts on the part of UNAMID to facilitate access to affected populations,[28] these efforts have been far less than what has been required, since the peacekeepers have been short on resources and have a weak mandate. In addition, as seen in the debate over more robust military action, there is also a worry that greater military action will jeopardise the humanitarian mission. It could invite further restrictions from the government. Further, NGOs are generally very wary about using peacekeepers as protection, since doing so could create a perception on the part of various parties to the conflict that they, too, have taken sides. While the former axis is purely domestic, the latter axis brings in an international element which puts humanitarians at the whim of geopolitical forces which are unpredictable. To combat this, NGOs must establish the trust of local leaders and populations by building up relationships on the ground, although this will obviously not work in all circumstances.

The criminal justice plane is defined by the IHOs, armed groups and ICC points. The addition of the ICC point creates problems for IHOs in their relationship with armed groups, since the ICC is a threat to armed groups and there will be worry on the part of such actors that IHOs may cooperate with the ICC. More broadly, however, as seen in Darfur, the ICC brings in another unpredictable international element, since IHOs were expelled from the local humanitarian space by one of the local armed groups (the government) to protest against the international actions of the ICC and generally exert their power. While Bashir may have just used the arrest warrant as an excuse to expel the NGOs, the application of international criminal justice norms directly impacted the application of international humanitarian norms and action. The perpetrators of crimes against humanity were targeted by the ICC, but it was the civilians who suffered.

The third plane is purely international, encompassing IHOs, peace-keeping and ICC points. It is on this plane where IHOs are most directly buffeted by the winds of geopolitics, as the international community debates how to address situations such as Darfur. In Darfur, the international community chose first the humanitarian response, then the criminal justice response and finally a very weak R2P/peacekeeping response. At the same time, regardless of what global powers were choosing, IHOs had made their own choice to be in Darfur, and while these same powers were deciding what to do, the IHOs had to deal with local forces, sometimes successfully, sometimes not. The insertion of the international element in one sense made their lives more difficult, as they had to deal with the fallout of the Bashir arrest warrant, as well as debates about the invocation of R2P. The final plane, or base, of the humanitarian space pyramid, is where various local armed groups, peacekeepers and criminal justice mechanisms all interact, with civilians in the middle. IHOs look down on this from their lofty humanitarian imperative peak and must figure out how to engage with this complex situation on the ground while negotiating labyrinthine local and global dynamics.[29]

Thus, humanitarian space has been both constituted and constrained in Darfur, as in many other situations, by both local and global forces. The IHOs themselves decide whether they want to be in Darfur. NGOs decide this based on their humanitarian mandate and available resources. UNHCR and similar organisations decide on similar bases, or have the decision made for them by their political masters in New York. It is armed groups which determine the basic level of security or insecurity on the ground. Peacekeepers can, at times, contribute to security, although their very presence can also politicise the conflict—and the IHOs—even further, and more generally potentially endanger humanitarian actors. The ICC places IHOs in an ambiguous and difficult situation because, while many will support the goals of the ICC, they become objects of suspicion once the ICC becomes interested in a situation. Further, as we have seen, humanitarian action can become a pawn in efforts to combat

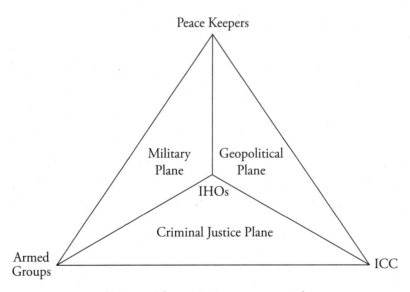

Figure 1: A humanitarian space pyramid

impunity and become objects of war crimes themselves, as they are either targeted by various military elements or ejected from the country by local political forces. Thus, the "space" for protection of individuals and the "space" for action on the part of IHOs is determined by who IHOs are and how they act, but also by perceptions of who they are and what they are doing on the ground, and to what political use they may be put by local and global political actors. And, as in the case of the response to the Bashir arrest warrant, they may also be "collateral damage." The pyramidal nature of the space in which humanitarian actors operate is thus a difficult and complex melding of local and global factors. While, as Hubert and Brassard-Boudreau argue at the beginning of this volume, humanitarian space may in fact be expanding globally, it is also becoming more complicated for humanitarian actors to navigate and can be both constituted and constrained by a constant interplay of local and global actors and dynamics.[30]

6

WORLD POLITICS AND HUMANITARIANISM IN KOSOVO

A SYMBIOTIC RELATIONSHIP?

Andrea Edoardo Varisco

In biology, two different species are in symbiosis when they live in close proximity and depend on each other in specific ways, each gaining benefits from the other. An excellent example of this type of relationship is the oxpecker, an African bird that lives in symbiosis with large mammals. Perching on the back of antelopes and zebras, oxpeckers pick ticks from the animals' fur, simultaneously cleaning them while feeding themselves. This chapter argues that, just as large mammals live in symbiosis with oxpeckers, world politics and humanitarianism were similarly connected during the Kosovo War in 1999, exploring the different consequences that this military intervention created for both world politics and humanitarianism. The chapter is divided into six parts with a parallel structure which analyses world politics and humanitarianism during the conflict, their symbiotic relationship and the consequences of this relationship on them.[1] The first section presents a brief account

73

of the historical context and a summary of the events that led to the conflict. The second and third parts investigate the main features of world politics and humanitarianism during the Kosovo War, respectively. The fourth section merges world politics and humanitarianism, explaining whether and how the relationship between them in Kosovo can be considered symbiotic. The fifth and the sixth parts examine separately the consequences that the Kosovo campaign and this symbiotic relationship had on both world politics and humanitarianism. These two parts lead to a final conclusion that further underlines how the Kosovo intervention affected the nature of world politics and humanitarianism, and, more importantly for the aims of this book, the original notion of humanitarian space as "an environment in which humanitarian agencies can operate independently of external political and other agendas."[2]

Historical context

The Kosovo emergency occurred in the wake of the Bosnian peace process: as the 1995 Dayton Peace Accords failed to address the Kosovo situation, the Albanians in the region felt ignored by the international community and abandoned the pacifist leadership of Ibrahim Rugova. The Kosovo Liberation Army (KLA) initiated a low intensity war against the Serb forces in the region, which responded with several offensives that sometimes ended in massacres of Albanian civilians.[3] Following the Serb refusal to sign the Rambouillet Peace Agreement, the North Atlantic Treaty Organisation (NATO) started a bombing campaign which lasted seventy-eight days from 24 March to 9 June 1999. Rather than compelling Milosevic to sign the agreement, the operation caused a violent reaction by Serbian paramilitary forces and precipitated a major humanitarian emergency that resulted in at least 10,000 deaths and 800,000 refugees and internally displaced people (IDPs) among the Kosovar Albanians.[4] United Nations Security Council (UNSC) Resolution 1244 ended the war, demanded the withdrawal of Serb military and police personnel from Kosovo and deployed a NATO-led international security force in the region.[5] Nonetheless, peace was not completely achieved after the resolution. Instead, the KLA filled the vacuum left by the Yugoslavian troops and expelled more than 250,000 non-Albanians from the region.[6] To date, the constitutional political status of Kosovo remains undefined, with ninety of the 193 United Nations member countries recognising its state independence.

A SYMBIOTIC RELATIONSHIP?

The war in Kosovo: world politics...

The 1999 NATO campaign was an external intervention in a sovereign state by a regional military alliance without UNSC approval, an action that deeply involved the international community: sovereign states, NATO, the UN and non-governmental organisations (NGOs), each playing a role on the Kosovo chessboard. Many states' interests were at stake during the campaign. For the United States, the NATO bombings in Kosovo represented an opportunity to prove to the world that in the hegemonic post-Cold War international system "world order and Pax Americana are roughly the same thing."[7] Neighbouring European countries, on the other hand, concealed their military weakness by supporting an intervention which alleviated fears of refugee influxes, conflict contagion in the Balkans and trade and tourism disruption.[8] For example, fear of refugee influxes and geopolitical considerations moved some NATO allies such as Italy, a country historically linked to Albania, that tried with the intervention to reassert its role in the region and its international ambitions.[9] Conversely, the campaign was strongly opposed by Russia, which sought to defend its national interests in the light of the Kosovo crisis,[10] and China, whose embassy in Belgrade was damaged during the NATO bombings.[11] For NATO, the Kosovo campaign was another step in its post-Cold War transformation from an organisation concerned with collective defence and deterrence to a more proactive peacekeeping and peace-enforcement actor. Furthermore, the campaign raised many questions about the legitimacy of a military intervention by a regional organisation that overrode national sovereignty in the name of humanitarian principles without UNSC consensus or approval. The crisis also challenged the nature of the UN, an organisation whose mission involves sometimes difficult diplomatic mediation between states' interests and human rights. While it is true that UNSC did not approve the NATO action, it is also true that before 1999, the UNSC passed three different resolutions, namely 1160, 1199 and 1203, which were increasingly specific about the violation of humanitarian standards occurring in Kosovo, the transgression of the Serb forces and appeals to states to act. Finally, despite a Russian request, the UNSC refused to condemn the use of force on 26 March 1999.

UNSC Resolution 1244 ended the NATO campaign and has been judged by some commentators as "political science fiction."[12] The resolution deployed "international civil and security presences"[13] and assured the security of the international civil personnel under UN authority—the United Nations Interim Administration Mission in Kosovo (UNMIK); a mission which still exists today, but now plays a minor role following the creation and deployment in 2008 of the European Union Rule of Law Mission in Kosovo (EULEX)—through the presence of a NATO-led Kosovo Force (KFOR). The resolution also called for the withdrawal of military, police and paramilitary forces, as well as the demilitarisation of the KLA, forecasting the return of an agreed number of Yugoslav and Serb military and police personnel. Furthermore, it did not avoid KLA-led counterattacks against Serbs and Roma, as Kosovar Albanians expelled more than 250,000 non-Albanians from Kosovo upon their return to the region. Finally, the status of Kosovo as a protectorate with substantial autonomy and meaningful self-administration, within the Federal Republic of Yugoslavia remained open to different interpretations, as demonstrated in 2008 when Kosovo's unilateral declaration of independence was recognised by only part of the international community and the International Court of Justice.[14]

…and humanitarianism

The Kosovo emergency occurred in the wake of the Bosnian peace process after years of humanitarian crises and ethnic conflict in the Balkans, which, in some cases, resulted in the massacre of civilians, as occurred in Srebrenica in 1995. The international community decided not to remain a passive bystander in another outburst of ethnic violence in the region and intervened to end the Serbian violence against Kosovar Albanians. Humanitarian concerns triggered a NATO intervention in the region; therefore, the Kosovo campaign has been portrayed by some scholars as a "humanitarian" war.[15] Yet, considering that the concept of humanitarianism entails assistance and protection, some evaluations demonstrate that no emergency assistance occurred before the NATO intervention. Instead, "the refugees were relatively better nourished, healthier and with better access to good resources […] than those in other emergencies."[16] The catalyst for the Kosovo campaign was instead a crisis of humanitarian protection. Nevertheless, the issue of protection was hardly addressed by the international community's intervention: the United Nations High Commissioner for Refugees (UNHCR) underlined that "on the protection side, there was a near-disaster at the outset of the emergency"[17] and:

A SYMBIOTIC RELATIONSHIP?

No framework was in place in which even the ICRC could carry out its protection activities from March to June 1999. No provision for protection was available for civilians, either on the ground or from the air.[18]

Protection was lacking before, during and after the campaign. At the outset of the emergency, thousands of refugees remained trapped at the Blace crossing point on the border between Kosovo and the Former Yugoslav Republic of Macedonia. During the intervention, "over one million people remained [...] with little or no international protection or assistance after the agencies withdrew in March 1999."[19] The ethnic cleansing against the Kosovar Albanians was indeed reinforced during the NATO bombings, and consequently the campaign produced the largest population displacement in Europe since the aftermath of the Second World War. In turn, Kosovar Albanian refugees returned after the intervention and exerted physical violence, intimidation and discrimination against the non-Albanians. Humanitarian activities in Kosovo focused on assistance to refugees and their return to the region at the end of the campaign. Before the international aid effort geared up, local humanitarian agencies such as the Mother Teresa Society played crucial roles in receiving refugees and distributing food and clothing.[20] On the other hand, international agencies did not forecast the large outflow of population and were indeed unprepared and surprised by the speed and magnitude of refugee movement. Even UNHCR had "reserves of basic relief items supposed to meet the immediate needs of 200,000–250,000 persons"[21] and an in-house capacity "totally inadequate in the Kosovo emergency without large-scale external support."[22] Moreover, the large flow of donor funds and intense media pressure multiplied the number of the agencies and actors involved in the intervention, constraining the capacity and the role of UNHCR as the lead relief agency and marginalising its coordination function.[23]

Confronting this account with the notion of humanitarian space as "an environment in which humanitarian agencies can operate independently of external political and other agendas,"[24] several reflections could be derived from the Kosovo experience. While the humanitarian space was almost non-existent during the campaign—with the violence against Kosovar Albanians increasing and the agencies with little or no access to the population at risk and being forced to withdraw from the region during the bombings—the post-war scenario was conversely characterised by an extensive presence of humanitarian actors. Nevertheless, this presence was far from being "independent of external political agendas,"[25] as the provision of aid was indeed driven by a high level of political interest and competition between donors. This politicisation of aid resulted in a lack of coordination and the multiplication of actors involved in humanitarian efforts. The large number of humanitarian actors across the region did not imply more professionalism: several of them lacked the necessary experience and competence to serve the people they intended to help. On one hand, it is undoubtedly true that the mortality rates were well below the generally accepted threshold for emergencies and that no refugees died from lack of food and shelter or from illness. On the other hand, this positive outcome was not the result of a ready humanitarian response, but was rather the consequence of fortuitous factors, such as:

The good pre-crisis health and nutritional status of the refugee population, the short duration of the emergency and quick return of the refugees, the fact that two-thirds of refugees stayed outside the camps and were supported by the local population.[26]

World politics and humanitarianism in Kosovo: a symbiotic relationship?

As has often occurred in several contemporary conflicts, political interests and humanitarian concerns were deeply intertwined during the Kosovo War. This interrelation can be considered a symbiotic relationship in which both world politics and humanitarianism met their reciprocal needs. For world politics, depicting the Kosovo campaign as a humanitarian intervention allowed participants to hide political actions behind the neutral, impartial and independent humanitarian flag. The emphasis on institutionalisation, self-government, international sovereignty and protection shows clearly that even before the war, the aims of the NATO action were not purely humanitarian, to the point that the mission rapidly transformed itself into a nation-building intervention that continues to this day. At the same time, humanitarianism took advantage of the presence of many political actors in the Kosovar landscape. Following the campaign, NGOs and international agencies rushed into the region in a number that had no precedence in other humanitarian crises. For a humanitarian agency, being in Kosovo implied competing for donors and media coverage and struggling for a place behind a TV camera. Like the zebras and antelopes cleaned by the oxpeckers, the interests and image of world politics were "cleaned" by humanitarianism, which provided the motivation and the justification for a military intervention in a sovereign country. Like oxpeckers feeding themselves on the back of the animals, humanitarian actors found in Kosovo their "food" for survival—a perfect environment crowded with donors and mass media to champion their cause. Yet, the apparently innocent concord of interests which underpinned this symbiotic relationship entailed many consequences for both world politics and humanitarianism.

The war in Kosovo: the consequences for world politics...

The main political debate that followed the campaign focused on the legitimacy of a military action undertaken by a regional organisation in a sovereign state. For example, if the Independent International Commission on Kosovo judged the campaign "illegal but legitimate,"[27] other more critical commentators considered the NATO bombings to be an imperialist intervention.[28] The international community answered the criticism by issuing the 2001 report entitled "The Responsibility to Protect,"[29] a doctrine which accepts military intervention by the international community in a sovereign country for humanitarian purposes. Since then, the responsibility to protect was subsequently adopted by 191 heads of state and government at the 2005 General Assembly World Summit and reaffirmed in two occasions by the UNSC.

Bellamy's chapter in this volume offers a deeper analysis of the responsibility to protect concept and of its implications for humanitarian interventions;[30] therefore, this chapter only underlines two issues related to the responsibility to protect with the goal to spur further discussion among scholars. First, although the report focuses on humanitarian intervention, it does not consider the issue of assistance—a core part of the humanitarian activities—a just cause for military action. The responsibility to protect is not a responsibility to protect and assist. Consequently, many humanitarian activities, such as the provision of assistance after a natural disaster, fall outside the framework of the report, as the debate about intervention after the Cyclone Nargis in Myanmar demonstrated. Second, the debate on the recent intervention in Libya and on the current situation in Syria show that some scholars doubt whether humanitarian interventions can be considered consistent with the norms of international society, pointing out how this principle is susceptible to double standards and high levels of subjectivity and selectivity.[31] Scholars further emphasise how humanitarian concerns and human rights have been disregarded when the main interests of the international community—mainly of the Western governments—were not directly at stake.[32]

...and for humanitarianism

The participation in the Kosovo humanitarian intervention, a campaign in which "for the first time military means were used to create a humanitarian space for the reconstruction of a country,"[33] also entailed many consequences for humanitarianism. These are the acceptance of war by humanitarian actors; the loss of their ideals of neutrality, impartiality and independence; and the cooperation of humanitarian actors with military personnel. The first consequence is the acceptance of war and the use of military force as an instrument to stop atrocities and promote human rights. When humanitarian actors accept a part in military operations, they participate in actions in which the boundaries between politics, military action, the state and power are blurred, becoming, in this way, a political actor. Having acquired a political status, "aid agencies are in no position to demand that governments separate aid from foreign policy when [they] are also 'doing politics' with aid."[34]

This transformation entails a second consequence: humanitarians' loss of their ideals of neutrality, impartiality and independence. With a few exceptions, these two consequences have been easily accepted by the agencies and NGOs which operated in Kosovo.[35] Aid agencies lost their independence from Western governments and their neutral, impartial and independent humanitarian space. This resulted in the creation of a morally defined hierarchy of "deserving and undeserving victims,"[36] which occurred in Kosovo when humanitarian actors were unable to assist non-Albanians targeted by Albanian-led counter-violence at the end of the campaign. The third consequence lies in civilian military cooperation, a sometimes tenuous and fraught partnership between civilian humanitarian actors and militaries during the humanitarian operations which may create problems for both the humanitarians and armed forces. On one hand, humanitarian personnel are no longer perceived as impartial by the people they assist; rather, they are considered to be a part of the military force and can, therefore, become a possible target for terrorists and guerrilla fighters, as many examples following the recent interventions in Afghanistan and Iraq demonstrate. On the other hand, humanitarian interventions require that militaries trained to fight wars not only focus on the provision of protection, but also mediate with civilians and assume a humanitarian role—tasks for which they were not necessarily trained or prepared to undertake successfully. As a consequence of the military's lack of expertise and experience in these activities, ineffectiveness in humanitarian efforts may undermine the humanitarian nature of a campaign and ultimately harm the people in need of assistance.

Conclusion

As this chapter sought to demonstrate, the relationship between world politics and humanitarianism in Kosovo can be considered a symbiotic partnership. The consequences of this intertwined relationship have affected world politics and humanitarianism differently. For world politics, the outcomes of Kosovo relied on the development of a framework of principles justifying military interventions for humanitarian purposes while, according to some critics, camouflaging the "business as usual" actions of states' interests behind the humanitarian flag. For humanitarianism, the Kosovo campaign resulted in more serious consequences. Many humanitarian actors in Kosovo accepted a role in the military intervention, working with, and sometimes under the command of, military forces. In so doing, they lost their claim to neutrality, impartiality and independence. This departure from these three humanitarian principles did not actually result in a better provision of humanitarian aid, but, according to some scholars, conversely led humanitarianism to progressively lose awareness of its role in future humanitarian interventions.[37]

This symbiotic relationship also entailed some consequences for the concept of humanitarian space, as defined, analysed and operationalised by Hubert and Brassard-Boudreau in Chapter One.[38] Almost all the definitions of humanitarian space provided in Chapter One use the three historical principles of humanitarian actions: neutrality, impartiality and independence. As demonstrated above, several humanitarian agencies accepted to disavow these principles in order to operate in Kosovo; yet, this did not necessarily result in a better or more efficient humanitarian intervention. With reference to the respect for International Humanitarian Law, the first dimension of humanitarian space, the campaign ended the violence against Kosovar Albanians, but the ethnic attacks were reinforced during the NATO bombings which, according to Human Rights Watch, resulted in 500 civilian casualties among the Yugoslav population but no fatalities among NATO troops.[39] In analysing the second dimension of humanitarian space, the security of the humanitarian personnel, this chapter argues that when humanitarian agencies accept an active role in highly politicised military interventions, they risk endangering the security of their personnel. Finally, the chapter indicates how, in Kosovo, there was a very large number of humanitarian actors, yet it also argues that this access—the third dimension of humanitarian space—was, is and will continue to be increasingly mediated by politics and diplomacy. The example of Kosovo seems to confirm Weiss's claim: the temperature in the humanitarian kitchen "is not going to get cooler or easier"[40] and symbiotic relationships between world politics and humanitarian actors will become increasingly common in future humanitarian operations.

7

SHIFTING SANDS

HUMANITARIAN RELIEF IN ACEH

Paul Zeccola

The 26 December 2004 Indian Ocean tsunami claimed the lives of some 167,000 people and displaced around 500,000 others in Aceh, an Indonesian province located on the northwestern tip of Sumatra. The disaster also shaped new physical and political contours in the province. Days after the tsunami the seaside town of Lampu'uk resembled a vast desert as the wave deposited tonnes of sand where there was once a sleepy fishing village and a few *losmen* (small hotels). The ocean enveloped the remains of private homes as well as parts of the national highway that hugged Aceh's coastline. The tsunami was a catalyst for one of Indonesia's most important political developments in recent history, namely the peaceful resolution of the violent conflict between the government of Indonesia (GoI) and the Free Aceh Movement (Gerakan Aceh Merdeka, GAM). The conflict had lasted for thirty years and came to an end on 15 August 2005 when the two groups signed a memorandum of understanding (MoU) in Helsinki. The tsunami also transformed the character of humanitarian relief in Aceh. Whereas previously local and international humanitarian groups were responding to the effects of the conflict, after the tsunami they were almost solely focused on tsunami relief. Such a shift is to be expected but it was also politically motivated and did lead to the creation of "competing" humanitarian spaces. In the first months after the tsunami, Indonesia allowed international NGOs to provide tsunami relief but restricted them from engaging in conflict-related assistance. Most NGOs were limited to tsunami-only issues despite the ongoing humanitarian needs in conflict-affected areas. This chapter explores opportunities and strategies for international NGOs in negotiating for an expanded humanitarian space to go beyond the "natural" and "apolitical" tsunami disaster response to include dealing with the "man-made," political conflict in Aceh between 2005 and 2007.[1] Many NGOs came to Aceh with plenty of internal resources to tackle the situation properly, yet how adept were they in contextualising the response in Aceh? The chapter attempts to answer this question, as well as to address conceptions of the character of humanitarian space, especially when "natural" and political disasters collide. The first section provides a background to the situation, including the pre-tsunami humanitarian response to the Aceh conflict (1998–2004). The second section assesses humanitarian approaches to conflict programming in the post-tsunami period (2005–2007).[2]

The Aceh conflict and humanitarian response

The Aceh conflict began in 1976 when Hasan di Tiro, the founder of GAM, "re-declared" Acehnese independence, claiming that Aceh was never completely colonised by The Netherlands, and that its transferral to Indonesian authorities in 1949 was illegal.[3] GAM was at its strongest in 1998 following the downfall of Indonesian president Suharto when many GAM fighters were released from prison under a government amnesty and took up arms again. Support for the movement grew amid Indonesia-wide political disorder and growing anti-Jakarta sentiment in Aceh. Clashes between the Indonesian security forces and GAM were common and GAM controlled much of the province. State infrastructure all but ceased to function and GAM established its own parallel government structure.[4]

Dissent in Aceh was underpinned by economic, civic and political transgressions and the pursuant conflict in turn caused widespread poverty, gross human rights violations and political repression. Levels of displacement fluctuated between 12,000 and 180,000 people between 1999 and 2003.[5] Local NGOs, student groups, international NGOs, UN agencies and the Red Cross movement provided a range of assistance in response to the worsening crisis. According to a 2002 United Nations World Food Programme report, the conflict exposed Acehnese internally displaced persons (IDPs) to higher rates of poverty, unemployment and poor health, "over 90 per cent of the households fell below the poverty line."[6] The six or so international NGOs operating in Aceh in the post-1998 period mostly supplied humanitarian relief to IDPs, livelihoods programmes for conflict-affected people and support for local NGOs.[7] Some, including the International Catholic Migration Commission (ICMC) also ran human rights programmes, while Peace Brigades International (PBI) accompanied local NGOs delivering humanitarian assistance and investigating human rights violations, and ran conflict transformation workshops. PBI's public slogan in Aceh was "making space for peace."

Human rights advocacy was at a peak in the post-1998 period, as Edward Aspinall noted, "the defining issue of this Acehnese political renaissance was human rights."[8] In August 1998, following widespread media exposure of human rights violations in Aceh, human rights advocacy and campaigns took centre stage in Aceh. Local media reports and victims' personal testimonies transformed the lives of many Acehnese who went on to become human rights defenders as the war continued. Most local NGOs targeted their human rights campaigns against the Indonesian state and pro-independence groups used human rights advocacy to strengthen their argument for independence. In the words of a former student leader, "Indonesia lost its moral right to govern Aceh because of human rights violations against the Acehnese."[9] GAM's strategy was to "internationalise" the conflict and one way to do so was through human rights rhetoric.[10] GAM played the human rights card to attract local and international support for the struggle and to direct criticism to the GoI. They were afraid that local NGOs linked to GAM would "trick" international NGOs into supporting GAM's "internationalising" strategy.[11] The political dynamic constrained humanitarian space in Aceh during this period whereby Indonesian military leaders and politicians linked support for human rights with support for GAM. Some humanitarian workers argued that humanitarian access would be jeopardised by human rights activities while others actively promoted human rights.

Two key challenges in responding to the Aceh conflict were maintaining neutrality and ensuring staff security. It was important to preserve the impression of neutrality because the Indonesian authorities were wary of human rights issues and foreign interference and were distrustful of the activities of some local NGOs. International NGOs tried to establish support at all levels of the Indonesian government to ensure the smooth running of their programmes. Most secured a MoU with a relevant ministry in Jakarta, such as the departments of education or health. International NGOs were always extremely cautious about which organisations to work with. PBI, for instance, deliberately selected a mixture of partners, including local humanitarian and human rights NGOs, in order not to appear over-political and to be focusing only on human rights issues. Such a "negative perception" could have jeopardised its access to Aceh. Perhaps more important for day-to-day operations, NGO staffers worked to cultivate personal relations with police, military and local government authorities in Aceh. This often involved direct negotiations with military leaders and field commanders.

Maintaining neutrality and staff safety were both critical to preserving humanitarian access. One international NGO director in Aceh in 2001–2003, who requested to remain anonymous, saw working on human rights as becoming politicised, and potentially jeopardising an entire programme. When asked about the NGO's position on human rights in Aceh, he replied: "It's a trade off. We maintain a low profile simply to maintain a presence." He perceived human rights work as having security repercussions: "Basically, we didn't want our staff to be harmed or threatened. It is important not to work on a political agenda, especially local NGOs' political agendas. The focus must be on humanitarian principles."[12] He saw the integration of human rights into humanitarianism as the politicisation of humanitarian aid, which could lead to the targeting of aid workers and to NGOs being forced to withdraw their programme. This threat was very real: some Oxfam local staffers were tortured in August 2000. Local NGO workers were systematically targeted by the Indonesian security forces and faced intimidation, detention and forced "disappearance."[13] Some humanitarian workers, most notably the large international NGOs, considered humanitarian space to be a practical and physical space in which humanitarian workers could access safely and thus correlating to the second and third concepts explained in the introduction chapter. In May 2003 when the peace process mediated by the Geneva-based Centre for Humanitarian Dialogue faltered and President Megawati Sukarnoputri declared Aceh to be under a military emergency, humanitarian activities in the province were restricted. By July 2003 international aid agencies were effectively forced out of Aceh. Most international NGOs made certain compromises, such as not raising human rights issues, in the interest of maintaining a presence in Aceh. However, these compromises were not sufficient to garner the support of the government to remain in Aceh during the military emergency.

Post-tsunami challenges

According to the Agency for the Rehabilitation and Reconstruction of Aceh and Nias (BRR), the humanitarian response to the tsunami included some 124 international NGOs, 430 local (and national) NGOs, eleven foreign militaries, donor and UN agencies, the International Federation of the Red Cross and Red Crescent Societies, the ICRC and the Indonesian Red Cross.[14] The contrast with the recent past was striking: there was a sudden increase from approximately ten expatriates working in Aceh at the height of the conflict in 2001 to literally thousands in early 2005. The Tsunami Evaluation Coalition (TEC), a multi-agency learning and accountability initiative, conducted several studies of the international response to the Indian Ocean tsunami. One of the studies, on the financial response to the tsunami, found that the tsunami appeal "was the largest international response to a natural disaster; the largest public response, but not the largest official response; involved the largest number of donors (state and private); had the largest number of implementing agencies involved in the response; [and] involved the largest amount of aid per affected person." In addition, it saw the fastest financial response: "the response from the general public was also extremely rapid. A record of £10 million in 24 hours was donated via the UK DEC [Disasters Emergency Committee] website."[15] Commitments to the reconstruction programme in Aceh and Nias for 2005–2009 totalled $8.85 billion. This figure includes money contributed by domestic governments, donors (multilateral and bilateral) and private entities (NGOs). NGOs had more funds ($2.5 billion) at their disposal than multilateral donors ($2 billion). Oxfam alone had $95 million in its tsunami fund for Indonesia in the period between December 2004 and September 2007.[16]

While the tsunami response, especially during the initial "emergency phase" was widely hailed as a success—with no major outbreaks of disease, and clean water, food, health care and shelter provided promptly— local groups and international evaluators make a number of criticisms of the response. Whereas local NGOs in Aceh had been responding to humanitarian crises since 1998, after the tsunami, international NGOs largely overlooked local NGOs in favour of direct implementation. The TEC found that in Indonesia and Sri Lanka "local ownership [...] was undermined and some local capacities were rendered more vulnerable."[17] Acehnese civil society leaders called for a comprehensive approach to assist victims of both the natural and political disasters equally and complained that most international NGOs were unwilling or unable to provide assistance to conflict victims, in most cases for up to two years in the post-tsunami period.[18] The TEC *Synthesis Report* showed that international groups had a "poor understanding of local contexts, including ongoing recovery processes and the dynamics of armed conflicts in Sri Lanka and Indonesia."[19] As a consequence of problems with contextualising, Michael Flint and Hugh Goyder noted that: "there is a major question of equity between war-affected IDPs in both Sri Lanka and Aceh, and people affected by the tsunami."[20]

The early international tsunami response forged certain norms, especially among NGO workers in Aceh. Due to the scale of the disaster, aid workers naturally went headfirst into a life-saving emergency response. Furthermore, recruitment was often internal to organisations to facilitate a rapid response, with most aid workers coming directly from "permanent emergencies" in the Horn of Africa and the Middle East. Mike Novell, regional director of SC-US, described the situation as "crazy" and "chaotic" for the first year after the tsunami; "things were being driven by a 'have-to-be-done' attitude."[21] Aid workers were mostly technical specialists working on infrastructure, water and sanitation, health and shelter programmes. Many of the people with whom this author worked knew each other from Afghanistan, Darfur (Sudan), Iraq, Kosovo or Pakistan. Aceh or Indonesia specialists were not in high demand or simply were not available. Even groups like Save the Children, which had been in Aceh since 1976, had difficulties in transitioning from pre- to post-tsunami: "We jumped from 23 to 600 staff within weeks. Many expats had little experience and almost all new staff had no historical knowledge of Indonesia."[22] Since the majority of the main offices of NGOs were in Banda Aceh, they did not get a sense of the militarised situation that existed in small towns and rural Aceh until after the August 2005 MoU. Many considered Aceh to be a tropical paradise in comparison to Baghdad (Iraq), El Fasher (Sudan) or Kabul (Afghanistan) and the diving resorts on the nearby Weh Island were highly popular among expatriates. For many, the conflict was a thorn in the side of the tsunami programme and Aceh's low-intensity conflict was simply not compelling.

In looking closer at some specific cases, even those NGOs that did attempt to engage in the conflict had trouble balancing their tsunami-related commitments. For instance, Catholic Relief Services (CRS)'s "human rights, reconciliation and peace-building programme" was stopped when it was forced to shift key personnel towards the problematic tsunami shelter programme.[23] Oxfam provides another example of the challenges NGOs faced in shifting towards any form of conflict response. On the eve of the tsunami, Oxfam had received permission to resume its conflict response in Aceh.[24] The tsunami, though, changed the course of events. Oxfam's donor restrictions,[25] as outlined by the Disasters Emergency Committee (DEC), a United Kingdom umbrella organisation that launches and coordinates responses to major disasters, meant that funding could be used only for programmes directly related to the tsunami and not for conflict-related issues.[26] On top of this was a highly sensitive political environment in the first few months after the tsunami. Illustrating the precariousness of the situation was the fact that the Oxfam office, Hotel Regina, where it ran its humanitarian programmes, was also being used as a police intelligence unit base. According to an Oxfam staff member: "[intelligence] agents still occupied one room within the Oxfam building."[27] Furthermore, "the conflict was still going on and there was a lack of confidence in the government of Indonesia supporting a long presence. We wanted to do work on peace. We developed an advocacy strategy around that but it was still too sensitive."[28] Following extensive internal debate within Oxfam regarding moves to work on conflict issues, Oxfam went beyond its tsunami-only focus by organising a one-off technical exercise to support the Aceh Human Rights NGO Coalition and other local civil society groups in drafting the LoGA.[29]

Indeed, the political sensitivities surrounding the conflict need to be taken into account. Following the tsunami, the 50,000 Indonesian security forces stationed in the province initially continued counter-insurgency operations. On 20 January 2005, the then chief of staff of the Indonesian National Armed Forces (Tentara Nasional Indonesia, TNI), Ryamizard Ryacudu, announced that the military had killed more than 120 GAM members in the previous two weeks.[30] When the tsunami struck, the Indonesian military did not want foreigners to meddle in the conflict. It was clear that foreign assistance was welcome in response to the tsunami, but it was most unwelcome in response to the conflict. In a meeting with an Indonesian army official in Aceh less than a month after the tsunami, this author was informed that internationals were only permitted to work on tsunami-related activities and should not get involved in the conflict.[31] Media statements indicated that all internationals would have to leave Aceh by the end of March 2005. Amnesty International was denied entry to Aceh and the United Nations High Commissioner for Refugees (UNHCR) was forced to withdraw on 24 March 2005 with millions of tsunami dollars unspent.[32] UNHCR was invited back to Aceh three months later, but without a "protection mandate."[33] This situation presented international NGOs with a dilemma: ignoring the directives of the Indonesian authorities could also jeopardise access to tsunami-affected areas because the authorities had the power to expel any international agency if it stepped out of line. Several international NGOs went to great lengths to mitigate this risk. The stakes were high, with several billion dollars of aid money to be spent and hundreds of international agencies on the ground in Aceh. NGO chiefs did not want to risk losing millions of tsunami dollars by ignoring the directives of the GoI and potentially face expulsion. The UNHCR incident was testimony to this real danger.

Still, the division of tsunami and conflict issues raised a dilemma regarding the principle of impartiality (equality, non-discrimination and proportionality). In Aceh, most international NGOs risked dividing communities by delivering assistance to tsunami-affected populations, while not being able to provide anything to their conflict-affected neighbours. One middle manager at Oxfam pointed out that "for over a year we were arguing that we could be exacerbating conflict and should be working with conflict-affected people if they are in a certain radius of tsunami communities. For the first year and a half we really moved away from the principle of equity."[34] Furthermore, according to the same aid worker: "Oxfam's mandate is to work with the poorest of the poor and to overcome poverty. There are bigger issues than the tsunami. If we stand by our mission we should work on poverty and make sure people have access to their rights."[35] Furthermore, numerous Acehnese civil society leaders, as well as some international aid workers, warned that failure to deal with conflict issues might undermine long-term tsunami reconstruction efforts and might even lead to a resumption of hostilities. As described below, this did not turn out to be the case.

Funding was another factor that narrowed the overall humanitarian space. According to one UN official "a key feature in Aceh after the tsunami was that NGOs had more money than the UN, which reduced the UN's capacity to coordinate the NGOs."[36] The NGO rush to spend money also likely lessened the willingness of NGOs to be coordinated. The large sums of money NGOs were responsible for also made them inflexible and risk averse. The comments of one international NGO director on this question are insightful: "large NGOs with millions of dollars in programmes will not risk jeopardising that. People will also look out for their own career. They do not want to be seen as making a mistake and losing all that money."[37] Other factors that contributed to an aversion to conflict-related programming included individual personalities and internal organisational office politics. The IRC, which had worked in Aceh since 1999, showed an early interest in working on human rights and conflict issues. In February 2005, it began recruiting a protection adviser and by mid-2005 it had also hired a land and property rights specialist and a gender-based violence (GBV) consultant.[38] Around the same time, though, the IRC Aceh director was replaced and any possible conflict response was postponed. The IRC Protection Unit in New York was eager to set up protection and access to justice programmes in Aceh, whereas the new Aceh director did not want to expand the IRC's Aceh response beyond the four core areas of health, livelihoods, water and sanitation, and child and youth protection and development.[39] On the one hand, the IRC Protection Unit saw a good opportunity to develop an innovative programme and to carve out a niche for the IRC as a pioneer among humanitarian NGOs working on protection, justice and GBV. However, the IRC Aceh director was concerned about exceeding the organisation's capacity and core strengths, and did not want to get into trouble with the authorities. According to

Margaret Green, the director of the IRC Protection Unit in New York: "protection is always a complicated and prickly topic at both HQ [headquarters] and [in the] field. Too many people don't like it. It is considered as an elective."[40] The internal struggle exposed a tension within the IRC regarding organisational identity and a disparity between perceptions held by staff working in the field and at headquarters. Some members of the IRC, such as Marcel de Brune, the deputy director for programs in Aceh, identify it as a humanitarian assistance NGO,[41] whereas Jana Mason, the director of government relations in Washington, DC, identify it as a protection agency.[42] The "green light" for the IRC to work in conflict-affected areas came at a UN coordination meeting in August 2006 when the head of UNORC, Eric Morris, urged NGOs to "stop differentiating between tsunami and conflict areas."[43] Twenty-one months after the tsunami, the IRC began working behind the "tsunami line" and including former rebels and conflict victims in community development programmes. According to Marcel de Brune: "the money is still explicitly coming from tsunami funds. People had fled their homes in conflict areas for the coast, only to be pushed back into their home areas by the tsunami. So although they live in conflict areas, and behind the five kilometre tsunami line, [the] IRC argues that they are also tsunami affected."[44]

'Re-entering' the conflict zone

Four major political breakthroughs in 2005 and 2006 represented a shift in context in Aceh. First was the lead up to, and the eventual signing in Helsinki of, the 15 August 2005 MoU between the government of the Republic of Indonesia and the Free Aceh Movement.[45] Second was the successful disarmament and demobilisation process, completed by December 2005. Third was the passing by the Indonesian parliament of the new Special Autonomy Law for Aceh, the Law on Governing Aceh (Law 11/2006, LoGA), in July 2006, cementing key provisions of the MoU in law. Fourth was Aceh's first direct elections for gubernatorial and regency offices in December 2006—a political dividend of the peace process—which saw GAM-backed independent candidates elected throughout the province.[46] In addition, there were growing signs that the GoI wanted NGOs to provide assistance in conflict areas: a December 2005 GoI report on progress made in the first year after the tsunami, containing a foreword by Indonesian president Susilo Bambang Yudhoyono, called for tsunami recovery programmes to be linked to conflict recovery and reconciliation efforts.[47]

Days after the tsunami, Médecins Sans Frontières (MSF) made international headlines for its highly controversial decision to stop accepting tsunami funds. MSF found that its Indian Ocean tsunami appeal was over-funded and saw an opportunity to channel funds to other parts of the world that were receiving far less attention and money. The organisation contacted each of its donors and asked for their permission to de-restrict their donations so that they could be used for other emergencies and forgotten crises. According to MSF, "of all the people contacted, one per cent asked for their money to be refunded rather than redirected," which meant that MSF programmes were driven by need alone, "and not by a desire to spend surplus funds."[48]

In Aceh, MSF was the first large international NGO to engage in conflict-related advocacy in the post-tsunami period. It provided emergency humanitarian relief and raised awareness of the plight of conflict victims, thus living up to its slogan "*soignez et temoignez*" (care for and testify). In coordination with local government authorities MSF began to provide medical relief in conflict areas in May 2005, just five months after the tsunami. MSF-Holland head of mission, Anne-Marie Loof, said: "while it took a little while for the areas to open up and be accessible there were no major challenges in shifting from tsunami to conflict-related work."[49] MSF also engaged in low-key advocacy on the Aceh conflict through a photographic exhibition entitled "Mental trauma and conflict in Aceh," which aimed to raise awareness of the negative effects of the conflict.[50] MSF believed the story of suffering as a result of conflict in Aceh should be told, however, it did come with extensive internal debate between MSF chapters on the risks associated with running the photographic exhibition, as well as a series of negotiations with local government authorities.[51] What set MSF apart from many other NGOs in Aceh was its ability to use unrestricted funds. In Aceh, MSF saw the conflict as a neglected crisis within the broader tsunami disaster.

A number of smaller international NGOs started to work on conflict issues immediately after the tsunami. One such group, Hivos (Humanistisch Instituut voor Ontwikkelingssamenwerking) focused on long-term institutional support for human rights NGOs such as the Commission for the Disappeared and Victims of Violence (KontraS

Aceh) and the Aceh Judicial Monitoring Institute. Dewi Suralaga, the Indonesia manager of Hivos, noted that: "there was so much money and so many internationals after the tsunami that we attempted to identify any gaps in the tsunami response. One was to strengthen the capacity of local NGOs for the long term, beyond tsunami reconstruction." Hivos was open to working on a broad range of issues: "anything from technical or peace support to gender mainstreaming; anything to allow local NGOs to respond to the situation but with an eye for new initiatives that dealt with the longer term. We did not want to disqualify NGOs for working beyond the mainstream donor priorities."[52] In other words, Hivos was conflict-sensitive and equipped local NGOs to meet locally derived priorities. A number of multilateral organisations also developed a range of post-conflict programmes in Aceh in 2005 and 2006.[53] The European Union (EU) was the most prominent, fielding some eighty observers to Aceh on the day of the signing of the MoU to cover the period until the full deployment of the Aceh Monitoring Mission (AMM) on 15 September 2005.[54] The AMM had a mandate to monitor the implementation of the MoU, including the demobilisation of GAM, the decommissioning of GAM weapons, the relocation of non-organic military and non-organic police forces, and the reintegration of active GAM members, as well as to rule on disputed amnesty cases and to deal with complaints and alleged violations of the MoU. In addition, it had a mandate to monitor human rights and to provide assistance in this area, yet this proved to be its weakest aspect.[55] Its initial mission was set to deploy for six months, but this was extended three times, before concluding on 15 December 2006.

The World Bank assisted the GoI's post-MoU reintegration activities for former GAM combatants through its existing national Kecamatan Development Program (KDP)—a "community-driven development" initiative run through the Indonesian Ministry of Home Affairs—which had facilitators in every village throughout Aceh. After a false start with the GoI-administered Aceh Reintegration Agency (Badan Reintegrasi Aceh, BRA), the World Bank stepped in, in late 2005, to assist reintegration efforts by providing block grants to villages through the KDP network. Villagers would then decide how funds should be allocated. The World Bank had staff members who had been working on conflict programmes for several years in Indonesia and the KDP did not stop in Aceh during the military emergency. However, personal and institutional rivalries, as well as the belief that individual claimants, not communities, should be recompensed, led to the discontinuation of World Bank involvement in reintegration assistance in June 2007.[56] In addition, the World Bank had a comprehensive research programme to support the peace process, involving for example a GAM reintegration needs assessment, a study of trucking and illegal payments, and an ongoing conflict monitoring update, based on newspaper conflict mapping and analysis.

The United Nations Development Program (UNDP) together with the International Organization for Migration (IOM), the United States Agency for International Development (USAID) and the World Bank, and in coordination with the Aceh provincial government, formed the Peace Socialisation Team (Tim Sosialisasi Damai, or Timsos) soon after the signing of the MoU. Timsos distributed peace posters, stickers and copies of the MoU, and organising peace concerts and a satirical radio drama as part of an information awareness campaign to promote peace in Aceh. According to former UNDP public information officer Imogen Wall, who worked on both the tsunami response and the peace process, "previously, we could not even mention the conflict out of fear of following UNHCR and being expelled."[57] Early on in the peace process, "the UN could not be visible because of Timor-Leste. Jakarta saw the UN as assisting Timor to break away."[58] Thus in the first weeks after the signing of the MoU, UNDP avoided all publicity. However, Imogen Wall suggests that "as the peace process solidified things became more open and UNDP went public and held peace-building workshops." She added that the Timsos project worked well "because it was a small group of people, all of whom became close friends and cared about what they were doing, and were not caught up in 'Jakarta (inter-agency) politics'. We also had money, thanks to the World Bank."[59]

Conclusion

Humanitarian space in Aceh was multifaceted, dynamic and contested. During the conflict period human rights came up against humanitarian needs as Indonesian government officials warned international NGOs against supporting the local human rights agenda. In the post-tsunami period, relief for the "natural" disaster was at odds with the "political" disaster. The tsunami was perceived by some to be a "pure" humanitarian problem, untainted by the political and human rights violations associated with "man-made" disaster. Local humanitarian actors suddenly found the ground had shifted with the arrival of hundreds of new humanitarian organisations. Some adapted to the new "tsunami-only" focus, while others, especially the more hardened activists that disputed the international tsunami-only focus, found donors that would support their conflict assistance and human rights niche. The scale of the tsunami disaster also meant that every possible kind of humanitarian organisation imaginable was present, and each brought its own identity and approach to humanitarian relief. A constant factor during both periods was maintaining humanitarian access, and key to that was the need to conduct regular and thorough political analysis and security assessments.

This chapter found that negotiating humanitarian access, and indeed negotiating access to different humanitarian needs, very much depended on political and security assessments, funding restrictions, organisational identity and individual personalities of NGO leaders. The GoI was apprehensive at first of having international NGOs in Aceh and the bulk of NGOs did not want to jeopardise lucrative tsunami programmes by developing conflict-related programmes and damaging relations with their new host. Many were burdened by capacity constraints and unable to respond adequately to the tsunami, let alone expand the scope of their work. The IRC case shows that there are also a number of internal organisational constraints related to human rights-based programming. MSF and the few small international NGOs that had flexible funding and did work on the conflict in the post-tsunami period were not expelled from Aceh, as some may have warned. However, such NGOs did "tone down" their activities in anticipation of government sensibilities. Perhaps surprisingly, it was primarily multilateral organisations working directly with local and national government authorities that provided the most significant response to the conflict. Individual personalities and political will among key donors were influential factors in each case. Both donors and NGOs need to be flexible in order to adapt to a changing political environment. Whereas access to Aceh in the immediate aftermath of the tsunami required acquiescence with respect to GoI concerns, these concerns were not unabated. Most humanitarian NGOs lost their independence and were no longer sovereign over their mission and mandate in Aceh, as they were unable or unwilling to channel tsunami funds to war-affected communities. Similarly, the funding regime must be flexible to adjust to situations where two disasters enter into an interdependent relationship, as happened in Aceh: peace in 2005 supported tsunami reconstruction efforts; and tsunami reconstruction efforts could aid, or undermine, post-conflict transformation in Aceh.

8

SPOTLIGHTS AND MIRRORS

MEDIA AND THE HUMANITARIAN COMMUNITY
IN HAITI'S DISASTER

Mark Schuller

Introduction

Humanitarian space has a direct, if often under-appreciated, relationship with media. As the chapter by Bleiker, Hutchinson and Campbell argues, how disasters are framed within media can powerfully shape the response. For example, calling Katrina survivors "looters" reinforced a racialised, militarised, police response while calling to bear familiar "blame-the-victim," racist narratives that can serve to excuse slow and inadequate response.

These tendencies were unfortunately exhibited in Haiti following the devastating earthquake. Arguably more than any other disaster before or since, Haiti's earthquake quickly dominated global media. CNN offered round-the-clock coverage for two weeks, and blogs carried a special link for Haiti earthquake coverage for more than three months. Again deploying a familiar racialised narrative of Haitians being unruly serving as a frame, images of raw suffering, human misery, and the unimaginable damage and scale portrayed a hell on earth, one that desperately needed foreign assistance and foreign control. Not surprisingly, the response was militarised; 22,000 US troops immediately mobilised to coordinate the emergency logistics, rebuilding the airport, clearing the rubble and assisting in the medical mission. Despite this role for which arguably the US military was singularly qualified to undertake, as a military response it was hierarchical and treated survivors as security risks. As a military, they prioritised the issue of security above all else, delaying aid and augmenting the culture of fear that divided non-Haitian aid workers from the aid recipients. According to WikiLeaked documents, security was not on the list of Haitian president René Préval's priorities outlined in a 16 January communiqué.[1] Yet, a day later, he requested the deployment of US troops (days after they had already been deployed) in a public relations effort to rationalise their de facto presence. On 20 January, Secretary of State Hillary Clinton issued a directive to embassies to discipline "irresponsible journalism" because it was important to "get the narrative right" about US intentions in Haiti. Most upsetting to many within the humanitarian community was that the US used its foothold in the airport as gatekeepers, promoting a US aid "shock and awe" to the detriment of other donors, NGOs and aid agencies. The US military infamously denied landing rights to French NGO Médecins Sans Frontières while allowing the Pennsylvania governor to airlift two twenty-somethings from his state who had started an orphanage out of Haiti.

There are many other examples of how the international media's framing of the disaster normalised the continuing foreign control that space constraints prevent mention here. However, the relationship between the international media and humanitarian agencies is far from one-sided, as Secretary Clinton's attempt to influence media reporting highlights. This chapter documents and theorises two examples of humanitarians' efforts to actively influence the international media and its story about Haiti and specifically the response. Media agencies, and particularly the people who work for them in-country as correspondents, have to constantly uncover stories that are newsworthy. Wire services that make their money by outlets purchasing their stories are particularly under pressure to compete with one another for uncovering the "scoop." In this context, humanitarian agencies have opportunities to send stories out through press releases and press conferences. Increasingly since the advent of electronic media, agencies have more tools to spread the message. The two examples in this chapter fall into two general approaches of training the foreign eye: "spotlights" and "mirrors," focusing attention either towards or away from a particular phenomenon and back at the onlooker. The first effort discussed, the spotlight, was a direct approach to infuse the media with specific facts and a "spin" about how to interpret the facts. The mirror approach is more indirect; this second case arose not from official channels such as press releases or press conferences but an individual effort. The mirror case deflected attention away from critical on-the-ground realities as well as criticism.

Following a ten-year project of studying impacts of development aid on NGOs in Haiti, this chapter draws upon interviews and three rounds of quantitative research conducted in July–August 2010, January 2011 and June–August 2011. Quotes and statistics not otherwise attributed are based on this ongoing research.

Spotlight: the "light at the end of the tunnel"

As the first anniversary of the earthquake loomed, it was predictable that the international media would produce a story of "one year later" which would undoubtedly offer an assessment of the progress of the international response. Preparing for this media event, in fact creating it, agencies put out reports and press releases about the year in review. Many NGOs took the opportunity to detail their outputs: how many people received food distribution, how many litres of water in how many camps, and so on. Reuters' AlertNet, a PR website for NGOs, assisted in this effort putting out these statistics. So-called "new media"—notably blogs like *Huffington Post*—offered humanitarians a more direct tool for shining the spotlight on their efforts. *Huffington Post* alone, in an effort to expand their coverage of Haiti, invited scores of new bloggers with some connection or expertise in Haiti. A few were independent scholars including the author, however the majority of *Huffington's* new bloggers were NGO employees, most often directors or public relations staff. The majority of the stories coming out from *Huffington Post* sent to media search engines as "news" were simply NGOs' PR. In early 2011 it was purchased by media conglomerate AOL, and so became the highest-circulation source of online news, surpassing even the *New York Times*.

In addition to NGOs' direct reporting on the their efforts, the International Organization for Migration (IOM), who had taken the lead in coordinating the many IDP camps, under the rubric of the Cluster for Camp Coordination and Management (CCCM), sent stories out. One of the primary tools of the CCCM is a database of the officially recognised camps, the Displacement Tracking Matrix (DTM). In addition to being a tool for humanitarian agencies to coordinate their efforts, it was also a census of how many people were still living under tents or tarpaulins. The Water, Sanitation and Hygiene (WASH) cluster used the DTM and camp ID to identify NGO actors providing WASH services.

Late on the morning on 11 January 2011, one day before the earthquake's anniversary, Haitian president René Préval and his dauphin Jude Celestin were metres away from a camp in Kanaran, which was to be the site of a day of reflection for a network of social movement organisations including FRAKKA (the Reflection and Action Force for the Housing Cause), BAI (International Lawyers' Office), Batay Ouvriye (Workers' Struggle), Bri Kouri Nouvèl Gaye (Noise Travels, News Spreads), Invèsite Popilè (Popular University) and a range of constituent groups, including camp committees. The sun was hot, the wind blowing dust from the eroded mountains. People stayed in their makeshift homes dotting the jagged landscape, possibly to ensure their belongings didn't gust away. But the paltry attendance was more attributable to politics.

In this camp—not officially recognised—where some 60,000 people live, there is not one but two official committees. In one "turf" was the camp's only water supply and toilets. On the other sat an empty and ripped UNICEF tent, on which graffiti denouncing the other committee representative was written. In the neutral zone, dwarfing everything around it, including the tents, toilets and the wood structures that were to replace a makeshift school made on one side of the camp, people were building a sound stage using professional building materials and not merely scrap. "We're going to have a big crusade tomorrow," boasted one committee member. While not wanting to be too direct, I asked who was going to come. He continued, saying that international organisations, the government and NGOs were going to be there today. A barber whose shop sat across from the sound stage said what was inevitably on many people's minds: "Instead of spending thousands driving people here, renting the equipment and all this, they could just give us food. We're starving."

Most of the groups who staged events on 12 January were NGOs, to attract some foreign media attention to their efforts. Groups as divergent as Catholic Relief Services, CARE, World Vision and Oxfam held press events highlighting their achievements, but watchdog groups such as Amnesty International, Institute for Justice and Democracy in Haiti and Disaster Accountability Project published reports critical of the lack of progress. Some progress was made in some areas. More children went to school in 2011 than in 2010; a little more of the rubble had been cleared; more people had moved into homes, mostly temporary or "T-shelters." Despite figures coming from NGOs and individual success stories, life for the overwhelming majority of people in Port-au-Prince, especially the million-plus IDPs, only got much worse.

One index is cholera. The official count put out in January 2011 cited 3,600 people dead and 170,000 cases of cholera, barely two months after the outbreak began. According to UN cluster officials, this was very likely an under-count and was still not at its "peak." "Cholera changed everything," said a government official. Almost immediately the official population of the IDP camps plummeted. Said a sanitation expert, "Cholera most definitely played a role in individual families' migration decisions. People are, have been, and will continue to move around. Cholera tipped the balance in favour of leaving the camps." In a camp in Carrefour informally called Ti Bato (Little Boat), thirty-three cases of cholera were recorded out of 350 residents. As of January 2011, almost a year after the quake, the camp still lacked a single toilet. People defecated in the open air, twenty metres from the shelters.

Also in Carrefour, at an Adventist church, there were still no toilets when the cholera outbreak began in late October, ten months after the earthquake. Church leaders had been giving verbal warnings for people to leave. People stayed until, one day in November, eight cases of cholera were recorded in the camp. The next day, all 546 people fled the camp. Where did they go? Some went to another camp. Others pitched what was left of their tent after ten months of tropical weather in front of a friend's house. Some may have squatted in an empty house. Some may have gone to unofficial camps like Kanaran. Others may have created a whole new camp recently "discovered" by aid officials.

In short, no one knows. "The thing is, IOM has responsibility to officially registered displaced people, not just people who live in camps. They have a responsibility to do some follow-up," decried a Haitian government mid-manager. Many other examples can be cited about people abandoning their camp following the cholera outbreak, especially if the camp did not have essential water and sanitation services. In one camp in Tabarre called Levi, only thirty of 486 people remained in January 2011 following the cholera outbreak. The camp never had a toilet, so people went to a neighbour's house. Neighbours' generosity has limits, especially after the outbreak of the faecal-borne disease.

Supervising a team of eight State University of Haiti students, the author conducted a study of a random sample of over 100 camps, one in eight of those in the Port-au-Prince metropolitan area. Of this sample, as of August, 30 per cent of camps lacked a toilet, and 40 per cent lacked water provision.[2] Since the cholera epidemic, and the $173 million UN flash appeal, almost no progress was made. In January 2011, follow-up research from the author recorded that only four additional camps had water or toilets: 26 instead of 30 per cent of camps still didn't have toilets, and 37 instead of 40 per cent of camps didn't have water.[3] Eight camps closed because of the lack of services. Still another three closed because landowners—all three of them churches—forced people off their land. In all, one in four camps had closed between August 2010 and January 2011.

Water was a more serious concern: donors cut off emergency water rations at the end of 2010 in at least four camps studied. The last water distribution for Cité Soleil camps Tapis Vert (20,000 people) and Camp Nielo (763 people) was 31 December. "This doesn't make sense. We're in a crisis!" said a WASH cluster employee. "To turn the spigot off while we're in the middle of a cholera epidemic is tantamount to genocide."

Explaining this lack of progress requires attention to structural deficiencies in the system, and how aid was instrumentalised following the earthquake.[4] Aid coordination was attempted by the Haitian government and the IOM, but to sum up, according to an IOM official, "The bottom line is we have no carrots and sticks. NGOs are private agencies and pretty much can do what they want."

The IOM declared the 31 per cent decrease in camp population a success, hailing it a "light at the end of the tunnel." This line was repeated by UN special envoy Bill Clinton on 12 January 2011, and hence appeared in dozens of news accounts. The facts discussed above argue that IDP's flight from the camps was a symptom of failure to protect, wherein people moved into more precarious situations and became more vulnerable to cholera. Rather than seeing this as a light at the end of the tunnel, this massive exodus was an oncoming train. The spotlight trained the eye of the international media to the numbers that put the international response effort in the best light—the statistics about services—as well as an interpretation and a catch-phrase to declare the fact of the IDP population reduction as a hopeful sign.

Possibly in response to critiques, the IOM later qualified this language, however this was only cited in a single article in March 2011. The spotlight already was turned off, with the official story being progress, equating the mere existence of IDPs as a failure. As of the submission of this chapter almost two years after the earthquake, rehabilitation or construction was only completed on 5,000 houses, whereas an estimated 175,000 houses were fit for demolition or required serious rehabilitation, according to a structural evaluation team. But the spotlight of the international media was already onto other stories, including other disasters such as the earthquake and nuclear meltdown in Fukushima, Japan.

Mirrors: redefining the death toll

This housing survey, conducted by the Ministry of Public Works with financial support from USAID and technical support from a private engineering firm, was another important tool in the reconstruction effort. In total, 382,256 housing units were evaluated. Of these, 205,539 were tagged "green," ready for human habitation, 99,043 "yellow," requiring significant repair, and 77,674 "red," which were so damaged so as to require demolition. As is typical with donor-funded projects, USAID commissioned an evaluation. Anthropologist Timothy Schwartz led the team contracted with conducting and writing the report. The report contained some important warnings to the donor and NGO community. Despite its technical successes and easy-to-understand coding system, the programme didn't noticeably alter people's decisions to move back into the homes. Most alarmingly, 73,846 of 115,384 (sic.) "red" houses had been re-inhabited by January 2011.

In addition to these carefully researched findings, Schwartz included others that were not a part of his mandate from USAID, about the official estimates of the death toll and the "legitimate" IDPs. According to his own blog on *Slate*, USAID denied publication of the report because it attempted to distance itself from these controversial claims. But Schwartz persevered, leaking the draft report to the press. One journalist, Agence France-Presse's (AFP's) Emily Troutman, published a story about it on 27 May 2011.

This story triggered a heated debate on a subject that for most Haitians was only marginally relevant and disrespectful. Blogs and public lists such as the 8,000-member "Corbett List" registered scores of email commentaries that degraded into *ad hominem* attacks. Like many other peoples displaced by the holocaust of the middle passage, Haitian culture grants a central role to its ancestors whose spirits return home, to *ginen*, Africa. The Haitian government's official estimate of the dead from 12 January was 230,000, which was repeated by the NGOs and the media. As the first anniversary loomed, without citing additional research or proof, Haitian prime minister Max Bellerive announced that the earthquake killed 316,000 people. As Schwartz blogged, this was a deliberate inflation aimed at loosening up more funds for the relief and reconstruction effort. Dozens of news stories, including in large-circulation publications *Washington Post, New York Times, Newsweek* and *Time*, repeated this finger-wagging, more editorialising than news reporting.

While basing Schwartz's critique of the Haitian government on its lack of transparency in its research methods, the leaked report was similarly opaque. For its part, USAID distanced itself from the most controversial claims, citing inconsistencies and irregularities within Schwartz's research methods. Only two stories that made it to Google's daily news alerts reported this critique, despite the dozens that used the leaked report to lodge a critique against the Haitian government, many drawing on familiar narratives of Haitian incompetence, adding to Haiti's unending bad press.[5] The damage was already done. True, Schwartz was acting as an individual, not USAID, but as a humanitarian actor nonetheless. This attempt is primarily to deflect attention, as a mirror deflects light. Also as a mirror, Schwartz's crusade was aimed at a clear, if unflattering, gaze back at the humanitarian effort, particularly NGOs who he argued were complicit in the inflation of the death toll for self-interested ends.

As a study of the impact of the housing evaluation, it was an important intervention. But the report that was leaked to the press—and uncritically repeated—did not explain the methodology for Schwartz's un-commissioned campaign: for example, what sampling criteria were used, both in terms of neighbourhoods and individuals, how this sample represents larger trends, and so on. There seems to have been no recognition of the possibility that entire structures levelled to rubble would have been impossible to number, whose family members were all either dead or living in the IDP camps. The report cited precise numbers, not rounded, to estimate both the numbers of dead and the "legitimate" IDPs, despite the conventions of rounding based on significant digits within statistical research, declaring there to be from 46,190 to 84,961 dead, giving an average of 65,575, a little more than a fifth of the government's estimate. Part of the study's argument rests on contrasting its precision with the Haitian government's lack of precision. Conclusions were reached about IDP camps without researchers visiting the camps. The report estimated 258,085 "current" IDPs (range of 141,158 to 375,031 compared to the IOM's estimate of 680,000 from the DTM), with 42,608 "legitimate" IDPs.

Researchers with the Small Arms Survey conducted an independent much more methodologically grounded, study of the death toll, with the result lower than the Haitian government's estimate but significantly higher than Schwartz's—158,000. This estimate first appeared in a *Los Angeles Times* editorial on 12 July 2011, eighteen months after the earthquake and a month and a half following the Schwartz report.

The debate was primarily focused on the death toll, leaving the other unsubstantiated claims about the "legitimate" IDPs, incendiary statements of people only in the camps for the free access to services unaddressed, and the most troubling finding of a majority of "red" houses being reoccupied. The total silence, the attention deflected away from this discussion of the "illegitimate" IDPs, was an insidious outcome of this mirror. With the public debate focusing on what most Haitian people consider a red herring—with nothing to be done about the dead, no one ultimately responsible for their deaths—the inflammatory and controversial allegations about living IDPs—whose rights were actively being challenged by a range of actors—became tacitly accepted by the lack of scrutiny.

Unfortunately, these allegations were not true. The DTM continued to enumerate just under 600,000 IDPs as late as November 2011, six months after the Schwartz report. The IOM contracted with French NGO ActEd to survey 15,446 IDPs about their intentions, publishing a report in early August 2011 when there were 630,000 IDPs still in the camps. According to this report, 94 per cent of IDPs wanted to leave the camps. The author's survey of 800 families within eight IDP camps yielded a similar result, that 92 per cent of IDPs wanted to leave as of summer 2011. Since there was only 5,000 housing units built, and since 79.5 per cent of residents were renters before the earthquake, the IDPs can't leave because they have nowhere to go.

In addition to not being able to leave, the "free services" that ostensibly were the magnet to the camps, notably water and toilet services, were being shut off as NGO contracts ended. As of October 2011, only 6 per cent of IDP camps had water services, and in November water trucking services had to stop per government decree. To the oft-repeated quote—amplified and justified by the Schwartz report—of people suddenly appearing in unused tents whenever a distribution was made, the author's eight research teams spent five weeks in the same camp and noticed a constant level of comings and goings, economic activity and social life. In other words, they were all "real" camps. To the concern about the free aid being a magnet pulling tens of thousands of people from the provinces, the survey showed only 3.5 per cent came since 2010, with the mean year of migration to Port-au-Prince being 1993, which seems to follow the general pattern of Haiti's rural exodus. In other words, all but 3.5 per cent are "real" IDPs.

Whether or not this deflection was intentional, certainly by a maverick humanitarian such as Schwartz who has published critical accounts of NGOs and missions,[6] the unchallenged discourse has utility for many actors. Landowners and government officials such as Delmas mayor Wilson Jeudy, having lost the bid for Haiti's presidency to Michel Martelly, who actively sought to close IDP camps, found justification. If the vast majority of IDPs and camps are not "legitimate," a heavy handed, violent, response in reclaiming land could be arguably justifiable. The day following the APF's story, Jeudy again destroyed an IDP camp on public land in his municipality, his second violent act within two weeks, citing a similar refrain of the IDPs being criminals. Jeudy employed armed irregular forces not formally employed by the police to rip people's tents and destroy their belongings.

In addition to those who would reclaim land from IDPs despite their rights to life-saving services, this unchallenged discourse of "illegitimate" IDPs was also useful to humanitarian agencies increasingly on the defensive following billions in aid spent and little evident progress. If the number of IDPs were artificially inflated and the majority of those dwelling in under-serviced IDP camps are not "legitimate" victims, humanitarian agencies have lower obligations. For its part, USAID was the target of a bipartisan probe from the US House of Representatives, H.R. 1016, on 10 May 2011, calling the agency to account for the billions and apparent lack of progress. Indeed, members of Congress who represent large Haitian communities sent a scathing critique of the Haitian government for not protecting IDPs two days before AFP leaked the draft Schwartz report.

Whether or not Schwartz acting as an individual had intended these outcomes, the mirror the AFP article provided deflected attention and criticism against both the Haitian government and USAID and offered ideological support for reactionary positions, justifying forced evictions and lack of progress for IDPs. As a mirror deflects light away, redirecting it, this general approach works when there is already light shone in a particular area. It is a risky approach, because the elected official or agency holding a mirror and turning it to deflect attention somewhere else is under the spotlight. In this case, the agencies that most benefited from this attention being deflected away were not the ones holding the mirror.

Concluding reflections

As Kurt Mill's chapter on Darfur reminds us, the media framing of disasters wields a powerful influence on humanitarian space. As one of the most mediated disasters in recent history, the earthquake in Haiti raised the expectations and scrutiny for the humanitarian response. This chapter has shown that the relationship between media and humanitarian actors is complex. The structure of the international media offers opportunities to humanitarians to feed stories to stringers who need to produce. In addition, since the advent of blogs, humanitarian actors have become media agents as well. Given this iterative relationship, humanitarians who understand that financial flows to their agencies depend in part on their positive reflection in the media attempt to train a spotlight on the stories that put their work in the best possible light. The media also provides ideological cover to agencies that do not want the spotlight, and stories can act as mirrors deflecting attention, redirecting it somewhere else. Whether or not this spotlight or mirror approach only works because of the competition inherent in the for-profit media, the media's reflection of the humanitarian enterprise can increase or decrease humanitarian space. In Haiti's case, both efforts recuperated or defended space for humanitarian action. This chapter highlights some of the negative impacts of this effort to aid recipients who too often remain in shadows.

9

LEAP OF FAITH

NEGOTIATING HUMANITARIAN ACCESS
IN SOMALIA'S 2011 FAMINE

Ken Menkhaus

Somalia has a long and unhappy history as the site of recurring humanitarian emergencies, routinised humanitarian response and complex, non-permissive environments for relief agencies to navigate. In the war and famine of 1991–1992, an estimated 240,000 Somalis perished and a million refugees fled the country. During that period, Somalia was one of the first of what came to be called "complex political emergencies" and was widely considered to be one of the most difficult sites in the world for relief agencies. It was also one of the first instances in which diversion of food aid by armed militias grew to such levels that emergency relief was accused of fueling a war economy—an assertion that contributed to the decision to mount a major United Nations peace enforcement operation in Somalia in December 1992. But the challenges of humanitarian action in Somalia in the 1980s and 1990s pale in comparison to the extraordinary difficulties faced by relief agencies in the devastating 2011 famine in southern Somalia. In previous decades, humanitarian agencies were generally able to negotiate access to communities at risk; the main obstacles they faced were related to their inability to fully control distribution, due to systematic diversion of aid by the Somali state (in the 1980s) and predatory armed groups (in the 1990s). In 2010–2011, relief agencies confronted a far more daunting array of impediments, including basic problems of access and new types of externally imposed political and legal constraints. As a result, humanitarian actors were very limited in their ability to respond effectively to the world's worst famine in twenty years. An "alarming void in international humanitarian aid" emerged at precisely the moment when relief aid was needed most.[1] Agencies that did manage to maintain some access to the famine zone were in very weak positions to maintain standards of accountability and monitoring, and thus exposed themselves to potentially serious charges of violating counter-terrorism legislation in Western countries. This in turn produced a dilemma for the humanitarian community and some of their donors. In order not to compromise what minimal access some aid agencies enjoyed, all had to maintain silence about the extent to which control over distribution was lost. The claim that "humanitarian space" could be negotiated by skillful and influential local partners was frequently invoked, more as a leap of faith than a statement of fact. The reality was that southern Somalia remained for the most part, in the words of NGO officials, "an accountability free zone."

Western media coverage of the Somali famine tended to lay blame for the famine on the Somali radical Islamist group al-Shabaab, which blocked most international food aid into its areas of control in southern Somalia. Shabaab's obstructionist policies were indeed a major factor in the famine, and the group bears principal responsibility for presiding over the world's worst famine in twenty years. But it was not the sole bottleneck. In reality, external aid efforts of all types—including Western NGOs, UN specialised agencies, the International Committee of the Red Cross (ICRC), international Islamic charities and Somali diaspora relief projects—faced five distinct impediments to effective famine relief. These included: Shabaab's refusal to permit most international relief agencies to operate in the famine zone, and its sharp restrictions on the few that were granted access; US suspension of food aid into areas of Somalia controlled by Shabaab, and other constraints on aid agencies related to counter-terrorism legislation; chronic insecurity pre-dating Shabaab and

US policies, which led most aid agencies to suspend or close operations in southern Somalia by 2009; diversion of food aid by armed groups and corrupt officials in the Transitional Federal Government (TFG) which controlled the capital Mogadishu; and a "privilege gap" in Somali society, in which low status groups lacked the social capital to access relief aid, remittances and lateral transfers from fellow Somalis.

Any one of these obstacles alone would have posed a serious problem for humanitarian response, but the combination of all five created an operating environment that proved impossible for humanitarian agencies to navigate successfully. Some, like Somali diaspora groups, Islamic NGOs and the ICRC, were better able to negotiate access than others, but all were severely constrained in their ability to monitor distribution. Their limited presence probably saved many lives, though proof for this may never be available. The net result of these multiple constraints on humanitarian relief was catastrophic. Large sections of southern Somalia were hit hard by famine conditions. As many as 100,000 Somalis died, and the crisis produced many hundreds of thousands of internally displaced persons (IDPs) and refugees. Largely sidelined in the midst of a major famine, frustrated humanitarian actors also found themselves under fire from all directions. This was perhaps inevitable in a highly polarised and violent political setting in which humanitarian aid had become a top priority and powerful players sought to harness famine relief to advance their own interests. Shabaab accused them of spying for the US, threatened or assassinated their staff and eventually banned them. Sharp tensions flared between relief agencies and Western governments over counter-terrorism legislation that essentially criminalised aid operations in areas controlled by Shabaab. The UN Political Office for Somalia, Western donors and the TFG publicly criticised humanitarian agencies for working around, rather than with, the corrupt and obstructionist TFG in the capital Mogadishu. And Western and UN humanitarian agencies were accused by Somali and international critics of a bewildering array of often contradictory charges—that they were late and inadequate with emergency response; that they were exaggerating the famine for fundraising purposes; that they were over-paid "Lords of Poverty" who preferred the comforts of Nairobi to engagement inside Somalia; that they were complicit in corrupt arrangements with warlords to divert food aid; that they represented the international community's preference for humanitarian band-aids rather than durable solutions for the Somali crisis; that they supported terrorists; that they were proselytising to convert Somalis to Christianity; that they perpetuated dependence or that they undermined local farmers. Some of these allegations had merit; others did not. Criticism of Western humanitarian aid agencies—especially those dealing in food aid—was, it seemed, the only issue on which Shabaab, the TFG, the UN and Western governments could agree. This hostile political environment placed humanitarian aid agencies in an exceptionally weak bargaining position as they sought to maintain neutrality, protect their staff, and gain or maintain access to famine victims. It was a far cry from the privileged position and moral high ground that humanitarian actors had enjoyed in the 1991–1992 famine relief operations in Somalia.

Background: the Somali context

Understanding the politics behind the 2011 famine in Somalia requires appreciation of contextual factors that helped to produce the famine and shape the behaviour of key actors in the crisis.

Geographic setting, livelihoods and food insecurity

The eastern Horn of Africa is semi-arid and exceptionally prone to extreme variation in rainfall, with severe droughts or flooding occurring every few years. Local populations have coping mechanisms for these extreme weather patterns, but those adaptive strategies have been eroded by years of insecurity, displacement, land alienation and population growth. In consequence, rural Somalia has been the site of severe and worsening food insecurity for decades. Malnutrition rates are chronically high even in years of good harvests, and external food aid and supplemental feeding has become routinised and institutionalised since the 1970s. Even in years of good rains, local harvests account for no more than 40 per cent of national consumption needs, with food imports accounting for 20 per cent and food aid providing an extraordinary 30 per cent.[2] Some observers have argued that the international community has become inured of Somalia's extremely high levels of humanitarian need, "normalizing" levels of severe malnutrition that in any other setting would be considered a "loud" humanitarian emergency.[3] The Inter-Agency Standing Committee put the 2011 famine in the context of the wider problem of food insecurity in Somalia by describing it as "a crisis within a crisis."[4] Most of Somalia's rural population engages in pastoralism or agro-pastoralism, which, thanks to the mobility inherent in that mode of production, is generally better equipped to cope with drought. Rainfall levels are high enough in parts of southern Somalia to sustain small-holder farming; those communities are the most vulnerable to both drought and insecurity, and have been at the epicentre of Somalia's humanitarian crises since 1991. The farming communities have also historically been a weak, low status social group in Somalia, a factor of no small consequence when food aid is controlled and diverted by more powerful groups in the country.

State collapse, insecurity and the political economy of food aid

Somalia has not had a functioning central government since early 1991, when the government of Siyad Barre fell to multiple clan-based armed groups. In some locations, regional or municipal authorities have emerged; in the rest of the country, communities rely on hybrid local governance arrangements that draw on customary clan law and sharia courts. Armed groups—usually clan-based in composition—control fiefdoms in the capital and countryside. While not anarchic, Somalia is highly insecure. Somalia has experienced several periods of armed violence that qualify as civil war; the rest of the time the country is in a state of chronic but variable insecurity, thanks to communal clashes, armed criminality and, more recently, insurgency. In some locations, war economies have emerged, in which local political leaders and merchants have developed a powerful interest in perpetuating conditions of disorder and insecurity. This has had implications for humanitarian aid. The introduction of resources—including humanitarian and development aid—into areas controlled by an armed group invariably provides both direct and indirect benefits to those groups. A political economy of food aid developed in this setting, in which a small number of powerful local businesspeople have benefited from lucrative contracts—estimated at about $200 million per year—to ship food into the country.[5] Accusations of corruption and collusion between some of the major international providers of food aid and these local contractors have tarnished the image of humanitarian relief and highlighted the extent to which routinised humanitarian aid has become part of the fabric of political and economic life in Somalia. Accommodating these local realities has been viewed, rightly or wrongly, as "the cost of doing business" in Somalia. But that has come at a real cost, especially to relief agencies working with high value food aid. As Laura Hammond and Hannah Vaughn-Lee argue:

The political economy of aid—the complex inter-weaving of legal and illegal business transactions, diversion, taxation, etc., and the power dynamics that govern these activities—has become so entrenched that it has eroded trust between stakeholders and increased insecurity for humanitarian personnel and civilians living in conflict zones, severely constraining humanitarian space.[6]

Put another way, "negotiating humanitarian space" in Somalia has involved compromises that have long been tacitly justified on utilitarian grounds, but which have implicated relief agencies in a wider system of resource diversion that is increasingly viewed by both Somalis and external actors as unacceptable.

Refugees, IDPs and the remittance economy

Years of armed conflict, ethnic cleansing and the erosion of rural livelihoods have produced very high levels of internal displacement, urban drift and refugee flows in Somalia. The number of internally displaced persons (IDPs) has spiked dramatically in the insurgency and counter-insurgency violence in the capital Mogadishu since 2007. By 2011, Somalia had an estimated 1.5 million IDPs.[7] This created an entire category of households with limited livelihoods and social safety nets—a very large group that was particularly vulnerable in the event of a severe humanitarian crisis. The 1 to 1.5 million Somali refugees living outside the Horn of Africa play an essential role in the Somali economy. They remit between $1.5 and $2 billion each year back to family members in the country. Remittances dwarf any other source of income or hard currency in Somalia, and are literally the lifeline of the country. This dependable source of purchasing power meant that some Somali households—mainly more privileged, urban households—were always able to buy food, which was readily available in the markets (though expensive) even at the height of the famine. The diaspora also engages in fundraisers to support local NGOs. The spike in diaspora remittances and community fundraising no doubt was a major factor in reducing famine fatalities. But, as is argued below, social factors in Somalia limited the extent to which the weakest and most vulnerable groups could make claims on remittances.

Political turmoil and radicalisation since 2006

Somalia's political and security situation has plummeted since 2006, creating a highly polarised and insecure setting for humanitarian response. A series of battles in Mogadishu in early 2006 pitting pro-Western militias against a coalition of Islamist militias resulted in the rise to power of the Islamic Courts Union (ICU) across all of southern Somalia. The ICU, a loose umbrella movement of sufis, non-violent salafis and violent extremists, effectively governed southern Somalia and Mogadishu for a six-month period, earning it a strong measure of support and legitimacy in the eyes of most Somalis. But extremists in the coalition, centred in a small but powerful militia that came to call itself al-Shabaab, marginalised the moderates in the group and pushed the ICU into taking more radical positions, including provocations of neighbouring Ethiopia. In December 2006 the Ethiopian military mounted an offensive which routed the ICU in days. Ethiopian forces then occupied the capital Mogadishu. The Transitional Federal Government, which until then had been blocked from entering the capital, entered Mogadishu under Ethiopian protection. The Ethiopian military occupation of Mogadishu was the crossing of the Rubicon—the point of no return for Somalia. Somalis vigorously resisted, and the armed insurgency which ensued came to be led by Shabaab. The vast majority of Somalis saw the Ethiopian military occupation as illegal, unacceptable and a humiliation, and viewed armed resistance as a legitimate form of national self-defence. Shabaab's popularity soared among Somalis as a result; it enjoyed strong financial support and recruitment locally and in the diaspora. Its asymmetrical, urban guerilla warfare tactics were countered with heavy handed counter-insurgency attacks by the Ethiopian forces, producing massive damage, tens of thousands of casualties and the dislocation of 700,000 Somalis in the capital. Somalis were furious and many were radicalised by this destruction. Anti-Ethiopian and anti-Western sentiment spiked across much of the population.

Shabaab gradually recaptured most of southern Somalia and over half of the capital by 2008, pushing the TFG into a corner of Mogadishu patrolled by Ethiopia forces and a growing African Union peacekeeping force tasked with protecting the TFG. For humanitarian aid agencies, this meant that almost all of their area of operation was either highly insecure or under the control of Shabaab. By March 2008, the US government designated Shabaab—which had earlier announced its ties to al-Qaeda—a terrorist organisation. This immediately created a potentially serious legal trap for aid agencies operating in Shabaab-controlled zones, as their assistance unavoidably provided some material benefit to Shabaab, placing them at risk of charges of violating the Patriot Act and related counter-terrorism legislation in the US and elsewhere. In 2007–2009, this uncomfortable reality went largely unspoken by aid agencies and donors; few wanted to raise attention to an issue which had the potential to lead to a cessation of humanitarian aid into deeply stressed regions of southern Somalia. Donor states sometimes complained, but acquiesced to humanitarian pragmatism in securing access. At the time, humanitarian aid agencies faced a more immediate problem—deteriorating security. In some areas, local Shabaab leaders protected and facilitated the work of aid agencies and even operated the airstrips used by relief agencies, though the price of admission was strict submission to Shabaab operating rules and a "quietening" of aid agencies on matters of civilian protection.[8] In other locations, hardline Shabaab groups either expelled, threatened or attacked relief workers. This made operating in Shabaab-controlled areas a delicate diplomatic game. At the same time, humanitarian agencies were also targeted by the TFG, which accused them of channelling food aid and colluding with "the enemy," Shabaab. Many security incidents involving aid agencies were suspected of being the work of TFG officials and their paramilitaries, not Shabaab. The operating environment was thus not only much more dangerous and non-permissive, but unpredictable. As one local civil society figure put it, "we used to know what direction the bullets were going to come from; now we're getting shot and don't even know which side has targeted us."[9] By 2008, one-third of all humanitarian casualties globally occurred in Somalia, making it one of the most dangerous places in the world for relief workers.[10] Between 2007 and 2009, seventy-one aid workers were killed in Somalia in 139 separate security incidents.[11] Nearly all of the casualties were Somali national staff. The chronic and worsening insecurity, combined with exceptionally high operating costs (basing offices in neighbouring Nairobi was expensive, as was the cost of private security inside Somalia), make it more and more difficult to justify maintaining programmes in south-central Somalia. One by one, agencies opted to suspend or severely curtail operations; some withdrew altogether.

In early 2009, hopes were raised that an end to the political violence was near, when Ethiopian forces withdrew and the former head of the ICU, a moderate Islamist named Sheikh Sharif, was appointed as the new TFG president. Instead, a prolonged violent stalemate ensued. Shabaab continued to launch attacks against the TFG and the forces of the African Union Mission to Somalia (AMISOM). Political assassinations, suicide bombs, roadside bombs and AMISOM counter-attacks in densely populated neighbourhoods continued to make Mogadishu one of the most insecure places in the world. In Shabaab-controlled areas of the countryside, the jihadist group maintained good security but imposed draconian interpretations of sharia law. It also focused on revenue generation, mainly from taxes on charcoal exports and consumer goods imported through the seaport of Kismayo, and from taxes levied on local populations. Shabaab's legitimacy and support began to wane among Somalis who were repelled by their gratuitous level of violence, repeated targeting of civilians in terror attacks, and open linkages to al-Qaeda. But the TFG's popular support was even weaker. Despite the change in leadership, the TFG continued to be one of the most corrupt administrations in the world, and made almost no progress in advancing the transition or governing areas nominally under its control. It also made life difficult for external aid agencies, which sought to avoid working with the TFG both as a matter of principle (to protect their neutrality, as the TFG was an active party in an ongoing civil war) and effectiveness (the TFG was both so ineffective and corrupt that partnering with it guaranteed failure). TFG officials and their external backers—especially the United Nations Political Office for Somalia, which took the lead role in promoting state-building—insisted that humanitarian aid be coordinated by and delivered through the TFG, in order to help legitimise it in the eyes of the Somali people.

Relief agencies resisted this push to subordinate humanitarian aid to a political stabilisation agenda. The result was rancorous relations between the humanitarian agencies and the donor and UN offices tasked with state-building.[12] The special representative of the secretary-general to Somalia, Ahmedou Ould-Abdallah, repeatedly emphasised the need for permanent, long-term political solutions to the Somali crisis, criticising humanitarian response as little more than a band-aid and a diversion from the greater task of political reconstruction. Part of this line of argument involved challenging the entire notion of humanitarian neutrality, which the SRSG did overtly in a 2009 opinion editorial. Implying that Shabaab finances itself by controlling humanitarian aid in the interior of the country, Ould-Abdallah charged that "those who claim neutrality can also be complicit."[13] Humanitarians' relations with Shabaab plummeted at the same time. In 2010, the split within Shabaab over the presence of UN and Western aid agencies in its areas of control was eventually resolved in favour of the hardliners. The shabaab central *shura* created an Emergency Relief Committee which expelled some aid agencies and imposed sharp restrictions on the rest. Shabaab leaders who possessed clan constituencies in their area of control (and who had to answer to those constituencies) tended to favour the continuation of aid operations, but lacked control over revenue flows in Shabaab and were made to fall in line.

What made Shabaab's policy shift on international relief agencies unusual and, on the surface, irrational is that it was driving away a lucrative source of funding. According to the most authoritative assessment, the UN Monitoring Group's bi-annual report on Somalia, Shabaab imposed a variety of fees and taxes that totalled on average $90,000 per aid agency every six months.[14] Why would a jihadi group walk away from that kind of revenue? The answer, it appears, is personal security fears of the top Shabaab leadership—especially among the foreigners—and genuine ideological revulsion at Somali dependence on food aid from the West overrode the opportunity to profit from the relief operations. The UN Monitoring Group offers an additional potential explanation as well. Its July 2011 report estimates that Shabaab generates between $70 to $100 million per year in revenues from taxes and extortion, port revenues, trade and contraband, and external contributions.[15] Put in this perspective, the money to be made on relief agencies was a relatively small slice of Shabaab's financial portfolio. The benefits to Shabaab simply did not merit the risk that some NGO staff might be passing information to the West. At the same time Shabaab's hardliners were expelling international relief agencies, the US government was growing increasingly concerned about the likelihood that some of its food assistance, routed mainly through World Food Programme (WFP), was falling into Shabaab's hands. The worry was not so much that this was giving Shabaab a decisive advantage financially—it was that a legal concern that the provision of any material benefit to a designated terrorist group was in contravention of the US Patriot Act and related counter-terrorism legislation, and that USAID officials were themselves potentially liable. In September 2009, the Obama administration temporarily suspended shipments of US food aid to Somalia pending a policy review. The public position taken was strictly legal. "We were compelled to hold up [food aid shipments] once there were legitimate concerns that aid might be being diverted," explained one USAID official. "We have to follow the law."[16] In December 2010, the WFP announced it was suspending operations in southern Somalia. It cited unacceptable levels of insecurity as the reason, but close observers claim that it was the result of US political pressure. Any doubts about the possibility that Shabaab was benefiting from Western food aid deliveries were put to rest when the UN Monitoring Group released a detailed report in March 2010 that documented the extent to which food aid was enriching WFP contractors and their sub-contractors who were in some cases financial supporters of Shabaab.[17]

Thus by 2010 southern Somalia was largely depopulated of relief agencies. Some UN specialised agencies and international NGOs—mainly those dealing in health care, nutrition and agricultural livelihood support—were able to maintain a low level, discrete presence, either directly or through local partners. Shabaab was fully aware of this work through local partners, of course, but was willing to tolerate it. Some food aid was still delivered as well—mainly by the ICRC, which maintained a carefully negotiated arrangement with Shabaab via its partnership with the Somali Red Crescent, as well as by some smaller Islamic NGOs. But the suspension of WFP food shipments was huge. Some observers worried that, given Somalia's long and deep dependence on external food aid, the sudden suspension of WFP shipments would plunge the already impoverished country into famine. But very good rains in the spring (or *gu* season) of 2010 produced a bumper crop of cheap staple grains. This, it turned out, only bought the country time before the real crisis hit in 2011.

Key features of the Somali famine

The conditions that produced famine in parts of southern Somalia in 2011 constituted a perfect storm. Severe drought was the precipitating cause, but by no means the only one. In neighbouring areas of eastern Ethiopia and northern Kenya the drought was just as severe, but famine was averted. It was only in southern Somalia where the drought led to famine. What were the other factors? They included several sources of food insecurity and shortage already noted here, including the expulsion of aid agencies by Shabaab and the suspension of US food aid into Shabaab-controlled areas. Other factors were chronic in nature, not causes of famine but sources of worsening food insecurity. Insecurity in the countryside disrupted pastoral movements, restricted farmers to plots close to their villages and raised the cost of commercial movement of foodstuffs. Years of state collapse meant that basic agricultural exten-sion services were not available, reducing smallholder production and rendering many irrigation canals unusable. And high levels of displace-ment from years of warfare created 1.3 million IDPs, who constitute a special class of vulnerable persons in the famine. In addition, a spike in global prices of food and fuel drove prices of imported food up beyond the reach of many poorer Somali consumers. In 2011, the price of the cheapest staples—sorghum, millet and maize—reached the same price in the Somali market as rice, a "luxury" grain that is normally out of reach for poorer Somalis. Prices for sorghum and maize jumped to 350 per cent of their prices from 2010.[18] A market failure ensued. Demand for low value grains was high, but merchants were reluctant to import large quantities of foodstuffs with such limited market value. The pur-chasing power of the poorest Somalis was weakened further by inflation of the Somali shilling.

The result was that basic foodstuffs were available in markets across southern Somalia, but at prices well beyond the reach of destitute farm-ers, pastoralists and IDPs. Because most of these drivers of the famine were chronic, not a sudden onset, the 2011 crisis has been described by some emergency aid workers as a "slow motion" famine. This was a very different famine from the one that ravaged southern Somalia in 1991–1992. That famine was caused by a sudden political collapse and the rapid rise of a predatory civil war in which farming communities were repeatedly plundered, producing famine conditions within six months. In 2011, Somalis' famous coping mechanisms enabled households to stave off famine for a year, but at a cost of a gradual decline into severe malnutrition for much of the population. A variety of factors—remit-tance flows from the Somali diaspora foremost among them—gave por-tions of the Somali population the purchasing power to secure food even at inflated prices. Families also reduced the number of meals they took to one per day, and turned to wild edibles for sustenance. But eventually these and other coping mechanisms broke. The tipping point came in July 2011, when the UN announced famine conditions across several regions of southern Somalia. By then, emaciated Somali families were already pouring across the Somali-Kenyan border or into Mogadishu. For some farmers, their final act of desperation was to sell their riverine land in distress sales, in order to pay for transportation to the Kenyan border where they hoped to reach the Dabaab refugee camp.

Another feature of the 2011 Somali famine was its "patchiness." Though the drought was pervasive, the actual zones of concentrated famine were scattered across parts but not all of southern Somalia. One of the most telling aspects of the famine was that its epicentre was along much of the Shabelle river valley, normally the breadbasket of the country, and an area that one would expect to be better able to withstand a severe drought thanks to access to river water for irrigated agriculture. The fact that downstream portions of the river dried up partially accounts for the severe distress experienced in the lower Shabelle region. But there may have been political factors at play as well—irrigation water was said to be diverted to plantations and away from smallholders, because the plantations generated more tax revenues for Shabaab.[19] Famine early warning systems generally worked well in the 2011 crisis. Alerts were issued by November 2011, a full seven months before actual famine occurred. Early warning response, however, was very inadequate.[20] This seems to have been due to a combination of donor fatigue with Somali humanitarian emergencies, scepticism or uncertainty about the quality of data given limited access, and a sense in some quarters that the humanitarian crisis was diverting energies away from state-building and stabilisation priorities. Some relief officials acknowledge, moreover, that they were taken by surprise at the scale of the disaster, which at one point placed 4 million Somalis—half or more of the total population in south-central Somalia—in need of emergency humanitarian aid. Yet only 2.2 million of those Somalis could be reached by relief agencies.[21]

By August 2011, UN OCHA predicted up to 750,000 excess mortalities could occur. The greatest fear was that severely weakened and malnourished populations would succumb to waterborne diseases such as cholera with the arrival of the short (*deyr*) rainy season in October. In the end, far fewer died, in part because the *deyr* season rains were excellent and, many suspect, the combination of ICRC food aid and Somali remittances were just enough to keep many alive. No reliable estimates are available because of lack of access to Shabaab-controlled areas. Aid agencies have been reluctant to even hazard a guess, though some have made broad statements estimating that 50,000 to 100,000 Somalis died in the famine. The lower than expected casualty figures have led some to question whether the crisis was exaggerated and should have in fact been labelled a famine, especially since humanitarian monitoring systems were not in a position to collect the kind of data needed to declare a famine. Others make the opposite claim, arguing that the UN's declaration that the famine "ended" in February 2012 is a distinction without a difference for the 2 million or more Somalis believed to be still in need of humanitarian aid. When the famine was declared in July 2011— accompanied by brief but intense media coverage, including a front page photograph of a starving child in the *New York Times*—a predictable scramble by international donors and aid agencies ensued.[22] International NGOs and UN specialised agencies came under heavy pressure from headquarters to expand operations; "traditional" donors ramped up pledges of aid; the so-called "non-traditional" donors and aid agencies, mainly from the Islamic world (and especially Turkey), rapidly expanded their activities, to the point that about one-third of aid pouring into Somalia in the latter half of 2011 came from non-Western donors;[23] and the Somali diaspora mobilised additional funds for their own formal and informal relief operations, mainly working through local contacts to disperse cash and food. Collectively, this produced a crowded humanitarian playing field, as a flood of aid agency personnel and resources poured into Mogadishu. This created a rash of predictable problems. Coordination was elusive; the seaport was congested and chaotic; the need for security swelled the number of private security companies, sometimes with lethal results. But the main problem was that these agencies and their donors confronted five critical bottlenecks impeding the flow of their emergency aid to populations in need.

The five bottlenecks

Shabaab policies

As the humanitarian crisis worsened in 2011, Shabaab initially appeared to shift towards a responsive and constructive approach. It collected money from local businesspeople and others as a form of *zakat* to redistribute to the needy, and in July 2011 it announced that it welcomed Western famine relief "with no strings attached." But it quickly rescinded that statement—arguing that it had been "mistranslated"— and affirmed that only a small number of aid agencies would be allowed to operate in its area of control.[24] With the largest purveyors of food aid—WFP and CARE—banned from Shabaab areas, only the ICRC had the capacity to move large quantities of food. This placed an enormous burden on ICRC, which had to shoulder the task of moving food aid into southern Somalia for a targeted population of one million people, all the while negotiating continuously with a very nervous and increasingly unpredictable and internally divided Shabaab leadership. As the crisis worsened, Shabaab's policies became more pathological. Its spokesman denied that a famine existed, and blamed the UN for trying to fabricate a crisis to embarrass Shabaab. It tried, with limited success, to block famine victims from fleeing to Kenya or Mogadishu. Accounts from refugees and IDPs of Shabaab efforts to block them from leaving, and its efforts to hurriedly bury the dead to hide the scale of fatalities occurring on its watch, badly damaged Shabaab's legitimacy in Somalia. Shabaab initially tried to collect drought victims in its own relief camps, to prevent them from leaving to areas beyond its control. But the group adamantly opposed vaccinations in those camps, until a devastating measles outbreak in several of their camps led them to reconsider. In late September, it suddenly announced that drought victims had to return to their fields to prepare the ground for the next rainy season—a forced relocation by truck that, given the weakness of the population, turned into a death sentence for some, and made it much more difficult for populations to access what little medical and nutritional aid making its way into southern Somalia. Shabaab also forced rural households to either pay a tax or offer up one of their sons as a fighter. Given the destitution in the community, this was a thinly veiled form of forced conscription, and one which was deeply resented. Some of these boys deserted and fled to the Dabaab refugee camps.

Over the course of the crisis, Shabaab's leadership appeared more and more intent on hiding the extent of its own responsibility for the famine, blaming the disaster on others and claiming credit for successful aid delivery, whether or not it was true. Ironically, on this score Shabaab had much in common with the international donors and aid agencies it despised. NGOs still on the ground quietly expressed frustration that Shabaab was seeking to manipulate efforts to provide famine victims with direct purchasing power in the form of vouchers. Shabaab first sought to stamp all vouchers with the word "Shabaab" to give the impression it was responsible for the vouchers. Then, in late September, it forbade the vouchers altogether. This was the point when Shabaab famine policies swung into a much more hardened position, a shift some NGO officials claimed was a backlash against Western governments and media publicly blaming Shabaab for the famine. Shabaab figures in the National Drought Committee (renamed the Resettlement and Recovery Committee by September) demanded that remaining international NGOs and their local partners and Islamic charities hand over all relief goods; forbade any documentation such as registration, photographs or beneficiary lists; exerted sole control over the distribution of relief aid; and forbade monitoring and evaluation by aid agencies.[25] The foreign relief agencies and their local partners were essentially told to hand over relief supplies and step away.

For some of the new and inexperienced Islamic charities, handing over truckloads of food to Shabaab was not seen as unreasonable or objectionable. But for Western and local NGOs, it was an agonizing dilemma. To reject these terms meant cutting off medical and food aid to famine victims. Most aid workers were convinced that Shabaab's relief committees were relatively honest and committed to delivering aid to those in need; this was not an instance of wholesale diversion of emergency relief. But the demands Shabaab made undermined core commitments to accountability and due diligence, violated humanitarian principles of neutrality (as Shabaab leaders were strengthening themselves from controlling distribution of aid) and placed aid agencies in jeopardy of violating Western counter-terrorism laws by knowingly allowing their resources to benefit Shabaab. This dilemma was short-lived, however. In late November, Shabaab shut down almost all remaining relief agencies in southern Somalia. Its Office for the Supervising of Foreign Agencies issued a lengthy communiqué, based on what it claimed was a "meticulous year-long review and investigation," that charged these international (and in some cases Somali) aid agencies and UN specialised agencies with misconduct that included spying, fostering tribalism, undermining Islam, proselytising, mobilising communities against Shabaab, undermining sustainable livelihoods, conspiring to exploit Somalia's natural resources and failing to remain neutral.[26] Only ICRC was able to continue to operate, serving as a critical lifeline for southern Somalia. But on 30 January 2012, Shabaab expelled ICRC as well. In a statement, Shabaab claimed that "despite being offered unrivalled access to all the regions governed by the Mujahideen in south and central Somalia, the International Committee of the Red Cross has repeatedly betrayed the trust conferred on it by the local population," and specifically accused the group of distributing expired food aid that was "unfit for human consumption" to Somalis.[27] It then claimed to have burned 2,000 metric tons of food aid, in the midst of a famine.

Western counter-terrorism restrictions

The suspension of US humanitarian assistance into Shabaab-controlled areas of southern Somalia in late 2009 had immediate implications for food security across southern Somalia, as the US is the main source of food aid globally. But it also had a wider impact on humanitarian agencies, even those not dealing with food aid. It forced donor states and relief agencies to openly address a dilemma that they would have preferred to leave unspoken—the fact that counter-terrorism laws applied to Somalia essentially criminalised almost all flows of remittances and aid into areas controlled by Shabaab. Aid agencies, Somali groups sending emergency aid to home towns and officials in donor institutions (including USAID) were all potentially vulnerable to charges of providing material benefits to a terrorist group. When famine was announced in July 2011, the US government officials found themselves in a serious bind.[28] Many, especially those in USAID, wanted to reduce or eliminate any legal obstacles to the release of food aid into the famine zones. But others in the administration either privileged security priorities—the imperative not to provide Shabaab with an infusion of resources at a time when it was showing growing signs of distress—or took a legal approach and argued that, like it or not, the Patriot Act was the law of the land. Lurking beneath the competing positions were the inevitable political calculations as well. The Obama administration was keen to avoid being blamed for the famine, but it was also loathe to give its political rivals an opportunity to accuse it of aiding and abetting terrorists. The divisions within the US government on the issue were, by all accounts, sharp, and cut across different departments in the government.

Making matters worse for all concerned parties was the enormous complexity and ambiguity of the laws and executive orders. Confusion reigned in the aid community over the wording of laws and the scope of liability for individuals and organisations. Lawyers came to play a prominent role in the discussions, which did not advance the cause of clarity. Humanitarian aid agencies sought to negotiate with the US government for a waiver, which would provide them with legal protection while working in areas controlled by a designated terrorist group. There was precedent for waivers of this sort in southern Lebanon and the West Bank. Over the course of the summer and autumn of 2011, international NGOs met repeatedly with US diplomats in an effort to reach an agreement. It was a bridge too far. US government officials offered the NGOs a memo that they insisted provided them with sufficient guarantees that they would not be liable to criminal prosecution as long as they made good faith efforts to prevent aid from benefiting Shabaab, and as long as they self-reported when unintentional benefits did accrue to Shabaab. The US officials were adamant that they wanted to see aid get to the famine victims, and were not about to play a game of "gotcha" with humanitarian organisations trying to save lives, and were taken aback by the reluctance of humanitarian agencies to accept these assurances. More than anything else, they argued vigorously that the bottleneck to humanitarian access was Shabaab's policies, not US counter-terrorism laws. Some suspected that the US was being scapegoated by a humanitarian community that was ideologically opposed to the securitisation of US foreign policy since the 9/11 attacks.

For their part, humanitarian agencies' lawyers concluded that the written assurances offered by the US government did not in fact provide them with adequate legal protection, and that the verbal assurances meant nothing. They argued that the government wording was intentionally confusing. While the NGOs needed clarity, the government wanted ambiguity. Established international NGOs were not only worried about the fate of individuals in their organisation; they argued that a public accusation that they aided a terrorist group could destroy the reputation and funding sources of the entire NGO. Much more was at stake than their operation in Somalia. The humanitarian agencies also complained that the US and UN seemed intent on redirecting humanitarian aid to the "newly liberated" areas as a form of peace dividend. Agencies objected to this effort to harness humanitarian aid to a stabilisation agenda, and were critical of aid agencies like WFP that appeared too eager to move back into areas recently vacated by Shabaab. In the end, a handful of UN agencies and Western NGOs remained in southern Somalia in the summer and autumn of 2011 until expelled by Shabaab; they opted to risk running foul of counter-terrorism legislation. But the groups that were most impervious were the Islamic NGOs, from Turkey and elsewhere. The restrictions had little impact on them, allowing them to operate as freely as they could in Shabaab-controlled areas.

Insecurity

As noted above, by 2009 most aid agencies had taken actions in response to unacceptable levels of insecurity for their staff. They had either withdrawn from Somalia, suspended operations, reduced operations to very low levels or subcontracted out work to local partners. In all of these cases, the adaptation to insecurity had the net effect of dismantling or eroding important networks and trust relations with local communities. The longer operations were suspended, the worse this problem became. This constituted a serious but underappreciated bottleneck to rapid famine response. Aid agency personnel quietly anguished over the fact that even if restrictions by both Shabaab and Western states were removed, their NGOs would not be able to "scale up" operations in time to save many lives. In order to move aid effectively in the politically complex and highly dangerous environment of southern Somalia, they argued, relief agencies had to have well-established trust relations and dense networks with civic leaders and others across their areas of operation. Access and security in this environment was typically negotiated "village by village" and required close and accurate knowledge of the political landscape. Hasty operations that introduced large shipments of aid into areas without those trust networks virtually guaranteed trouble—in the form of looting, diversion and potentially lethal security threats. Arrangements with local leaders took time to negotiate—time the relief operations did not have. This sobering admission by aid agencies pointed to a disquieting conclusion—that by September 2011, there was very little that external aid agencies could do for the drought victims. This was a line of argument that exasperated donor states, which were placing strong pressure on the humanitarian community to "scale up" operations in areas liberated from Shabaab.

TFG obstructionism

Shabaab controlled an estimated 95 per cent of the territory where famine victims were located. But the 5 per cent that was beyond Shabaab's direct control—most of the capital Mogadishu—was home to tens of thousands of drought victims flooding into IDP camps in the city. Mogadishu was under the nominal control of the TFG, which received extensive foreign aid and diplomatic support from the international community and which was beholden to the international community for its security (thanks to the 12,000 peacekeepers in AMISOM). It was not unreasonable, therefore, to assume that the UN and Western donor states would be in a position to exert strong pressure on the TFG to facilitate and protect the flow of humanitarian aid to the drought victims fleeing into its areas of control. It was also not unreasonable to assume that the beleaguered TFG leadership would seize the opportunity to demonstrate to the Somali people that it could provide essential services and protection during a time of great need—earning badly needed "performance legitimacy" and creating a clear contrast between its famine relief policies and those of Shabaab. For aid agencies, this should have been a relatively permissive environment in which to negotiate both access and effective monitoring of distribution.

Those assumptions were unfortunately wrong. The TFG leadership and many (though not all) of the Somalis formally or nominally a part of the TFG as civil servants, security forces, paramilitaries, district commissioners, parliamentarians and ministers, approached the flood of famine relief pouring into Mogadishu as an opportunity to enrich themselves. Corruption in the TFG had been epic in scale since the creation of the government in late 2004, earning Somalia the annual distinction as the most corrupt country in the world in Transparency International's rankings, so the TFG's predatory approach to famine aid came as little surprise to observers familiar with Somalia. The TFG's diversion of aid occurred at all phases of aid delivery. At the seaport, relief supplies were stranded unless and until healthy payoffs in cash or in kind were made to port authorities. This was a problem not only for UN and Western agencies; Islamic charities were also held up in this manner.[29] The delivery of food aid from seaport to IDP camp must pay "taxes" to any of the 336 militia checkpoints that food convoys pass in TFG controlled areas of Mogadishu.[30] And TFG officials and their militia backers treated the IDP camps as bait to attract and divert food aid. The diversion of aid from IDP camps has been a long-standing practice in Somalia; "camp managers" known locally as "black cats" take a substantial portion of rations from each IDP, and in some cases have blocked IDPs from leaving the camp. But the fact that TFG district commissioners and others were all setting up their own IDP camps to attract and divert aid made the TFG culpable in this unseemly enterprise. A political quarrel within the TFG over whether or not to concentrate the IDPs in a few large camps had nothing to do with efficiency and everything to do with a struggle to control the food aid flowing in and then back out of the camps. International and local aid organisations were furious with the diversions and with the TFG's culpability and indifference. Many Somali civil servants in the TFG were equally appalled. Because the diversions occurred after the aid was distributed, there was very little the aid agencies could do. The "black cats" in these cases were backed by armed groups that NGOs were simply not in a position to negotiate with. In the end, the relief agencies had to live with the rationale that as long as enough aid was getting through to the IDPs, the fact that TFG-affiliated armed groups were diverting portions of it was "the cost of doing business." In fairness to the TFG, many of the political figures and their paramilitaries engaged in division were part of the TFG in name only; in reality, they were autonomous armed groups and political entrepreneurs who were in the process of carving Mogadishu up into fiefdoms. In 2011, a leaked UN report documented the existence of seventeen autonomous clan-based militias in Mogadishu, each presiding over its own chunk of the city. Some of the leaders of these militias were also sitting members of parliament. For Somalis, this was not only further evidence of the illegitimacy and weakness of the TFG, but also a worrisome sign of the return of warlordism as both the TFG and Shabaab weakened. For aid agencies, this meant a return to a depressingly familiar operational landscape, that of Somalia pre-2006, when gaining access in southern Somalia was a matter of neighbourhood-by-neighbourhood, village-by-village negotiations with different armed groups.

Thus the TFG was too weak to control its own limited territory, and was the major impediment to delivery of food aid at the seaport and IDP camps. Yet the TFG and its external backers in the UN continued to insist that all humanitarian aid be channelled through the TFG, as a way of building up its legitimacy and capacity. The UN also criticised NGOs for employing private security guards in Mogadishu rather than relying on the TFG police as armed escorts; one UN office went so far as to accuse the humanitarian agencies of reviving warlordism in the capital by financing private armed security. These claims exasperated humanitarian aid workers, who were convinced that they possessed a much more accurate assessment of the TFG than did the UN Political Office for Somalia, and who were not about to risk kidnapping or assault by the TFG security forces. They were also appalled at the fact that donor states and the UN were seeking to tether life-saving humanitarian aid to what they saw as a sinking ship in the TFG. On this issue, the humanitarian actors did have some bargaining leverage; they were generally able to circumvent the TFG and ignore the UN's insistence that they fold their humanitarian work into the broader goal of stabilisation.

The "privilege gap"

All humanitarian assistance involves a leap of faith. At some point in the chain of distribution, aid agencies can no longer monitor the distribution and consumption of the food aid. Whether it is at the level of a regional administrator, of village chiefs or heads of household, someone has to be entrusted to do the right thing and see that the aid gets to those in need. One of the most troubling but least discussed aspects of Somalia's recurring humanitarian crises is the low sense of social and ethical obligation to assist Somalis from weak lineages and social groups. This stands in sharp contrast to the very powerful and non-negotiable obligation Somalis have to assist members of their own lineage. Somalis possess an impressive array of means to make claims on one another for help; they are rich in social capital, and use that to give and receive aid from one another. This has been one of the most effective social safety nets in the country. But Somalis of low status—members of weak lineages in strong clans, or members of low caste social groups—lack the means to make claims on their more privileged neighbours. This is most in evidence when humanitarian crises occur. Somalis from low status groups are consistently unable to make claims on other Somalis for assistance, whether in the form of remittances received or food aid distributed. Too often, in the many deals struck over allocation of food aid locally, the weakest lineages are given short shrift. They are also the principal victims of diversion of food aid by "black cats" and others.

When one asked the clarifying question "Who died?" in the Somali famine, the privilege gap in Somalia becomes apparent. In the 1991–

1992 famine, the victims were almost all from the poorly armed Digle-Mirifle clans and the Bantu farming communities, all of whom have been treated as second class citizens in Somalia. In 2011–2012, we have only anecdotal evidence, but it again points to disproportionate deaths among the Maay speaking farming communities and low status groups. This is a major bottleneck for humanitarian relief, because external aid agencies are never in a position to monitor who low status groups are and whether they have received—and been able to keep—assistance. Many Somali national staff, as well as Somali NGOs, are well aware of the marginalisation of these low caste groups and attempt to target aid to them, but are often up against powerful local forces which embrace a different set of priorities about aid distribution. The privilege gap is a social—not a political, security or legal—impediment to humanitarian access. It is in no way unique to Somalia—weak social groups, including women as well as minority groups—routinely face difficulties accessing assistance in emergency circumstances. Social obstacles to humanitarian access are much more difficult to negotiate than legal or political impediments, and are typically much more difficult to change. They can involve deeply ingrained attitudes and cultural practices, and are often very sensitive to broach. But Somalia is badly in need of a frank and open discussion about this particular impediment to emergency aid. The "black cat" phenomenon is emblematic of this problem—a fracture in the social compact among Somalis that allows for some to routinely divert food aid from starving countrymen with no social consequences. Interestingly, the one group that made a real effort to overcome this lethal form of discrimination was Shabaab, which for a time specifically sought to empower minority groups in southern Somalia. That did not last long however, as by 2011 those same weak social groups were the principal victims of a famine over which Shabaab presided.

Conclusion

Humanitarian actors of all types—ICRC, UN specialised agencies, Western NGOs, Islamic NGOs and Somali NGOs—were forced to engage in multiple negotiations to gain access in the Somali famine. None of the most powerful actors in the Somali drama—Shabaab, the TFG, the UN, the US and Ethiopia—facilitated this effort—all, in varying degrees, were impediments to humanitarian access. The result was very limited space for aid agencies to operate and maintain minimally effective control of distribution of aid. The ICRC fared best, by working through Red Crescent to placate Shabaab until early 2012. Local NGOs backed by diaspora funding were sometimes able to push back against local Shabaab authorities and protect humanitarian space, but had no clout once high level Shabaab figures got directly involved. In TFG controlled areas, all humanitarian actors enjoyed better success negotiating space, mainly by working around TFG. But this access did not solve the problem of lack of control over distribution. Negotiations between humanitarian actors and the UN and others prioritising stabilisation objectives broke down badly, resulting in exceptionally poor relations between the two. Unfortunately, by early 2012 humanitarian space was virtually eliminated for all humanitarian agencies, and humanitarian actors appeared to have very little bargaining leverage to alter that fact. This puts southern Somalia in an exceptionally precarious position in the event of another setback to food security.

PART III

CONTESTED SPACE
INTERVENTIONS AND DILEMMAS

10

ETHICAL COMPLEXITY AND PERPLEXITY

HUMANITARIAN ACTORS, DISASTERS AND SPACE

Heather M. Roff

Humanitarianism is a widely studied and frequently invoked concept. The language of humanitarianism is used to legitimate causes, assuage fears, signal intent or, in more malevolent moments, employed to conceal imperialistic motives. Yet, the use and abuse of this term leaves many, academics and practitioners alike, feeling as though the concept is over-stretched. Indeed, because this concept is so broad, attempts to apply it in more practical endeavours, like identifying the kinds of ethical complexities humanitarian actors might face, may appear ad hoc and random. This is due to the fact that ethical judgements presuppose a clear theoretical framework of the practice or concept in question, and only when a clear framework is present can we position ourselves to make normative prescriptions or identify potential problem areas. Therefore, before we can begin to identify the ethical complexities of humanitarian action, we must first and foremost understand the moral frameworks from which we make such judgements, what kinds of disasters require humanitarian assistance, who the actors involved in such assistance are and finally what "humanitarianism" means. In this chapter I will attempt to demarcate carefully the different issues involved when invoking the term "humanitarian," and I will also argue that depending upon where one stands, the ethical challenges may be very different. That is, ethical complexities arise from a number of vantage points, but only when we have a clear understanding of where the horizon sits can we even begin to identify them.

Moral frameworks

Ethical judgements assert that some action is right or wrong according to a particular standard, usually a standard that is set by a system of principles or rules (moral frameworks) used to guide an agent's deliberation and action. The two most widely used moral frameworks are consequentialism and deontology. Depending upon the set of principles by which one abides, different actions may be right or wrong according to that set. Consequentialism, and its offspring utilitarianism, roughly states that an act is right if it maximises the best consequences (or in utilitarianism's version, utility) more than any other act, all things considered.[1] This maximisation is of some sort of predetermined non-moral good, like happiness, pleasure, wellbeing or flourishing. Deontology, on the other hand, claims that the right act is that which is done in accordance with one's moral duty. Kantian versions of deontology claim that one can determine if one's action (and maxim) is in accordance with duty by proceeding through several "tests." These tests are laid out in Kant's famous categorical imperative, where each formulation acts as a sort of litmus test for permissibility. For example, one formulation considers a maxim's universalisability and another questions whether one's act would violate the "humanity" within oneself or another.[2] Deontologists claim that any act that violates one's duty is wrong, no matter what the consequences. Thus, a short-hand way of understanding these two frameworks is that consequentialism privileges the "good" over the "right," while deontology privileges the "right" over the "good."

Another track that one could use to determine the morally right act when undertaking humanitarian action is international legalism. This framework posits that a humanitarian actor ought to abide by international laws, norms or standards. Such laws, norms or standards could range from: international humanitarian law, as enumerated in the 1949 and 1977 Geneva Convention and Optional Protocols; to norms, such as the "Responsibility to Protect" doctrine; or to standards such as those outlined in the 1997 Sphere Project that attempts to develop a minimum set of operating procedures and baselines for humanitarian non-governmental organisations. Adopting this framework, though, is not without its problems. For instance: international humanitarian law is not applicable in natural disaster situations; norms are easily misinterpreted or ignored; and, creating operational standards risks prioritising bureaucracy over victims.[3]

As noted at the outset, the morally correct act could be different depending upon which moral framework one adopts. For example, if one's goal is to minimise the overall suffering of a target population, then violating the rights of a portion of this population is morally permissible, if the overall population's suffering is actually minimised. Such rights violations might take the form of refusing aid to a rebel group within a country adversely affected by a natural disaster for fear that providing assistance will fuel civil war or provide the rebels with a political platform on the international stage.[4] As long as the majority of the victims receive aid, then any suffering or harm done to the rebels will be seen as morally correct. Contrarily, if one is a deontologist, violating any person's rights to minimise the overall suffering of a population would be a moral wrong, regardless of the "good" to come out of such violation.[5] If one is an international legalist, then the correct answer is to abide by the laws, norms or standards, whatever the outcome may be. Of course, in practice, these three frameworks often become intertwined, and following strict frameworks is nearly impossible, especially if one abides by a principle of "do no harm."[6]

Types of actors and assistance

Up until this point, we have been as general as possible when using the term "humanitarian actor." Yet, we cannot continue this for long. Philosophers, practitioners or policy makers must explicitly identify the agents they are referring to when making ethical judgements, or attempting to identify any potential ethical quagmires. Identifying the actors is extremely important, as some actors will face vastly different situations than others, and so sweeping generalisations will be at best of little use or at worse exacerbate crises. Humanitarian actors come in a variety of forms: states, nongovernmental organisations, international organisations, soldiers, relief workers and even donors. While each type of actor faces unique situations and choices, for our purposes, I will focus on two broad classifications: combatants and noncombatants.[7]

Combatants, traditionally, consist of all those men and women in a state's or a regional organisation's armed forces. Combatants are those men and women who are trained soldiers "set apart from the world of peaceful activity; they are trained to fight, provided with weapons, [and] required to fight on command."[8] Combatants are considered a "dangerous" class. They are dangerous because war is their "enterprise" and through some mechanism they all have been forced to fight.[9] This is the traditional understanding; however, there are other types of actors that gain combatant status, particularly guerilla groups or other insurgents. Whether these groups gain the rights of belligerents depends upon several factors, such as wearing their arms openly, having a fixed emblem denoting their status (such as a uniform) and being under some sort of hierarchical command structure.[10] Some, like Walzer, also claim that if guerrillas gain material and political support from the people, then this grants the guerillas belligerent status as well.[11]

Noncombatants are all those agents not engaged in the "business of war".[12] That is, noncombatants "have done nothing, and are doing nothing, that entails a loss of their rights."[13] They have not taken up arms, and they are not part of a class of people making munitions or other material goods directly related to the supply of weapons.[14] Civilians working in government are a problematic case; however, for like all other civilians, they retain their rights not to be killed or harmed.[15] Aid workers are seen as noncombatants, while peacekeepers are combatants. The operations that each undertakes can be decidedly different, but this is not always the case. For example, aid workers might run refugee camps, deliver food, engage in job training programmes or provide medical attention. Peacekeepers, on the other hand, can also deliver food and provide medical attention, but they may also undertake military operations to protect civilian lives or stop two warring parties from fighting. Operations undertaken by soldiers, thus, presuppose a war torn area, where security, for relief operations or the civilian population, is lacking.

Humanitarian disasters

We must also identify the type of emergency in which a humanitarian actor might find oneself so that we can understand the potential ethical complexities one might face. Accordingly, we must ask: is this a natural disaster? Is it a political disaster? Or, are both present? Each situation presents itself with different challenges, and so one cannot make blanket judgements that apply to all three scenarios. In the case of natural disasters, actors are faced with the scourging effects of typhoons, hurricanes, floods, earthquakes or droughts, and the ability for humanitarian actors to get access to disaster victims may not be as compromised or challenged by issues of institutional legitimacy or violence. As Albala-Bertrand notes, the resulting emergencies from natural disasters erupt without, or with little, warning and are usually short term.[16] Thus, responses to such disasters are typically short term and focused on restitution and rebuilding to the status quo ante. Political disasters, otherwise known as complex humanitarian emergencies, are not as concerned with restitutive responses.[17] Complex emergencies erupt because of dissatisfaction with the current societal structures, and so response mechanisms must also change.[18] In these instances, humanitarian actors are not only faced with issues of displacement and fulfilling basic needs, they are also faced with problems associated with peacemaking and peacekeeping, development and political legitimacy.[19] Even more complex is when a natural disaster has exacerbated an ongoing political conflict or struggle. A case in point is the 2004 Indian Ocean tsunami. When the tsunami struck Sri Lanka, the long held political struggle between the government and the Liberation Tigers of Tamil Eelam (LTTE) reached a boiling point. Both parties called on international society for aid, and both accused the other of using that aid against the "people." The LTTE claimed that if the government was granted aid, the Tamil people would see none of it, and the government claimed that any aid given to the LTTE would fund an illegitimate insurgency and harm the Sri Lankan people.[20] Thus aid became a highly politicised tool and humanitarian agents were seen to endorse or legitimise one side over the other.

Ethical complexities and the meaning of humanitarianism

It should now be apparent that identifying a list of possible ethical complexities for humanitarian actors is no easy task. Indeed, that task becomes even more difficult when the meaning of "humanitarianism" or the notion of "humanitarian space" comes into the equation. In terms of what it means to be "humanitarian" we are faced with the litany of questions and distinctions noted above: are we speaking of combatants or noncombatants? Are we in a natural disaster or a political one? Are the lines blurred with regard to agent and situation?

What it means to be a humanitarian combatant will be couched in terms of mission mandates, international law and the questions of moral importance not outlined in handbooks and treaties. These humanitarian soldiers must be sensitive to the unexpected and unintended consequences of their presence. One such example is well documented by Peter Andreas and his work on the rise of black markets associated with the United Nations's overtaking of the Sarajevo airport during the 1992–1995 siege of Sarajevo. Andreas notes that:

[A]s the [UN run] airlift helped to keep the city from starving, it also made the siege tolerable and therefore internationally acceptable—reducing the likelihood of it being lifted. Humanitarian action became, in effect, a new form of containment. It also provided a mode of managing the situation without having to resort to direct military force. [...]The result of this process, as Michael Ignatieff puts it, is that 'the U.N. allowed itself to become the administrator of the Serbian siege of Sarajevo.'[21]

However, these unintended and unexpected effects are only one type of ethical complexity. There are other, perhaps unintended, but not unexpected effects of combatants. For instance, in war torn and ethnically divided areas, such as the Democratic Republic of Congo, the presence of combatants does not necessarily guarantee safety. In 2010, reports emerged of UN-backed Congolese troops murdering and raping women.[22] The report specifically noted that the UN "has previously been criticised by human rights groups for supporting the Congolese army despite its record of violations."[23] In such a case, the question arises as to whether the UN should have taken additional measures to protect these women and children, or refused to provide logistical support to the Congolese troops.

Furthermore, combatants may not merely find themselves amidst the power plays of states or international organisations but instead faced with personal ethical choices. Such choices can range from whether to fire on child soldiers, who are traditionally categorised as moral innocents, to taking on greater risk to ensure the safety of noncombatants in a war zone. The moral import of either an act or an omission depends upon the moral framework from which one is operating. In the case of child soldiers, if the combatant is a deontologist, there is a strict prohibition against killing the innocent. If the combatant is a utilitarian, there may be no such prohibition. International legalism is of little help in this situation as well, as many of the international treaties on the protection of the child do not provide guidance on the rules of engagement with twelve-year-old coerced combatants.[24]

For noncombatants, especially aid workers, the ethical complexities are perhaps even more opaque, and the meaning of "humanitarianism" even more abstruse. On the surface, the "humanitarian imperative" to provide assistance where needed is traditionally circumscribed by three principles: impartiality, neutrality and independence. Impartiality ought to guide relief efforts by not distinguishing among recipients "because of nationality, race, religion or other factors."[25] Neutrality requires aid workers to refrain from taking part in hostilities or "from undertaking any action that furthers the interests of one party to the conflict or compromises those of the other."[26] Independence ought to "ensure that humanitarian action is exclusively concerned with the welfare of humanity and free of all political, religious or other extraneous influences."[27] Conceptually these principles seem quite straightforward; however, applying them is not. Given a choice between the LTTE and the Sri Lankan government, there can be neither impartiality nor neutrality. In such a situation, then, should aid be withheld? If one attempts to answer "yes," then one is faced with yet another moral question: is omitting aid in this instance as morally culpable as delivering aid to one side or both? The answer to this question, again, depends upon one's moral framework. The deontologist might answer in the affirmative, while the consequentialist in the negative.

However, there is, of course, the argument that all aid is inherently political, and so attempts at impartiality, neutrality and independence are misguided. Indeed, the politics of aid have become so pervasive that aid is almost always contingent upon sustaining "comprehensive, durable, and just" resolutions of conflict.[28] Failure to reach resolutions can result in such actions as closing borders to refugees, withdrawing aid when conflicting parties fail to reach agreement or making aid conditional upon cooperation with intervening military forces.[29] Yet, "humanitarianism" can be more politically nuanced than insisting on terms of conditionality. As Jennifer Rubenstein concludes, "it is precisely human-itarian action's disconnection from more structural issues that gives it its particular brand of political power, and that enables humanitarian actors to sometimes do what more 'political' actors cannot."[30] In other words, labelling an action humanitarian can be, in itself, a strategic choice because of all of the notions embedded in the concept of "humanitarian-ism." Politics, therefore, can happen on many levels and need not occur solely between governments and rebels.

There may be, however, an even darker side to aid about which NGOs, donors and relief workers must be made aware. It is the very notion of perpetuated victimhood through bureaucratisation. As Elizabeth Dunn argues, "to make something, humanitarianism demands the subordination of the subject to the recognition of the violence done to him or her."[31] Yet, this continual recognition undermines the attempts at rebuilding the self, that is, to no longer be a victim. Any relief effort, then, is premised on a false note:

> Humanitarianism is generally thought to produce something. In the grinning photos and sentimental anecdotes found in humanitarian agencies' brochures, it is something good: material well-being, livelihood, social order, human rights, and reconstructed identities. In much of the scholarly literature, humanitarian-ism produces something bad: a pretext for militarism, an extension of brutal conflict, poverty, illness, and a social order that disciplines and oppresses.[32]

As Dunn argues, the production of humanitarianism is its continued existence through increasing levels of bureaucracy. NGOs are caught up in perpetuating themselves, and to do this they require subordinating the victims of crises to their own end: perpetuity.

All of this, though, is subject to even further difficulty. Even if we fully understand what humanitarianism requires, there is no agreement on what "humanitarian space" is and what its (potential) effects on humanitarian action might be. Even within this very volume there is disagreement on its precise definition. Thomas Weiss, for instance, argues that humanitarian space is the "physical arena within which relief and protection can be effectively and safely provided to victims of armed conflict," while Hubert and Brassard-Boudreau define it in terms of "dimensions" where respect for International Humanitarian Law (IHL), physical space and "humanitarian action writ large" are all components of the concept.[33] Each definition, however, proves problematic for the ethicist. Weiss's definition, for instance, risks being too narrow because he limits it to violent political conflicts and does not take into consideration natural disasters. Moreover, limiting the concept's application to physical space may be a disservice, not only to humanitarian actors, but also to the study of humanitarianism. Case in point, if humanitarian space is "shrinking" what does that mean in terms of physicality and geography? Surely, the physical space is not shrinking. Somalia is the size it always has been. Rather, what we are describing is the actor's ability to have access to affected populations, access to other relief workers or undertake effective relief strategies. Contrarily, we should not commit the opposite fault and define the concept too broadly, such as Hubert and Brassard-Boudreau attempt to do. For attempting to define a concept by including too many factors endangers it to becoming vacuous and over-stretched. When a concept becomes "over-stretched" there is so little precision available with which to make meaningful claims because other determinants might be responsible for the outcome. For instance, if we attribute respect for IHL as a dimension of humanitarian space (and its subsequent enlargement), while simultaneously noting that attacks on relief workers are increasing, we might ask what such incongruous outcomes are telling us. What, in other words, is "doing the work" in such a concept? Is it respect for law? If so, then why are there attacks on relief workers? Or, even more generally, why are humanitarian actors there to begin with, as surely if one respects IHL, then there would be no need for humanitarian assistance.[34] If we over-stretch humanitarian space, then we have no footing on which to make theoretical, empirical or even ethical claims. There are just too many cooks in the kitchen.

The ethical complexities that result from humanitarian action are, therefore, so vast that it would be naïve to attempt to list a set of possible situations that humanitarian actors might face. This is because much depends upon which ethical framework one adopts, one's status as a combatant or noncombatant, the type of emergency with which one is faced, and whether one abides by the notion that all humanitarian action ought to be impartial, neutral and independent, and all of it is compounded by how one views one's position in "humanitarian space." There is no easy answer here. There is no perfect definition. We must be cautiously optimistic when the "right answers" are provided, and we must remember that every situation is different and full of ambiguity. This ambiguity is, of course, a result of the very notion of ethics. To be an ethical person is to understand the right action, at the right time, and have the right motivations. One cannot be told ahead of time what one will encounter and how one should react. Quite the opposite: ethical action requires human beings to think through particular situations, their roles in the situation, the moral codes by which they abide and then to freely choose to act in accordance with all of these factors. Ethics, therefore, requires us not to make things too easy, and much depends on the meaning of the word "right."

11

THE RESPONSIBILITY TO PROTECT

OPENING HUMANITARIAN SPACES?

Alex J. Bellamy

Adopted unanimously by heads of state and government at the 2005 UN World Summit and reaffirmed twice since by the UN Security Council, the principle of the "Responsibility to Protect" (R2P) rests on three equally weighted and non-sequential pillars.[1] The first pillar refers to the primary responsibility of states to protect their own populations from genocide, war crimes, ethnic cleansing and crimes against humanity and from their incitement. The second refers to the international community's responsibility to assist the state to fulfil its R2P. The third pillar relates to the international responsibility to take timely and decisive action, in accordance with the UN Charter, in cases where the state has manifestly failed to protect its population from one or more of the four crimes. In 2008, UN secretary-general, Ban Ki-moon challenged UN members to translate their commitment from "words to deeds."[2] This challenge was taken up by the General Assembly in 2009 when it agreed to give further consideration to the Secretary-General's proposals for implementing the principle.[3] R2P has also become part of the diplomatic language of humanitarian emergencies, used by governments, international organisations, NGOs and independent commissions alike to cajole governments and non-state actors to refrain from committing atrocities, take steps to protect endangered populations and grant humanitarian access. The principle's greatest strength in this regard is the global consensus that underpins it. Indeed, some of the governments that have actively used the principle include some of its chief critics: Egypt (calling for an international force to protect the people of Gaza), Russia (justifying intervention in Georgia) and India (reminding Sri Lanka of its protection responsibilities).

This chapter examines R2P's role in opening humanitarian space. The key, it argues, lies in the principle of sovereignty as responsibility which underpins R2P and the capacity of international actors to persuade governments and non-state actors to accept this responsibility. The chapter begins by examining sovereignty as responsibility and then turns to some recent cases where R2P has played a role in negotiating humanitarian access (Myanmar) and persuading actors to step back from the brink of mass atrocities (Kenya). The final section notes some lessons that might be learnt from these cases.

Sovereignty as responsibility

An important precursor to R2P, sovereignty as responsibility rests on three foundations: the inalienable human rights of individuals, the idea that governments have primary responsibility for protecting those rights and the claim that when states abuse those rights or fail to protect, international society acquires a responsibility to step in. During the 1999 Kosovo crisis, UN secretary-general Kofi Annan wrote an article in which he contrasted two visions of sovereignty. Traditional accounts held that states enjoyed sovereign privileges (non-interference and so on) irrespective of how they behaved. But, the secretary-general continued:

[S]tate sovereignty, in its most basic sense, is being redefined[…]States are now widely understood to be instruments at the service of their peoples, and not vice-versa. At the same time individual sovereignty—by which I mean the fundamental freedom of each individual, enshrined in the Charter of the UN and subsequent international treaties—has been enhanced by a renewed and spreading consciousness of individual rights. When we read the Charter today, we are more than ever conscious that its aim is to protect individual human beings, not to protect those who abuse them.[4]

According to this view, sovereignty entails both rights and responsibilities. Only those states that protect the fundamental rights of populations in their care are entitled to the full panoply of sovereign rights.

The notion of sovereignty as responsibility was first developed by Francis Deng, the UN secretary-general's special representative on internally displaced people (IDPs), appointed in 1993. Unlike refugees, who enjoy international legal protection, the internally displaced remain under the jurisdiction of the state that caused—either by will, neglect or incapacity—them to flee in the first place. The principal challenge confronting Deng—and his colleague Roberta Cohen—was how to persuade governments to protect IDPs and find a way to navigate around the denial of humanitarian assistance to them. The starting point for sovereignty as responsibility was therefore recognition that the primary responsibility for protecting and assisting IDPs lay with the host government.[5] No legitimate state, Deng and Cohen argued, could quarrel with the fact that they were responsible for the well-being of populations in their care and in practice no governments did quarrel with this proposition. This opened an important diplomatic avenue because, having acknowledged their responsibilities, states found it more difficult—though certainly not impossible—to refuse international assistance in cases where they were obviously unable or unwilling to offer protection. Deng and Cohen argued that when a state was unable to fulfil its responsibilities, it should invite and welcome international assistance. Such assistance strengthened sovereignty by enabling states to discharge their responsibilities. During major crises, troubled states faced a choice: they could work with international organisations and other interested outsiders to realise their sovereign responsibilities, or obstruct those efforts and sacrifice their good standing and sovereign legitimacy—risking diplomatic censure and potential punishment or intervention.[6] To translate "sovereignty as responsibility" into protection for IDPs, Deng and Cohen developed a series of "guiding principles," released in 1998. The principles recognised that primary responsibility for displaced people rested with the local authorities but that access to international humanitarian aid should not be "arbitrarily withheld" especially when the local authorities were unable or unwilling to provide the necessary assistance.[7] They were adopted by the UN's Inter-Agency Standing

Committee (IASC), the UNHCR's executive committee, the OSCE and the AU. ECOWAS called upon its members to disseminate and apply the principles. Thus, "sovereignty as responsibility" focused on the responsibilities of governments towards their own population and maintained that effective and legitimate states were the best way to protect vulnerable populations. International assistance should in the first instance support the sovereign's efforts. But if the sovereign proved unable or unwilling to discharge its responsibilities, international society acquires a duty to assume responsibility for protecting populations from genocide and mass atrocities. The association between sovereignty as responsibility and R2P is evident in the latter's three pillars which affirm the state's primary duty and international society's responsibility to assist the sovereign's efforts as well as maintaining that the responsibility to protect endangered populations shifts to international society when the state manifestly fails to fulfil its obligations.

Before R2P arrived on the scene, critics complained that sovereignty as responsibility constituted interference in the internal affairs of states on the grounds of "self interested" Western concepts of human rights and ideologies held by "a few countries."[8] Cuba linked Deng's ideas with humanitarian intervention and argued that both constituted an attempt "to forcibly impose certain ideological conceptions of human rights on a number of countries, chiefly, though not exclusively, in the Third World."[9] Others worried that by advocating sovereignty as responsibility, the West was setting itself up as both judge and jury in relation to a doctrine that lent the veneer of legitimacy to self-interested coercive interference. Although many of these concerns and criticisms remain, with their unanimous commitment to R2P states have formally and unambiguously recognised their sovereign responsibilities. With their own commitments to R2P, both the General Assembly and Security Council have done likewise. This point cannot be stressed enough. Whatever its critics might claim, R2P is not a "Western construct" imposed on the rest but a commitment that all the world's governments have freely entered into—and this is an important development that creates new pathways for opening humanitarian space and persuading parties to step back from the brink of mass atrocities.

Opening humanitarian space: Myanmar

The case of Cyclone Nargis in Myanmar is particularly interesting, because although R2P did not apply because it is limited in scope to genocide and mass atrocities, the principle featured in international debates about humanitarian response and some claim that this contributed to the opening of humanitarian space. On 3 May 2008, Cyclone Nargis struck Myanmar, devastating the Irrawaddy delta area and leaving much of the region under water. Approximately 138,000 people were left dead or missing and 1.5 million people were displaced by the cyclone. Despite the massive scale of the humanitarian catastrophe and the government's obvious inability to respond effectively, Myanmar's military regime initially denied access to humanitarian agencies, inhibiting the delivery of urgently needed supplies and medical assistance. The disaster occurred shortly before a constitutional referendum aimed at legitimising the military government, which the regime decided to proceed with. Organisations already present in the country were able to get relatively small numbers of aid workers into the affected areas but reported a tightening of travel restrictions. Other NGOs, UN agencies and states offered assistance but Myanmar was slow to issue visas and insisted on distributing aid itself—raising fears that much of it would be siphoned off by the military and never reach their intended recipients. The junta also insisted on restricting the movement of aid workers, fearing that they might distribute pro-democracy propaganda and encourage social unrest. Independently of one another, some ten days after the cyclone struck, the UN's Office for the Coordination of Humanitarian Affairs (OCHA) and Oxfam reported that, at the most, only a quarter of the required aid was being allowed into Myanmar and that the aid that did arrive was not being effectively distributed.

Frustrated by this lack of progress, French foreign minister, Bernard Kouchner, proposed that the UN Security Council invoke R2P to authorise the delivery aid without Myanmar's consent. When the EU met to discuss its response to the cyclone and the French proposal to invoke the R2P, France's junior minister for human rights, Rama Yade, told reporters that "we have called for the 'responsibility to protect' to be applied in the case of Burma."[10] EU ministers failed to reach a consensus on the French proposal, but the EU's high representative for the common foreign and security policy declared that the international community "should use all possible means to get aid through to victims of Myanmar's cyclone."[11] Some media commentators in the US, UK and Australia echoed Kouchner's call for R2P to be invoked to justify the delivery of aid without the government's consent. Kouchner's proposal was flatly rejected by China and ASEAN, which argued (correctly) that the R2P did not apply to natural disasters. ASEAN governments also maintained that Myanmar must not be coerced into accepting humanitarian assistance. This view was shared by senior UN officials, including John Holmes (under-secretary-general for humanitarian affairs) and Edward Luck (special adviser to the secretary-general on R2P). The British minister for international development, Douglas Alexander, rejected Kouchner's argument as "incendiary" and Britain's UN ambassador, John Sawers, expressed his support for the view that R2P did not apply to natural disasters and therefore should not be invoked to coerce the Myanmar government or justify the forcible delivery of aid.[12]

ASEAN and the UN secretary-general used diplomacy to secure the regime's acquiescence to the delivery of international aid and organised a joint UN-ASEAN relief effort. There has since been speculation that the "threat" of R2P encouraged the regime to grant access and anecdotal evidence from multiple sources points in this direction. According to one account, Indonesia's foreign minister, Hassan Wirajuda, told his Myanmar counterpart that if his government rejected the proposed UN-ASEAN humanitarian relief effort, ASEAN governments would not be able to prevent the UN Security Council from invoking R2P and authorising the forcible delivery of aid without the government's consent. If this was indeed the case, it was more likely the regime's paranoid fear of Western invasion rather than a calculated concern about R2P itself that prompted this shift, given that there was never much chance that Russia and China would do anything other than veto any proposals for coercion brought to the Security Council. Although painfully slow, uncoordinated and ad hoc, the diplomatic effort, which made use of R2P, if only indirectly, secured humanitarian access and the delivery of relief that helped prevent the much predicted second round of deaths due to disease and malnutrition.

Back from the brink: Kenya

The diplomatic response to the ethnic violence that erupted in the aftermath of the disputed 30 December 2007 elections in Kenya is widely trumpeted as the best example of R2P in practice.[13] Whilst up to 1,500 people were killed and 300,000 displaced, a coordinated diplomatic effort by a troika of eminent persons mandated by the AU, spearheaded by Kofi Annan and supported by the UN secretary-general persuaded the country's president, Mwai Kibaki and main opponent, Raila Odinga, to conclude a power-sharing agreement and rein in the violent mobs. This prevented what many feared could have been the beginning of a much worse campaign of mass atrocities. Reflecting on his successful diplomatic mission, Annan later observed that he:

Saw the crisis in the R2P [Responsibility to Protect] prism with a Kenyan government unable to contain the situation or protect its people. I knew that if the international community did not intervene, things would go hopelessly wrong. The problem is when we say 'intervention,' people think military, when in fact that's a last resort. Kenya is a successful example of R2P at work.[14]

Ban Ki-moon was also quick to characterise the situation as relevant to R2P and to remind Kenya's leaders of their responsibilities. On 2 January 2008, the Office of the Secretary-General issued a statement reminding: "the Government, as well as the political and religious leaders of Kenya of their legal and moral responsibility to protect the lives of innocent people, regardless of their racial, religious or ethnic origin" and urging them to do everything in their capacity to prevent further bloodshed.[15] The secretary-general's newly appointed special adviser for the prevention of genocide, Francis Deng, also called upon Kenya's leadership to exercise their responsibility to protect, reminding them that if they failed to do so they would be held to account by the international community.[16] It is worth noting that several other senior UN officials also weighed in: under-secretary-general for political affairs, Lynn Pascoe expressed concern about ethnic violence and the high commissioner for human rights, Louise Arbour, demanded that there must be no impunity for those responsible. Significantly, these efforts were given strong diplomatic support by the UN Security Council, which issued a presidential statement reminding Kenya's leaders of their "responsibility to engage fully in finding a sustainable political solution and taking action to immediately end violence."[17]

It is widely acknowledged that this concerted diplomatic effort prompted the two leaders to stand down and saved Kenya from a much worse fate. Reflecting afterwards on this case, Edward Luck told reporters that: "The only time the UN has actually applied this [the R2P], was in the case of Kenya, early in 2008 after the disputed elections. When there's seven or eight hundred people killed, it was not clear there was full-scale ethnic cleansing, but it could well become that or even something greater, and the UN decided to apply R2P criteria and to really make it the focus of the efforts there."[18] But whilst those involved contend that Kenya provides an illustration of what R2P can deliver in terms of preventive action, others, such as Pauline Baker (Fund for Peace) argue that R2P itself played a marginal role.[19] Another note of caution was sounded by AU Commissioner Jean Ping, the General Assembly president who had guided R2P through the 2005 World Summit. Ping questioned whether it was appropriate to apply R2P in this case, suggesting that it raised serious questions as to the threshold of violence that constituted an R2P situation and about potential selectivity when the response to Kenya is compared with the lack of response to the much more serious situation in Somalia.[20]

R2P and humanitarian space

Whilst it is still too early to make definitive judgements about R2P's role, some early lessons can be identified. Most notably, it seems that R2P is most effectively employed as a diplomatic tool to encourage political leaders to cooperate with international actors or step back from the brink of mass atrocities. Where R2P has been used by diplomats to remind governments of their responsibilities this has often proven to be effective. To the aforementioned cases might be added Sri Lanka, where Indian diplomacy referred to R2P and encouraged at least a degree of moderation on the part of the government, and Guinea where R2P was not specifically referred to but where the pattern of response mirrored that of Kenya. This is in sharp contrast to cases where R2P has been used, almost entirely without success, to call for military intervention—as in the cases of Darfur, the Democratic Republic of Congo and Somalia.

Although compliance with international demands was neither complete nor unhindered when R2P was used as a diplomatic tool, widely anticipated atrocities and other forms of suffering did not happen on the scale feared. Critically important in all these cases was the relationship between the UN and regional actors, including regional organisations and regional hegemons. In Myanmar and Kenya (as well as Guinea), the lead was taken by regional actors (ASEAN and AU/Annan respectively) who commanded considerable regional respect and legitimacy, but was supported by both UN officials and the Security Council. This helped to create the impression that should regional-led efforts fail to deliver humanitarian access or restraint, the matter would likely be taken up by the UN Security Council which could bring the full weight of its authority to bear. This is an important development and one that needs further research to elucidate more precisely the factors that make the use of R2P more or less likely to succeed in this fashion. What is clear, though, is that R2P has changed the politics of humanitarian diplomacy for the better.

12

HUMANITARIANISM, INTERVENTION
AND THE UN

A WORK IN PROGRESS

Conor Foley

The ancient city of Anuradhapura, in north-west Sri Lanka, is the site of some of the most important monasteries in the Buddhist world. On the day before I visited it, in March 2009, my wife had discovered that our then un-born baby Daniel, would be a boy. The monks gave me a special blessing for his future health and happiness and I kept the ribbon that they tied around my wrist for the next six months. I had not meant to visit Anuradhapura at all. But we got held up for so long at an army check-point coming out of Vavuniya that my Sri Lankan colleagues suggested spending the night. The conflict in Sri Lanka was sliding towards its shocking *denouement* and I was carrying out an evaluation of the "protection" projects of a humanitarian agency there. The harmony inside the monastery was a sharp contrast to the bloodbath taking place outside.

Between January and May of that year hundreds of thousands of Sri Lankan civilians were blockaded into an area the size of New York

Central Park, where the International Crisis Group estimates that tens of thousands of them were killed.[1] The area was shelled incessantly and hospitals and food-distribution points appear to have been deliberately targeted. Many more died from starvation and disease because the government blocked humanitarian access. Others were summarily executed during the final assault. When a staff member for the agency that I was working for was killed, the Ministry of Defence released a false statement saying that he was a terrorist. Dozens of Sri Lankan aid workers were arrested as "suspected terrorists," while many international staff were thrown out of the country when their visas ran out. Since the conflict ended the government has blocked all calls for an independent inquiry and mounted a campaign of overt physical intimidation of the United Nations mission in the country.[2]

Although the available evidence suggests that the Sri Lankan government may be guilty of a far larger crime than the massacre at Srebrenica in 1995, it has faced little of the international opprobrium that attached itself to the Bosnian Serbs. In May 2009, the UN Human Rights Council adopted a resolution praising its victory and humanitarian assistance efforts. Brazil joined China, Cuba, Egypt and Pakistan in voting down calls for an international investigation into possible war crimes.[3]

There is little doubt that the world has lost its enthusiasm for "humanitarian interventions." In 1996 Fergal Keane, a BBC foreign correspondent, recorded a letter to his own new-born son, Daniel, which became the most requested broadcast in the corporation's history. He told him that:

I am pained, perhaps haunted is a better word, by the memory, suddenly so vivid now, of each suffering child I have come across on my journeys. To tell you the truth, it's nearly too much to bear at this moment to even think of children being hurt and abused and killed. And yet looking at you, the images come flooding back.[4]

This was the era of the humanitarian narrative and the public reaction to Keane's broadcast showed that he had touched a live chord. Journalists were expected not just to report on conflicts, but to tell us how they felt about them. Readers were invited to share emotionally with the subject matter and to feel their authors' projected pain. There was a "perfect triangle" of victims, perpetrators and by-standers, which crowded out more complicated analysis.[5] Although I felt some similar emotions at the birth of my own son, I simply cannot imagine writing something about anywhere that I have worked which could be so devoid of context.

This type of pathos was not just pitched for journalistic effect. Human rights and humanitarian agencies used the language of legal certainty to mobilise their supporters. There was an "obligation to intervene" in conflicts to prevent human suffering. One writer claimed that the UN's failure to prevent genocides in Rwanda and Bosnia-Herzegovina demonstrated its "complicity with evil," rather than just a malfunctioning of mission mandates and breakdown of logistical support operations in two messy conflicts.[6]

Some things are simple. The number of refugees in the world peaked in the mid-1990s, reflecting a huge upsurge of people displaced by conflicts from their homes. The world's most powerful nations deliberately looked the other way while civilians were being massacred in their hundreds of thousands. But far from "disgracing itself by passivity," the UN began transforming itself into an interventionist institution in response.[7] The Security Council mounted almost twice as many peace-keeping or peace enforcement operations between 1988 and 1994 as it had done over the previous forty years and the upward trend has continued since.[8] There are now more peace-keeping UN soldiers, police and civilian personnel deployed in conflict zones than ever before. Resolutions authorising interventions often refer to human rights and humanitarian concerns as a trigger, which marks a significant shift in how the UN itself, and others, perceive its role.[9]

The origins of the UN are firmly rooted in the post-Second World War global order. Article 1 of its Charter states its primary purpose to be the collective maintenance of international peace and security. Membership of the UN is open to all "peace-loving nations" irrespective of the nature of their government providing that they accept the obligations of the Charter. Article 2 states that even the UN shall respect the principle of "non-interference" in a member state's internal affairs. The promotion of respect for human rights is listed as a purpose in Article 1(3) of the UN Charter, although the wording indicates that it is a more aspirational goal. Articles 55 and 56 also state that the UN shall promote "universal respect for, and observance of, human rights"—which are deemed to contribute to conditions of peace and stability—and that all members of the UN "pledge themselves to take joint and separate action" to achieve these purposes.

These rights have been spelled out in more detail in a variety of international human rights treaties that have been drafted in the intervening years and by the decisions of international courts and tribunals. When the totality of the UN Charter is read together with these legal instruments, it can therefore be argued that states are restricted from inflicting harm on people within their own territorial borders by virtue of the UN Charter.[10] Nevertheless there is no reference to human rights in Article 2 of the UN Charter and so it is difficult to see how the principle of non-intervention can lawfully be set aside solely on this basis. The only explicit exceptions to the prohibition of the threat or use of force in the Charter is the "inherent right of self-defence" recognised by Article 51,[11] or an operation authorised by the Security Council under Chapter VII.[12] The latter permits the Security Council to use force, in discharging its responsibility for upholding international peace and security, when the specific methods, envisaged in Chapter VI are deemed insufficient. For most of the Cold War the Security Council was extremely reluctant to invoke Chapter VII. However from the start of the 1990s it began to take a more expansive view of its powers. A series of resolutions were adopted authorising interventions on the basis that gross violations of human rights and humanitarian law even when within the borders of a state, might destabilise peace and security in a region, for example, by provoking a refugee crisis in neighbouring states.[13] Essentially, Chapter VII was being used to circumvent Article 2.[14]

There were two obvious problems with this type of humanitarian activism. First of all, as Victoria K. Holt and Tobias Berkman have noted, a military intervention designed expressly to protect civilians from mass killing is fundamentally different from a traditional UN peace-keeping operation.[15] Previously these had mainly been deployed to support negotiated ceasefires and prevent a return to interstate warfare. Such interventions were usually based on the principles of consent, impartiality and limited use of force; often with only Chapter VI mandates. Multidimensional peace operations became more common in the 1990s and these sought to support stability in countries emerging from civil war. Some included robust "peace enforcement" elements. However, this was usually balanced with numerous other goals, which often stretch the capacity of a mission beyond its limits. The presence of internationally mandated forces in conflict zones clearly raised expectations about what they could achieve—particularly on the part of civilians whose lives were threatened and the aid workers and journalists covering the conflicts in their professional capacities. Very often the UN forces were simply unable to cope. Francis Briquemont, for example, one of the early commanders of the UN force in Bosnia-Herzegovina complained publicly in 1993 about the "fantastic gap between the resolutions of the UN Security Council, the will to execute these resolutions and the means available to commanders in the field."[16] This complaint has been echoed many times since.

Secondly, while it is widely accepted that Chapter VII authorisation confers international legality on a "humanitarian intervention," this poses a key question: is the intervention legitimate purely because the Security Council has declared it to be so or do some independent principles exist against which its legitimacy can be judged? It is easy to think of a theoretical case where a genocide or other situation of mass killing of civilians is taking place, but one of the five permanent members of the UN Security Council exercises its veto power to prevent action. In such cases, some argue, unilateral intervention to prevent another "Rwanda, another Holocaust or even acts of mass killing that cannot be characterised as genocide, must be permissible under customary international law."[17] The UN is under an obligation to intervene, they maintain, and if it fails to discharge this responsibility then it passes to others.

Geoffrey Robertson QC, a noted human rights lawyer and former president of the Special Court for Sierra Leone, for example, argues that decisions on intervention "cannot be the sole prerogative of the UN, because its defective procedures have blocked it [intervention] on many appropriate occasions."[18] He claims instead that there is an "evolving principle of humanitarian necessity" in which states may in exceptional, conscience-shocking situations use "proportionate force" to intervene in other states' internal affairs in order to uphold certain basic rights or end gross violations.[19] Tony Aust, a former legal counsellor for the British Foreign Office, has stated that according to customary international law "in extreme circumstances a state can intervene in another state for humanitarian reasons."[20]

The obvious riposte to these arguments was given in a policy paper by the British Foreign Office, a few years earlier, which warned that "the case against making humanitarian intervention an exception to the principle of non-intervention is that its doubtful benefits would be outweighed by its costs in terms of respect for international law."[21] "The best case that can be made in support of humanitarian intervention is that it cannot be said to be unambiguously illegal [...] But the overwhelming majority of contemporary legal opinion comes down against [it]."[22] Allowing individual states to act as judge, jury and executioner in deciding when, where and whether to invade other countries is destabilising and such decisions are likely to be driven by a variety of political and strategic considerations; humanitarian arguments may just be a convenient excuse.

This debate is not new. As Robert Keohane has observed: "Saying 'humanitarian intervention' in a room full of philosophers, legal scholars and political scientists is a bit like crying 'fire' in a crowded theatre."[23] However, it took on an added urgency in the 1990s. At the end of the first Gulf War in 1991 the Security Council passed Resolution 688, which demanded "humanitarian access" to the Kurds whose abortive rising against Saddam Hussein's regime had just collapsed. Fearing another chemical weapons attack, like the one at Halabja in 1988, 2 million people fled towards the Turkish border, but arrived to find it sealed off by the Turkish government. The world had just witnessed US air power annihilate the Iraqi armed forces and Western public opinion refused to accept that nothing could be done to prevent another act of genocide. Britain, France and the United States deployed ground troops to turn back the Iraqi army and persuade the refugees that it was safe to come down from the mountains.[24]

UN Security Council Resolution 688 was not in fact adopted under Chapter VII, nor did it explicitly authorise military intervention. However, it used similar language, describing the refugee crisis as constituting a threat to international peace and security in the region. More interventions followed as the 1990s wore on, of which the best known were: the former Yugoslavia, Liberia, Somalia, Haiti, Angola, Rwanda, Burundi, Zaire, Albania, the Central African Republic, East Timor, Sierra Leone and the Democratic Republic of Congo. Their success rate can probably best be described as mixed.

NATO's intervention in Kosovo in 1999 may be regarded as the high watermark of humanitarian interventionism. Since the UN had not authorised it, the British government again claimed legal justification on the grounds that it was "an exceptional measure on the grounds of overwhelming humanitarian necessity."[25] Britain's newly-elected prime minister, Tony Blair, became one of the most articulate champions of the humanitarian creed. His speech in Chicago, in April 1999, setting out the interventionist case was hailed at the time as marking his transition from political leader to international statesman.[26]

The Kosovo crisis also led to the publication of a report by the International Commission on Intervention and State Sovereignty (ICISS), "The Responsibility to Protect," which subsequently received a general endorsement at the UN World Summit in September 2005. However, its substantive proposals, such as amendments to the UN Charter and reform of the Security Council, have gone unheeded. The R2P norm (as it has become known) has also aroused the suspicion and hostility of many UN member states who fear its "neo-imperialist" implications. These suspicions have heightened since the invasion of Iraq, and Blair's attempts to re-package it as a "humanitarian intervention." During the discussions on Darfur in 2007, for example, the pro-interventionist International Crisis Group despairingly dubbed him a "false friend of the responsibility to protect doctrine."[27] Supporters of the R2P doctrine now concede that the "sensitivities" surrounding it are widely viewed as having "needlessly politicised" the Security Council's work in this area.[28]

The interventionists have been criticised not just by traditional defenders of state sovereignty, but by humanitarian actors as well. The threat by Bernard Kouchner, France's former foreign minister, to use military force to distribute aid in Myanmar in 2008, for example, and the indictment of Sudan's president on genocide charges by the International Criminal Court in 2009, clearly increased the difficulties of those engaged in delivering life-saving assistance. As the line between politics and humanitarian action has become increasingly blurred, many agencies have also concluded that abandoning their traditional neutrality caused more problems than it solved.[29]

At the same time the concept of "protection" has become more mainstream in the humanitarian discourse. Most aid agencies involved in relief distribution accept the need to consider how their activities impact on the rights of their beneficiaries—using international law as a basic reference point. The concept has been used to evaluate whether projects may inadvertently discriminate against people, or fail to address the particular needs of vulnerable groups. It has also provided a framework for assessing the political impact of the independent and impartial delivery of relief supplies in a conflict zone.[30] Interrogating the notion of "protection by presence" has also forced agencies to consider whether they should continue to implement assistance projects in a country even if this means that they are unable to report on grave violations of human rights and humanitarian law.

Some humanitarians argue that protection is "not our job." Marc DuBois of Médicins Sans Frontières (MSF), for example, highlights the gap between the "everyday understanding of the word and the special-ised meaning given to it by humanitarian NGOs—the gulf between the protection people need and the protection we humanitarians can offer."[31] Unarmed aid workers cannot physically prevent attacks on people in conflict zones and may only advocate that those who have the military capacity should take such action. Yet MSF sometimes seems to face in opposing directions on this issue. The organisation famously took out advertisements in relation to Rwanda in 1994 stating that "one cannot stop a genocide with doctors." Yet in its "Activity Report for 2000–2001" MSF states: "We have emphatically denounced any kind of military intervention that calls itself 'humanitarian'."[32]

Meanwhile the UN has been giving increasing attention to the pro-tection of civilians, in the context of improving the effectiveness of peacekeeping operations.[33] In 1999 the Security Council authorised an operation in Sierra Leone, UNAMSIL, using the following language:

Acting under Chapter VII of the Charter of the United Nations, decides that in the discharge of its mandate UNAMSIL may take the necessary action to ensure the security and freedom of movement of its personnel and, *within its capabilities and areas of deployment, to afford protection to civilians under immi-nent threat of physical violence taking into account the responsibilities of the Gov-ernment of Sierra Leone.*[34]

This was the first time that a peace-keeping operation had been spe-cifically tasked with the protection of civilians and similar language has been included in the mandates of subsequent operations. The UN mis-sion to southern Sudan (UNMIS) in 2005, for example, was tasked under Chapter VII "to take the necessary action, in the area of deploy-ment of its forces and as it deems within its capabilities, [...] and with-out prejudice to the responsibility of the Government of Sudan, to protect civilians under imminent threat of physical violence." By 2009, most of the nearly 100,000 uniformed UN peacekeepers deployed worldwide were operating with such mandates.[35] The protection of civil-ians in armed conflict (POC) is also now debated at an open bi-annual session of the Security Council and this has resulted in a steady stream of statements, resolutions and reports. When the Security Council revised the mandate of the UN mission to the Democratic Republic of Congo (MONUC) in 2007 it stated that "the protection of civilians must be given a priority in decisions about the use of available capacity and resources."[36]

The caveats and ambiguities in these resolutions are obvious and, even so, UN missions still struggle to turn the ambitions of their drafters into realities on the ground. A recent independent review, commissioned by the UN, found that "the presumed 'chain' of events to support protection of civilians—from the earliest planning to the implementation of mandates by peacekeeping missions in the field is often broken."[37] Nevertheless it concluded that "strong leadership can counter-balance some of the tensions in peacekeeping and integrated missions and encourage collaborative work practices under challenging circumstances."[38]

The language is cautious and the ambition moderate. Realpolitic on the Security Council will continue to shelter serial human rights abusers where these are allied to powerful states. Other conflicts will continue to go largely unnoticed because they are not in places of strategic significance. The office of the prosecutor of the International Criminal Court, whose creation was hailed by human rights activists, has got off to a disappointing start.[39] Humanitarian agencies will continue to struggle with the dilemma of how to preserve their neutrality during bitterly politicised conflicts and find their independent "space" squeezed by mission integration. Yet this is the messy world of modern-day humanitarianism. Twenty years on from the creation of the Kurdish safe haven, we are still learning from our many mistakes. The best we can probably say is that it is still a work in progress.

13

THE DILEMMAS OF
PSYCHOSOCIAL INTERVENTIONS

Phil O'Keefe, Janaka Jayawickrama and Geoff O'Brien

This chapter explores the dilemmas of psychosocial interventions in disaster and conflict, focusing on humanitarian delivery by what might be broadly described as Western aid agencies. These Western aid agencies deliver a model of psychosocial interventions assuming that individuals can be diagnosed and treated along the lines of conventional psychosocial medicine. The focus on the individual coupled with the assumption that treatment can "cure" the diagnosed condition lead to interventions that might best be viewed as inappropriate, but at worse, may well restrict community recovery from disaster and conflict. Reporting about conflicts or disasters will quite regularly refer to disaster and/or conflict-affected communities as being "traumatised," "psychosocially scarred," "emotionally injured" or "psychologically damaged." The psychosocial wellbeing of conflict and disaster affected communities has come to the forefront of humanitarian interventions. In most humanitarian situations psychosocial and trauma interventions even displace food and shelter as the most pressing issue in the humanitarian sector.[1]

Psychosocial interventions are assumed to be relevant to the needs of all societies. However, these interventions are largely based on Western psychological theories from Europe and North America.[23] Although the Inter Agency Standing Committee's Guidelines on Mental Health and Psychosocial Support in Emergency Settings (IASC Guidelines) were finalised in 2007, the underlying clinical and philosophical assumptions of psychosocial interventions remains Western science. In this chapter, we discuss the dilemmas of psychosocial interventions, which are based on Western concepts delivered to non-Western societies. The discussion is based on fieldwork in Sudan, Malawi, Pakistan, Jordan and, in particular, on Sri Lankan case materials. We argue that disaster and conflict-affected communities are resilient and capable of mobilising their traditional knowledge systems to improve their wellbeing through the uncertainties of disasters and conflicts. The core contention of our argument is that dilemmas raised in the title of this chapter are predominantly raised by Western interventions because of their disassociation from traditional social systems. The dilemma is threefold; namely whether psychosocial interventions, primarily based on a model of Post Traumatic Stress Disorder (PTSD) are appropriate for diagnosis and treatment of human suffering in disaster and conflict situations. The second dilemma is that the focus on the individual rather than the community does not draw on existing resources to address suffering. The third dilemma is whether the promotion of such Western practice in non-Western countries is significantly problematic.

From hero to zero: the need for a paradigm shift

In 1966, a catastrophe shook the society of the United Kingdom. A coal waste tip devastated a school in the Welsh village of Aberfan. This disaster killed 144 schoolchildren and teachers. There were no reported psychosocial interventions and the surviving children resumed their studies two weeks later. Some months later those survivors appeared normal and well-adjusted.[4] The newspapers commended the villagers for rehabilitating themselves so admirably with little outside assistance. After such an incident today, the assumption would be that survivors were traumatised—some for life—and needed expert psychosocial interventions from psychologists and other professionals.[5]

Before and during the Cold War, refugees and torture survivors who came to the West were generally few in number and frequently presented as examples of individual courage. Refugees, such as Albert Einstein, Milan Kundera and Elias Canetti, were not treated as traumatised victims, but heroic individuals. However, such heroic images of disaster and conflict changed with the end of the Cold War. One agency in particular, the United Nations Refugee Agency (UNHCR) charged with a legal obligation to help refugees, saw its caseload increase from some thousands in the Cold War to one of 20 million refugees and 40 million internally displaced people.[6] It was UNHCR within its responsibility for camp management, which spearheaded initial psychosocial interventions.

Definitions of "psychosocial"

There are various definitions of the word "psychosocial." The common understanding of the term suggests an active relationship between psychological and social worlds. The psychological world is internal; this includes thoughts, feelings, emotions, understanding and perception. The social world is external; this is comprised of social networks, community, family and environment. It is important to remember that what happens in one of these areas will affect aspects of the other. The Reference Centre for Psychosocial Support of the International Federation of Red Cross and Red Crescent Societies (IFRC) defines the term "psychosocial support" as:

An approach to victims of violence or natural disasters to foster resilience of both communities and individuals. It aims at easing resumption of normalcy and to prevent pathological consequences of potentially traumatic situations.[7]

According to the Psychosocial Working Group, which is based at the Refugee Studies Centre of Oxford University and the Centre for International Health Studies of Queen Margaret University College, psychosocial issues link to wellbeing:

The psychosocial well-being of an individual is here defined with respect to three core domains: human capacity, social ecology and culture & values. These domains map in turn the human, social and cultural capital available to people responding to the challenges of prevailing events and conditions.[8]

The IASC Guidelines suggest that mental health and psychosocial problems in emergencies are highly interconnected, but may be either social or psychological in nature.[9] Most of the definitions of the term psychosocial present two significant identifiers: they are focused on the individual; and expect the consequences of disaster or conflict to be pathological. As Summerfield points out:

It is a category fallacy to assume that, just because similar phenomena can be identified in various settings worldwide, they mean the same thing everywhere [...] We need to remember that the Western mental health discourse introduces core components of Western culture, including a theory of human nature, a definition of personhood, a sense of time and memory, and a secular source of moral authority. None of this is universal.[10]

At the heart of this argument is a critique of the IASC Guidelines, by implication the United Nations as the first provider of global humanitarian relief that they are not following the core instruction of the medical Hippocratic oath "Do No Harm." The Guidelines are the assumption that the suggested interventions are models of good practice. Apart from the assumption that the Western approaches to mental health are universal, most psychosocial interventions ignore the fact that disaster and conflict-affected communities have been living through these difficulties for generations. They have developed more effective, yet sophisticated methods to deal with issues around conflicts and disasters. Most of the time however, these traditional knowledge systems are being labelled as un-scientific by experts.

Table 1 below shows the distinctive difference between traditional knowledge systems, which are employed by a majority of disaster and conflict-affected communities, and the scientific knowledge systems that are developed in the West and employed by most humanitarian agencies. It shows the differences between traditional knowledge and scientific knowledge systems of mental health. While traditional knowledge systems perceive mental health from a spiritual, community-centred, integrated, intuitive, holistic, subjective and experiential point of view, the understanding of mental health within the scientific knowledge system comes through a secular, individual-centred, analytical, model-based, reductionist, and objective and positivist perspective. These two different understandings of mental health certainly create major tension in interventions. The scientific knowledge system—predominantly a Western way of understanding—creates confusion in a traditional knowledge system—predominantly a non-Western way of thinking:

One morning a team of 'psychosocial specialists' came to our camp. We were told that they are from the US and here to help us to provide psychosocial activities. All of us gathered in the community hall and through translation they told us the importance of sharing our sadness and grief about our losses from the tsunami. Then the man and the woman who came from the US started hugging us. I felt very uncomfortable and irritated. During the tea break I went home and told my mother and she told me to keep away from them.[11]

Table 1: Mental Health and Wellbeing: Traditional vs Scientific Knowledge Systems

Traditional Knowledge on Mental Health and Wellbeing	Scientific Knowledge on Mental Health and Psychosocial Wellbeing
• Assumed to be the truth	• Assumed to be a best approximation
• Spiritual	• Secular only
• Teaching through storytelling	• Didactic
• Learning by doing and experiencing	• Learning by formal education
• Community-centred	• Individual-centred
• Oral or visual	• Written
• Integrated, based on a whole system	• Analytical, based on subsets of the whole
• Intuitive	• Model or hypothesis-based
• Holistic	• Reductionist
• Subjective	• Objective
• Experiential	• Positivist

Experience after the Rwandan genocide, psychosocial interventions to "treat" traumatised victims became popular within the humanitarian discourse.[12] It became common in war torn societies such as Western Darfur, Sri Lanka, Afghanistan and Iraq to implement psychosocial interventions with the assumption that affected communities were psychologically damaged and needing help without much empirical evidence. Psychosocial interventions became a core aspect of the humanitarian responses in all these cases.

The new conceptualisation of traumatisation is based on the experience of the Vietnam War.[13] The Diagnostic and Statistical Manual of the American Psychiatric Association (DSM III, 1980) adopted a conceptualisation and notion of post-traumatic stress disorder (PTSD) as a psychiatric condition. This provided Vietnam War veterans, with a diagnosis of PTSD access to social security, which many had been denied before diagnosis. We do not wish to comment on the efficiency and effectiveness of PTSD diagnosis and treatment of Vietnam War veterans, what we wish to note, however, is that this particular intervention was projected onto a world stage in an entirely different context of risks from that of war. Essentially it was a solution in search of a problem. The relationship between disaster and conflict-affected communities and mental health focuses on trauma rather than communities.[14] This is an indication that research in the field of conflict and disaster affected communities has been more theory driven than problem driven.

Individual vs collective: assumptions behind psychosocial interventions

Undoubtedly, psychological intervention to alleviate the symptoms of trauma is a first order of business especially since the prevalence of trauma-related disorders is exceptionally high among war-torn populations. A large percentage of functionally impaired trauma victims is presumed to significantly slow down the affected community and to compromise its ability to recuperate from its conflict and conflict-related problems.[15]

The most striking aspect about disaster and conflict intervention reports is the assumption that all conflict and disaster affected communities are traumatised and need psychosocial interventions. Even if the agencies, which include the United Nations, acknowledge how different cultures and traditional belief systems respond to uncertainties and dangers of life, there is nevertheless an assumption that communities in disaster and conflict-affected areas must be traumatised and require psychosocial assistance.[16]

Exposure to a massive disaster, and its aftermath, is not generally a private experience. It is in a social setting that those affected and in need of help reveal themselves and this process, which determines how victims become survivors (as the majority do), plays out over time. The assumption that violence or disaster immediately increases the risk of psychological trauma within entire communities has to be rejected. This assumption has been the core of inappropriate mental health interventions after the tsunami in Sri Lanka. This uniform approach to disasters and mental health is an all-consuming globalisation, that comes into disaster and conflict-affected developing nations.

Do communities request psychosocial interventions?

The short answer to this is a resounding "no." Our experience of most field level discussions with communities is that they have not sought counselling; instead they argue that their shattered homes and liveli-hoods need assistance. The children have been observed as sad, and a few with nightmares, but most are well functioning and keen to have their schools rebuilt. Experience from the tsunami-affected Sri Lanka is that people who turned up at mental health centres were actually pri-marily concerned with issues like livelihoods.

Despite community concerns and longstanding scholarly arguments about the limitation of Western medical models of mental health, inter-national agencies continue their misplaced psychosocial activities around the world. Our field interview with a fisherman from tsunami-affected Sri Lanka gives a sense of local frustration:

He came in to our village after the tsunami with an assistant. We were told [by the local NGO] that he is a mental health expert from the UK. They said that they are going to treat us with our mental health problems. Then this man sat down in front of my wife and started pointing a finger at her eyes. Yes, we are sad and upset about all what happened. I thought that they are going to help us to re-build our lives, but I got really mad when I saw this strange man point-ing a finger at my wife. When I questioned this in an angry tone, the translator said that my anger is the mental health problem and I need special support. What nonsense! I asked them to leave my place immediately.[17]

The discussion with this fisherman needs a level of explanation. The Western mental health expert and his assistant were trying to use Eye Movement Desensitization and Reprocessing (EMDR) therapy for his wife. This was, in short, experimental material. The personal and moral qualities of the practitioner stress the personal dimension and the qual-ity of the relationship in therapy rather than a technique. Further, "Counselling and psychotherapy are thoroughly ethical activities, in the deepest sense of the term "ethical." They are concerned with the process of discovering the good life."[18] However, the above statement by the Sri Lankan fisherman does not tally with this sense of ethics, because the intervention he received did not assist him or his family to discover the good life. The process lacked transparency and accountability as well as treated this fisherman as an unintelligent person.

Issues in field interventions

There are many guidelines and ethical supervision in the USA and Europe for psychological interventions. The critical issue is that none of these are practised or monitored in the field. The real complication is when local practitioners receive training from Western experts and start "thinking" as counsellors or psychotherapists. Most of the time, they confuse the psychosocial or counselling tools that they receive in this training with the living realities of their communities. At heart are the three dilemmas outlined earlier in this chapter, namely: whether psychosocial interventions primarily based on a model of PTSD are appropriate for diagnosis and treatment of human suffering in disaster and conflict situations; that the focus on the individual rather than the community does not draw on existing resources to address suffering; and whether the promotion of such Western practice in non-Western countries is significantly problematic. Take for example this interview with a local practitioner in Western Darfur, Sudan:

I received two weeks training from the psychologists from the headquarters of my organisation [a European-based NGO] about a year ago. This training mainly focused on how rape or torture victims can express their feelings and how counsellors like me can help them to get in touch with their feelings. This is a rewarding job and almost all the women come in to this counselling room freely talk about their feelings and cry. But the real problem is men. They don't cry and do not like to talk about their feelings and emotions.[19]

With two to three weeks' training, most field practitioners become counsellors in countries like Sri Lanka, Sudan or Malawi. This is a totally different situation to Europe or the USA. To become a member of any professional counselling association in a developed country requires successful completion of postgraduate training with a reasonable amount of practical training, in some cases, for about five years. In addition, these membership categories provide continuing professional development, ethical supervision and monitoring, as well as opportunities to meet peers from the field.

Counselling training in the field does not provide any of the above opportunities to the counsellors they train:

After receiving a two and half weeks training, my organisation promoted me to senior counsellor of the organisation [a US-based NGO] in 2001. Since then I have participated in three more one week trainings. I am supposed to train new counsellors, supervise them and provide them support when they have difficulties. But I do not have any of that.[20]

The reality in the field does not reflect the psychosocial interventions conducted by most international agencies. Trainings conducted by

THE DILEMMAS OF PSYCHOSOCIAL INTERVENTIONS

European and North American experts have made local community practitioners believe that expressing feelings and emotions is the best remedy to improve people's psychosocial status:

the use of 'talk therapy' aimed at change through gaining insights into one's psychological life is firmly rooted in a Western conception of a person as a distinct and independent individual capable of self-transformation in relative isolation from social context.[21]

The cultures in Africa, Asia or the Middle East do not embody an individualistic perspective of life. In our experience many counsellors do not observe this fact and create attention to the individual by denying community existence. People in these regions always identify themselves related to another person in the society. This community-centred view of life contradicts the Western view of individual self. In all the field experiences, there is no evidence that communities request psychosocial interventions.

Conclusion

Using Western-style psychosocial programmes does not necessarily assist disaster and conflict-affected communities and sometimes can be a hindrance to recovery. The magnitude of this issue, and the severity of the impacts of these psychosocial interventions, is less known. It is also uncertain how, if local communities continue to receive the burden of these impacts, this will affect Western and non-Western relationships in the long term. Changes must be made in the existing mental health approaches, within the humanitarian discourse, so that negative impacts become more unlikely. Part of the issue is the lack of initiatives in place to improve the transparency, accountability and participation in humanitarian assistance by psychosocial professionals. Although there is an increasing literature that is critiquing the core assumptions of psychosocial interventions, there seems to be little momentum in the field to transform the status quo.[22] Collaboration with the local population—Western-type specialists or not—is imperative at some stage of project implementation. Easterly notes that diverting power to local, on-the-ground efforts is difficult because:

The officials who talk about participation and local ownership can't seem to let themselves shift power to the locals [...] Unfortunately, decades of participation rhetoric have not changed the balance of power in foreign aid.[23]

NEGOTIATING RELIEF

There are two avenues by which Western mental health and psycho-social interventions can increase their effectiveness, efficiency and accountability: stricter evaluation processes and qualified ethical committees. Mental health delivery, however, must start and end with a community diagnostic of their own needs.

14

THE IMPACT OF CRIMINALISING THE ENEMY ON HUMANITARIANISM

Fabrice Weissman

Could a doctor working for a humanitarian organisation be sentenced to life imprisonment in the United States for having offered his "expert advice" to people linked to a "terrorist organisation?" That is what is feared by a number of civil rights organisations in the US since the Supreme Court declared on 21 June 2010 that the legislation known as the Material Support Statute was constitutional. Adopted by the US Congress in 1996 and amended twice since 9/11, the legislation is intended to provide a framework to crack down on "material support" for organisations and individuals identified by the State Department as "terrorists" or a "threat to US national security and foreign policy."[1]

These laws adopt a broad definition of the concept of "material support," to cover "training," "services," "expert advice or assistance" and "personnel." They apply to all United States individuals or organisations (through their board members) as well as to foreign persons physically present on US soil.[2] The constitutionality of the statute had been contested by the Center for Constitutional Rights (CCR). In 2005, it had

177

brought a case before the Supreme Court on behalf of a group of organisations and individuals who feared criminal prosecution under the Material Support Statute if they engaged in "political and humanitarian activities" for the Kurdistan Workers' Party (PKK) in Turkey and the Liberation Tigers of Eelam Tamoul (LTTE) in Sri Lanka (two organisations included on the State Department's list of terrorist organisations).[3]

Distinguishing political solidarity and humanitarian aid

In its ruling of 21 June 2010, the Supreme Court confirmed that training members of the PKK and LTTE to use international humanitarian law and other peaceful means to defend their cause was a federal crime that could be punished by up to fifteen years in prison. The decision has been denounced by the CCR as an unjustified attack on the freedom of expression and freedom of association guaranteed by the US constitution.[4] The ruling has also been criticised by international human rights organisations, which consider it as a risk of criminalising not only their activities but also humanitarian aid. In a brief sent to the Supreme Court in 2009, the Carter Center and the International Crisis Group emphasised that "the provision of humanitarian aid often requires working with and providing expert advice to local actors," activities that could be covered by the sanctions set out in the Material Support Statute however tenuous the link between these local actors and an organisation identified as "terrorist."[5]

Whilst their fear is legitimate, it is important to emphasise that the cases brought before the Supreme Court did not relate to humanitarian aid delivered to a population but rather to political support to a rebel movement. According to the complaint filed by the CCR, organisations and individuals it represented "sought to associate and provide support to the PKK and LTTE."[6] In the first case, the human rights NGO, the Humanitarian Law Project, sought to "advocate for the PKK in the interest of protecting human rights of the Kurds in Turkey, and to provide the PKK and persons associated with them with training and assistance in human rights advocacy and peacemaking negotiation."[7] In the second case, a group of doctors and US citizens of Tamil origin sought to "provide humanitarian aid and services and political support to the LTTE," primarily with the aim of accessing international funding intended for the victims of the tsunami.[8] The CCR pointed out that "the plaintiffs oppose terrorism and seek to associate with and support only the lawful, nonviolent activities of the PKK and the LTTE. Yet they are deterred from doing so by [anti-terrorist legislation], because any activities in conjunction with or for the benefit of the PKK or the LTTE might cause them to be designated or subject to investigation."[9] It is therefore non-violent support for a foreign political and military organisation that is being targeted, rather than the direct distribution of humanitarian aid to a population by an international NGO.

The CCR's ongoing confusion between political solidarity and humanitarian action is in this respect a source of some regret. The expression "support the humanitarian activities of the PKK and LTTE" is misleading if humanitarian action is taken to mean the impartial distribution of essential aid with no other aim than helping a population to survive the consequences of a conflict. However legitimate and useful, the socially-oriented activities of the PKK and LTTE are neither impartial nor divorced from political and military aims. In this respect, they are not more humanitarian than the campaign of psychological warfare carried out by NATO's "Provincial Reconstruction Teams" in Afghanistan or the distribution of food and water by the Sri Lankan army in the internment camps for Tamil civilians at the end of the conflict (February–December 2009).

Nonetheless, although the Supreme Court ruling confirms, first and foremost, a prohibition on any propaganda and political support for the enemies of the United States, its argument contains the seeds of criminalising humanitarian action. Echoing the argument made by the US Congress, namely that "foreign organisations that engage in terrorist activity are so tainted by their criminal conduct that any contribution to such an organisation facilitates that conduct," Judge John G. Roberts Jr maintained in his recitals that, "it is not difficult to conclude, as Congress did, that the taint of [the PKK and LTTE's] violent activities is so great that working in coordination with them or at their command legitimizes and furthers their terrorist means."[10] He continued:

Designated foreign terrorist organisations do not maintain organisational firewalls between social, political, and terrorist operations, or financial firewalls between funds raised for humanitarian activities and those used to carry out terrorist attacks. Providing material support in any form would also undermine cooperative international efforts to prevent terrorism and strain the United States' relationships with its allies, including those that are defending themselves against violent insurgencies waged by foreign terrorist groups.[11]

Applied literally, this argument amounts to the criminalisation of any relief provided to help populations living in areas administered by rebel groups identified as "terrorists." Setting up aid operations necessarily involves negotiating directly with the de facto authorities ("working in coordination with them") and providing indirect material support to their political economy. Like most guerrilla movements and governments, the Tigers benefited from taxes applied on local staff's wages of aid organisations as well as on service contracts (for transport, construction and supplies). Taking responsibility for the welfare of the population (by providing medical care, water, accommodation and food) allows rebel groups (and governments) to outsource the control and management of their population whilst saving their own resources for the war effort. Even though humanitarian action does not aim to "support the activities" of the PKK or LTTE or any other political or military organisation, there is no getting away from the fact that it does to some extent help to strengthen them—only marginally in most cases, but sufficiently in the eyes of Supreme Court Judge John G. Roberts Jr. to constitute a federal crime.

Braving government prohibitions

The Court's arguments are part of the discourse of total war traditionally used by warring parties hostile to the deployment of humanitarian aid in the enemy's territory. It recalls the Cold War era when the criminalisation of humanitarian assistance in rebel-controlled areas was the norm rather than the exception. From Afghanistan to Angola and Ethiopia to Cambodia, the governments of the time put up radical opposition to any form of negotiation between humanitarian organisations and rebel groups and *a fortiori* to the deployment of aid outside government-controlled areas. The ICRC was paralysed, and most aid was delivered to refugees on the periphery of the conflict. It was primarily as a reaction to being locked out in this way that the "without borders" movement began in the early 1970s. Following in the footsteps of the (primarily religious) pro-Biafran organisations in Nigeria, MSF decided to sidestep government prohibitions to assist "hostile populations" by clandestinely crossing the borders of Afghanistan, Ethiopia and Angola, and later Sudan and Burma.

At the time, braving government prohibitions was possible because of a combination of at least three conditions: the existence of armed movements controlling particular regions and populations (the mujahedeen in Afghanistan, the EPLF and TPLF in Ethiopia and UNITA in Angola); the tacit acceptance of neighbouring countries, which tolerated illegal border crossings (Pakistan, Sudan and Zaire); and finally a decision by the "without borders" organisations to give up neutrality insofar as they found themselves embedded in the rebellion and were therefore rarely in a position to operate in government-controlled areas. In most cases, Western governments and their public opinion backed what was in fact a breach of state sovereignty for the sake of humanitarianism. Governments saw the "without borders" movement as an influential ally in the ideological battle against communism, insofar as the states that criminalised humanitarian assistance all happened to be allies of the Soviet Union (the MPLA in Angola, the DERG in Ethiopia and the pro-Soviet government in Afghanistan).[12]

The early 1990s were an interlude when many nations, particularly in Africa, were more inclined to enter into international negotiations involving at least a degree of recognition of rebel movements, particularly in the context of arrangements for the deployment of humanitarian aid. The shift had begun in 1988 with the creation of Operation Lifeline Sudan (OLS), the first agreement on delivering humanitarian aid signed by a United Nations agency (UNICEF), a rebel movement (SPLA) and a government (Sudan). Yet, the criminalisation of "spoilers" of international peace agreements—like the RUF in Sierra Leone from 1997 onwards and UNITA in Angola after 1999—has led to a return to denied access, based on the argument of the "criminal" nature of the enemy, and any assistance provided to it, including by humanitarian organisations whose sole aim is to help civilian populations. This is how people living in RUF and especially UNITA areas were deprived of any kind of assistance by a particularly effective embargo on humanitarian relief that cost thousands of lives.[13]

Since 9/11 and the United States's entry into the war along with its allies in Afghanistan and Iraq, the rhetoric of the war on terror has revived the figure of the enemy of mankind—*hostis humani generis*—in its transnational, tentacular form, rejecting the fundamental laws of humanity and therefore unable to claim protection under them. Criminalising humanitarian assistance to "enemy terrorists" is re-emerging in countries at war inside or outside their own borders (Iraq, Afghanistan, Pakistan, Somalia, Sri Lanka… and the United States).[14]

The decision of the Supreme Court will be used to legitimise, on the national and international stage, the reluctance of national governments to fulfil their humanitarian obligations.

Gaining clandestine access to populations living under the authority of "terrorist" organisations is now much more complicated than it was during the Cold War. The movements concerned (Pakistani, Afghan, Somali, Sri Lankan… rebels) do not necessarily have enough territorial control to protect humanitarian workers from central government. Few neighbouring countries are inclined to allow humanitarian workers to cross their borders illegally alongside "terrorist" organisations (either because they respect their international commitments in relation to the "war on terror" or because they are trying to hide the fact that they have broken them). Militants have little inclination to open their territory to international organisations, whose head offices are based in countries that are waging war on them. Furthermore, there is generally open hostility from Western public opinion and governments for such clandestine missions seen nowadays as supporting "terrorists" (as opposed to "freedom fighters" during the Cold War, thought they might be the same groups as illustrated by the case of the mujahedeen in Afghanistan). It is therefore through negotiation and building political leverage—and less and less through clandestine action—that humanitarian organisations must resist the trend that criminalises their activities.

Defending policies of humanitarian assistance

Countering the rhetoric that denies the right to provide aid impartially to all victims of a conflict, including when they are on the "wrong side" of the front line requires being transparent and articulated. Humanitarian organisations firstly need to recognise that the risk of humanitarian aid being co-opted materially or symbolically in the war effort is real and that it has been taken into consideration when setting up operations. Access to populations in danger is not solely rooted in the legal and moral authority of humanitarian principles. It is the product of repeated transactions with local and international political and military forces. Its scope depends largely on the relief agency's ambitions, the diplomatic and political support it can rely on and the interest taken in its operations by those in power. In other words, the political exploitation of aid is not a misuse of its vocation, but its principal condition of existence.

Ideally, aid actors should be able to say in all honesty: "We are conscious of the political and strategic benefits that the de facto authorities (government, anti-government and "terrorist") may derive from our actions. We will do our utmost to limit the impact of this and ensure that aid is not being used against the populations, that it is not diverted (to support violence, amongst other things). In order to carry out this evaluation, we require from the existing authorities a minimal degree of freedom that includes the ability to move around freely and engage in direct dialogue with the local population, as well as to plan, implement and monitor our operations. Finally, we commit ourselves to suspending our operations if we believe we are not in a position to know what we are doing or if we consider that the effects of our action are so far removed from our intentions that it is doing more harm than good." This, in short, is the message that should be conveyed to authorities which accuse humanitarian organisations of providing criminal assistance to "terrorist" organisations. A commitment to transparency— which is too often reduced to financial transparency, keeping political and operational decisions aside—is crucial for governments to at least tolerate, if not trust humanitarian organisations.

The next step is to defend the legitimacy of a policy of humanitarian assistance, starting by reminding national governments that they have made a commitment to respect the impartiality of humanitarian organisations, conscious of the fact that this carries with it a political cost— indirectly supporting the political economy of warring parties—and a benefit—ensuring the survival of as many people as possible. Aid organisations may choose to emphasise the fact that the support of the war effort by humanitarian assistance is generally marginal in light of the resources derived from the belligerents' involvement in the global economy, including funds raised from diaspora networks, political support and earnings from legal and illegal trade.[15] The failure of counter-insurgency strategies based on an overtly political use of "humanitarian" aid by Western forces to "win hearts and minds" of the people of Afghanistan, Pakistan and Iraq illustrates the limited impact on the course of the war of the (massive and highly questionable) co-option of aid organisations.

Lastly, it is important to emphasise the sheer inconsistency of criminalising "material support" for "terrorism." Classifying an organisation as "terrorist" is eminently liable to change, as shown by the turnaround in the situation in Afghanistan or Somalia (where the United Nations and Western governments are now supporting the government led by Sheikh Sharif, having previously fought him as a terrorist). By the time humanitarian workers could be judged for providing "material support" to terrorism, it is likely that the political assessment of the status of the movement has changed. A trial on the legality of a humanitarian operation to support people living under the authority of a "terrorist" organisation could potentially have positive outcomes: it would create a political and media arena where the legitimacy of impartial humanitarian assistance policies would be defended, and its autonomy vis-à-vis *raisons d'etat.*

15

FOR HUMANITY OR FOR THE UMMA?

IDEOLOGIES OF HUMANITARIANISM AMONG TRANSNATIONAL ISLAMIC AID NGOS

Marie Juul Petersen

In January 2010, Islamic Relief set up three camps for victims of the earthquake in Haiti, providing 1,100 families with water, food and medicine. And later that year, the International Islamic Relief Organization (IIROSA) offered meals to more than 25,000 poor families in African countries, celebrating the month of Ramadan. These two examples illustrate the fact that transnational Islamic aid NGOs have become increasingly visible in the field of humanitarian aid. Today, there are approximately 400 transnational Islamic aid NGOs. Most of them are based in Britain and the Gulf countries, but work all over the world, getting their funding from individuals, governmental aid agencies, inter-governmental organisations, Islamic banks and businesses. There is very little research on these organisations as humanitarian actors. Especially since 9/11, much of the existing literature casts them as political actors, analysing them as front organisations for global militant networks such as al-Qaeda or as supporters of national political parties and resistance groups in Palestine, Sudan, Afghanistan and elsewhere.[1] Research on humanitarianism, on the other hand, has tended to focus on Western, secular actors and their conceptions of humanitarian aid, centering on notions of neutrality and universalism and predicated on a strongly secular understanding of aid. In the discussion of conceptions of "humanitarian space," for instance, the introduction to this volume includes actors such as the International Committee of the Red Cross, Médecins Sans Frontières and Oxfam; not Islamic Relief or IIROSA.[2]

Directing attention to some of these humanitarian actors, this chapter seeks to decanter Western, secular interpretations of humanitarian aid, emphasising instead the pluralism and heterogeneity of the contemporary humanitarian space.[3] Tracing the historical and ideological trajectories of transnational Islamic aid NGOs, the chapter explores the ways in which conceptions of aid change over time, emphasising the historical specificity and temporality of humanitarian ideologies. The analysis is based on micro-sociological case studies of four of the largest transnational Islamic aid NGOs: Islamic Relief and Muslim Aid from Britain, the International Islamic Charitable Organization (IICO) from Kuwait, and IIROSA from Saudi Arabia.[4]

The birth of Islamic humanitarianism

Islamic traditions of charitable giving (*sadaqa*) have existed since the early days of Islam, just like the obligatory alms tax, *zakat*, and the religious endowment, the *waqf*, have historically been important Islamic institutions of aid provision to the poor and suffering.[5] But like Western humanitarianism, contemporary Islamic humanitarianism (in Arabic *igatha*), is a modern phenomenon, shaped in particular by twentieth century colonialism and wars. However, while Western aid ideologies have grown out of an experience of power and hegemony, of imperialism and victory,[6] Islamic aid ideologies have been shaped by experiences of marginalisation and colonisation—first by Western powers and later by new Arab regimes, perceived to be protégés of Western states. This has influenced the ways in which aid has been conceptualised among Islamic organisations. As Abdel Rahman Ghandour notes, it is perhaps easier to be a proponent of universalism and neutrality when one is in a position of dominance than when one is in a position of inferiority.[7]

In more concrete terms, contemporary Islamic aid came to be shaped by a number of factors. Perhaps the most important was the emergence of the Muslim Brotherhood, established in Egypt in 1928, a few years after Egypt's independence. Especially in its first years, the Brotherhood focused primarily on social welfare, health services, education and relief, seeking to present an alternative to the largely unsuccessful state.[8] The founder, Hassan al-Banna, was a schoolteacher with a strong social awareness, and he saw the provision of aid to the poor as an important religious responsibility of the Brotherhood and of any Muslim, building the foundation for a strong link between Islam and aid.

From the 1960s onwards, the Gulf countries also started playing an important role in shaping contemporary Islamic aid. Articulated as a counterweight to Nasser's secular Arab nationalism, King Faisal would promote the idea of pan-Islamic, transnational solidarity, claiming that all Muslims were one people with a responsibility to support each other in times of crisis.[9] A crucial factor in facilitating this new movement of transnational aid was the emergence of Islamic economics. Increasing oil prices in the 1970s placed large sums of money in the hands of governments, businesses and individuals in the Gulf countries, boosting efforts to create distinctively Islamic financial institutions.[10] As a way of purifying interest money (prohibited in Islam), many of these institutions would convert interests into charitable work, releasing large sums of money for Islamic humanitarian organisations.[11]

Finally, a third factor paving the way for transnational Islamic aid NGOs and Islamic aid was the migration of Muslims from Middle Eastern and Asian countries to Europe and the USA, starting in the 1960s. Muslim migrants wanted organisations to which they could pay their *zakat*, at once fulfilling religious obligations and helping people in their home countries. Initially, people would distribute their *zakat* through relatives or make their payment to the local mosque, but with the emergence of a well-educated Muslim middle class came demands for more professional aid organisations, ensuring the effective collection and distribution of *zakat* and other donations.

The first generation of Islamic humanitarianism: Islam, solidarity and justice

Against this background, the first transnational Islamic aid NGOs emerged at the beginning of the 1980s, many of them in the Gulf countries. One of them was IIROSA, established in 1979 by a group of wealthy Saudi men. IIROSA quickly grew to become one of the world's largest Muslim NGOs, with an annual budget near $100 million in the late 1980s. Another was the IICO, founded in Kuwait a few years after.

In the first decades of their existence, these NGOs tended to operate in parallel networks outside or at the margins of the mainstream humanitarian space, cooperating with the Muslim Brotherhood, the Muslim World League and the Organization of the Islamic Conference (now Organization for Islamic Cooperation) rather than the UN, USAID or Oxfam.[12] They had no pressing need to cooperate with these actors, insofar as they were getting sufficient funding from pious Muslims, governmental *zakat* institutions and religious ministries, Islamic banks and businessmen. Further discouraging cooperation, Western humanitarian actors would often actively avoid Islamic aid organisations, whether because of suspicions of political involvement, secularist scepticism of religion, or cultural and language barriers.[13] Shaped by their particular history and context, these organisations promoted a distinct humanitarian ideology, in many respects fundamentally different from mainstream Western ideologies of humanitarian aid. Whereas the latter tend to centre on concepts of universalism and neutrality, often based on secular conceptions of aid, the first generation of Islamic humanitarianism came to turn on notions of Islam, solidarity and justice.

"It's all in Islam!"

First, the aid ideologies of the first generation of NGOs were based on a very visible, all-encompassing notion of Islam, echoing the Muslim Brotherhood's slogan "Islam is the solution." Islam influenced all spheres of organisational life: founders and trustees were Islamic dignitaries, staff members were all practising Muslims, the sources of financing were Islamic, and activities were shaped by Islamic traditions and principles. Aid and Islam were closely intertwined, based on a conception of suffering as simultaneously material and spiritual: aid was not only about building wells, distributing medicine or teaching children to read and write—it was also about building a mosque, preaching and teaching children to memorise the Qur'an. Likewise, Islam was not just about praying, going to the mosque and dressing the right way—it was also about education, health services and relief.

FOR HUMANITY OR FOR THE UMMA?

The Islamisation of humanitarian aid manifested itself in explicitly religious activities such as the construction of mosques and Qur'an schools—in the IICO, for instance, at least one-fifth of the budget was spent on mosque building and maintenance. But religion would also influence other activities. IIROSA's distribution of dates during Ramadan illustrates this inseparability of relief and Islam, serving at once as humanitarian food distribution to many thousands of poor families, and as the celebration of an important Islamic tradition. Likewise, when building a mosque, many organisations would also build a well, at once facilitating the Islamic tradition of ablution (ritual purification before praying), and offering poor people access to clean water.[14]

Helping Muslim brothers and sisters

The first generation of Islamic humanitarianism turned on notions of brotherhood and Islamic solidarity, binding Muslims together in a global community, the *umma*. In this perspective, all Muslims are part of the same religious brotherhood, and as such, are closely connected, mutually interdependent and obliged to help one another. One of the first disasters to attract the attention of Islamic organisations was the famine in the Horn of Africa at the beginning of the 1980s. For many people, Islamic solidarity was a major reason for engaging in this disaster—a wish to translate the theoretical and much talked-about Islamic solidarity into a practical Islamic aid, by demonstrating compassion with the starving Muslims.[15] While mainstream humanitarian aid is predicated on notions of the "distant sufferer," this emphasis on solidarity created an image of the recipient as a "Muslim brother," subjectified within an overall framework of the Muslim *umma* rather than an abstract global humanity. In concrete terms, this meant that Muslim organisations would work almost exclusively in countries with large Muslim populations, or with Muslim minorities in non-Muslim countries.

Inherent in the first generations of Islamic humanitarianism was also an element of competition and defiance of Western hegemony.[16] As a board member of Muslim Aid says: "Everyone was there [in Africa] but the Muslims. We saw it on TV and we were ashamed." For some organisations, this was a competition not only in terms of aid, but also in terms of souls. Among Islamic aid NGOs, there was a widespread perception of Western aid NGOs as crude embodiments of Christian missions and secularist decadence, threatening the faith and identity of the Muslim community by their proselytising attempts at converting the poor, whether to Christianity or secularism.[17] At least in part as a way of challenging this alleged dominance of Western organisations, some Islamic NGOs would start engaging in missionary activities themselves, entering into a sort of competition. A former staff member in IIROSA notes that the expansion of Christian organisations in Africa was an important factor in prompting IIROSA to engage in aid provision. Likewise, the establishment of the IICO was also a response to Christian missionary efforts. Yusuf al-Qaradawi, a prominent Islamic scholar and founder of the IICO, launched the campaign "Pay a dollar and save a Muslim," explicitly alluding to a conference of missionary organisations in Colorado in 1978 at which Christian missionaries had announced their intention of investing a billion dollars in an effort to convert as many Muslims as possible.[18]

Aid as a tool for justice

A third important characteristic of early Islamic aid ideologies was the conception of aid as a tool for justice. For many transnational Islamic aid NGOs, the provision of humanitarian aid was a way of realising and extending sentiments of solidarity in order to protect fellow Muslims from external threats, whether in the form of dominant colonial powers or oppressive, secular regimes—or atheist communism, as was the case in the 1980s Afghanistan, which became another important area of intervention for transnational Islamic aid NGOs, parallel to the involvement in the Horn of Africa. Many of these NGOs did not see the involvement in humanitarian aid as contradictory to political activism but closely related to this. This has much to do with the fact that they had grown out of political movements and organisations. For instance, founders of the IICO and Islamic Relief were both related to the Muslim Brotherhood; Muslim Aid was established by members of the Bangladeshi political party Jama'at-e Islami; and IIROSA was part of the Muslim World League, supported by the Saudi government.

This coupling of aid and political involvement was particularly clear in Afghanistan: many people saw the 1979 Soviet occupation as an atheist attempt to intimidate a pious Muslim population, and felt obliged to support fellow Muslims in this struggle. Thus, whereas the provision of aid in Africa was sometimes simultaneously relief and *da'wa* (mission), in Afghanistan it was sometimes relief and *jihad*. Qaradawi, for instance, proclaimed that:

Jihad is *fard 'ain* [an obligation] for military and medical experts or anyone with a special skill that the *mujahidin* need. They should help the *mujahidin* in the field of their competence and capacity. In general, it is incumbent on all Muslims to provide material and intellectual help in order to live with them in the heart even if they cannot live with them in the body.[19]

While most transnational Islamic aid NGOs, together with Qaradawi himself, took this to mean non-violent and indirect jihad through *da'wa* and relief, others interpreted it as a call to directly engage in the armed struggle of the mujahedeen. In particular Saudi NGOs would provide support to the fighters parallel to their provision of aid, blurring the boundaries between relief and militant jihad. IIROSA, for instance, allegedly supported training camps in Afghanistan. Likewise, some staff members joined the mujahedeen. As a former IIROSA staff member says: "In Afghanistan everything was mixed up."

If the use of aid as a tool to support the mujahedeen was initially endorsed by Western governments, in particular the USA, this changed at the beginning of the 1990s. With the victory of the mujahedeen, support for Islamic movements and groups would wane, including Islamic NGOs. The alleged involvement of some transnational Islamic aid NGOs in the 1993 and 1998 attacks on American territories—first the World Trade Center and then the bombings of the US embassies in Kenya and Tanzania—only led to increased control with this group of organisations, manifested in a decrease in public funding, arrest of individuals and ban of certain organisations.

9/11 and the "war on terror"

With the attacks on New York and Washington on 11 September 2001, the situation worsened for many transnational Islamic aid NGOs. After it became clear that the attacks had been carried out by radical Islamist groups, suspicions quickly rose as to the involvement of certain Islamic NGOs in planning and financing the attacks. In the name of the "war on terror" a range of measures were introduced by the US and other governments to prevent transnational Islamic aid NGOs from funding militant Islamic groups, including restrictions, control and ultimately, designations. Gulf-based organisations were especially hit. The Saudi organisations Al Haramain and Benevolence International were designated, just like two country offices of IIROSA were closed down due to suspicions of terrorist connections. Other organisations were not banned outright, but experienced a serious decline in funding and popular support.

However, for some Islamic NGOs, the "war on terror" became a window of opportunity, leading to a tremendous growth. Since 2001, for instance, the annual budget of Islamic Relief has increased from approximately $20 million to $96 million in 2009, and that of Muslim Aid from $5 to $72 million.[20] "Hard" measures to crack down on "terrorist" NGOs were coupled with "softer" counter-terrorism approaches seeking to encourage cooperation with so-called "moderate" Muslim NGOs in order to prevent radicalisation and to strengthen relations with potential bridge builders.[21] Organisations such as Islamic Relief and Muslim Aid would receive public praise from governmental authorities for their efforts in "building links within communities and promoting tolerance,"[22] and they were invited to participate in governmental committees and advisory councils. As a staff member from Islamic Relief notes with some amusement: "Because it's Muslim, our organisation enjoys greater access to funding. It's included everywhere, people listen, they have access to the government. In these times, people want to be seen to be involving Islam."

This coincided with a general interest in so-called "faith-based organisations" among Western aid agencies, in particular in Europe.[23] As the new "magic bullets" in aid provision, faith-based organisations are expected by aid agencies to have a great potential as implementers of development and humanitarian aid, capable of reaching large constituencies that may otherwise be unreachable. Different initiatives testify to this sudden interest in faith-based organisations in general, and Muslim NGOs in particular. In 2005, the British Department for International Development (DfID) launched a research programme on religions and development, paralleled by an increase in cooperation with Christian and Muslim NGOs. Likewise, the German aid agency GTZ has launched programmes on aid and Islamic values in Asia, and the Swedish International Development Cooperation Agency (SIDA) has published a report on the role of religion in the provision of aid.

Thus, after 9/11 transnational Islamic aid NGOs were navigating in an environment of increasing regulation and control, but with simultaneous openings for cooperation and funding. It was no longer desirable—or indeed possible—for these NGOs to remain isolated from the mainstream humanitarian space, relating to Western humanitarian actors solely by way of competition or conflict. Instead, the situation called for new repertoires of action, prompting the emergence of a new generation of Islamic humanitarian aid.

New ideologies of Islamic humanitarianism: secularism, universalism and neutrality

While Gulf-based Islamic NGOs such as IIROSA and IICO dominated the first generation of Islamic aid, the second generation is to a much larger degree defined and shaped by European Islamic NGOs such as Islamic Relief and Muslim Aid, which have both been particularly successful in seizing the opportunities provided by the "war on terror." This is witnessed most clearly in the increase in funding from mainstream aid agencies such as ECHO, DfID and SIDA: Islamic Relief's institutional funding has grown from close to zero before 2001 to almost 25 per cent in 2009. And in Muslim Aid, institutional funding today makes up as much as 75 per cent of the total budget.[24] Different factors may explain this success: naturally, the geographical proximity to mainstream humanitarian organisations plays an important role, facilitating access to these actors, but their ability to transform their ideologies of aid, aligning these with mainstream humanitarian principles of secularism, neutrality and universalism, has been equally imperative.

"A professional humanitarian organisation"

First, Islamic Relief and Muslim Aid have rejected conceptions of aid as justice, emphasising instead political neutrality as an indispensable condition for humanitarian legitimacy. Framing themselves as "professional humanitarian organisations," they pledge allegiance to Western principles of accountability and transparency as the only legitimate way to respond to allegations of political connections and terrorist financing. Muslim Aid and Islamic Relief have both introduced strict mechanisms for accountability and control of partner organisations, they have fired much of their politically inclined staff and employed young and explicitly non-political aid experts instead. In Muslim Aid's office in

Bangladesh, management has even introduced a complete ban on political discussions during lunch breaks!

In their efforts to promote their organisation as neutral and professional, staff in Islamic Relief and Muslim Aid dissociate themselves from other Islamic organisations. Distinguishing between "traditional" and "modern" Islamic organisations, a staff member says:

The modern accept the Western system and they give it an Islamic flavour, an Islamic spirit. By Western I mean internal management systems […] The traditional organisations depend only on personal accountability. It's about you as a spiritual person, about whether you are trustworthy or not. It's not about the system, it's about the person.

A person who used to work in a Gulf-based NGO but now works in a UK-based NGO tells me that he left the organisation precisely because of this: "There was a clash between the way I needed to work as a professional and the way they worked. Their set-up is not professional." According to some people, this lack of professionalism has to do with the fact that these organisations are led by religious people; not humanitarian professionals. In this perspective, a visible, orthodox religiosity becomes the antithesis of professionalism.

"The humanitarian spirit of Islam"

Rejecting the orthodox religiosity underlying conceptions of aid in other organisations, Islamic Relief and Muslim Aid instead promote a more secularised version of Islamic aid, based on a sharp distinction between religion and aid, echoing principles of Western humanitarianism. As a staff member puts it: "In the day-to-day programmes, there is no influence by Islamic principles. There's more of an echo of Western principles and donor wishes." In this perspective, religion is acceptable as the source of individual values, underlying principles and motivation, but not as public rituals and collective practices influencing the ways in which aid is provided and to whom it is given. This conception of religion is reflected in the frequent use of airy terms such as "Islamic flavour," "Islamic charitable values" and "the humanitarian spirit of Islam" denoting an interpretation of Islam as an invisible, "ethical reference" rather than an orthodox, visible religiosity.[25] A person says: "We don't want to distinguish ourselves as Islamic, the humanitarian principles that we base our work on, are universal. We don't need to raise the

Islamic flag when we do humanitarian work, we don't need to say that we are more humanitarian because we are Islamic."

This secularisation of aid is visible in several ways. First, organisations such as Islamic Relief and Muslim Aid increasingly employ non-Muslims and development experts in their staff, making claims to a professional rather than a religious legitimacy. It is about the services they provide, not the values they possess.[26] Second, there are few religious practices internally in the organisations. Most offices have a prayer room, but there is no pressure to use it: "Some pray, and others don't," says the director of one of Islamic Relief's schools in Bangladesh. And third, few aid activities are shaped by religious traditions. The organisations do not build mosques or finance religious education and staff rarely speak with recipients about religion. "We talk more about practical things," says a participant in one of Islamic Relief's projects. A staff member adds: "Our main objective is to provide an input to beneficiaries—what they are doing in relation to Allah, to their God, that's their own business, that's not really our business." Even the celebration of religious holidays is thoroughly secularised and adjusted to mainstream principles of aid provision. In Muslim Aid, for instance, the slaughtering of meat for the celebration of Eid al-Adha is integrated into the organisation's microfinance projects.

Aid for humanity

Because aid is not religiously defined, it can be given to all. In the past, Islamic Relief and Muslim Aid may have talked of "the Muslim umma," and "Muslim brotherhood,"[27] but now these organisations explicitly emphasise their work with non-Muslims. According to both, the provision of aid is not restricted to Muslims, but extended to "disadvantaged people across the globe, irrespective of their faith, colour and race."[28] This universalist approach is legitimated by reference to Islamic principles: "If you look at it from the side of Islam, most instructions from the Prophet Muhammad and the Holy Qur'an are about motivating people to help others, to support and help especially the poor," says an Islamic Relief manager. "And they don't mention what kinds of poor—they don't say what gender, what race, what religion."

This is manifested in increasing efforts to include non-Muslims in the Muslim countries where the organisations work. In Muslim Aid's microfinance project in Bangladesh, staff emphasise that 10 per cent of the participating women are Hindu, reflecting the general composition of the population. Likewise, Islamic Relief's orphan sponsorship programme includes Christian children and donors; several recipients of microfinance loans are Hindus; even Ramadan food packages are distributed to non-Muslims. Furthermore, both organisations have intensified their involvement in non-Muslim countries. After the Haiti earthquake in January 2010, Islamic Relief set up camps for victims of the earthquake, as noted at the beginning of this chapter. Likewise, after the Japan earthquake in March 2011, both organisations launched emergency appeals for victims of the disaster.[29]

Conclusions

Overall, this brief history of Islamic humanitarianism has contributed to a decentring of mainstream humanitarian ideologies by directing attention to alternative conceptions of aid, promoted by actors at the periphery of the humanitarian space. At the same time, however, the analysis has pointed to the hegemony of mainstream humanitarian ideologies, displaying the ways in which (some) transnational Islamic aid NGOs have adjusted their ideologies to principles of secularism, neutrality and universalism in order to carve out a place for themselves in the humanitarian space. These changes are not entirely unproblematic. First, in their attempts to demonstrate allegiance to principles of neutrality, universalism and secularism, transnational Islamic aid NGOs may gain acceptance among mainstream humanitarian aid agencies and NGOs, but they risk losing credibility among (certain) Muslim donors, expecting these organisations to protect and promote what they consider to be authentic Islamic traditions of charity. In other words, and paraphrasing Michael Barnett, religious organisations that increasingly drift towards rational, professional principles as a way of defending their humanitarian legitimacy may jeopardise the unique moral authority inherent in their religious identity.[30] Second, and perhaps more importantly, this second generation Islamic aid may not always meet the needs of recipients. In a study of Islamic Relief's work among Rohingya refugees in Bangladesh, Victoria Palmer found that while the organisation's work may very well resonate with mainstream humanitarian principles, it did not always meet expectations of individual Muslim recipients. She quotes a Rohingya refugee as saying: "We want Islamic Relief to establish a mosque inside the camp as we think they are Muslim and they should understand our needs. We can live without food but we can't live without our religion."[31] Thus, from the perspective of (some) recipients of humanitarian aid, a thoroughly Islamised aid such as that of first generation of Islamic humanitarianism may in fact be preferred over the secularised aid of the second generation.

PART IV

NEGOTIATED SPACE
DIPLOMACY AND GEOPOLITICS

16

HUMANITARIANS AND DIPLOMATS

WHAT CONNECTIONS?

William Maley

On 28 April 1945, a Reuters report surfaced that the reichsführer-SS in Nazi Germany, Heinrich Himmler, had met with Count Folke Bernadotte of the Swedish Red Cross to canvass an unconditional surrender of German troops to the Western allies.[1] Himmler had first met with Bernadotte on 12 February, and had had further meetings on 2 April and 21 April before the dramatic meeting on 23–24 April in the Swedish Consulate in Lübeck that led to the Reuters report. The news of Himmler's betrayal struck the surviving Nazi leadership—sheltering in the Führerbunker below the streets of Berlin—like a bombshell. As Adolf Hitler's biographer put it, "The bunker reverberated to a final elemental explosion of fury;" it was, screamed Hitler, "the betrayal of all betrayals."[2] Himmler's ludicrous endeavour to save his own skin got him nowhere, and he was finally to commit suicide on 23 May after being captured by the British. Bernadotte's endeavours, however, were not entirely fruitless. He had been drawn into negotiations with Himmler and the SS in the hope of saving some of the surviving inmates of Nazi concentration camps. And some were saved: as Martin Gilbert recorded, on 14 April, Bernadotte "negotiated the release of the 423 Danish Jews who had been held, unharmed, at Theresienstadt, and they were returned to Denmark."[3]

This particular episode highlights both some of the dimensions and some of the challenges of humanitarian diplomacy, and the following remarks are designed to flesh these out. The first section of the chapter deals with different forms of humanitarian diplomacy. The second identifies some of the key agents and actors in these kinds of diplomacy, and the third highlights a number of the major challenges that can arise in the relationship between humanitarianism and diplomacy. The final section offers some brief conclusions.

Forms

Humanitarian diplomacy comes in varying forms.[4] A first is what one could call rescue diplomacy, and Bernadotte's activities in 1945 offer an obvious example. Here, the distinctive feature of the endeavour is that it involves an attempt to extract a vulnerable group of people from the control of one power, and to place them under the protective mandate of another. The range of beneficiaries can be quite diverse. At the extreme, it may involve negotiating the release of hostages, whose needs may be classed as humanitarian even if their seizure hardly amounted to a humanitarian emergency.[5] It can also involve the use of diplomatic resources to facilitate the flight of the vulnerable, with envoys such as the renowned Raoul Wallenberg of Sweden and the less well-known but equally remarkable Chiune Sugihara of Japan working tirelessly to spirit vulnerable Jews to safety during the Second World War.[6] In some circumstances, the negotiation of resettlement arrangements for refugees may also amount to rescue diplomacy, although states are often driven by selfish motives.[7]

A second type of diplomatic activity involves what one might call access diplomacy. Here, the aim of negotiation is not to extract people from the control of a power, but rather to secure access to them so that support services of various kinds can be delivered. This is related in some ways to Rony Brauman's notion of "humanitarian space," which in its most meaningful sense refers to a set of access opportunities created and sustained by processes of engagement and negotiation. This kind of activity captures the bulk of what many aid workers would consider humanitarian diplomacy to involve, and is both arduous and challenging. It can have many dimensions, ranging from the starkly political to the mundane. At the highest level, it can be conducted at the government-to-government level or through regional organisations, as one saw in Southeast Asia in May 2008 when ASEAN and its members sought access to Burma in order to deliver relief in the aftermath of the devastating Cyclone Nargis. But it can also be carried out in multiple localities by those in aid convoys seeking to reach isolated populations, as occurred frequently in Bosnia in the early 1990s.

Third, a great deal of effort has been devoted to what one might call coordination diplomacy, that is, efforts to apportion responsibilities between different actors and to establish structures through which decisions in times of need can be taken, communicated, and implemented. Coordination diplomacy can occur as an ad hoc response to an immediate problem, or with a view to preparing for future problems. Coordination goes further than mere cooperation, which can emerge as a reflection of actors' pursuit of their interests;[8] in ordinary language it suggests the existence of coordinating actors. This is where the trouble can start: on occasion when actors speak of the importance of "coordination," it is all too clear that what they really mean is that they should be free to lead, and others should be willing to follow. This is unsurprising given the asymmetries of power in world politics, but a consequence is that negotiations over coordination can be particularly fraught. The United Nations has sought to address this in a number of ways: by designating particular bodies as "lead agencies" for the purposes of humanitarian action, as occurred with the office of the United Nations high commissioner for refugees (UNHCR) in Bosnia in the 1990s; and through General Assembly Resolution 46/182 of July 2002 on "Strengthening of the coordination of humanitarian assistance of the United Nations."[9] Yet no one would seriously suggest that problems of coordination have disappeared. On the contrary, as humanitarian actors proliferate, the need for effective coordination diplomacy has arguably risen hugely.

Given the messiness of the real world, these different forms of humanitarian diplomacy should best be seen as ideal types. Representatives of states, and other humanitarian actors, may find themselves shifting between them on a daily and sometimes hourly basis. Humanitarian diplomacy of this kind may also overlap with other kinds of "new diplomacy," where actors that previously were excluded from the diplomatic realm now enjoy some kind of place at the table. As Michael Barnett has highlighted, "humanitarianism" in recent years has changed in complex ways, and navigating these new waters requires considerable "diplomatic" skill.[10]

Actors

Humanitarian diplomacy involves a diverse range of actors. Despite notable recent movements away from "club" models of diplomacy in favour of models that put more emphasis on networks, states remain actors of profound importance.[11] In the face of large-scale emergencies, it is states alone that can mobilise the resources that are required to undertake mass-relief operations, although the resources themselves may be forwarded to non-state implementing agencies. Major powers typically have dedicated development agencies within or associated with their governmental structures—bodies such as the British Department for International Development (DfID), the US Agency for International Development (USAID), and the Deutsche Gesellschaft für Internationale Zusammenarbeit (GIZ)—and at the technical level, officials from such agencies are likely to play the most active roles in humanitarian diplomacy. Yet for a number of reasons, high political leaders are likely to become involved as well. Responding to sudden needs may require commitments of additional resources, not simply adjustment in intra-agency priorities, and depending upon the precise nature of the challenge, there may be major political ramifications, both domestic and international, that need to be taken into account in deciding how to proceed. Political leaders are unlikely to leave such decisions in the hands of technocrats.

In addition to states, different components of the United Nations system are also major participants in humanitarian diplomacy. However, it would be a grave error to treat the term "system" literally, as if it implied organisational coherence or cohesion. While there is a "United Nations System Chief Executives Board for Coordination," it has not succeeded in producing the kinds of inter-agency coordination one might wish to see. To this day, the UN remains more a "dysfunctional family" than a system.[12] This problem has been widely recognised for decades: it was the central focus of Sir Robert Jackson's famous "Capacity Study" in 1969, which still offers one of the most insightful appraisals of the UN that has ever been written. Unfortunately, Jackson was equally insightful in outlining why procuring systemic reform would prove nearly impossible.[13] The United Nations Office for the Coordination of Humanitarian Affairs, currently headed by Baroness Amos, under-secretary-general and emergency relief coordinator, heads the UN Inter-Agency Standing Committee that was established in the wake of the General Assembly's adoption of Resolution 46/182. However, no matter how well this committee works, it confronts the ongoing problem that humanitarian crises invariably have political dimensions, with the potential to engage the interest of the Security Council. I shall return to this problem shortly.

A third actor of significance is the International Red Cross movement comprising national Red Cross and Red Crescent societies, the International Federation of Red Cross and Red Crescent Societies, and the International Committee of the Red Cross (ICRC). The ICRC has special rights and responsibilities under international humanitarian law, and its emblems are protected not just by international law, but by the domestic laws of many states. Guided by long-established principles of which the most important are arguably neutrality and impartiality, it has a creditable history of negotiating for operating space which makes it one of the most effective international humanitarian actors. But that said, its officials may have relations with states that can affect how they are seen. When Count Bernadotte was in Germany in 1945, he was asked by Ernst Kaltenbrunner, head of the Reich Main Security Office (*Reichssicherheitshauptamt*) whether he had an official order from his government. Bernadotte replied as follows: "That I do not have, but I can say that not only the Swedish Government, but also the Swedish people, share the views that I have outlined here."[14] Support from states, either tacit or explicit, is one of the factors that allows the Red Cross to work. This, however, entails real dangers, as we shall shortly see.

Finally, humanitarian diplomacy can draw in a wide range of other actors. One type of obvious importance consists of not-for-profit non-governmental organisations (NGOs) that tend to proliferate in areas where humanitarian needs are great, and often defy the attempts of other actors to coordinate what they do. This is hardly surprising, since the ethos of many NGOs emphasises accountability to their donors, and to the populations they assist, rather than to governments and bureaucracies (which can be corrupt and ineffectual) or to international organisations (which may lack the local knowledge garnered through field experience that NGOs can often claim). NGOs, however, come in many shapes and sizes, and to some degree this determines their capacity to engage in humanitarian diplomacy.[15] Some of these actors are deeply problematic participants in humanitarian action because of the inscrutability of their motivations, and this raises a question as to whether the negotiations in which they engage should really be seen as "diplomacy." Jönsson and Hall have argued that "reproduction of international society" through recognition and socialisation is one of the key dimensions of diplomacy, and this at the very minimum requires fidelity to certain norms. Yet this is not necessarily found with all actors that now litter the landscape.[16]

Challenges

This is not simply a theoretical problem. It raises practical challenges as well. Diplomatic activity works when it is nested within a framework of norms and understandings that prescribe how actors should behave, and ensure that they honour their commitments. In March 1998, following a physical attack by a Taliban leader on a UN official, the UN suspended its humanitarian activities in southern Afghanistan. As UN envoy Lakhdar Brahimi put it, the "international community has a standard and if you want to be a member of the club you have to abide by the rules."[17] Unfortunately, humanitarian actors are routinely confronted with actors that have no understanding of such rules, and no commitment to them. In certain circumstances such actors might be socialised into acceptable forms of behaviour,[18] but it would be naïve to count on this always happening.

A second, connected, challenge relates to the mandate or authority of negotiators. In many humanitarian negotiations, it can be hard to know exactly with whom one is dealing, and what they can realistically promise. Sometimes complete charlatans can insinuate their way into talks, as occurred in 2010 in Afghanistan, when a man subsequently alleged to have been a grocer from Quetta was given a place at the table.[19] Yet even if this is not the case, negotiating with an actor that cannot deliver at the end of the day runs the risk of enhancing that actor's standing (by signalling that the actor is worth engaging in the first place) without necessarily achieving any desirable outcome. This can easily prompt anger on the part of other actors, and a string of unintended consequences that can leave vulnerable individuals and communities worse off than they otherwise might have been.

A third challenge is that of having to deal with actors who are morally unappetising. This is a problem that crops up regularly in state-to-state relations, where the issue of how to deal with enemies is a live one.[20] It occurs just as pressingly in humanitarian diplomacy. The argument in favour is consequentialist: that better results can be obtained through engagement than by keeping one's distance. This certainly underpinned Bernadotte's engagement with the likes of Himmler and Kaltenbrunner. Those encounters, however, occurred in unusual circumstances. The war was lost, and senior SS figures had strong reasons of self-interest to make humanitarian concessions that would have been unthinkable even shortly before. But the wider issue of Red Cross engagement with Germany before its defeat was imminent has proved far more controversial. The effective head of the German Red Cross was an active SS officer, Ernst Grawitz, who committed suicide at the war's end, and critics have charged that the ICRC's commitment to neutrality and impartiality caused it to squander an opportunity to expose the horrors of the Holocaust.[21]

A fourth challenge is how to avoid seeing the wood for the trees. One danger is that humanitarian action can become an excuse for political inaction. As David Rieff wrote with respect to Bosnia, "Fundamentally, the better the job UNHCR and the NGOs that worked with it did in Bosnia—and, given the appalling, impossible circumstances, the job they did was magnificent—the more cover they provided for the great powers to avoid doing anything to stop the slaughter."[22] Another danger is that of tunnel vision, fully on display in some UN dealings with the Taliban in the late 1990s. Tunnel vision can lead humanitarian actors to overlook key norms in the rush to negotiate access. One such example occurred on 13 May 1998 when a UN negotiator signed an agreement with the Taliban stating that "women's access to health and education will need to be gradual." This led to furious reactions from agencies involved in promoting norms of gender equity to which the UN was committed as a result of the September 1995 Fourth World Conference on Women, held in Beijing.[23] A third, related, danger is that humanitarian negotiators will lose a sense of the political consequences of their actions. The UN Security Council and its key member states may conclude that the interests of international peace in the long run are best served by signalling firmly to an actor that it needs to modify its behaviour. Humanitarian actors can end up disrupting this strategy if they then engage with such an actor because it seems important in the short term to do so. When UN secretary-general Kofi Annan in December 1999 raised the serious question of the use of child soldiers by the Taliban, the UN emergency relief coordinator in Islamabad took it upon himself to express public regret that "the Taliban believed Annan was personally responsible for the report, which he himself had not actually written."[24] Humanitarian actors, with the best of intentions and bolstered by a burning conviction that they know best, can sometimes opt for "principled engagement" without appreciating that this inevitably has political and reputational consequences, as the ICRC discovered during the Second World War.

In the end this comes to the question of when, and in what circumstances, it is appropriate to make compromises. Here, the distinction drawn by Avishai Margalit between sanguine compromises and rotten compromises may be useful: according to Margalit, a rotten compromise "is an agreement that establishes or maintains an inhuman political order based on systematic cruelty and humiliation as its permanent features."[25] It is tragically the case that humanitarian action may work to the advantage of those with nothing whatsoever to redeem them from a moral point of view, and that aid to vulnerable individuals may have the simultaneous effect of sustaining destructive structures or networks of power This was one of the factors that prompted the French section of Médecins Sans Frontières to withdraw from refugee camps in Zaire in 1994.[26] Whether a compromise is, in fact, rotten will depend on the specifics of a situation, but it pays for humanitarian diplomats to bear the risks of rotten compromise in mind.

Humanitarianism and diplomacy

Humanitarian diplomacy has come a long way since 1945. Institutions for the delivery of humanitarian assistance are much more advanced, and globalisation of communications means that some crises that might otherwise have gone unmarked now have the potential to capture the attention of compassionate people in remote reaches of the world. There is now a Convention defining the crime of genocide, and the doctrine of a global responsibility to protect has emerged to prompt state actors to confront the challenge of mass-atrocity crimes.[27] While hideous humanitarian disasters have continued to surface, from Biafra in the 1960s to Rwanda in the 1990s and Somalia in the second decade of the twenty-first century, there has been progress on some key fronts.

One person who was not able to witness these developments was Count Bernadotte himself. In the aftermath of the Second World War, he was widely viewed as one of the most notable humanitarians of his time, and he served as president of the International Red Cross Conference in Stockholm in August 1948.[28] This proved to be his swan-song. The next month, he travelled to Palestine as United Nations mediator, and it was there, on 17 September, that he was murdered by an assassin from a radical Zionist group known as Lehi. The plan to assassinate him had been put to Lehi's central committee, where it met no opposition.[29] Bernadotte's standing as a humanitarian offered him little protection in the vicious climate of the times. Nonetheless, his memory lives on, not least through the work of the Folke Bernadotte Academy, a Swedish government agency concerned with conflict, crisis management and peace operations. Its activities serve as a reminder that the challenges that create the need for humanitarian diplomacy remain very much alive, and are likely to prompt the continuation of the kinds of diplomatic activity with which this chapter has been concerned.

17

FROM ARROW TO PATH

INTERNATIONAL RELATIONS THEORY
AND THE HUMANITARIAN SPACE

Mathew J. Davies

In 2008 I was asked by Professor Raymond Apthorpe to speak to a group of students of the Australian National University, many of whom worked or wished to work in humanitarian agencies, about the relationship between international relations theorising (IRT) and humanitarian assistance. I was unsure what to say, and why it would be relevant. Surely those interested and/or engaged in humanitarian activities would have little time, and even less inclination, to listen to the supposed wisdom of theoreticians. When engaged in the hectic and often hostile humanitarian space what possible utility could the cool abstraction of realism offer those who were not only getting their hands dirty but regularly risking their lives? Reviewing the literature it was clear that there certainly was a relationship between IRT and humanitarianism but the then shape of this relationship was not particularly useful for my audience. Humanitarianism was an area of action that those theoretically

211

minded studied for useful pieces of evidence to support, critique or develop particular theoretical concerns (see for example the work of Alex Bellamy who writes passionately that certain critical theoretical lenses are preferable to others or Michael Pugh who seeks to use peacekeeping as evidence of the utility of Critical Theory).[1] This, whilst interesting, seemed inappropriate and inadequate for the task set me where the emphasis had to be on what they, in the room, could use IRT for.

As I pondered what to say an answer started to emerge. Regardless of the different forms, arguments and approaches that exist in IRT, all theoretical arguments are ultimately predicated on assertions about the motives, interests and identities of actors. Was it possible that humanitarian actors could benefit from what theorising suggested shapes and drives actors? A knowledge of the different arguments and positions that a range of theoretical perspectives takes may equip the practitioner with at least a set of possible expectations that both help delineate the feasible and practicable in the humanitarian space and stands as a basis to interrogate the motives and interests of not only others but also themselves. What I was thinking then, and shall expand on here, is that the relationship between IRT and humanitarianism is not an arrow that points in one direction. Instead, it is a path that can be travelled in either direction. IRT benefits from studying humanitarianism but through appreciating the arguments about the motives and interests of actors so humanitarians can benefit from theory. To illustrate this utility I shall first investigate how IRT can be realised as a practical endeavour before discussing realism, liberalism and constructivism in turn.

IRT as an ethical enterprise: how and why should we act?

The first step that needs to be taken is unpacking how theories of international relations reveal arguments about the motives and interests of actors. This can be achieved by looking at what contemporary theoreticians have suggested IRT is about. Christian Reus-Smit and Duncan Snidal in the *Oxford University Press Handbook on International Relations* published in 2008 suggest that regardless of other differences, all theoretical positions seek to answer the question "how should we act?"[2] Reus-Smit and Snidal are suggesting here that IRT is an ethical, although not always necessarily moral, enterprise. This revelation is useful for two reasons. First, asking how should we act is a strategic question. It requires us to consider what we need to do to achieve our goals. Second, if theories ask how should we act then there is a deeper question that theories must also address. There can be no consideration of "how should we act" unless there is an answer to "why do we act" as it is this question which informs why one course of action is preferable to any other.[3]

IRT as an ethical concern is a discipline that clearly talks about questions of strategy and questions of motive. Theories are abstract to different degrees, yes, but each is also a discrete package of arguments about why actors act, how they act and how to engage with those actors successfully. If we accept, as others in this volume indicate, that aid agencies and others are engaged in "evolving tactics" to rescue strangers then an awareness of theorising may help to hone those tactics by illuminating other participants in the arena.[4] The humanitarian space is nebulous, ill-defined and contorting under the pressure of the actors, ideas and interests that populate it. IRT can offer practitioners ways of thinking that help delineate those actors and the interests that may have. This argument is not only intended for the NGO's that have evolved into "a crucial pillar of the international humanitarian architecture"[5] but for all participants whether governmental or otherwise. The greater the refinement with which humanitarian actors understand their environment the more likely it is that they will be successful in their labours. Far from being superfluous or even indulgent an awareness of IRT offers crucial insight and advantage into the means and methods of contemporary humanitarianism.

Realism: egoism and power

Realism is less a discrete theory and more a discourse within which many differing approaches are in creative tension. William C. Wohlforth has identified that regardless of the particular strain of realism in play (and we can choose from among Classical, Structural, Neo-Classical, Defensive, Offensive and more) there are four essential propositions that define a realist: groupism; egoism; anarchy; and power politics.[6] These concerns appear in the classical realism of Hans Morgenthau in Hans Morgenthau's famous "Six Principles of Political Realism" of 1948 just as much as they do in the structural realism of Kenneth Waltz some thirty years' later, albeit in a different configuration.[7] The ethics of realism are not wedded to states, but are instead arguments about how collectivities act in the political realm. It is just such a leap that has powered realism's investigation into phenomena as diverse as terrorism and civil war.

These commitments to the nature of the world offer and provide a focused analysis on the motives of actors within that world. Actors are self-regarding and egoistical, pursuing their own interests in ways which ultimately protect their own survival. Murielle Cozette has written powerfully how Morgenthau's work is concerned with illuminating what forms of behaviour are "ethically right" within this world view.[8] Perhaps the most famous of these ethical insights would be a sustained scepticism of the use of moral arguments to justify actions. Jack Donnelly indicates that it is not that realists reject all notions of morality of justice, rather that they claim "instead that these standards either do not apply to international politics or are appropriately overridden by other considerations."[9] What this results in is a further scepticism about the voracity of actors' claims to be acting in pursuit of moral ends. Actors often make recourse to moral arguments as justifications for choosing particular courses of action over alternatives, and in assigning that behaviour a sense of "right" and we should be sceptical of such claims. Morgenthau notes that there exists an "ineluctable tension between the moral command and the requirements of successful political action" and that the "moral aspirations of a particular nation [cannot be equated with] the moral laws that govern the universe."[10] Realism is often thought of as a "tragic vision" of politics. There can be no progress towards alleviating competition and any effort to pursue ones interests in ways other than through the eternal edicts of power and state security leads inevitably to falling victim to those actors who have listened more carefully to the instructions of anarchy.

Realism suggests that actors are not motivated by human rights, human security or democracy. Instead they are solely preoccupied with power and position, never forgetting their own partisan political ends. Acting in the humanitarian space may not indicate any great commitment to humanitarian principles, despite our aspirational beliefs that humanitarianism ideally is nonpolitical.[11] The International Committee of the Red Cross has decried the politicisation of the humanitarian space. Realism suggests that this is inevitable, not some "mistake" that needs to be corrected. Realism counsels that politically selfish action always has a role to play in what ideally we may seek to define as a selfless and apolitical arena. The relationships between organisations within the humanitarian space is not harmonious, as perhaps one would expect were all participants unselfconsciously committed to the principles of humanitarianism. Instead the humanitarian space is "dysfunctional" given the enduring "organisational insecurity, competitive pressures and fiscal uncertainty" actors face.[12] Whether that be in competition for resources, or to "be on the ground first," or to carve out a separate territorial or bureaucratic enclave to call ones own, there is much evidence that political motives characterise participation in humanitarian action.

Liberalism: cooperation and institutionalisation

The great contender to realism's claim to hegemonic status within the discipline was for a long time liberalism, and just like its rival, liberalism was and remains more a unifying label than a particularly precise term. Classical liberals focus on transnational relations and the fraying centrality of states, neoliberals in the wake of Waltz's neorealist re-articulation of the purposes and practices of theories, focus only on states in anarchy. Contemporary liberals such as Andrew Moravcsik discuss the interplay of domestic political constituencies and international political behaviour.

Underpinning this variety liberal IR thinkers make no great claim about the altruism of the individual or collective, and do not seek the quick and radical reorientation of political behaviour, although some who study the related field of democratic peace research often do aim for such a transmogrification of world politics. They remain convinced that actors are selfishly motivated and constantly concerned with their own position. However, liberals cluster around the belief that the cooperative ethos permeates political behaviour as the logical response to the self-help imperatives of international anarchy.[13] Gone is the realist belief that the pursuit of ones interests can only be conducted in the language of security and insecurity, and instead liberals suggest that the undoubted preoccupation with self-interest can lead to cooperation under specified conditions. The cooperative endeavour and the ability of actors to come to reasoned, and thus reasonable, beliefs about what to do and how to do it offers a rather less pessimistic view than does realism. Moravcsik notes that because of this, liberal theory rejects the cyclical view of the realist and in its place is comfortable with the notion that over time the self interest of actors under circumstances of economic and political modernisation can lead to a future that is better than the past.[14] Liberalism therefore "highlights the scope for human action and choice" in a fuller way than their realist counterparts, but always insists that the "constraints that are emphasised, indeed overemphasised, in theories such as realism [...] Be taken very seriously."[15]

Key in the liberal vision of world politics is the presence and role of institutions in international politics, where the "raw power" of states is "replaced by institutional networks involving rules and moderation" that become the vehicles for international cooperation.[16] The international architecture of overlapping organisations attracts not just states but a variety of civil society actors who cluster around specific issues, enjoying the benefits of greater predictability than the convergence of state interests provides. In turn these oases of cooperation become lynchpins for the establishment of international law that provides both procedural regularity and normative aspiration to international political behaviour.

What then can a humanitarian make from this? Liberalism offers humanitarian practitioners a more complex, but not necessarily more optimistic, view of humanitarian space. It emphasises the role of actors such as the UN or EU and notes that states may well seek to operate through collectivities to maximise effectiveness. Liberalism serves to reaffirm the importance of remaining aware of the self-interest of actors, but not to assume that self-interest is necessarily deleterious to the possibility of humanitarian outcomes. Whilst to realism those claiming humanitarian motives are always hiding their self interest with no real interest in humanitarianism, to a liberal humanitarian, goals may well emerge as genuine within the context of self-interest. This is of significant consequence for arguments that focus on the negative associations of politicisation. Politicisation is inevitable but liberalism suggests that it is not inevitably bad. Actors in the humanitarian space would be well advised to recognise this fact, and work to ensure that the politicisation that occurs is constructive, through the clear explication of the linkages between political goals and the humanitarian outcome. Many humanitarian efforts have withered on the vine of declining political engagement and a more proactive effort to embrace politicisation in certain forms may forestall such occurrences. Liberalism suggests that this is best achieved through enmeshing actors in organisational settings that can help sustain cooperation and mitigate the negative consequences of inevitable competitive drives. The inclusion of actors such as the UN and EU into the humanitarian space serve to cement the participation of states as well as provide greater degrees of coordination and should be embraced and fostered.

Constructivism: complexity and ideas

Building on the infusion of Marxism into international relations by the critical theorists of the 1980s, constructivism has become a key theoretical approach in the discipline. If the heterogeneity of realism and liberalism is daunting, then the differences displayed between those who call themselves, or are labelled as, constructivists may lead us to question the utility of the collective noun at all. All constructivists agree the world is "socially constructed," and would further agree with Alexander Wendt when he noted that the fact "500 British nuclear weapons are less threatening to the United States than five North Korean nuclear Weapons," indicates the utility of a focus on ideas and inter-subjective meaning and that material facts are the starting point, not the final word, for any analysis.[17] Constructivists, however, disagree bitterly on how to respond to that insight.[18] They disagree on where exactly to focus attention. Wendt himself suggests that international and domestic politics can be bracketed separately from each other (the distinction between corporate and social identities).[19] Others have broken this dichotomy and suggested that domestic politics is crucial to explanation, a far more popular position.[20] Epistemologically, US-led constructivism has retained an explicit or quasi positivist methodological position whilst elsewhere constructivism has come to focus far more on methods more usually associated with arch post-positivists.[21]

Out of this array of competing research agendas, epistemological commitments and methodological proclivities certain commonalities do remain, and it is these islands of agreement that allow me to look at what constructivism may offer the humanitarian. Constructivism does not offer a singular argument about what actors will do, but it does suggest a common reason for why they will do something (although as investigated by Richard Price this very fluidity impacts the constructivist position on establishing a particular ethic in the sense that Reus Smit and Snidal suggest).[22] Whilst the realists suggest permanent pursuit of egoism and a fascination with power with the result that the possibility for moral action is crowded out, and the liberal remains committed to the selfish motive but with the possibility of a greater range of actions that fulfil that desire, constructivism is far more open to idea, even ideal, driven behaviour. Constructivists believe that prevalent ideational structures determine the particular politics of actors. They further suggest that these structures are in constant renegotiation as actors engage with each other, learn from each other and promote new standards. This mutual constitution of the interests and identities of actors is driven forwards by the interplay of actions, intentions and interpretations in a delicate and ever swirling dance where states, NGO's, individuals and the ideas and norms themselves all participate.

What this means is that the humanitarian space is not necessarily just another realm of selfish egoism, but may be populated with actors pursuing what is right and morally justified. The particular value of constructivism comes when we realise that different actors may be chasing divergent ends because they hold different ideas about what is right. That motivation is ideational is not the same as arguing that it is uniform. Humanitarian actors should recognise that those they work with, or against, are enmeshed in deeply held ideas of probity which may be at odds with those they hold and assume others should share. Even if we limited our horizons to the chapters in this collection we would see the wide variety of ideas of what humanitarianism has meant, does mean and should mean in the future. Participation in the humanitarian space does not automatically mean commitment to the same understanding of humanitarianism. Broader still, constructivism suggests that those who oppose humanitarianism do so because of their own set of beliefs about right and wrong which whilst we may fundamentally disagree with, we should not dismiss arbitrarily.

Given this, and if motives are ideational and shifting, then constructivism suggests something about how actors can engage successfully with each other. Constructivist scholarship has emphasised the importance of ongoing discursive engagement with actors to persuade them to engage in, or refrain from, certain actions.[23] Deep seated ideational affiliations are not quickly abandoned, and actors need to be convinced that new ways are better ways. Successful action may require long-term commitments to understand, engage with and learn from others through processes of open dialogue and mutual respect.

IRT and humanitarianism

An appreciation of IRT by those who engage in humanitarian activities is not a panacea for their ills, nor some alchemy which ensures every endeavour is successful, but recognising and appreciating the lessons it contains offers new and hopefully useful ways to approach the questions of motive and identity which form the basis of action in the humanitarian space. I do not argue that in all cases an awareness of theoretical arguments about actor motivation will ensure humanitarian actors will be successful in fulfilling their tasks, nor do I argue that realism, liberalism, constructivism or any of the alternative theoretical positions that have not been discussed here, represent the "right choice" over potential alternatives. Theories offer a sensibility with which to interrogate the world. Realism reminds you to think about selfish motivation. Liberalism suggests that cooperation may well play a fuller role than the realists suggest, but that it does not come at the expense of self-interest. Constructivism hints that an understanding of the matrix of ideas and interests that bind different actors together may enhance success. Obviously the benefits offered by a single theory of International Relations are magnified if we utilise multiple theoretical frameworks. Instead of asking simply "what would realism have to say about this" we should ask "what would IRT have to say about this?" This trend known technically as analytical eclecticism, has emerged as a methodological innovation advocating the benefits of using different theories as "lenses" through which to view issues.[24] Moreover, I personally believe that these arguments serve not only to enquire about others, but to help understand more fully our own actions and interests. Why am I animated to help this or that concern? Why do I participate in the way that I do, how is it that I think I am helping and why would others agree and disagree with that assertion? Am I truly motivated by selfless interest or is there egoism in play here?

This is the message I tried to convey in 2008 in that classroom. We can look at individual theories and start to reveal a picture. However, as thinkers and practitioners, we can step outside of that ivory tower. An awareness of theorising and the braided streams within it, helps illuminate the murky recesses of the humanitarian space and give form and substance to those beasts that populate it. Individual theories may emphasise various notes and chords, whether those are harmonious or somewhat off-key, but an awareness of international relations theories more generally furnishes us not only with an appreciation of the orchestra itself, but vitally with a firmer and more reasoned answer to why we may seek to place ourselves in the role of conductor.

18

INTERSECTING DISASTERS

ESCHEWING MODELS, EMBRACING GEOPOLITICS

Jennifer Hyndman

This chapter makes the argument that humanitarian crises should be approached as the outcome of multiple disasters, not just singular ones. Crises may be serial in a given place, or temporally coincident, but they tend not to exist in isolation. Humanitarian response, in turn, cannot be framed as a singular approach or solved with a model that excludes consideration of other disasters—past or present. Humanitarian space, in short, is not bracketed off from the political, environmental and development projects that co-constitute the context of responses to disasters. To the extent that humanitarian response and analysis focus only on managing the crisis at hand, they are bound to miss their mark.[1]

Increasingly, disasters are not discrete events but violent human-made and environmental events that overlap with one another, what I have called "dual disasters."[2] In 2011, *The Huffington Post* posted the headline, "Dual Disasters," with reference to the earthquake, tsunami, and related nuclear meltdown at the Fukushima plant in Japan. In January 2010, the Haiti earthquake devastated a politically fragile and economically impoverished country while an event of similar magnitude in Chile produced much less loss and damage, given its more stable standing and history of quakes that led to greater preparedness. In this example, the world witnessed how existing vulnerabilities due to one humanitarian crisis are usually exacerbated with the onset of another. And yet, the intersection of disasters can also open up new political spaces for change and reconciliation where it might be needed. "Disaster diplomacy" refers to the extent to which disaster-related activities—including prevention and mitigation activities or response and recovery—induce cooperation between enemy parties on national or international scales.[3] Just eight months after the 2004 Indian Basin tsunami, a peace agreement was signed between Acehnese rebels in Northern Sumatra and the government of Indonesia. The tsunami did not cause peace, but it accelerated the process and put Aceh on the international map, after years of foreign visitors and journalists being banned from the region.[4] In short, the tsunami opened up new political spaces at the same time as it killed more than 200,000 people.

I begin the chapter with a brief overview of recent humanitarian crises that exacerbated existing vulnerabilities, disparities and fragilities. Certainly, no group of people can experience several humanitarian crises without such hardship eroding their capacity to survive. I then highlight how conflict-sensitive aid in response to humanitarian disasters is more important than ever. What is needed is disaster-sensitive assistance that acknowledges existing tensions, vulnerabilities and political landscapes when its purveyors arrive to deliver it. When dual or multiple disasters coalesce, humanitarian aid may fuel existing conflict, which is problem enough. If international aid is provided for a major disaster with high visibility, but with little or no regard for the context of a pre-existing humanitarian crisis that may have lower visibility, the success of the interventions and humanitarian aid provided and the people for whom they are intended remain at risk.

Dual disasters

In July 2011, the UN high commissioner for refugees (UNHCR), Antonio Guterres, declared Somalia "the worst humanitarian disaster" in the world after he met with refugees in the Dadaab refugee camps of northeast Kenya.[5] Somalia faces the most acute drought in six decades, and experiences continued political instability as al-Shabaab persists in challenging the authority and control of the country by a Western-backed, if precariously perched, president and government. This example illustrates two points: that the thousands of people crossing the border into Kenya are fleeing violence as well as drought, and that similar conditions of drought and displacement almost two decades earlier precipitated the first significant wave of Somali refugees to Kenya. I surmise that the resources and assets of Somalis living in Somalia have diminished over this twenty-year period, reducing both their capacity to stay in their homes but also prospects for peace. Clearly, careful research on whether this has played out needs to be done. The humanitarian crises spawned by the politics in and of Somalia are dual disasters in terms of both conflict and the environment, and they are serial in terms of recurrence.

The 2010 earthquake in Haiti devastated an already shaken country. The adverse effects of the earthquake on the Haitian people were acute, but they could not be separated from its colonial history with France, its imperial occupations by the United States, the rise of authoritarian government throughout much of the twentieth century and the political coups that have characterised the past twenty years of rule in Haiti. These political relationships of conflict at many levels contributed to the poverty in Haiti before the 12 January 2010 quake. Haiti is defined as much by pre-existing layers of political instability and economic privation as by the earthquake that has now shattered the nation. Humanitarian crisis is not an event, but an accumulation of sediment layers of conflict, displacement, privation and environmental destruction.

The question remains whether Haiti will be "built back better"—a common refrain among housing and reconstruction experts—or whether the future of the country depends on more than new schools, hospitals, roads, government buildings, economic advice and loans. Caribbean historian, Melanie Newton comments that:

> [...] reconstruction efforts must aim at eliminating Haiti's terrible reality of *la misère*, the Haitian Kréyol word for the abject poverty that dominates the lives of most Haitians. As long as Haiti remains one of the world's most socio-economically unequal countries, reconstruction efforts in Haiti are likely to re-create the structures exacerbating the current catastrophe.[6]

Instead of simply building back better, an approach that risks recreating disparities that existed before the earthquake, experts, expatriates and others have called for a new strategy that addresses the political crisis, not just the broken infrastructure and rubble that remain in Haiti. Humanitarian disasters and their responses do not occur in a political or economic vacuum. Local geographies of inequality, poverty, gender relations, ethnicity, and social and economic marginalisation shape response and recovery for those who survive them. Yet, international responses will also bear the imprint of geopolitical designs and strategic considerations. There is simply no such thing as a purely "natural" disaster. The earthquake in Gujarat in January 2001 was even stronger than the one measured in Haiti, if less deadly, killing over 20,000 people and injuring some 167,000. Patterns of discrimination in the reconstruction initiatives that followed related to broader patterns of extant social polarisation.[7]

On 26 December 2004, a tsunami captivated the world's attention; the huge waves washed away family members, homes and hotels in the dramatic devastation. While Aceh was the hardest hit and closest to the epicentre of the shock that created the tsunami, the plight of people there received far less attention because foreigners were not allowed into the province. Unlike Thailand, a tourist mecca during holiday season, the destruction and loss experienced in Aceh came much later from local news media and people's cell phone footage. In the Maldives, far fewer died—only 108 people perished in the tsunami—but the estimate of damage and loss was nearly 80 per cent of a year's gross national income.[8] An almost exclusively coastal tourist economy meant that a great deal of infrastructure was destroyed. The human impact of the tsunami also varied dramatically across space, based on proximity to the epicentre, population density and quality of housing structures: in Aceh the ratio of dead to injured was 6:1, falling to 1.5:1 in Sri Lanka.[9]

The destruction of Hurricane Katrina—a "First World" disaster—followed the tsunami in August 2005. While the number of those who died was much lower than those of the other crises, the cost of reconstruction was by far the greatest. Commentators asked how such human calamity could be created in the world's remaining superpower. Some called the survivors of Katrina "refugees" because of the US government's inability to protect its citizens, both before the levees broke and after the hurricane hit. Others protested the refugee label, stating that its racialised connotations conjured an orientalist image of displaced people from places in Africa inappropriate for American citizens. Later that year in October 2005, the Pakistan earthquake in Kashmir hit, but did not get the same attention as the tsunami or Hurricane Katrina, despite the death of almost 80,000 people and the displacement of millions more. The uneven global media coverage and world attention these environmental disasters generate is a vital factor shaping international responses to crisis. Postcolonial ties, Cold War allegiances, economic reliance and diasporic influence also help shape international responses to humanitarian disasters, whether they are human-made or tectonically-derived.[10]

Disasters are, then, not simply "natural." Building codes, zoning policies, environmental regulations and their enforcement (or not) shape the outcomes of major weather events, earthquakes and tsunamis. Human vulnerability to these calamities and resilience in the face of them are conditioned by human factors, a commonsensical point but one that often gets lost in the shuffle during humanitarian responses. So just as there are no real "natural" disasters, there are no simple or "natural" humanitarian responses.

Learning from disaster: if/then…

In 2004, an earthquake off the tip of Sumatra Island, Indonesia generated a momentous tsunami in the Indian Ocean Basin, affecting some twenty countries. Had these events occurred in the South Pacific where tsunamis are quite common, early warning systems would have been in place, notifying people of impending waves and saving lives. If the countries affected by the 2004 tsunami were more affluent, they might also have afforded these preventative measures before the tsunami hit, and outcomes could have been much different. Given government restrictions on access to Aceh for foreigners, images from that region took longer to emerge.

Less than a year after the 2004 tsunami, a major earthquake levelled homes in the contested Kashmir border region of Pakistan, and to a lesser extent, India, rendering 3.3 million survivors homeless.[11] International public attention to and funds for the earthquake were significantly less than those for the tsunami, raising important questions of which "optics" foster giving from charitable strangers who witness such disasters from afar.[12] The media coverage and visibility of the earthquake in remote Kashmir were far less than that for the tsunami in Thailand and Sri Lanka where foreign tourists videotaped the event.

Eight months later, in August 2005, Hurricane Katrina formed over the Bahamas, gained strength and struck the US coasts of Florida,

Louisiana and Mississippi. Despite expert knowledge that the levees protecting New Orleans needed $15 billion worth of serious repairs to make the city safe, they were never funded. Instead, the levees failed and much of New Orleans was flooded. Safety was disparately apportioned: those too infirm or poor to evacuate stayed put; those who could leave did. The confluence of racialised poverty, differentiated mobility, bad policy decisions (not to fund levee reconstruction) and global warming created an immense humanitarian disaster. Here the local conditions of relative privation cast shame on the government of one of the wealthiest counties in the world, illustrating the messiness of disaster and the ways in which a "politics of scale" at local, state and national levels plays into the diversity and intensity of disasters and their manifestation.

Hurricane Katrina was a moderate Category One hurricane when it hit Southern Florida, but after gathering warmer water, wind and force from the Gulf of Mexico, it struck the Louisiana coast as lethal Category Three or Four hurricanes. Evidence shows that hurricanes are getting stronger due to global warming.[13] This means that dual, or multiple, disasters are likely to increase in the future, assuming current rates of global warming and conflict duration.

When Cyclone Nargis hit Burma (known as Myanmar in official parlance) in May 2008, 130,000 people along the Irrawaddy Delta were killed and over two million people displaced. This violent storm became a full-blown humanitarian disaster in part because of government policy. The military government, or junta known ironically as the State Peace and Development Council (SPDC), has ruled with impunity since 1990 when it ignored the outcome of elections. The subsequent regime has had scant regard for human life, let alone human rights. It permitted very little coverage of the cyclone's destruction to be seen in the international media and virtually no international aid or staff was allowed into the area to assist those affected until almost one month after the cyclone hit. The idea that disaster is conditioned by existing policies and practices challenges the "naturalness" of a so-called "natural disaster."

On 12 May 2008, a massive earthquake of magnitude 7.9 hit Sichuan Province, China. Some 90,000 people were killed, among them 19,000 children who were crushed in poorly built school buildings that collapsed at the time of the quake.[14] Since 1976, when the Tangshan earthquake in China killed over 240,000 people, the government has required that new structures be built to withstand major quakes. Yet, the collapse of schools, hospitals and factories in several different areas around Sichuan raised serious questions about whether such codes were enforced during China's recent building boom.[15] The alleged corruption of Chinese government officials, who were accused of ordering the construction of inferior public school buildings in order to skim funds for themselves, created public outrage.

An earthquake of magnitude 8.8 rocked Chile in February 2010, prompting warnings in fifty-three countries ringing the Pacific Ocean. Yet, fatalities were in the hundreds, rather than the hundreds of thousands. Chile is a much wealthier country than Haiti. "On a per-capita basis, Chile has more world-renowned seismologists and earthquake engineers than anywhere else."[16] Chile possesses a robust emergency response capacity as well as a long history of managing seismic disasters. "Earthquakes don't kill—they don't create damage—if there's nothing to damage," according to Eric Calais, a Purdue University geophysicist.[17] The country has earthquakes regularly, and the country was prepared for this one. In 1960, after Chile's worst earthquake of magnitude 9.5, 1,655 people were killed and some two million left homeless. Haiti's last earthquake was 250 years ago, so readiness and a lack of resources to create capacity were both issues in that context. In both cases, however, crises was precipitated or averted by the landscapes of privation or readiness that preceded the earthquakes. Adequately accounting for these relations of power, politics and practice is vital to conceiving of the most effective humanitarian response.

Catastrophe as opportunity?

Human displacement, due to conflict, earthquake, or a tsunami, is tied to other social, cultural and economic displacements: the loss of existing authority structures, livelihoods and daily routines. Such losses can increase people's vulnerability to hunger, violence and homelessness.

Struggles over interethnic justice, neo-liberalism, economic distribution the disempowerment of "women, caste bigotry and such have shaped the [Sri] Lankan political landscape in significant ways over the last decades [...] even the tsunami cannot wipe out the imprint of these fault lines."[18]

"Fault lines" are produced by human as well as by geophysical forces. Yet, they can also open up space for other, more positive changes. Humanitarian actors could do a much better job of analysing these "fault lines" and exclusions but also in excavating the new spaces of hope and possibility that are generated by crises and change. During the war between government troops and the Liberation Tigers of Tamil Eelam (LTTE) in Sri Lanka, government embargoes prevented basic staples like diesel fuel from getting in to LTTE-held territory in the north. Accordingly, mobility became more restricted for those who had relied on public transportation. Women's travel to local food markets in rural areas was severely impeded due to a lack of available public bus service and to a cultural context that frowned upon married women riding bicycles. Yet, slowly, women took up the two-wheeled option. Their mobility and autonomy increased, albeit in a context of conflict, scarcity and necessity. Gender relations were destabilised by the war and remade in the context of the conflict. The tsunami's destruction remade social relations in unexpected ways. If catastrophe breeds opportunities for social transformations and economic exploitation, it also generates new social and political openings and space for change.[19] As noted in the introduction, just eight months after the 2004 tsunami struck Aceh, Indonesia, a peace agreement was finalised between government and rebel forces after more than three decades of deadly conflict.

From conflict-sensitive to disaster-sensitive aid

For far more than a decade now, aid workers, government policymakers and international donors have been increasingly aware of the ways in which aid can both fuel and mitigate war when delivered in such a context. Hence, international humanitarian assistance must be "conflict sensitive" to avoid exacerbating violence or unwittingly aiding combatants. A good deal of research has also focused on the relationship of aid to conflict reduction.[20] Yet little is known about what happens when multiple humanitarian disasters intersect, and when aid to each is organised separately, often by different actors.

In research that Arno Waizenegger and I conducted between 2007 and 2008, we found that international organisations responding to the tsunami largely ignored the plight of those civilians displaced by the conflict that preceded the tsunami. The "two solitudes" of humanitarian activity, disparate as they were, were not coordinated or shared in accordance with need. Instead, we found that tsunami survivors were getting new houses, and in some cases several houses, whereas those who lost livelihoods and homes in the conflict received little attention.[21] Moreover, humanitarian organisations that eventually realised these gaps in assistance and unmet needs could not spend funds earmarked for the tsunami on those persons in need affected by the conflict. We argued that tensions created because of such drastic disparities between those affected by the conflict and those who survived the tsunami could threaten the peace agreement of 2005. Thankfully, we have been proven wrong so far. The current situation in Somalia, however, shows us that peace is still elusive after two decades, despite acute environmental drought at the same time as conflict continues. What these conditions are, how they dovetail (if at all) with environmental precarity and resource scarcity, and how successive crises in a given place affect the capacity of people to resurrect livelihoods when they have been lost are vital questions to which humanitarians must pay greater attention.

Conclusion

In a world increasingly characterised by global warming and environmental degradation, conflict, resource wars, human rights atrocities and subsequent human displacement are part of humanitarian crises that complicate and exacerbate such processes. Dual disasters, over time or at the same time, create the most complex of emergencies. Scale is thus an unavoidable matrix for analysing humanitarian crises, dual or multiple. As Philip Kelly puts it:

To speak of local, regional, national or even global processes is meaningless— social relations are in fact played out across scales rather than confined within them. Consequently, it makes little sense to privilege any scale as a primary referent for analysing particular social processes.[22]

An understanding of local conditions cannot be divorced from the national picture, and the regional/global geopolitics. The examples and approaches chronicled here aim to illustrate that disasters permeate the most personal and global scales of social and political space: from the human body and household, to the international community and global environment.[23] These scales are not discrete units that can be neatly separated out from one another, just as concomitant disasters cannot be treated in isolation. As in Aceh, how the survivors of one humanitarian crisis are treated in relation to another just up the hill can shape prospects for peace in a larger sense. Disasters intersect in place and over time. Explicitly articulating how they overlap, link or contradict one another is important. Planning coordinated and comprehensive approaches that acknowledge these connections, political histories and conflict implications is vital. Probing the effects of crises over time in a given place and on a group of people is also key to understanding livelihoods and their restoration. Environmental change continues apace, and global warming will only exacerbate existing challenges of drought, flooding and weather events. Understanding the ways in which extant humanitarian crises interact with environmental disasters is critical to planning for such contexts in future.

19

HUMANITARIANISM, DEVELOPMENT
AND THE LIBERAL PEACE

David Chandler

In the new humanitarian order, interventions are posed in the language of individual empowerment, freedom and capacity-building. This chapter considers this humanitarian discourse of empowerment and freedom in relation to the problematic of development in contexts considered to be illiberal. Rather than a material view of development, human agency is placed at the centre and is seen as the measure of development in terms of individual capabilities. In the words of Amartya Sen, the winner of the 1998 Nobel Prize for Economic Science, freedom is increasingly seen to be both the primary end and principal means of development: "Development consists of the removal of various types of unfreedoms that leave people with little choice and little opportunity of exercising their reasoned agency."[1] In this humanitarian discourse, "human development," freedom and autonomy are foregrounded but development lacks a transformative or modernising material content. Development is thereby taken out of an economic context of GNP growth or industrialisation or a social and political context in which development policies are shaped by social and political pressures or state-led policies. The individualised understanding of development takes a rational choice perspective of the individual or "the agent-orientated view," in which development concerns enabling individuals to make effective choices by increasing their capabilities.[2]

Change does not come from above but through the agency of individuals, who act and make choices according to their own values and objectives. The outcome of development can therefore not be measured by any universal framework as different individuals have different development priorities and aspirations and live in differing social and economic contexts. While a critique of top-down state-led approaches to development, the post-liberal framing should not be confused with advocacy of the free market. Markets are not understood as being capable of finding solutions or leading to development themselves and are seen to depend on the formal institutional framework and the informal institutional framework of social culture and ideas or "behavioral ethics."[3] Although the individual in need of empowerment and capability, or capacity-building, is at the centre, both the allegedly illiberal post-colonial state and the society are understood to have secondary and important supporting roles in developing the institutional and cultural frameworks to enable individuals to free themselves or to develop themselves.[4]

The humanitarian framing of development in terms of empowerment and capacity-building centred on the individual responsibility of the post-colonial or post-conflict subject has been critiqued for its emphasis on "non-material development" which has tended to reinforce global inequalities of wealth and as marking "the demise of the developing state" as the poor are increasingly seen to be the agents of change and poverty reduction rather than external actors.[5] Vanessa Pupavac highlights that as development has come to the forefront of international agendas for state-building and conflict prevention, there has been a distancing of Western powers and international institutions from taking responsibility for development, with a consensus that the poor need "to find their own solutions to the problems they face."[6] This chapter draws out the changing nature of humanitarian discourses of development and the understanding of policy practices as promoting the empowerment of the post-conflict Other.

THE LIBERAL PEACE

Background

The problem of development has always been linked to a humanitarian discursive ethos as it has been one of the most sensitive and awkward questions raised in the external intervention in, and regulation of, the colonial or post-colonial state. Humanitarian discourse, as highlighted here in relation to development, has arisen defensively, in the context of apologia: in the negotiation of the ending of formal colonial rule and, subsequently, as a way of rationalising support for one-party rule in post-colonial Africa and for the limited aspirations of external powers in the post-Cold War era. In the days when colonial hierarchies were unquestioned, development was not a question of humanitarian concern regardless of the nature of economic crisis. For example, in response to the Irish potato famines of the 1840s, British administrators did not blame colonial economic policy but saw Irish habits and lifestyles as the cause of poverty and famine. Questions of poverty and development were not discussed in humanitarian terms but as racial or cultural problems connected to diet, overpopulation or laziness and indifference. In this context, Britain's mission in Ireland was seen not as one to "alleviate Irish distress but to civilise her people."[7]

The discourse of development only arose defensively, in the context of external avoidance of responsibility for the inequalities which critics alleged were being reproduced and reinforced through the hierarchies of international power or the pressures of the world market. It is for this reason that the problematic of development has always tended to be linked with the questions of humanitarianism, local ownership and empowerment and has sought to shift the understanding of development away from a universalising perspective of modernisation to exaggerate the differences between the West and the post-colonial world, where the attenuation of development aspirations has been held to be a way of empowering post-colonial societies themselves.

The liberal peace paradigm of international state-building builds on earlier discursive framings of development, stressing the need for ownership, but is distinct from earlier framings in that it ruptures the classic modern framing, which understood economic development and political autonomy as mutually supportive aspects of liberal modernity. Earlier discourses of apologia sought to problematise liberal approaches to the colonial or post-colonial world through the emphasis on the problems of material development. The state-building paradigm inverses the problematic—the framing of the relationship between development and autonomy: posing the autonomy of the post-colonial or post-conflict subject as a problem for development rather than the lack of development as a problem for political autonomy. This means that development in relation to state failure or state fragility becomes a process of external relationship management and explanation for inequality and intermittent crisis but without an end goal in which this situation is seen to be alleviated. In this chapter, the humanitarian paradigm of development as freedom, central to discourses of development within liberal peace interventions, will be traced out in relation to two earlier framings of the problematic of development and autonomy. These three framings of the problem of development can be seen from the viewpoint of Western policy-makers or international interveners and in their differing relationships to the object of intervention—the colonial or post-colonial state—and the different rationales in which development fitted into the paradigms within which this relationship of domination or influence was conceived.

The historically defensive and limiting nature of discourses of development is drawn out here through an initial focus upon the rise of the development problematic in the colonial era. In fact, it first arose with the problematisation of colonialism in the wake of the First World War. Development as a set of policy practices was used both to defensively legitimise colonial rule and to help further secure it. The classic example of discussion of development under the period of late colonialism was that most clearly articulated by Lord Lugard under the rubric of the "Dual Mandate," where development discourse operated to reveal the different and distinct development needs of illiberal colonial societies and therefore to indicate the need for a different set of political relations and rights than those of liberal democracies. The dual nature of the development discourse helped to shift the focus of policy-making away from the export of Western norms, such as representative democracy, and towards support for traditional elites, empowering more conservative sections of society in the attempt to negotiate imperial decline through preventing the political dominance of pro-independence elites.

The second period where development discourse comes to the fore in international debates is that of negotiating relations with the post-colonial world. Here, too, the discourse was a defensive one, with an awareness of the lack of direct interventionist capacity and a need to respond to the perceived threat of the Soviet Union gaining influence in many states which were no longer formally dependent on Western power. From the late 1950s to the early 1970s development was presented as necessitating a centralising state role as Western governments sought to bargain with post-colonial elites, facilitating a strong state to prevent rebellion led by movements sympathetic to the Soviet cause. The geopolitical division of the world and the competitive balance of power, made the post-colonial state an important subject in its own right, with the possibility of choosing (and playing-off) competing external patrons. The Western approach to development was one that argued that Western standards of democracy and governance were not applicable for the management of post-colonial development needs.

From the late 1970s until the end of the 1990s, development and humanitarian framings of policy intervention were largely off the agenda as models of state-led development failed and the Soviet model became discredited. In this period, the international financial institutions were much less defensive and, under the "Washington Consensus" framework of structural adjustment, sought to increasingly assert regulatory control over the post-colonial state, gradually extending the reach and focus of economic policy conditionality, focusing on financial and monetary controls and attempts to "roll back the state." The lack of defensiveness meant that there was little focus on development as a precondition for political equality—either in terms of independence or liberal-democratic frameworks of domestic rule—in this period, therefore, there was also little concern with the ownership of development. Rather than focusing on the empowerment of the post-colonial state and society, the international financial institutions openly claimed the mantle of development expertise and had little concern regarding the humanitarian or social impact of their financial stringency or about advocating the market as the framework which would provide solutions. The lowering of the priority of development meant that from the late 1970s to the 1990s the development sphere became the sphere of non-governmental activity as voluntary bodies stepped in to fill the humanitarian gap left by the decline of official institutional concern.[8]

Today the development of the post-colonial state and society has made a comeback as a central humanitarian concern of international institutions and leading Western states. The precondition for development becoming more central to Western concerns is a new defensiveness in relation to the post-colonial world as Western powers have sought to withdraw from policy responsibility. This discourse of withdrawal has taken place within the rubric of anti-modernisation frameworks, shaped by concerns over the environment and global warming. This defensiveness is reflected in the shifting focus away from the open dominance of international financial institutions and away from the market as a means of resolving the problems of development. Instead, development discourse focuses on empowering post-colonial states and societies in similar ways to the earlier discourses of the colonial and post-colonial periods. Once again, post-colonial states and societies are held to be the owners of their own development, but in the very different context of western regulation and intervention in the twenty-first century.

Today's development discourse of the importance of empowering the post-colonial subject was well described by Gordon Brown, in 2006, when still the UK Chancellor of the Exchequer:

A century ago people talked of 'What can we do to Africa?' Last century, it was 'What can we do for Africa?' Now in 2006, we must ask what the developing world, empowered, can do for itself.[9]

In today's discourse of development, it is often asserted that what is novel about current approaches is that of empowering the post-colonial world in relation to the needs of development. Many critiques of this approach have suggested that the discourse of empowerment and ownership is a misleading one considering the influence of Western powers and international financial institutions—this is no doubt the case.[10] The focus of this chapter, however, is how the discourses of humanitarianism and development are historically linked and how this discourse transforms and inverts the earlier attempts to explain differential policy frameworks, which understood development to be a precondition for autonomy; asserting a claim that it is autonomy which is problematic for development. It is this distinctive framing, emphasising the autonomy of the post-colonial subject, which facilitates development interventions aimed at indirectly influencing the autonomous choices of the poorest and most marginal sections of post-colonial societies.

Indirect rule in Africa

In the British case, the African protectorates were already, in effect, a postscript to the glory of empire. The African states were "protectorates"

236

not colonies, which already highlighted a defensive, contradictory and problematic approach to the assumption of colonial power over them. The distinction lay not so much in the power which the British government could exercise but in the responsibilities which it accepted. In 1900 the British courts (Kings Bench) definitively ruled that:

East Africa, being a protectorate in which the Crown has jurisdiction, is in relation to the Crown a foreign country under its protection, and its native inhabitants are not subjects owing allegiance to the Crown, but protected foreigners, who, in return for that protection, owe obedience.[11]

Colonial administrators were conscious of the fragility of their rule and nowhere more so than in sub-Saharan Africa. It was in order to address this problem that the discourse of development and the policy-making frameworks associated with it, particularly in the administrative conception of indirect rule, developed in an attempt to shore up external administrative authority through talking up the autonomy and independence of native chiefs, who they sought to rule through and develop.

The insight that Lugard had was to make a virtue out of development differentials as an argument for recasting British policy requirements in ostensibly neutral terms. Rather than an overt act of political reaction, Lugard's attempt to stave-off the end of colonial rule through the empowerment of native institutions was portrayed to be in the development interests of the poor and marginal in colonial society. Through the rubric of interventionist administrative "good governance," native institutions were to be built and simultaneously external control was to be enhanced. As Lugard describes:

The Resident [colonial official] acts as sympathetic adviser and counsellor to the native chief, being careful not to interfere so as to lower his prestige, or cause him to lose interest in his work. His advice on matters of general policy must be followed, but the native ruler issues his own instructions to subordinate chiefs and district heads—not as the orders of the Resident but as his own—and he is encouraged to work through them, instead of centralising everything in himself.[12]

Further, for Lugard, the native authority "is thus *de facto and de jure* ruler over his own people," there is not "two sets of rulers—British and native—working either separately or in co-operation, but a single government. It is the consistent aim of the British staff to maintain and increase the prestige of the native ruler, to encourage his initiative, and to support his authority."[13] Development was key to legitimating Lugard's strategy of indirect rule, with the reinvention of native authorities with modern administrative techniques which could assist in developing trade through introducing a wider use of money, rather than barter, and could expand the scope of political identification beyond personal social connections.

The discussion of development and its link with the mechanisms of indirect rule was the first attempt made to extend the policy framework of intervention with the humanitarian goal of empowering and capacity-building the colonial Other. This framing of empowerment developed in response to the negotiation of colonial withdrawal and the desire to use development as a discourse to undermine the legitimacy of the nationalist elites through posing as the representative of the poor and marginal, in whose interest development had to be managed through the maintenance of traditional institutions. In order to counterbalance the elites, British colonisers sought to become the advocates of development centred on the needs and interests of the poorest. The voices of the poor became the subject of British advocacy to suggest that development needs to focus on their needs rather than on the aspirations of the elites. The question of development and its relationship to empowerment and local ownership was revived in terms of content, but in a very different form, in the post-colonial era. Here, as considered in the next section, similar arguments to those put by Lugard, about the need for separate and distinct political forms to overcome the problem of development, were forwarded while arguments which insisted on measuring the post-colonial state according to the standards of Western liberal democracy were seen to be problematic in relation to development needs. Again the defensiveness of the discourse of critiques of liberalism can be seen in relation, not to the threat of anti-colonialism, but to the much broader problematic of support for the Soviet bloc and resistance to Western influence per se rather than just to Western rule in its most direct colonial form.

Post-colonial development

In the 1960s there was a general awareness of the weakness and fragility of the post-colonial state and development discourse focused defensively upon distancing the problems of the post-colonial state from the history of colonial rule. This defensive concern deepened with the perception that development might lead to the growth of influence of social forces which would be more sympathetic to Soviet rule. Whereas the discourse of development and local ownership had focused on the poor in an attempt to undermine the legitimacy of ruling elites, in the 1960s, development discourse focused on ownership at the level of state elites in order to prevent the masses from becoming a destabilising force capable of aligning the regimes to the Soviet sphere of influence.

In terms of policy responses, the problem of development was seen to be a unique dilemma which had only arisen in the post-colonial period. It was clear that while democracy was a central motif of the Cold War divide, the West was in no position to break from supporting "illiberal" post-colonial states on this basis if it wished to keep them outside of the Soviet sphere of influence. In post-colonial "transition" societies, Western Cold War norms of judgement needed to be rethought. This sense of defensiveness is well expressed by Pye:

Is the emergence of army rule a sign of anti-democratic tendencies? Or is it a process that can be readily expected at particular stages of national development? Must the central government try to obliterate all traditional communal differences, or can the unfettered organisation and representation of conflicting interests produce ultimately a stronger sense of national unity? Should the new governments strive to maintain the same levels of administrative efficiency as the former colonial authorities did, or is it possible that [...] because the new governments have other claims of legitimacy, this is no longer as crucial a problem? The questions mount, and we are not sure what trends are dangerous and what are only temporary phases with little significance.[14]

Samuel Huntington's 1968 book, *Political Order in Changing Societies*, concretised the post-colonial perception of the problem of development and stands as the classic text for this period. Whereas previous analysts had suggested that instability and authoritarian rule could be inevitable, Huntington proposed a much more state-led interventionist approach to prevent instability and maintain order. He also inverted the late-colonial understanding of the problem being that the state institutions were in advance of society, suggesting that the issue should be seen from a new angle. Rather than seeing the lack of economic development as causing the state-society gap, he argued that it was the development process itself which was destabilising:

It is not the absence of modernity but the efforts to achieve it which produce political disorder. If poor countries appear to be unstable, it is not because they

239

are poor, but because they are trying to become rich. A purely traditional society would be ignorant, poor, and stable.[15]

Rather than being the potential solution, rapid economic progress was held to be the problem facing non-Western states, creating an increasingly destabilised world, wracked by social and political conflict:

What was responsible for this violence and instability? The primary thesis of this book is that it was in large part the product of rapid social change and the rapid mobilisation of new groups into politics coupled with the slow development of political institutions.[16]

It was not the case that the political institutions of the post-colonial state were ahead of their societies (in terms of representing a national collectivity which was yet to become fully socially and economically integrated). The problem lay with the institutions of the state rather than with society. Huntington's state-building thesis consciously sought to privilege order over economic progress, as both a policy means and a political end. Huntington was clear in his critique of the export of universal Western norms, asserting that the promotion of democracy was not the best way to bring development or to withstand the threat of communist takeover. The barrier to communism was a strong state, capable of galvanising society, possibly through the undemocratic framework of one-party or authoritarian rule: "the non-Western countries of today can have political modernisation or they can have democratic pluralism, but they cannot normally have both."[17] He suggested, as did the colonial advocates of indirect rule, that focusing purely on organic solutions to development, waiting for economic growth to develop a middle class basis for liberal democracy, would result in "political decay" and weak states falling to communist revolution.

The institutional focus for Huntington, as for Lord Lugard, was not a bureaucratic one, but a political one. This much more "political" approach to development reflected the Cold War framework of US foreign policy which sought to support "friendly" authoritarian regimes in order to maintain international stability and order, rather than concern itself with questions of narrow economic policy or with representative democracy. It was not until the late 1970s and 1980s that the international financial institutions and the former colonial powers concerned themselves with the domestic politics of African states once the threat of Soviet competition and the resistance movements which they sponsored became increasingly lifted. In this period the discourse of development and local ownership went into abeyance, to return in the late 1990s.

Climate change

From the 1990s onwards, development and local ownership have returned to the top of the international agenda and local ownership has been key to reinterpreting development in a humanitarian problematic. In many ways, the discourse draws upon the past: on the late-colonial discourse of emphasising the poor as the central subjects of development but also on the post-colonial discourse problematising the dangers of development and its destabilising effects. Sub-Saharan Africa is particularly vulnerable to climate fluctuations because of a lack of development. The lack of development means that 70 per cent of the working population (90 per cent of Africa's poor) rely on agriculture for a living, the vast majority of them by subsistence farming.[18] It is no coincidence that the continent with the lowest per capita greenhouse gas emissions is also the most vulnerable to climate change. Rather than the problems of Africa being seen as a lack of development resulting in dependency upon climate uncertainties, the problem of development has increasingly been reinterpreted in terms of the problem of individual lifestyle choices and the survival strategies of the poor.

The framework of intervention in the new humanitarian order views African development in terms of external assistance to an "adaptation agenda" essential to prevent the impact of climate change from undermining African development.[19] According to the UK government white paper on development, *Making Governance Work for the Poor*, "climate change poses the most serious long term threat to development and the Millennium Development Goals."[20] The humanitarian poverty agenda and the climate change agenda have come together in their shared focus on Africa. In the wake of international support for poverty reduction and debt relief, many international NGOs, international institutions and Western states have called for climate change to be seen as the central challenge facing African development. African poverty and poor governance are held to combine to increase Africa's vulnerability, while the solution is held to lie with international programmes of assistance, funded and led by Western states, held to be chiefly responsible for global warming.

241

The "adaptation agenda" brings together the concerns of poverty reduction and responses to climate change by understanding poverty not in terms of income or in relation to social or economic development but in terms of "vulnerability to climate change." This position has been widely articulated by the international NGOs most actively concerned with the climate change agenda. Tony Jupiter, executive director of Friends of the Earth, argues that, "policies to end poverty in Africa are conceived as if the threat of climatic disruption did not exist."[21] Nicola Saltman, from the World Wide Fund for Nature, similarly feels that, "All the aid we pour into Africa will be inconsequential if we don't tackle climate change."[22] This position is shared by the UK Department for International Development, whose chief scientific adviser, Professor Sir Gordon Conway, states that African poverty reduction strategies have not factored in the burdens of climate change on African capacities. He argues that: "there are three principles for adaptation: 1) Adopt a gradual process of adaptation; 2) Build on disaster preparedness; 3) Develop resilience."[23] The focus of the adaptation agenda puts the emphasis on the lives and survival strategies of Africa's poor. Professor Conway argues that, with this emphasis:

Africa is well prepared to deal with many of the impacts of climate change. Many poor Africans experience severe disasters on an annual or even more frequent basis. This has been true for decades. The challenge is whether we can build on this experience.[24]

The focus on the survival strategies of Africa's poor is central to humanitarian notions of strengthening African "resilience" to climate change. This approach has been contra-posed to development approaches which focus on questions of socio-economic development dependent on the application of higher levels of science and technology and the modernisation of agriculture. As the NGO Working Group on Climate Change report states:

Recently the role of developing new technology has been strongly emphasised [...] There is a consensus among development groups, however, that a greater and more urgent challenge is strengthening communities from the bottom-up, and building on their own coping strategies to live with global warming.[25]

Despite the claims that "good adaptation also makes good development," it would appear that the adaptation to climate change agenda is more like sustained disaster-relief management than a strategy for

African development.[26] In re-describing poverty as "vulnerability to climate change," there is a rejection of aspirations to modernise agriculture, instead there is an emphasis on reinforcing traditional modes of subsistence economy. Rather than development being safeguarded by the modernisation and transformation of African society, underdevelopment is subsidised through the provision of social support for subsistence farming and nomadic pastoralism. Once poverty is redefined as "vulnerability" then the emphasis is on the survival strategies of the poorest and most marginalised, rather than the broader social and economic relations which force them into a marginalised existence. The Working Group argues that community and individual empowerment has to be at the centre of the adaptation agenda:

[I]t has to be about strengthening communities from the bottom up, building on their own coping strategies to live with climate change and empowering them to participate in the development of climate change policies. Identifying what communities are already doing to adapt is an important step towards discovering what people's priorities are and sharing their experiences, obstacles and positive initiatives with other communities and development policy-makers. Giving a voice to people in this way can help to grow confidence, as can valuing their knowledge and placing it alongside science-based knowledge.[27]

African "voices" are central to climate change advocacy as the science of climate change leaves many questions unanswered, particularly with regard to the impact of climate change in Africa.[28] Information to support the urgency of action in this area is often obtained from those in Africa, and is held to have a "deeper" understanding than that which can be provided by "Western" science. For example, the views of Sesophio, a Maasai pastoralist from Tanzania are given prominence in the *Africa— Up in Smoke 2* report:

It is this development, like cars, that is bringing stress to the land, and plastics are being burnt and are filling in the air. We think there is a lot of connection between that and what is happening now with the droughts. If you bring oil and petrol and throw it onto the grass it doesn't grow, so what are all these cars and new innovations doing to a bigger area? Every day diseases are increasing, diseases we haven't seen before.[29]

Climate change advocates patronisingly argue that they are empowering people like Sesophio by "valuing" his knowledge and giving him a "voice" rather than exploiting Sesophio's lack of knowledge about climate change and the fears and concerns generated by his marginal existence.

The focus on the "real lives" of the poorest and most marginalised African communities has gone along with the problematisation of autonomy and the individual choices made by the African poor. The NGO Working Group suggests that the problems of African development lie with the survival strategies of the most marginalised in African society:

To survive the droughts, people have had to resort to practices that damage their dignity and security, their long-term livelihoods, and their environment, including large-scale charcoal production that intensifies deforestation, fighting over water and pastures, selling livestock and dropping out of school.[30]

The view of climate change, rather than underdevelopment, as responsible for poverty, results in an outlook that tends to blame local survival strategies, such as cutting down trees to make some money from selling charcoal. When these views are reflected back to Western advocates, African poor reflect Western views that they are part of the problem:

In nearby Goobato, a village with no cars, no motorcycles, no bicycles, no generators, no televisions, no mobile phones, and dozens of $5 radios, Nour, the village elder, said increased temperatures bake the soil [...] Nour also said villagers share the blame: 'We cut trees just to survive, but we are part of the problem.'[31]

The strategy of adaptation tends to problematise African survival strategies because, by talking up isolated positive examples of adaptation under international aid, it inevitably problematises the real life choices and decisions which African poor have to make. The "adaptation agenda" allows Western governments, international institutions and international NGOs to claim they are doing something positive to address the impact of global warming but the result is that African poor are problematised as responsible for their own problems. "Learning from the poor," "empowering the poor" and strategies to increase their "resilience," end up patronising Africa's poor and supporting an anti-development agenda which would consign Africa to a future of poverty and climate dependency.

Conclusion

The discursive framing of development within the humanitarian paradigm is that of understanding social and economic problems, most sharply posed by the problems of subsistence agriculture in sub-Saharan

Africa, as those of individual lifestyle choices. The framework of engagement is not to see the lack of development as a problem but the institutional framework in which these lifestyle choices are made. "Development as freedom" understands the problems of a lack of development, most clearly highlighted in the dependence on climate stability in sub-Saharan Africa, in terms of the freedom of the individual to make the right choices in response to the external environment. Rather than push for material development, the paradigm of "development as freedom" suggests that the solution lies with the empowerment of individuals and communities and that therefore it is their lack of agency or inability to make the right autonomous choices which is the problem which external humanitarian intervention needs to address. In this respect, the current framing of development solutions seems little different from that of the colonial period, discussed at the start of this chapter, where Britain's mission was not "to alleviate Irish distress but to civilise her people."[32]

20

HUMANITARIAN DIPLOMACY

THE ICRC EXPERIENCE

Fiona Terry

In the early afternoon of 7 April 1994, a vehicle belonging to the International Committee of the Red Cross (ICRC) was stopped at a roadblock in the Rwandan capital, Kigali. The ICRC's then head of delegation, Philippe Gaillard, recalls:

> Drunken government soldiers stopped us and demanded our car. I got out of the vehicle and introduced myself to their commander, who was especially drunk [...] I shook his hand and asked him his name. He refused to give it to me. In situations like that, it is vital not to let on that you are dead scared. You must keep your nerve, look people straight in the eye and find convincing arguments, no matter how you express them [...] I coolly told him that I lived in the same neighbourhood as [...] the Minister of Defence and [...] his chief of staff, and that I would not fail to inform them of their troops' unruly behaviour... The soldier allowed us to pass. I could not get over it; two minutes earlier he had been aiming his machine-gun at my stomach.[1]

And so began one of the most extraordinary episodes in humanitarian diplomacy ever seen. Over the following days and weeks, as the frenzied killings took shape as a planned extermination of the Tutsi minority, Gaillard and his team negotiated an island of humanity in a raging sea of inhumanity: a hospital and ambulance run to treat and transport genocide survivors. There were many more roadblocks during the next three months through which Gaillard would "chat, cajole and plead"[2] passage for ambulances, sometimes having to leave the vehicle and its patients before a murderous militia to cross town and obtain a paper—from the same authorities behind the killing—granting the ICRC safe passage. Maintaining contact with everyone was at the core of Gaillard's strategy—leaders of the Interahamwe militias, the Rwandan Armed Forces, the Rwandan Patriotic Front and the announcers of Radio Mille Collines who incited the masses to murder. "Dialogue was the cornerstone of our security," Gaillard said, "more important than protective vehicles or bullet-proof vests which are signs of fear and aggression."[3]

Such dialogue, in Rwanda and elsewhere, is made possible by the ICRC's adherence to several interrelated principles and practices in its humanitarian operations. The actors with whom the ICRC negotiates for respect of humanitarian laws and norms are extremely varied and require a myriad of different approaches. For certain activities, such as visits to detainees, the ICRC negotiates explicit agreements with senior officials before beginning to ensure that its delegates are permitted to talk privately with those at risk of disappearance and ill-treatment, and to inspect all areas of the detention facility. For other activities, such as distributing food or seeds to a farming community, implicit deals are struck with elders and those with guns along the road over the safety of staff and supplies travelling through: relief will cease if personnel or property are harmed or prevented from reaching their destination. And many discussions launched by ICRC delegates involve no deal at all, simply an attempt to persuade fighters, on the basis of arguments that resonate in their local context, to treat captured enemies with dignity, cease recruiting child soldiers or spare civilian lives and property in territory held by the opposing side.

This chapter explores some of the ideas and strategies behind these various types of dialogue and negotiation in which the ICRC engages. The ICRC's broad mandate to protect and assist victims of armed conflict is inscribed in international law, which, together with its reputation, lends its presence in a country or prison a particularly affirming quality. This can work in the organisation's favour if the authorities seek to enhance their international image as behaving responsibly. But this status also bestows particular responsibility on the ICRC to ensure that what it is able to achieve in the humanitarian field is balanced by, or preferably outweighs, the benefits its presence accrues to those in positions of authority.

Neutrality as an over-arching strategy

Neutrality is a fundamental principle of the Red Cross movement, yet is more akin to a strategy than to a principle that must be upheld as an end in itself. A neutral stance in conflict has no intrinsic moral value; indeed it would be reprehensible to remain neutral between genocidal killers and their victims. Instead, neutrality has a practical purpose: as the wording of the principle explicitly states, the Red Cross does not take sides in hostilities or engage in controversies "to enjoy the confidence of all." By being perceived as unbiased towards adversaries, the ICRC aims to gain their trust and acceptance so that they allow the organisation to operate effectively and safely in the territory they control. By consistently considering how words and actions might influence perceptions of neutrality, the ICRC tries to avoid giving belligerents a pretext to refuse, block or hinder its work and opens space for dialogue. And by continuing to speak with everyone, not only to the "good side," the ICRC strives to reach all those in need of humanitarian assistance on whichever side of a front line they may be found.

The continued pertinence of neutrality as a strategy to guide humanitarian action was thoroughly tested in Afghanistan since the US invasion of 2001. Neutrality was derided as "old-fashioned" and even morally contestable by many actors, and most aid agencies abandoned a neutral approach, directing their aid in accordance with the political priorities of the Coalition forces and Karzai regime.[4] The killing of an ICRC delegate in Afghanistan in 2003 because of what he symbolised as a "westerner," seemed to underscore the difficulty of being accepted as neutral, particularly as his murder was ordered and carried out by two men familiar with the ICRC—both wore an ICRC prosthesis on one leg. But rather than cede to the pressure to work only in government-held areas, the ICRC sought more engagement with the Taliban, to understand both why this had occurred and how to regain the acceptance necessary to assist Afghans in opposition-held zones. Through innovative and sometimes risky strategies, touched on below, the ICRC slowly expanded its contacts and dialogue with the Taliban and other opposition groups, which has permitted it to operate in areas of great need, such as Helmand and Kandahar Provinces, without coming under attack. As the insurgency expands, many other aid organisations are having to scale back or withdraw from areas of the south, east and north, putting a stop to the activities they gave up their independence and neutrality to implement. Now many are rethinking their approach and wondering how they can realign their actions to avoid being seen as part of the Western-driven agenda.

The ICRC's active pursuit of dialogue with all sides also reaped results in the Libyan conflict more quickly than anyone had anticipated. Having never had a solid presence in the country, the ICRC had to build a network of contacts from scratch once the war broke out. It mounted an emergency response to the fighting in the eastern port city of Benghazi in February, while simultaneously reaching out to Libyans still reporting to Gaddafi's regime in different embassies around the world. These contacts helped the ICRC to enter Tripoli in April, and the ICRC successfully negotiated a memorandum of understanding on its role as a neutral intermediary in the conflict. The ICRC was active on both sides, providing medical and other assistance to those affected by the fighting as well as visiting Gaddafi forces held by the opposition, and opposition fighters held by the regime. These achievements further reinforce the continued pertinence of neutrality as a strategy in today's conflicts.

Credibility and effectiveness

Holding dialogue with all sides is an important first step in negotiating humanitarian space, but the ICRC has long recognised that words and promises are not enough: aid organisations must have something concrete to offer to gain acceptance within the broader community. The difficulty lies in overcoming a Catch-22 in many contexts, in which security guarantees depend upon the effectiveness of operations, yet the ability to operate depends upon security guarantees. The ICRC's broad range of assistance activities (in health, water, nutrition, livestock, agriculture, micro-economic support and orthopaedics) allows it to tailor assistance to the needs of different communities and show the tangible benefits to all sides of having a neutral intermediary in conflict. In

Afghanistan, for instance, first-aid training courses for Taliban and police alike has met a pressing need to stabilise the wounded before evacuation to hospital whilst simultaneously providing a forum in which to discuss essential principles of international humanitarian law (IHL), such as respecting the red cross emblem—even when on a military heli-copter—or the right of wounded combatants to receive medical assis-tance. Providing drugs and materials to medics in opposition-controlled regions and delivering Red Cross messages to families of suspected Taliban detained by government or Coalition forces eased the suffering of many Afghans while opening channels of communication with fight-ers who would have otherwise remained inaccessible. Although govern-ment officials were initially reluctant to see the ICRC engage with the opposition, they also soon realised that it was useful to have an interme-diary to facilitate the release of hostages; gain security guarantees for Ministry of Health staff to undertake polio vaccinations in opposition-held areas; and repatriate the mortal remains of dead policemen from behind enemy lines so that they might have a proper burial in accor-dance with Islamic customs.

The ICRC's assistance activities also facilitated its acceptance in the Darfur region of Sudan where it had little exposure before the outbreak of conflict in 2003. Once Khartoum allowed aid agencies access to the region in 2004, the ICRC established camps for those displaced by Khartoum's brutal counter-insurgency campaign and met their immedi-ate needs. But once other aid organisations arrived, the ICRC handed over responsibility for the camps and commenced food distributions to outlying villages in order to prevent further displacement of farmers. By also assisting pastoralist communities with repairs to water sources and livestock vaccinations, the ICRC countered the simplistic stereotype prevalent within the media and aid community that cast all Arab nomads as "janjaweed militias" responsible for the atrocities committed. This gained the ICRC respect in the eyes of Arab groups, reduced secu-rity threats and permitted the ICRC to reach outlying villages without exacerbating tensions among the various communities.

Sometimes the breadth of the ICRC's mandate, however, can lead to difficult trade-offs between competing objectives. While providing assis-tance often opens avenues for discussion of protection issues, sometimes a choice must be made between the two. The government in Khartoum, for instance, has never opened its prisons to the ICRC's scrutiny, despite requests over many years to do so and the benefit its own soldiers gained by being registered and followed-up by the ICRC when held by opposing forces in the south or in Darfur. Yet the ICRC has not insisted on this important part of its work for the sake of retaining sufficiently good relations with Khartoum to ensure continued visas and authorisations for operations in Darfur, the south and in the east. The ICRC had to weigh up the gravity of the needs in conflict zones versus prisons and the likelihood of addressing them in each, against the potential cost of antagonising this difficult regime. It chose to prioritise assistance to Darfur—which continued to include visiting Sudanese government troops held by opposition groups and delivering Red Cross messages to their families.

The success of negotiations depends greatly on an organisation's credibility, and the ICRC puts considerable effort into ensuring delegates are well informed about who's who in the structure of armed groups and governments to ensure that concerns and requests are directed to the appropriate level of the hierarchy.[5] Delegations conduct extensive analysis with local specialists to identify those with a stake in the conflict, and listen to the beliefs and grievances expressed by all sides in order to adapt the organisation's arguments accordingly. ICRC delegates are pragmatic in their approach, using sophisticated legal argument when dealing with, for instance, the Israeli Defence Forces, while appealing to a sense of community spirit and honour when dealing with armed groups in a favela of Brazil. They adapt their arguments to their audience but avoid being seen to "renegotiate" or soften international standards when faced with cultural relativism. The standards remain applicable in all circumstances: the challenge is to find an argument which will put an interlocutor on the path to respecting them.[6]

Balancing confidentiality with transparency

The ICRC follows two seemingly contradictory policies to maximise its powers of negotiation in the field: transparency and confidentiality. The practice is encapsulated in the maxim learned by all new delegates, "the ICRC says what it does but not what it sees." In other words, the ICRC strives to be transparent and consistent in what it does so as to be predictable, while at the same time treating its findings confidentially so that these may be raised bilaterally with the relevant authorities without the risk of manipulation and politicisation that may arise when aired more broadly, particularly in the public domain. Officials tend to be more open in their dialogue about constraints to improving standards or admitting to violations of international law when they have confidence that their statements will not make the news the following day, or be used against them some time in the future. For this reason, the ICRC has negotiated immunity from testifying before the International Criminal Court in spite of its support for this mechanism of international justice. It cannot be made to handover evidence it collected whilst carrying out its humanitarian work so as to protect its ability to enter frank discussions with victims and perpetrators of abuses alike.

Over the last decade or so, the ICRC has placed increased importance on being actively transparent in its motives and methods. Whereas the organisation once pursued a top-down, rather elitist approach, assuming that agreements signed with national authorities would flow down to the local level, it now engages all levels of the hierarchy, religious and community leaders, militias and other armed groups, delivering the same consistent message to each in order to allay suspicions about its activities before they take hold. This approach has helped the ICRC to weather many storms, such as in 2008 over the indictment of Sudanese President Bashir by the International Criminal Court. By proactively addressing the issue with a wide array of players throughout Sudan, the ICRC succeeded in explaining its support for the Court's efforts to judge IHL violations without being expelled from the country.

The ICRC's policy of confidentiality has given rise to controversy, particularly following incidents like that of prisoner abuse in Abu Ghraib prison in Iraq in 2004, about which the ICRC knew much but said little publicly. It was only once an ICRC confidential report to the US authorities was leaked to the media by someone from within the US administration,[7] coupled with graphic photographs taken by the abusers themselves, that the issue captured the media spotlight. The ICRC was sharply criticised, particularly in the Arab world, for having failed to publicly denounce the crimes committed. But such criticism is premised on two assumptions that warrant questioning, especially in light of the Wikileaks phenomenon which is premised on the general public's "right to know."

First, there is a tendency in this age of constant noise, to assume that if something is not mentioned in the media, then it is not happening. It is true that a statement saying that an issue "is being dealt with behind closed doors" can ring hollow and raise suspicion that nothing is being done. But it is equally true that news of successful closed-door negotiations are not provided to the media either. The ICRC archives, by contrast, contain thousands of instances where confidential dialogue has improved conditions of detention; lead to the release of prisoners on humanitarian grounds; curbed abuses by armed forces; and gained access to people in vital need of assistance. What is less clear in the case of Abu Ghraib and others is how long the ICRC waits for improvements to occur before it raises the stakes, and whether it would be prepared to jeopardise its access to other prisons in Iraq (and potentially other sites of US detention) to expose what was going on in Abu Ghraib.

Second, public exposure of an issue is sometimes viewed by the public and aid community as an end in itself—whether or not it leads to improvements—rather than as one of several ways to influence behaviour. Sometimes a combination of public exposure and dialogue reaps results, with public statements by one actor complementing the ICRC's bilateral dialogue. When dialogue is unsuccessful, the ICRC sometimes tries to mobilise third parties to raise vital issues in their discussions with the perpetrator. Public denunciation is a last resort, once other strategies to pressure for change have failed or run their course. It is not entered into lightly since it can have adverse consequences for the victims—either directly as punishment or indirectly if the ICRC is prevented from continuing its work—and is likely to tarnish the ICRC's reputation for confidentiality in other parts of the world, giving other regimes reason to restrict the ICRC's access to prisons or troubled regions. All these considerations must be weighed against the unpredictable impact of public criticism.

Nevertheless, confidentiality is part of a deal that the ICRC strikes with authorities and as such is not unconditional.[8] If the other party does not adhere to its side of the bargain, by failing to make progress on any of the issues raised, or entering dialogue in bad faith, then the ICRC will consider raising its concerns publicly. This was the case in Myanmar in 2007, when the organisation denounced at a press conference the major and repeated violations of international humanitarian law by the military regime.[9] For several years prior to this, the ICRC had enjoyed relatively good cooperation with the junta, which had opened its prisons, labour camps and conflict-affected border regions to ICRC scrutiny. But an internal purge in October 2004 ousted Prime Minister Khin Nyunt in favour of hardliners who sought to curb the "interference" by international organisations. Access and dialogue ceased or made no headway on serious issues such as the army's use of detainees as porters and the suffering inflicted by the military on civilians in conflict-affected areas. After efforts to mobilise Myanmar's allies to influence the regime failed, the ICRC felt that it owed it to the detainees with whom it spoke to halt the charade. With few illusions that public condemnation would improve conditions in this authoritarian state, the ICRC nevertheless broke with its tradition of confidentiality and brought its criticism out in public.

While this act of defiance showed that the ICRC was not prepared to be a silent witness to what was occurring, the Myanmar case raises more questions than it answers. Why Myanmar and not Zimbabwe, Algeria, North Korea, Syria or Kashmir where the ICRC faces similar stonewalling and impediments to its actions? Is there criteria for public criticism which is applied consistently to all countries, democratic and non-democratic alike? What progress is the ICRC making in visiting Chinese or Turkish prisons, and what is the quality of dialogue in the Russian Federation? Would these issues warrant public exposure? Do concerns about donor funding curb public criticisms of major contributing nations? And is it only once access is denied and the ICRC has nothing more to lose that it will go public with its concerns?

The answers to these questions are far from clear. The ICRC is present in many countries where it is unable to fulfil its core mandate yet seems to have no clear bottom line for how long it will remain against the progress achieved. How long can the ICRC justify "being present" with the kudos this unavoidably bestows on a regime, in the hope of doing more? Is a "foot-in-the-door" really crucial to access in the event of a life-threatening event? Both Libya and Darfur suggest not.

The North Korean context brings these questions into stark relief. For many years the ICRC has run an orthopaedic project there, which no doubt meets some needs in this impoverished, authoritarian state but certainly not the most pressing ones. Its presence does, however, permit the ICRC to keep a finger on the pulse and build relationships with future expansion of activities in mind. The strategy recently met with some success: after years of patient operations and six months of solid negotiations, the ICRC signed an agreement in early 2011 to assist three hospitals with high rates of amputations. This is an achievement of sorts in this tightly closed country, particularly as 70 per cent of patients treated at one of the hospitals sustained injuries in the nearby coal mines and are thus unlikely to belong to the privileged class.

But these small successes do not change the fact that there is no dialogue possible with the North Korean regime and that the ICRC, like all other international organisations, is controlled in everything it does and sees. There is no possibility of having non-monitored contact with ordinary North Korean citizens or to know what is occurring elsewhere in the country. As long as there is no major crisis, this relationship-building (if genuinely possible) might have some merit in allowing for a gradual expansion of activities over the long term. But what if another famine occurs, like that of the late 1990s, when aid organisations were present in the country but only allowed to assist those deemed worthy of life by the regime in Pyongyang? Can a humanitarian organisation accept to assist some but not others, particularly when the "others" are those most in need? Will the ICRC continue its orthopaedic programme and support to select hospitals if it cannot successfully negotiate permission to assist people starving elsewhere in the country? Or will it draw the line and try to bring international pressure (for what it is worth) to bear on the regime to allow aid organisations to help those most in need? Ought it stay in the country to have "a-foot-in-the-door" and a shot at good relations with the government or refuse to engage with a regime which shows such contempt for the values on which humanitarian action is based? The ICRC does not seem to have clear answers to these questions.

Conclusion

Having a mandate bestowed by states and an official role as guardian of international humanitarian law, the ICRC has a unique set of factors to consider when entering into negotiations. All its activities are directed towards protecting the safety and dignity of victims of conflict and other violence, but these extend from the level of individual care on the ground, right up to developing the laws of armed conflict in high-level conferences attended by representatives of every state in the world. Hence it needs to take into account the implications of its actions and statements at every level from the local context to the world stage. Public criticism of the actions of a particular regime might be the most morally-sound course of action but not necessarily the best strategic one if it provokes rejection of the ICRC's attempts to assist victims of conflict in neighbouring states, or sabotages the ICRC's attempts to get certain states to ratify important laws. The ICRC must navigate a path through the competing demands and expectations of victims, state and non-state armed actors and the political forces that control them, while striving to minimise the manipulation and instrumentalisation of the ICRC's actions for political purposes.

While many aid organisations pay lip-service to the importance of humanitarian principles to guide their practice, the ICRC is adamant that these principles are the best framework that it has for negotiating access to those in need of humanitarian assistance. Each situation is unique yet adhering to some key principles and practices helps to provide consistency and coherence to the choices made, and builds confidence, even under the harshest of circumstances. Philippe Gaillard's courage during the Rwandan genocide was extraordinary, but his negotiation strategy was not—it followed the ICRC's standard ways of working to create understanding and acceptance of the ICRC's actions in every context. The team's defiant humanitarian spirit opposed the logic of genocide and even inspired some killers to stop. Before fleeing the city when they knew they were defeated, some militiamen brought a Tutsi nurse they had held captive for the last three months to the hospital to release her. "We have decided not to kill her despite the fact that she is a Tutsi," they said to Gaillard, "as a nurse she will be more useful in your hospital than dead."

21

ON "OPENING" HUMANITARIAN DIPLOMACY

A DIALECTIC SPACE

Michele Acuto

Negotiating relief is a practice of tremendous complexity and Byzantine political effects. Yet this should neither deter solid scholarly analysis nor should it prompt us, both in academia and practice, to keep away from opening humanitarian spaces. Ultimately, I hope, the collection stands as testament that there is much to be learnt from a careful and critical unpacking of this often oversimplified field of world affairs. This is because many commentators, wary that this move might unseal the mythical Pandora's box (or the more proverbial "can of worms"), still steer clear of such a critical quest and find refuge in more cautious thematic or managerial examinations. Seeking to redress some of this risky circumspection, the authors gathered in this book have therefore ventured through the "dialectics" of humanitarian spaces. Focusing on the negotiated nature of these geographies, the contributors have presented us with several critical investigations of the contradictions of humanitarian aid. However, if the classical and Hegelian arts of dialectical reasoning aim at discovering an ultimate synthesis of apparent oppositions, our effort here has certainly been more modest and wary of the "fragility of truths" in the "diplomatic" synthesis of humanitarianism and international politics.[1] Rather than aiming at an ultimate rejoinder on the condition of humanitarianism and its negotiations, the collection has therefore attempted to unveil the complex bundle of often contrasting processes that underpin them, and the wide ranks of those who engage in the spaces they create. I believe that the lesson one could draw from this quest is that, when we look more closely to its core dynamics, we are reminded that humanitarianism is a fundamentally social undertaking. While this assumption might in general represent a commonplace truism in both field and academia, little critical analysis and (not least) praxis conscious of its inherent "socialisations" is available to scholars and humanitarians.

To prevent these limits we might be required to "open" humanitarian spaces that too often stand "black boxed" in the midst of wider considerations on humanitarianism and scrutinise the human geography that sustains them.[2] Here the utility of considering the overlaps and frictions between humanitarianism and political negotiations have provided us with a charted course to find our ways into such complexity, without shielding off from its most thorny challenges. Looking back at the major lessons from the previous four parts, I therefore attempt to offer some preliminary thoughts learnt from opening humanitarian spaces, both theoretically and practically, and the possible pathways that the many authors gathered in the collection have pointed at. Far from representing a definitive primer on the practice of humanitarian diplomacy, this chapter more modestly aims at presenting a summary of their manifold responses to the three queries set up in the introduction, thus flagging some unappreciated areas of inquiry which could open further paths for both practice and research. Scrutinising the themes raised in the collection and taking into account these authors' experiences in the field, this last commentary seeks to provide some preliminary conclusions that look forward to prompt more critical and practice-oriented understandings of humanitarianism, its spaces and its negotiations.

Investigating humanitarian negotiation and its social nature

It might be convenient, at least for analytical purposes, to think of the diplomatic role of humanitarianism as a practice of engagement and mediation both among humanitarian actors, whatever their nature might be, and more crucially between these and other political entities capable of defining (but not necessarily being situated in) their field of action. We can then start here from the problem of unpacking what the phrase "humanitarian space" actually means, and what sort of geographies it charts. Certainly, across the collection there seems to be an almost universal agreement on what we might call the "materiality" of humanitarian spaces. Examples abound: from the deployment grounds of UNAMID in Sudan, to the food distribution shelters of the Mother Theresa Society in Kosovo, to the extensive livelihood support system in the wake of the 2004 tsunami—almost all of the authors have reminded us of how real the spaces of humanitarianism are. Yet there is another facet to this assessment, which might at times remain implicit in the authors' narrative, that is no less "real" and tangible.[3] It is the social dimension of these practices that also emerges loudly from the collection's analyses, whether they are concerned with illustrating the cross-boundaries' echoes of humanitarian crises, as in Bleiker, Hutchinson and Campbell's emotional responses; Weissman's legal quandaries or Donini and Chandler's concerns with Western subjugation; or with highlighting the socio-political construction of the contexts for relief, as in Mills's pyramidal take on space; or in Hyndman's dual disasters. Humanitarian spaces are therefore also, if not predominantly, social spaces: they are crafted, negotiated, challenged and recast not just in the sand and tents of refugee camps, but also in the words and deeds of humanitarians and in their relations with both locals and wider audiences far beyond the specific crisis.[4] This understanding, however, presupposes an emphasis on relationships over substances, and a mutually constitutive link among the social and the physical aspects of such spaces. In fact, as noted by Jose Albala-Bertrand, "attention to issues related to the social structure and dynamics of countries under emergency seems unavoidable for understanding conflict and induced emergencies" and, conversely, elaborating solutions to these.[5]

In this sense, when we see humanitarian spaces as socially-constructed (and thus negotiated) environments where the delivery of relief takes place, we might find some analytical "relief" in the distinction that British geographer Kevin Cox drew between spaces "of engagement" and "of dependence,"[6] Cox sought to elaborate a "dialectic duo" capable of underlying the contingent localising and globalising nature of social relations across space, and cope with the increasing complexity of a networked society, to differentiate the transitory and fluid essence of certain "engagements" from the institutionalised structures on which many depend. Accordingly "spaces of dependence" represent "those more-or-less localised social relations upon which we depend for the realisation of essential interests and for which there are no substitutes elsewhere; they define place-specific conditions for our material well-being and our sense of significance."[7] In humanitarian crises, traditional dependences such as those of states or of tribal and kinship support systems tend to break down, fail or even turn against those who depend on them, as we have respectively seen in the cases of Somalia, Aceh and Kosovo. These, however, can coexist with other socially-constituted political engagements which represent, in Cox's terms, the "space in which the politics of securing a space of dependence occurs."[8] These latter are the milieux where political engagements take place, which are constructed through networks of associations that might be more or less stable, more or less ad hoc, and certainly more or less confrontational, but that all commonly represent a social setting that is constituted beyond the boundaries of the status quo in order to reinforce this latter, or contest it, or even seek to create new dependences. Moreover, as engagements become institutionalised and their presence becomes rooted in society, they can themselves become dependences, as the long-lived system of refugee camps in the Middle East, or many relief systems set up in protracted crises such as Somalia might aptly demonstrate. Seen as engagements, humanitarian spaces underline once again the exceptionality and precariousness of the humanitarian enterprise, its mediated character and its necessary relation with pre-existent socio-political structures (like states, tribes, market institutions or colonial subjugations) upon which people have depended for far longer than humanitarians are often willing to admit.

A changing political geography

Humanitarian spaces, seen as social spaces, are not just embodied in the material divisions created in the field, but also transcend them. This take delineates a geography of humanitarian affairs as equally ordered by the relief actors' relations with each other and with those in need, depicting an image of a global society that surpasses traditional state boundaries, which is at the same time deeply embedded in the physical manifestations through which these are concretised. As such, the operational environments within which humanitarians operate are not solely forged by them, but are also products of both "external" and "internal" pressures. Exogenously, determinants like international audiences and media (in Bleiker, Hutchinson and Campbell's, as well as Schuller's cases), or global political processes (like the R2P institutionalisation noted by Bellamy and Foley), pull the geography of humanitarian spaces transnationally, eroding its localised boundaries and extending its porosity for a multiplicity of foreign actors. Endogenously, forces like individual and societal claims (as narrated by Mills or Jayawickrama, O'Keefe and O'Brien), as much as a large array of governmental and quasi-governmental actors (as in Menkhaus or Chandler's analyses), push for a redefinition and levelling of the localised playing ground of humanitarianism, producing much more complicated geopolitics than the idealistic relief-giver/aid-taker divide could ever illustrate. The spaces that we have encountered in the collection are thus not only situated in areas on our world political atlases, like Darfur and Aceh, but also situated practices linking people across multiple geographies, as in the cases of the networks of Muslim solidarity mapped by Petersen or the problematic Western-centric relief-crisis links unravelled by Donini. In short, the geography on which humanitarian diplomacy stands, and indeed in which it unravels its negotiations, is a far messier landscape whose multiple determinants should not be overlooked by one-way accounts. These spaces exist and evolve as a plurality of actors interact both in and off the "field" where, at the same time, pre-existent political geographies also add to such mutating complexity.

In this sense, we could stipulate here "humanitarian diplomacy" as all of those negotiations that deal with access for relief purposes, whether they are concerned with establishing maintaining, extending, or modifying such access. Like several of the authors of this collection remind us, the problem is not so much one of identifying these mediations, but rather to recognise their limits as well as to define what counts as "access" or, even more broadly, as "humanitarian." To put it simply, if the fields of diplomacy and humanitarianism have been both expanding and mutating, then the real crux of the matter will be to find where the two overlap at present. The question of who "humanitarian diplomats" are and what counts for "humanitarian diplomacy" is thus a basic problem that set the course of many contributors in this book. Yet this endeavour needs to be more effectively situated in the socialised nature of the geography of humanitarianism to provide us with a useful analysis for practitioners and scholars.

Highlighting the "ocial" does, however, not equate, assuming that the material aspects of humanitarianism are irrelevant, as the chapters by Weiss or Davies remind us. To think of humanitarian spaces without taking into account the social structures that underpin them, and the capacity for humanitarian agency that can shape them, is to miss much of the whole gamut of humanitarian experience as embedded in the social context where humanitarianism takes place. It is this overlooked aspect, several of the authors argued, which gives us a truly holistic snapshot of the manifold dynamics of humanitarianism as a precarious, shapeshifting and heterogenous world. In such a complex landscape, as many of the contributors pointed out, the role of humanitarian negotia-tion is an increasingly valuable one. Diplomacy offers key tools to open spaces both within the localised contexts of crisis, as Terry's Rwandan example shows us, as well as in their globalising world political echoes, as for instance in Bellamy's international confrontations around the Responsibility to Protect. Most crucially, diplomacy is often an indis-pensable forte required to cope with the intricacies of humanitarian emergencies for all of those that seek to forge and maintain spaces that provide vital connections, which often means medical aid, protection and, more generally, survival in exceptional times for tens of thousands. Nonetheless, as the volume has repeatedly hinted at from Maley's intro-duction, to Zeccola and Mankhaus's cases, humanitarian negotiation itself is an intricate enterprise.

To begin with, most of the accounts reported here confirm that the genus of humanitarian diplomats is expanding: if traditional players in the field, such as the ICRC or the UN, still dominate much of the scene, there is a quite evident tendency towards a proliferation in the genus of humanitarian actors and institutions. Yet it is not so much in the enlarge-ment of the cohorts of those providing, or seeking to provide, relief in crisis situations that the most challenging trend can be found. Arguably, this consideration is nothing short of representing a truism across all literature and policy writing, as the majority of analysts (and indeed near totality of contributors here) would agree on such growth of the humani-tarian enterprise. Scholars and practitioners might in this sense better focus now on the oft-overlooked corollary of this issue: it is perhaps in the almost unavoidable confrontation between a multiplicity of diverse actors that the greatest test for the endurance of the whole field might play out. All of this presents an obvious challenge to diplomatic practice and, more specifically, to the stability and functionality of the humanitarian system: the basic frames, institutions and norms on which these are based are strained, if not called into question, by the mounting variety of engagements that shape today's humanitarian spaces.

Humanitarian government officials, either voluntarily or forcefully, are for instance called upon to partake in a mounting variety of "hybrid" diplomatic engagements, where they are required to undertake "polylateral" negotiation with players that, at least legally, might not be "like units."[9] While this has long been true for agencies engaging "local" sub-state actors like rebel groups or autochthonous NGOs, fairly similar dynamics are unfolding today among the "humanitarians" themselves, as a quick glance at any recent relief coordination meeting such as those in the wake of the 2004 tsunami might evince.[10] At the same time, the "playing field" is not solely levelled, but also recast in its political geography by the contemporaneous initiative of these "non-traditional" actors, which in turn develop alternative socio-political structures complicating the nature and extent of humanitarian spaces.

This growing "architectural" complexity is confirmed by what might be considered as the key geopolitical dynamic that has been underpinning the humanitarian enterprise in the past few decades. In the past the so-called "classic" (the ICRC model) humanitarianism, via its Dunantist principles, originally took a depoliticised stance on aid in order to acquire legitimate space for relief where it could act rapidly as a palliative to "halt" emergencies and assist those harmed by these. However, this original space for action has, according to many, narrowed since the field went through the crises of the 1990s, aligned itself more explicitly with international political processes and has had to be rethought along post-Cold War lines.[11] As a corollary, several new approaches to relief have argued in favour of acquiring these spaces by themselves, an undertaking that mostly took shape through armed interventions, a "militarisation" of NGOs from within, and more and more frequent civil-military cooperation.[12] These political entanglements to protect aid workers are, however, progressively seen as either unavoidable or tantamount to "humanitarian war," an oxymoron which according to many may have become a dangerous reality in a number of cases from Kosovo to Libya.[13] Protection, rather than assistance, becomes in these views, as well as in the eyes of its many critics, the key matter of humanitarianism, overshadowing all the activities of the "old" approach with the necessities of the "new" context. This practical and conceptual evolution can be deceptive because, as several commentators underlined, it might provide a translation of an old dilemma into a potentially confusing new terminology, and thus not eliminating the problem but possibly renaming it in what Eric Dachy called a "variation on a misleading theme."[14] Likewise, it can overshadow the fact that what is often labelled as "old" is as actual and well-rooted in today's humanitarian spaces that the deceptively "new" forms of relief: the ICRC, for instance, has adapted well to the socio-political earthquakes of the 1990s and of 9/11, and much of the same could be argued for several key Islamic aid organisations. Likewise, "new" actors such as transnational campaigns are not solely relying on innovative tools to cement their global relief agency.

In terms of the overall geopolitical architecture of the humanitarian enterprise, this means a "shrinking" of humanitarian space only if this latter is taken as absolutely incompatible with politics.[15] On the contrary, as we have seen in many chapters, there is much political activity in today's spaces of humanitarianism, whether in the form of negotiation or in the shape of the essential context "humanitarians" have to deal with. A majority of chapters seem to agree then, albeit with at times differing motivations, that is indeed the case and that humanitarianism, whether political or not, is increasingly entangled in the dynamics of world politics.[16] So, if the desirability of political action on behalf of "humanitarians" remains the crux of a well-rehearsed debate that shapes much of the background to the authors' work, there is an almost cross-cutting consensus here that the spaces of the humanitarian enterprise have become inherently political.

Besides, this also points us towards the inevitable fact that "reductionist" views of humanitarianism as necessarily dissociated from politics (nowadays a minority, I would argue) tend to be blind to evident fact that, as the cases and critiques collected here evince, there are far more determinants to humanitarian space than just humanitarianism. As Collinson noted in Part I, the humanitarian system is not in any way unitary or cohesive as it showcases a growing and multiplex structure populated by a Gordian array of actors. In this sense, the international

266

system that upholds the humanitarian enterprise might, quite like that of global environmental governance, be expanding into an increasingly prolific "aggregate'" dimension which stands partly as an alternative and partly as a complement to the core norms and institutions of the system (such as the UN family, the Inter-Agency Standing Committee or the Sphere standards).[17] This complex policy realm is mostly clustered around the core international processes and is principally pinpointed on this latter's hybridisation with non-governmental entities that are no longer just occupying advocacy roles "on the side" of the multilateral world, but also carrying out key implementation and adaptation tasks. This is not just the world of growingly central NGOs such as Oxfam or MSF, but also that of a vast landscape of smaller but progressively active organisms, not all "humanitarian" by mandate or definition, which populate humanitarian spaces. Moreover, this not only covers the actual provision of aid, but also all of its ancillary activities, extending into financing or protection to aid workers.[18]

This, as justly underlined by Hubert and Brassard-Boudreau, as well as several other authors henceforth, means that we should debunk myths that see humanitarian spaces as "shrinking." Rather, what is perceived by restriction by some, might on the contrary represent an extension in reach for others. Spaces of humanitarianism have been broadened in aggregate but this should not be taken (as in the so common eulogistic sense) to mean that humanitarianism has per se improved. Rather such a transition to more polylateral relations, more pervasive linkages between situated crisis contexts and places and societies far beyond these, as well as more complex political architectures upholding the whole humanitarian machinery, epitomises a widening in the social reach of humanitarianism and its practitioners. This, in practical terms, equates an expansion in the geography of humanitarianism, and thus a clarion call on the importance of navigating, politically as much as logistically, the complexity of this field. Not surprisingly this is mirrored in several calls for pragmatism in the face of growing complexity and mounting need for coherence in the field. As David Rieff put it as early as 1997: "perhaps, after a long period of untrammelled growth, aid agencies now need to take a more cautious approach, and realistically reassess what they can and cannot accomplish."[19] Yet this might not be unique of humanitarianism: a large cohort of international practitioners and students alike have also been pushing towards a more down-to-earth practical approach to, borrowing James Der Derian's popular definition, "mediating the estrangement" among peoples, and thus actors that construct links and networks that, whether temporary or not, in turn create contexts for engagements such as humanitarian spaces.[20] Confronted with such a complex scenario, humanitarian diplomacy becomes, at least in my view, a prime instrument to navigate the intricacies of humanitarian spaces worldwide.

Diplomacy, after all

The move towards a more geopolitically complex humanitarian world is not just a structural one. This transformation also feeds back into the evolution in the diplomatic nature of humanitarian actors, which are consequently prompted to devise the new and polylateral negotiating strategies noted above. As such, humanitarian practitioners and analysts need a more nuanced understanding of the negotiated dynamics that are shaping the field. Twenty-first century humanitarian mediators, and those who study them, therefore have to adapt to a context where the diplomatic practice is changing substantially, whilst the quest to mould new methods of engagement has also been taken on by non-state organisations and even private actors.[21] As tensions mount in the realm of world politics, an increasing spectrum of participants begin to voice their personal interests and lobby for their own solutions to be put on the negotiating table. This analytical shift, then, pushes both scholars and activists to acquire an appreciation towards both developing a diplomatic "understanding" of the humanitarian enterprise, as well as consciousness of the diplomatic "thinking" that underpins this latter's spaces. As Paul Sharp argued:

A *diplomatic understanding* emphasises the extent to which the world is always in flux and how the struggles to be represented in it are ongoing. *Diplomatic thinking* suggests ways in which broadly peaceful relations can be conducted even in the midst of these struggles and in the absence of any final resolution in them.[22]

A critical sensibility towards the context and corpus of diplomacy thus allows us to focus "on how [political] relations are maintained between identities that are continuously under construction in conditions that, if not anarchic, are characterised by very thin social contexts."[23] In this view, the focus of the collection on "diplomacy" broadly understood allowed many of the authors to put particular emphasis on relations, power structures and social connections. This progressive or "new" view of diplomacy, mostly derived through an ontology of practice and a study of the qualitative dimensions of negotiation, allows us to scrutinise the dynamics that take place in a practice of politics particularly focused on interaction, mutual constitution and social relations.[24]

In this sense, what we can also learn from several of the analyses above is the essentially shared and negotiated nature of humanitarian space: what often remains overshadowed in the considerations on the "widening" or "shrinking" of the environment in which humanitarians operate is the inevitable participation of a multiplicity of actors and factors linked through a plurality of scales. Yet, there remains, not least due to the field's heavy dependence on the superstructures of world politics, a reliance on top-down interventions from an "outsider" intervention towards the "endangered" local—a dynamic that of course presents several practical (if not ethical) concerns. From a diplomatic viewpoint, locals are actively engaged in the production of aid delivery mechanisms and the spatialisation of the humanitarian enterprise. As such, as we learn from Part III of the collection, the dynamics extending this field are not solely exogenous impositions but also processes that are born deep into the interaction between the agents of the humanitarian enterprise and those who mediate its linkages with world affairs more generally. On the contrary, the leitmotif of aid workers today is often represented by commercial and diplomatic jargon: humanitarianism, referred to as "industry," is concerned about getting "deliverables" to "clients," often forgetting that the "targets" of the relief are people like those who decide to dispense them "charitable" aid.[25]

An understanding of the negotiated nature of the social relations "spatialising" humanitarianism is fundamental because it prompts three critical moves towards a better "diplomatic thinking" on the contemporary practice of relief.[26] First, the inherent precariousness of the humanitarian enterprise, entangled in ever-changing and often very sudden crises as well as characterised by a multifaceted need to link with a plurality of political-economic structures that define the spaces in which it operates, certainly begs for a tactful and prudent management of relations in the field, as well as beyond. Second, by engaging diplomatically with the mounting genus of actors (humanitarian and not) in the field, humanitarians can effectively manage the heterogeneous nature that presently characterises the field without having to give away their essential nature. Third, humanitarians need "diplomatic" approaches in order to cope with the shifting boundaries of the operational environments in which they act by producing temporary spaces of engagement.

Humanitarian diplomacy, in fact, does not solely relate to humanitarian operating environments: as several ICRC commentators have noted and the collection has proven, diplomacy also "becomes space."[27] As humanitarian negotiations respond to variations in the field, they also partake in producing alternative and often ad hoc links between relief actors, local organisations and international forces, which in turn become (at least in a social sense) additional spaces that can, ultimately, materialise in the field. Likewise, as a practice based on developing bargaining ties on evolving and hypothetical scenarios, diplomacy also strikes at the very heart of that "abstract" and immaterial dimension that constitutes humanitarian spaces as "figurative structures" imposed upon pre-existing socio-political geographies.[28] Humanitarian space is therefore necessarily a shared space because it is negotiated, and thus found in the midst of competing claims, needs and strategies, which all take part in the figuration and materialisation of the geography of negotiating relief—a spatiality that this collection has only just begun to unpack.

NOTES

PREFACE: THE POLITICS OF HUMANITARIAN SPACE

1. Barnett, Michael, *Empire of Humanity: A History of Humanitarianism*, Ithaca, NY: Cornell University Press, 2011.
2. Barnett, Michael and Weiss, Thomas G., *Humanitarianism Contested: Where Angels Fear to Tread*, London: Routledge, 2011.
3. Forsythe, David P., *The Humanitarians: The International Committee of the Red Cross*, Cambridge: Cambridge University Press, 2005.
4. Pictet, Jean, *The Fundamental Principles of the Red Cross*, Geneva: ICRC, 1979. See also Terry, Fiona, *Condemned to Repeat? The Paradox of Humanitarian Action*, Ithaca, NY: Cornell University Press, 2002.
5. Weiss, Thomas G., "Principles, politics, and humanitarian action," *Ethics & International Affairs* vol. 13 (1999), pp. 1–22.
6. ICISS, *The Responsibility to Protect*, Ottawa: International Development Research Centre, 2001; and Weiss, Thomas G. and Hubert Don, *The Responsibility to Protect: Research, Bibliography, Background*, Ottawa: International Development Research Centre, 2001. For interpretations by commissioners, see Evans, Gareth, *The Responsibility to Protect: Ending Mass Atrocity Crimes Once and for All*, Washington, DC: Brookings, 2008; and Thakur, Ramesh, *The United Nations, Peace and Security: From Collective Security to the Responsibility to Protect*, Cambridge: Cambridge University Press, 2006. See also Bellamy, Alex J., *Responsibility to Protect: The Global Effort to End Mass Atrocities*, Cambridge: Polity Press, 2009; Badescu, Cristina, *Humanitarian Intervention and the Responsibility to Protect: Security and Human Rights*, London: Routledge, 2010; and Thomas G. Weiss, *Humanitarian Intervention: Ideas in Action*, 2nd edn, Cambridge: Polity Press, 2012.
7. *2005 World Summit Outcome*, UN General Assembly Resolution A/RES/60/1, 24 October 2005, paras 138–40.

8. Minear, Larry, *The Humanitarian Enterprise*, West Hartford, CT: Kumarian Press, 2002.

9. Weiss, Thomas G., *Military-Civilian Interactions: Humanitarian Crises and the Responsibility to Protect*, 2nd edn, Lanham, MD: Rowman & Littlefield, 2005.

10. Kent, Randolph, "International humanitarian crises: two decades before and two decades beyond," *International Affairs* vol. 80, no. 5 (2004), pp. 851–69.

11. These figures were drawn from a 2003 OCHA roster (which is no longer updated).

12. Development Initiatives, *Global Humanitarian Assistance 2003*, London: Overseas Development Institute, 2003, p. 56.

13. James, Fearon, "The Rise of Emergency Relief Aid," and Janice Gross Stein, "Humanitarian organizations: Accountable—Why, to Whom, for What and How?" in Barnett M, and Weiss T. (eds), *Humanitarianism in Question: Politics, Power, Ethics*, Ithaca, NY: Cornell University Press, 2008, pp. 49–72 and 124–42.

14. McCleary, Rachel, *Global Compassion: Private Voluntary Organisations and U.S. Foreign Policy since 1939*, Oxford: Oxford University Press, 2009, p. 16 (and especially pp. 3–35).

15. Stoddard, Abby, Harmer, Adele and Haver, Katherine, "Providing aid in insecure environments: trends in policy and operations," *HPG Report no. 23*, London: Overseas Development Institute, 2006, p. 16.

16. Loescher, Gil, Betts, Alexander and Milner, James, *UNHCR*, 2nd edn, London: Routledge, 2012; and Walker, Peter and Maxwell, Daniel G., *Shaping the Humanitarian Order*, London: Routledge, 2009.

17. Cooley, Alexander and Ron, James, "The NGO Scramble: Organizational Insecurity and the Political Economy of Transnational Action," *International Security* vol. 27, no. 1 (2002), pp. 5–39.

18. Harmer, Adele and Martin, Ellen, "Diversity in Donorship: Field Lessons," *HPG Report no. 30*, London: Overseas Development Institute, 2010, p. 1.

19. Relief Web, "International: Changes in Aid Pose Challenges," 15 April 2010, available at: www.reliefweb.int/rw/rwb.nsf/db900sid/VDUX-84JSAS?OpenDocument (last accessed 22 August 2011).

20. See Harmer and Martin, "Diversity in Donorship," quotes from p. 3 and p. 6, statistics from p. 7 and p. 5.

21. Global Humanitarian Assistance, "03/Global Humanitarian Assistance," in *Global Humanitarian Assistance 2009*, Somerset, UK: Development Initiatives, 2009, p. 14, available at: www.globalhumanitarianassistance.org/analyses-and-reports/gha-reports/gha-reports-2009 (last accessed 22 August 2011).

22. Global Humanitarian Assistance, "01/Executive Summary," in *Global Humanitarian Assistance 2009*, p. 1, available at: www.globalhumanitarianassistance.org/analyses-and-reports/gha-reports/gha-reports-2009.

23. Slim, Hugo, "Global welfare," *ALNAP Review of Humanitarian Action in 2005*, p. 21, available at http://www.alnap.org/initiatives/rha/2005.aspx (last accessed 31 August 2011).

24. Smillie, Ian, and Minear, Larry, *The Charity of Nations: Humanitarian Action in a Calculating World*, West Hartford, CT: Kumarian, 2004, pp. 8–10 and p. 195.

25. Global Humanitarian Assistance, "01/Executive Summary," p. 2.

26. Walker, Peter, and Ross, Catherine, *Professionalizing the Humanitarian Sector: A Scoping Study*, Report Commissioned by the Enhancing Learning and Research for Humanitarian Assistance, April 2010, pp. 11–12.

27. Sriram, Chandra Lekha, et al. (eds), *Surviving Field Research: Working in Violent and Difficult Situations*, London: Routledge, 2009.

28. Buchanan, Cate, and Muggah, Robert, *No Relief: Surveying the Effects of Gun Violence on Humanitarian and Development Personnel*, Geneva: Centre for Humanitarian Dialogue, 2005, pp. 7, 9.

29. Gall, Carlotta, and Waldman, Amy, "Under siege in Afghanistan, aid groups say their effort is being criticized unfairly," *New York Times*, 19 December 2004.

30. Independent Panel on Safety and Security of United Nations Personnel and Premises, Towards a Culture of Security and Accountability, UN document dated 30 June 2008, available at: http://www.humansecuritygateway.com/show-Record.php?RecordId=25173 (last accessed 22 August 2011).

31. Kaldor, Mary, *New & Old Wars: Organized Violence in a Global Era*, Stanford: Stanford University Press, 1999; Duffield, Mark, *Global Governance and the New Wars: The Merging of Development and Security*, London: Zed Books, 2001; and Hoffman, Peter J., and Weiss, Thomas G., *Sword & Salve: Confronting New Wars and Humanitarian Crises*, Lanham, MD: Rowman & Littlefield, 2006.

32. Roberts, Adam, "Lives and statistics: are 90% of war victims civilians?," *Survival* vol. 52, no. 3 (2010), pp. 115–36.

33. Inter-Agency Standing Committee, *Preserving Humanitarian Space, Protection and Security*, background paper for the 70th Working Group meeting, New York: IASC, 2008.

34. Stoddard, Harmer and Haver, "Providing aid in insecure environments," pp. 1, 13.

35. Hammond, Laura, "The Power of Holding Humanitarianism Hostage and the Myth of Protective Principles," in Barnett and Weiss, *Humanitarianism in Question*, pp. 172–95.

36. See the debate in *Harvard Human Rights Journal* vol. 17 (Spring 2004), and in particular de Torrente, Nicholas, "Humanitarian action under attack: reflections on the Iraq war," pp. 1–30; O'Brien, Paul, "Politicized humanitarianism: a response to Nicolas de Torrente," pp. 31–40; and Anderson, Kenneth, "Humanitarian inviolability in crisis: the meaning of impartiality and neutral-

ity for U.N. and NGO agencies following the 2003–2004 Afghanistan and Iraq conflicts," pp. 41–74.

37. Rieff, David, *A Bed for the Night: Humanitarianism in Crisis*, London: Vintage, 2002, p. 10.

38. Smillie, Ian, *The Emperor's Old Clothes: The Self-Created Siege of Humanitarian Action*, Medford, MS: Feinstein Institute (forthcoming), p. 15 of draft.

39. Slim, Hugo, *A Call to Alms: Humanitarian Action and the Art of War*, Geneva: Centre for Humanitarian Dialogue, 2004, p. 4.

40. Weiss, Thomas G., "The Humanitarian Impulse," in D. Malone (ed.), *The UN Security Council: From the Cold War to the 21st Century*, Boulder, CO: Lynne Rienner, 2004, pp. 37–54.

41. Chesterman, Simon, *Just Law or Just Peace? Humanitarian Intervention and International Law*, Oxford: Oxford University Press, 2001.

42. Weiss, Thomas G., "RtoP Alive and Well after Libya," *Ethics & International Affairs* vol. 25, no. 3 (2011).

INTRODUCTION: HUMANITARIAN PUZZLES

1. de Waal, Alex, *Famine Crimes: Politics and the Disaster Relief Industry in Africa*, Bloomington: Indiana University Press, 1997, p. xvi

2. Barnett, Michael, *Empire of Humanity: A History of Humanitarianism*, Ithaca: Cornell University Press, 2011, pp. 220–40. Also see Mamdani, Mahmood, *Saviors and Survivors*, New York: Pantheon, 2009.

3. de Waal, Alex, "The humanitarians' tragedy: escapable and inescapable cruelties," *Disasters* vol. 34, suppl. no. 2 (2010), p. 136.

4. Minear, Larry, "The Evolving Humanitarian Enterprise," in Weiss, Thomas G. (ed.), *The United Nations and Civil Wars*, Boulder: Lynne Rienner, 1996, pp. 89–106.

5. For a more extensive collection of viewpoints see Hubert, Don and Brassard-Boudreau, Cynthia, "Is humanitarian space shrinking?," this volume.

6. See Minear, Larry and Smith, Hazel (eds), *Humanitarian Diplomacy: Practitioners and Their Craft*, New York: United Nations University Press, 2007; and Farer, Tom J. (ed.), *Toward a Humanitarian Diplomacy: A Primer for Policy*, New York: New York University Press, 1980.

7. Only a less popular but excellent collection by McRae and Hubert has thus far applied a non-statecentric perspective to the realm of humanitarian diplomacy. See: McRae, Rob and Hubert, Don (eds), *Human Security and the New Diplomacy: Protecting People, Promoting Peace*, Montreal: McGill-Queen's University Press, 2001.

8. See for instance Belloni, Roberto, "The trouble with humanitarianism," *Review of International Studies* vol. 33, no. 3 (2007), pp. 451–74; and Stockton, Nicholas,

"The changing nature of humanitarian crises," in OCHA, *The Humanitarian Decade: Challenges for Humanitarian Assistance in the Last Decade and into the Future* vol.II, New York: OCHA, 2004, pp. 15–39.

9. A few relevant exceptions, as in some of the re-evaluation practices of ICRC and MSF, are nonetheless available in the literature. See for instance Magone, Claire, et al. (eds), *Humanitarian Negotiations Revealed: The MSF Experience*, London: Hurst & Co., 2011.

10. A relevant exception here is the work of those few geographers working on this theme, as represented in Hyndman's concluding chapter as well as more extensively in Hyndman, Jennifer, *Dual Disasters: Humanitarian Aid after the 2004 Tsunami*, Sterling, VA: Kumarian Press, 2011.

11. Apthorpe, Raymond, "With Alice in Aidland: A Seriously Satirical Allegory," in Mosse, D. (ed.), *Adventures in Aidland: The Anthropology of Professionals in International Development*, Oxford: Berghan Books, 2011, pp. 199–220.

12. Minear, Larry, *The Humanitarian Enterprise: Dilemmas and Discoveries*, Bloomfield: Kumarian Press, 2002, pp. 77–8.

13. Barnett, Michael, "Humanitarianism transformed," *Perspectives on Politics* vol. 3, no. 4 (2005), p. 728.

14. Charen, Mona, "Quick-fix humanitarianism," *National Review* vol. 37 (28 June 1985); and Kurt Mills, "Neo-humanitarianism: the role of international humanitarian norms and organisations in contemporary conflict," *Global Governance* vol. 33, no. 1 (2005), pp. 161–83.

15. See, respectively, Udombana, Nsongurua J., "When neutrality is a sin: the Darfur crisis and the crisis of humanitarian intervention in Sudan," *Human Rights Quarterly* vol. 27, no. 4, pp. 1149–99; and Wheeler, Nicholas, *Saving Strangers: Humanitarian Intervention and International Society*, Oxford: Oxford University Press, 2000, as well as Ignatieff, Michael, *The Needs of Strangers*, New York: Penguin, 1986.

16. Terry, Fiona, *Condemned to Repeat? The Paradox of Humanitarian Action*, Ithaca: Cornell University Press, 2002, p. 245.

17. Of help here is the excellent http://www.globalhumanitarianassistance.org/ (last accessed 6 September 2011).

18. Keen, David, *Complex Emergencies*, Cambridge: Polity, 2008, p. 7.

19. See Gleditsch, Kristian Skrede, "Transnational Dimensions of Civil War," *Journal of Peace Research* vol. 44, no. 3 (2007), pp. 293–309.

1. IS HUMANITARIAN SPACE SHRINKING?

1. For an overview of recurring arguments, see: Minear, Larry, "Humanitarian Action in an Age of Terrorism," International Council on Human Rights Policy Working Paper for conference on "September 2001: Impacts on Human Rights

Work," International Council on Human Rights Policy, 2002; Barnett, Michael, "Humanitarianism transformed," *Perpectives on Politics* vol. 3, no. 4 (2005), pp. 723–40; Donini, Antonio, et al., *Humanitarian Agenda 2015: The State of the Humanitarian Enterprise*, Boston: Feinstein International Center, 2008; Tennant, Vicky, et al., *Safeguarding Humanitarian Space: Review of Key Challenges for UNHCR*, report commissioned by the United Nations high commissioner for refugees, 2010; Steering Committee for Humanitarian Response (SCHR), *Changing environment, growing complexities, increasing demands—implications for humanitarian actors*, Global Humanitarian Platform Background Paper, 2010.

2. This chapter is a condensed version of an earlier publication where we also critique many of the assumptions surrounding the causes of current limits on security and access, see Hubert, Don and Brassard-Boudreau, Cynthia, "Shrinking humanitarian space? Trends and prospects for security and access," *Journal of Humanitarian Assistance* (November 24 2010). Online: http://jha.ac/2010/ 11/24/shrinking-humanitarian-space-trends-and-prospects-on-security-and-access/ (last accessed 23 August 2011).

3. See Loescher, Gil, "Humanitarianism and politics in central America," *Political Science Quarterly* vol. 103, no. 2 (Summer 1988), pp. 295–320. First published as a working paper in 1986.

4. Khambatta, Michael, "Humanitarian space and stability operations," On the Edges of Conflict Working Paper (2009), p. 1.

5. Wagner, Johanna Grombach, "An IHL/ICRC perspective on 'humanitarian space'," *Humanitarian Exchange Magazine* no. 32 (2005), available at www.odi-hpn.org/report.asp?ID=2765 (last accessed August 23 2011).

6. Ibid.

7. von Pilar, Ulrike, "Humanitarian space under siege: some remarks from an aid agency's perspective," background paper prepared for *Europe and Humanitarian Aid—What Future? Learning from Crisis*, Bad Neunhar, 22–23 April 1999, p. 4.

8. Oxfam International, *Policy Compendium Note on United Nations Integrated Missions and Humanitarian Assistance*, Oxford: Oxfam International, January 2008.

9. Ibid, p. 2.

10. United Nations Office for the Coordination of Humanitarian Affairs, *Glossary of humanitarian terms in relation to the protection of civilians in armed conflict*, New York: OCHA, 2004, p. 14.

11. Ibid, pp. 14–15.

12. von Pilar, "Humanitarian space under siege," based on Koenrad Van Brabant's analysis, draws a similar portrait of the various understandings of humanitarian space.

13. Wagner, "An IHL/ICRC perspective."

14. Khambatta, "Humanitarian space and stability operations," p. 1.

15. CARE International, "Aid Agencies warn of impending humanitarian catastrophe in Somalia as crisis deteriorates further," media release (October 30 2007).

16. Resolution 1, "*noting* a disturbing decline in respect for international humanitarian law…," ICRC, 25th International Conference of the Red Cross, Geneva, (October 23–31 1986).

17. Melander, Erik, Öberg, Magnus and Hall, Jonathan, "Migration before and after the end of the Cold War," *European Journal of International Relations* vol. 15, no. 3 (2009), pp. 505–36. On trends in armed conflict, see *1946–2008 UCDP/PRIO Armed Conflict Dataset* available online. On civilians as casualties, see Human Security Report, *War and Peace in the 21st Century*, part V, Oxford: Oxford University Press, 2005, pp. 146–58.

18. Kalyvas, Stathis N., "'New' and 'old' civil wars: a valid distinction?," *World Politics* vol. 54, no. 1 (2001), p. 116.

19. Ibid.

20. Roberts, Adam, "Lives and statistics: are 90% of war victims civilians?," *Survival* vol. 52, no. 3 (2010), p. 128.

21. See "Casualties of Conflict" (1991) cited in Roberts, "Lives and Statistics," p. 119; and Ruth Sivard, "World Military and Social Expenditures 1991," *World Prioritie* no. 20 (1991), available at http://www.ruthsivard.com/wmse91.html (last accessed August 23 2011). Roberts also notes that this unnecessary overestimation may have worked against its initial scope by "[obscuring] significant achievements in civilian protection resulting from actions by states, international organisations and non-governmental organisations (NGOs)," Roberts, "Lives and Statistics," pp. 128–9.

22. Melander, Öberg and Hall, "Migration before and after the end of the Cold War," p. 506. On civilians as casualties, see Human Security Report, *War and Peace in the 21st Century*, pp. 146–58.

23. Melander, Öberg and Hall, "Migration before and after the end of the Cold War," p. 507.

24. Human Security Report, *War and Peace in the 21st Century*, pp. 146–58.

25. Inter-Agency Standing Committee, *Preserving Humanitarian Space, Protection and Security*, Background Document for the IASC 70th Working Group meeting (IASC, 2008).

26. Stoddard, Abby, et al., "Providing aid in insecure environments: 2009 Update," *HPG Policy Brief 34*, London: Overseas Development Institute, 2009, p. 1.

27. Sudan, Afghanistan, Somalia, Sri Lanka, Chad, Iraq and Pakistan.

28. Stoddard et al., "Providing Aid in Insecure Environments," p. 4.

29. Ray, Deepayan Basu, "The challenges of providing aid in insecure environments," in *NGO VOICE*, Issue 10 (2009), p. 4.

30. Ibid.

31. Gassmann, Pierre, "Rethinking Humanitarian Security," *Humanitarian Exchange*

Magazine no. 30 (June 2005), available at www.odihpn.org/report.asp?id=2721 (accessed 22 August 2011).

32. Ibid.
33. Tennant, et al., *Safeguarding Humanitarian Space*, pp. 21–2.
34. For a similar argument, see Fast, Larissa, "Characteristics, context and risk: NGO insecurity in conflict zones," *Disasters* vol. 31, no. 2 (2007), pp. 130–54.
35. Stoddard, Abby, et al., "Providing aid in insecure environments," p. 10.
36. Weiss, Thomas G., *Humanitarian Intervention*, London: Polity Press, 2007, p. 74. For 2008 figure see Global Humanitarian Assistance, "Latest DAC data release reveals big rise in humanitarian expenditure in 2008," (GHA, Dec 18, 2009). Figures estimated from ODA expenditures and include disaster response. However, top recipients of humanitarian assistance indicate that most humanitarian expenditure was destined to war-affected countries.
37. Stoddard, Abby, et al, "Providing aid in insecure environments."
38. Borton, John, *Future of the Humanitarian System: Impacts of Internal Changes*, Boston: John Borton Consulting and Tufts University, November 2009, p. 8, also available at http://reliefweb.int/node/24660 (last accessed 23 August 2011).
39. See for example Adele Harmer on possible causes of rising number of attacks on aid workers: "Another factor could be the increased number of NGO operations in high-risk areas over the past few years. NGO concerns on the impacts of political and military influences can therefore be linked directly to their increasing exposure in the field." Harmer, Adele, "Integrated missions: a threat to humanitarian security?," *International Peacekeeping* vol. 15, no. 4 (2008), p. 534.

2. THE HUMANITARIAN SYSTEM: HOW DOES IT AFFECT HUMANITARIAN SPACE?

1. Hubert, Don and Brassard-Boudreau, Cynthia, "Is Humanitarian Space Shrinking?," this volume.
2. Collinson, Sarah, *The Role of Networks in the International Humanitarian System*, Report commissioned by USAID/OFDA, Humanitarian Policy Group, London: ODI, 2011.
3. Duffield, Mark, *Development, Security and Unending War: Governing the World of Peoples*, Cambridge: Polity Press, 2007, p. 25.
4. Crisp, Jeff and Slaughter, Amy, *A Surrogate State? The Role of UNHCR in Protracted Refugee Situations*, New Issues in Refugee Research, Research Paper 168, Geneva: UNHCR, 2009, p. 8.
5. Duffield, 2010.
6. Barnett, Michael, "Humanitarianism transformed," *Perspectives on Politics* vol. 3, no. 4 (2005), pp. 723–40.

7. Ibid., p. 734. For instance, that in 2010 World Vision raised $2.61 billion in cash and gifts-in-kind, and World Vision's total expenditures totalled $2.48 billion (http://www.wvi.org/wvi/WVIAR2010.nsf/maindocs/9AD45EB59002C 22E882576DC001F5A86?opendocument); UNHCR's annual budget reached $3 billion in 2010 (http://www.unhcr.org/pages/49c3646c1a.html); and Oxfam's total expenditures exceeded $842 million in 2009/10 (http://www. oxfamireland.org/pdfs/annual_reports/Annual_Report_2011.pdf?PHPSESSI D=ea13171abbca093bac109aff83d7ca51), compared with many countries, including Rwanda, Sierra Leone, Timor Leste and Central African Republic, with estimated annual government budget revenues of $1 billion or less (http:// www.nationmaster.com/graph/eco_bud_rev-economy-budget-revenues; http:// www.photius.com/rankings/economy/budget_revenues_2010_0.html). All sites last accessed 6 January 2012.

8. Borrel, Annalies, et al., *Ambiguity and Change: Humanitarian NGOs Prepare for the Future*, Report prepared for World Vision, CARE, Save US, Mercy Corps, Oxfam USA, Oxfam GB & Catholic Relief Services, Cambridge, MA: The Feinstein International Center, Tufts University, 2004, p. 64.

9. Smillie, Ian and Minear, Larry, *The Charity of Nations: Humanitarian Action in a Calculating World*, Bloomfield, CT: Kumarian Press, 2004, p. 236.

10. Hopgood, Stephen, "Saying 'No' to Wal-Mart? Money and Morality in Professional Humanitarianism," in Barnett, Michael and Weiss, Thomas G. (eds), *Humanitarianism in Question: Politics, Power and Ethics*, New York: Cornell University Press, pp. 98–123.

11. Slim, Hugo, "The continuing metamorphosis of the humanitarian practitioner: some new colours for an endangered chameleon," *Disasters* vol. 19, no. 2 (2007), pp. 110–26; and African Rights *Humanitarianism Unbound*, London: African Rights, 1994.

12. Edwards, 1996, p. 34; cited by Ebrahim, 2003, p. 13.

13. See for instance Dechaine, Robert, "Humanitarian space and the social imaginary: Médecins San Frontières/Doctors Without Borders and the Rhetoric of Global Community," *Journal of Communication Inquiry* vol. 26, no. 4 (2002), pp. 354–69.

14. Stokke, Kristian, *Humanitarian Response to Natural Disasters: A Synthesis of Evaluation Findings*, Oslo: Norwegian Agency for Development Cooperation, Norad, 2007.

15. Donini, Antonio, "The far side: the metafunctions of humanitarianism in a globalised world," *Disasters* vol. 34, no. 2 (2010), pp. 220–37.

16. See Humanitarian Policy Group, "Humanitarian Space in Sri Lanka: what lessons can be learned?," Meeting Summary: Roundtable Meeting, London, 18–19 November 2010, London: ODI; Available at http://www.odi.org.uk/events/ documents/2656-meeting-summary.pdf. (accessed 6 January 2012).

17. Duffield, Mark, *Development, Security and Unending War: Governing the World of Peoples*, London: Polity Press, 2007.
18. Ibid., pp. 3, 14.
19. Donini, Antonio, et al., *The State of the Humanitarian Enterprise: Humanitarian Agenda 2015 Final Report*, Cambridge, MA: The Feinstein International Center, Tufts University, 2008, p. 16.
20. Also see Harvey, Paul, et al., *The State of the Humanitarian System: Assessing Performance and Progress. A Pilot Study*, London: Active Learning Network for Accountability and Performance ALNAP, 2010.
21. Dobusch, Leonhard and Quack, Sigrid, "Epistemic Communities and Social Movements: Transnational Dynamics in the Case of Creative Commons," *MPIfG Discussion Paper 8/8*, Cologne: Max Planck Institute for the Study of Societies, 2008.
22. Ibid.
23. Collinson, *The Role of Networks in the International Humanitarian System*.
24. Leader, Nicholas, "The Politics of Principle: The Principles of Humanitarian Action in Practice," *HPG Report 2*, London: Overseas Development Institute, 2000.
25. Hammond & Vaughan-Lee, 2011.
26. Cooley, Alexander, and Ron, James, "The NGO scramble, organizational insecurity and the political economy of transnational action," *International Security* vol. 27, no. 1 (2002), p. 7.
27. Ibid, p. 12.
28. Ibid.
29. Available at http://www.dyn-intl.com/development.aspx (accessed 6 January 2012).
30. Hilhorst, Dorothea and Jansen, Bram J., "Humanitarian space as arena: a perspective on the everyday politics of aid," *Development and Change* vol. 41, no. 6 (2010), pp. 11131–2.
31. In the Pakistan context, for example, see Whittall, Jonathan, "'We don't trust that': politicized assistance in North-West Pakistan," *Humanitarian Exchange Magazine*, Issue 49 (February 2011), available at http://www.odihpn.org/humanitarian-exchange-magazine/issue-49/we-dont-trust-that-politicised-assistance-in-north-west-pakistan and Harroff-Tavel, Marion, "Principles under fire: does it still make sense to be neutral?," *Humanitarian Exchange Magazine*, Issue 25 (December 2003), available at http://www.odihpn.org/humanitarian-exchange-magazine/issue-25/does-it-still-make-sense-to-be-neutral. In the Afghanistan context, see, for example, Jackson, "Nowhere to Turn: The Failure to Protect Civilians in Afghanistan," A Joint Briefing Paper by 29 aid organisations working in Afghanistan for the NATO Heads of Government Summit, Lisbon, 19–20 November 2010, p. 18, Available at http://www.oxfam.org/sites/

www.oxfam.org/files/bn-nowhere-to-turn-afghanistan-191110-en.pdf   (all accessed 6 January 2012).

32. Cooley and Ron, "The NGO Scramble," p. 6.

33. Ibid, p. 27.

34. Polastro, Riccardo, Nagrah, Aatika, Steen, Nicolai and Zafar, Farwa, *Inter-Agency Real Time Evaluation of the Humanitarian Response to Pakistan's 2010 Flood Crisis*, Commissioned by the Inter-Agency Standing Committee (IASC), Madrid: DARA, 2011, pp. 36–7.

35. Jaspars, Susanne and Maxwell, Daniel, *Targeting in Complex Emergencies: Somalia Country Case Study*, Medford, MS: Feinstein International Center, Tufts University, July 2008.

36. Donini, Antonio, Minear, Larry and Walker, Peter, "The future of humanitarian action: mapping the implications of Iraq and other recent crises," *Disasters* vol. 28, no. 2 (2004), pp. 190–204.

37. For example, through doing the government's bidding without any effective or open challenge in suddenly withdrawing all international staff from the North in late 2008 (on the instructions of the government) and by accepting gross limits on the amounts and conditions of food assistance that they (WFP and others) were subsequently being allowed to deliver into the North.

38. Anderson, Mary B, *Do No Harm*, Boulder, CO: Lynne Rienner Publishers, 1999.

39. Hammond & Vaughan-Lee, 2011.

3. HUMANITARIANISM, PERCEPTIONS AND POWER

1. Case studies included Afghanistan, Iraq, Colombia, Sudan, Palestine, Sri Lanka, Burundi, Liberia, Georgia, Nepal, Northern Uganda, Pakistan earthquake and DRC. All case studies and the final report, *The State of the Humanitarian Enterprise* (2008) are available at https://wikis.uit.tufts.edu/confluence/display/FIC/ Humanitarian+Agenda+2015+—+The+State+of+the+Humanitarian+Enterprise (last accessed 10 September 2011).

2. Such as the "Listening Project," the MSF perceptions studies and the growing anthropological literature on the aid world.

3. Such as al-Qaeda in the Islamic Maghreb who is allegedly responsible for the killing of (at least) three French aid workers in Niger and Mauritania in 2009/2010.

4. See the report on perceptions of social transformation in Nepal and the country Briefing Notes issued by FIC in 2010–2011 at https://wikis.uit.tufts.edu/confluence/display/FIC/Publications (last accessed 10 September 2011).

5. This does not necessarily mean that aid agencies create their own (parallel?) reality. But it does mean that, because they have money and power, they are able to

define who is vulnerable and who isn't and where to intervene, thus contributing to the shaping of the contexts where they work.

6. On network power as a form of "imperialism" see Grewal, David S., *Network Power: The Social Dynamics of Globalization*, New Haven, CT: Yale University Press, 2008.

7. Extrapolating from Development Initiatives estimates, it can be said that between two-thirds and three-quarters of all recorded humanitarian assistance is provided through the UN system, ICRC and a cartel of five consortia of transnational NGOs (World Vision, CARE, Oxfam, Save the Children and MSF).

8. Slim, Hugo, "How We Look: Hostile Perceptions of Humanitarian Action," Presentation to the Conference on Humanitarian Coordination, Wilton Park Montreux, 21 April 2004, p. 5.

9. Ibid.

10. Between $10 and $18 billion per year over the last decade according to Development Initiatives.

11. Wallerstein, Immanuel, *European Universalism. The Rhetoric of Power*. New York: New Press, 2011, p. 40.

12. Anderson, Mary, "The Giving-Receiving Relationship: Inherently Unequal?," *The Humanitarian Response Index 2008*, Madrid: DARA, September 2008.

13. Terry, Fiona, *Condemned to Repeat. The Paradox of Humanitarian Action*, Ithaca: Cornell University Press, 2002.

4. IMAGINING CATASTROPHE: THE POLITICS OF REPRESENTING HUMANITARIAN CRISES

1. Julia Gillard comments on images of the catastrophic 11 March 2011 earthquake and tsunami that struck Japan. Julia Gillard, "Transcript of Doorstop Interview," The Prime Minister of Australia Press Office, 11 March 2011. Available at http://www.pm.gov.au/press-office/transcript-doorstop-interview-new-yok 15 March 2011).

2. Devereux, Linda, "From Congo: newspaper photographs, public images and personal memories," *Visual Studies* vol. 25, no. 2 (2010), pp. 124–34; Jan Pronk, "We need more stories and more pictures," 50 Years of World Press Photos, 8 October 2005. Available at http://www.janpronk.nl/speeches/english/we-need-more-stories-and-more-pictures.html (last accessed 14 March 2011).

3. Campbell, David, "The iconography of famine," in Gidley, Geoffrey, et al., *Picturing Atrocity: Reading Photographs in Crisis*, London: Reaktion Books, 2011; Kleinman, Arthur and Kleinman, Joan, "The appeal of experience; the dismay of images: cultural appropriations of suffering in our times," *Daedalus* vol. 125, no. 2 (1996), pp. 1, 7.

4. Hubert, Don and Brassard-Boudreau, Cynthia, "Is humanitarian space shrinking?," this volume.

5. Mitchell, W.J.T., *Picture Theory: Essay on Verbal and Visual Representation*, Chicago: University of Chicago Press, 1994.

6. Sontag, Susan, *Regarding the Pain of Others*, New York: Farrar, Straus and Giroux, 2003, p. 22.

7. See, for example, Tagg, John, *The Burden of Representation: Essays on Photographies and Histories*, London: Macmillan, 1988.

8. Zelizer, Barbie, "Death in wartime: photographs and the 'other war' in Afghanistan, *Harvard International Journal of Press/Politics* vol. 10, no. 3 (2005), p. 29.

9. Levi Strauss, David, *Between the Eyes: Essays on Photography and Politics*, New York: Aperture, 2003, p. 45; Perlmutter, David D., *Photojournalism and Foreign Policy: Icons of Outrage in International Crises*, Westport: Praeger, 1998, p. 28.

10. Friday, Jonathon, "Demonic curiosity and the aesthetics of documentary photography," *British Journal of Aesthetics* vol. 40, no. 3 (2000), p. 365.

11. Zelizer, Barbie, "Finding aids to the past: bearing personal witness to traumatic public events," *Media, Culture and Society* vol. 24, no. 5 (2002), p. 699.

12. See Hariman, John and Lucaites, John Louis, "Public identity and collective memory in U.S. iconic photography: the image of accidental napalm," *Critical Studies in Media Communication* vol. 20, no. 1 (2003), pp. 35–66.

13. Macleod, Scott, "The life and death of Kevin Carter," *Time*, 12 September 1994. Available online at http://www.time.com/time/magazine/article/0,9171,98 1431,00.html (last accessed 15 March 2011).

14. Sydney Morning Herald, "Big Pictures: Disaster in Japan," http://www.smh. com.au/environment/bigpics/japan-disaster (last accessed 25 April 2011).

15. Gillard, Julia, "Transcript of press conference," Canberra, 13 March 2011. Available online at http://www.pm.gov.au/press-office/transcipt-press-conference-canberra (last accessed 25 April 2011).

16. See, for example, Balaji, Murali, "Racializing pity: the Haiti earthquake and the plight of 'others'," *Critical Studies in Media Communication* vol. 28, no. 1 (2011), pp. 50–67; Lidchi, Henrietta "Finding the tight image: British development NGOs and the regulation of imagery," in Skelton, Tracey and Allen, Tim (eds), *Culture and Global Change*, London and New York: Routledge, 1999, pp. 87–101; Malkki, Liisa, H., "Speechless emissaries: refugees, humanitarianism, and dehistoricization," *Cultural Anthropology* vol. 11, no. 3 (1996), pp. 385–90; Manzo, Kate, "Imaging humanitarianism: NGO identity and the iconography of childhood," *Antipode* vol. 40, no. 4, pp. 632–57; Strüver, Anke, "The production of geopolitical and gendered images through global aid organisations," *Geopolitics* vol. 12, no. 4 (2007), pp. 680–703.

17. Baer, Ulrich, *Spectral Evidence: The Photography of Trauma*, Cambridge: The MIT Press, 2002, pp. 10–14; Kaplan, E. Ann, *Trauma Culture: The Politics of Loss in the Media and Literature*, New Brunswick: Rutgers University Press, 2005, pp. 95–100.

18. See Dauphinee, Elizabeth, "The politics of the body in pain: reading the tthics of imagery," *Security Dialogue* vol. 38, no. 2 (2007), pp. 139–55.

19. Cohen, Stanley, *States of Denial: Knowing about Atrocities and Suffering*, Cambridge: Polity, 2001, pp. 182–3; Miller, Nancy K., "'Portraits of grief': telling details and testimony of trauma," *Differences: A Journal of Feminist Cultural Studies* vol. 14, no. 3 (2003), pp. 112–35.

20. *New York Times*, 28 December 2004, p. 1, original caption.

21. Perlmutter, *Photojournalism and Foreign Policy*, pp. xiv-xv, 4–5, 20–9.

22. Moeller, Susan D., *Compassion Fatigue: How the Media Sells Disease, Famine, War and Death*, New York: Routledge, 1999.

23. Cohen, *States of Denial*.

24. Campbell, David, "Horrific blindness: images of death in contemporary media," *Journal of Cultural Research* vol. 8, no. 1 (2004), p. 62.

25. Johnson, James, "'The Arithmetic of Compassion': Rethinking the Politics of Photography," unpublished manuscript, pp. 5, 6. See also Berger, John, "Photographs of agony," in *About Looking*, New York: Vintage, 1980, pp. 41–4.

26. See Bennett, Jane, *Empathic Vision: Affect, Trauma and Contemporary Art*, Stanford: Stanford University Press, 2005; Kaplan, *Trauma Culture*.

27. For a more detailed elaboration, see Bleiker, Roland and Kay, Amy, "Representing HIV/AIDS in Africa: pluralist photography and local empowerment," *International Studies Quarterly* vol. 51, no. 1 (2007), pp. 139–63.

28. Hooper, Edward, *Slim: A Reporter's Own Story of HIV/AIDS in East Africa*, London: The Bodley Head, 1990.

29. Shapiro, Michael, *The Politics of Representation: Writing Practices in Biography, Photography and Policy Analysis*, Madison: University of Wisconsin Press, 1988, pp. 129–30.

30. See, for instance, Campbell, David, "Imaging famine," available online at http://www.imaging-famine.org (last accessed on 29 May 2008); Malkki, "Speechless emissaries," p. 388; Manzo, "Imaging humanitarianism," pp. 649–51.

31. See Manzo, "Imaging humanitarianism," pp. 632–57. On the notion of "colonial" photography, see Maxwell, Anne, *Colonial Photography and Exhibitions: Representations of 'Native' People and the Making of European Identities*, London: Leicester University Press, 1999.

32. Hall, Stuart, "The work of representation," in Hall, Stuart (ed.), *Representation: Cultural Representations and Signifying Practices*, London: Sage and the Open University, 1997, pp. 13–75.

33. Campbell, David, "Stereotypes that move: the iconography of famine," 20 October 2010, available at www.david-campbell.org, (last accessed 22 August 2011)

34. Ibid.

35. Manzo, "Imaging humanitarianism."

36. Hariman, John and Lucaites, John Louis, *No Caption Needed: Iconic Photographs, Public Culture, and Liberal Democracy*, Chicago: Chicago University Press, 2007, p. 21.

5. HUMANITARIAN SPACE IN DARFUR: CAUGHT BETWEEN THE LOCAL AND THE GLOBAL

1. Mills, Kurt, "Vacillating on Darfur: responsibility to protect, to prosecute, and to feed," *Global Responsibility to Protect* vol. 1, no. 4 (2009), pp. 532–59.

2. Calling it a responsibility (as the French government has), gives a sense of requirement or imperative, which might be perceived to vary from Tom Weiss's argument later in this volume that it is better to talk about an impulse rather than an imperative, since any humanitarian action will not be applied equally across all situations and requires prudential evaluation on how and when best to act. Yet, the argument here is that the international community has a responsibility, in the sense of duty or imperative, to act when it can, subject to such prudential and other calculations. On the French recognition of humanitarian responsibility, see Barnett Michael and Snyder, Jack, "The grand strategies of humanitarianism," in Barnett, Michael and Weiss, Thomas G. (eds), *Humanitarianism in Question: Politics, Power, Ethics*, Ithaca: Cornell University Press, 2008, p. 143.

3. Mills, Kurt, "Neo-humanitarianism: the role of international humanitarian norms and organisations in contemporary conflict," *Global Governance* vol. 11 (April–June 2005), pp. 161–83.

4. On the creation of the ICC see Schiff, Benjamin, *Building the International Criminal Court*, Cambridge: Cambridge University Press, 2008; Schabas, William A., *An Introduction to the International Criminal Court*, 3rd edn, Cambridge: Cambridge University Press, 2007; Leonard, Eric, *The Onset of Global Governance*, Ashgate, 2005; Roach, Steven C. (ed.), *Governance, Order, and the International Criminal Court: Between Realpolitik and a Cosmopolitan Court*, Oxford: Oxford University Press, 2009.

5. Bellamy, Alex, *Responsibility to Protect*, Cambridge: Polity, 2009; Evans, Gareth, *The Responsibility to Protect: Ending Mass Atrocity Crimes Once and for All*, Washington, DC: Brookings, 2008.

6. Mills, Kurt, "United Nations intervention in refugee crises after the cold war," *International Politics* vol. 35 (December 1998), pp. 391–424.

7. Respectively: International Commission of Intervention and State Sovereignty, *The Responsibility to Protect*, 2001, available at http://www.iciss.ca/pdf/Commission-Report.pdf (last accessed 16 June 2011); and United Nations General Assembly, "2005 World Summit Outcome," 15 September 2005, available at http://www.un.org/summit2005/documents.html (last accessed 16 June 2011).

8. I use this term to refer to all humanitarian organisations—both nongovernmen-

tal and intergovernmental—although these different types of organisations may have some different characteristics. In his chapter in this volume, William Maley outlines the diverse actors which might come under the heading IHO.

9. On the last point, see Barrs, Casey, "Preparedness support: helping brace beneficiaries, local staff and partners for violence," The Cuny Centre, November 2009.

10. For history of the conflict in Darfur, see Prunier, Gérard, *Darfur: The Ambiguous Genocide*, 2nd edn, Ithaca: Cornell University Press, 2007; Mamdani, Mahmood, *Saviors and Survivors: Darfur, Politics, and the War on Terror*, London: Verso, 2009.

11. International Crisis Group, *To Save Darfur*, Africa Report No. 105, (17 March 2006), pp. 14–15, available at http://www.crisisgroup.org/en/regions/africa/horn-of-africa/sudan/105-to-save-darfur.asp (last accessed 14 June 2011).

12. International Criminal Court, "Warrant for arrest of Ahmad Harun," 27 April 2007, available at http://www.icc-cpi.int/iccdocs/doc/doc279813.PDF (last accessed 14 June 2011).

13. International Crisis Group, *To Save Darfur*, p. 2. In 2006, there were 1,800 attacks on aid workers by militias, and between June 2006 and June 2007 attacks on aid workers increased 150 per cent. Ward, Olivia, "Aid workers endure growing threats," *The Toronto Star*, 13 March 2009, available at http://www.thestar.com/news/world/article/601634 (last accessed 15 June 2011).

14. "UNAMID celebrates deployment of tactical helicopters," Press Release, African Union—United Nations Mission in Darfur, 27 February 2010, available at http://unamid.unmissions.org/Default.aspx?tabid=899&ctl=Details&mid=1072&ItemID=7898 (last accessed 14 June 2011).

15. "Sudan lifts flight ban on UNAMID helicopters," *Sudan Tribune*, 18 June 2010, available at http://www.sudantribune.com/Sudan-lifts-flight-ban-on-UNAMID,35426 (last accessed 14 June 2011).

16. "UNAMID deployment on the brink: the road to security in Darfur blocked by government obstruction," Joint NGO Report, December 2007, available at http://hrw.org/pub/2007/africa/unamid1207web.pdf (last accessed 14 June 2011). It had also previously prevented AMIS from bringing in armoured personnel carriers and helicopters.

17. MacFarquhar Neil, and Simons, Marlise, "UN panels says Sudan expulsion of aid groups is 'deplorable'," *The New York Times*, 6 March 2009.

18. Flint, Julie and de Waal, Alex, "To put justice before peace spells disaster for Sudan," *The Guardian*, 6 March 2009, available at http://www.guardian.co.uk/commentisfree/2009/mar/06/sudan-war-crimes (last accessed 15 June 2011).

19. United Nations Security Council, "Secretary-General Report on African Union-United Nations operation in Darfur," S/2009/297, 9 June 2009, available at http://www.un.org/ga/search/view_doc.asp?symbol=S/2009/297 (last accessed 16 June 2011).

20. Interview with Oxfam official.
21. "Expelled US aid groups deny return to Sudan," *Sudan Tribune*, 12 June 2009, available: http://www.sudantribune.com/Expelled-US-aid-groups-deny-return,31485 (last accessed 15 June 2011).
22. Interview with Oxfam official.
23. Interview with International Rescue Committee official.
24. These included the Save Darfur Coalition (http://www.savedarfur.org), the Darfur Consortium (http://www.darfur-consortium.org), and Enough (http://www.enoughproject.org).
25. de Waal, Alex, "Why Darfur intervention is a mistake," *BBC News*, 21 May 2008, available at http://news.bbc.co.uk/1/hi/world/africa/7411087.stm (last accessed 16 June 2011); Evans, Gareth, "The responsibility or protect and the use of force," Presentation by Gareth Evans, President, International Crisis Group, to Seminar on International Use of Force, World Legal Forum, The Hague, 11 December 2007, available at http://www.worldlegalforum.org/Docs/Speech%20Gareth%20Evans.pdf (last accessed 16 June 2011).
26. As of June 2011, eighty-nine UNAMID personnel have died in Darfur. UNAMID, available at http://www.un.org/en/peacekeeping/missions/unamid/facts.shtml (last accessed 16 June 2011).
27. I give credit here for the pyramid analogy to Daniel Thürer who used the pyramidal structure in a different way to explore the ideational and normative basis for humanitarian space—"Dunant's pyramid: thoughts on the 'humanitarian space'," *International Review of the Red Cross* vol. 89, no. 865 (2007), pp. 47–61.
28. UNAMID, "Operation Spring Basket reaches more remote areas in North Darfur," Information Note, 12 June 2011, available at http://unamid.unmissions.org/Default.aspx?tabid=899&ctl=Details&mid=1072&ItemID=14003 (last accessed 16 June 2011).
29. Or "humanitarian impulse" as Weiss argues in "The politics of humanitarian space," this volume.
30. Elsewhere in this volume Maley ("Humanitarianism and diplomats: what connections?") highlights some of the dilemmas humanitarian actors face. Also see Part III of the collection.

6. WORLD POLITICS AND HUMANITARIANISM IN KOSOVO: A SYMBIOTIC RELATIONSHIP?

1. I would like to thank Prof. Raymond Apthorpe, Dr Michele Acuto, Ms. Kathryn Rzeszut and two anonymous reviewers for their comments and revisions on earlier drafts of the chapter.
2. Tennant, Vicky, Doyle, Bernie and Mazou Raouf, *Safeguarding humanitarian space: a review of key challenges for UNHCR*, Geneva: United Nations High

Commissioner for Refugees Policy Development and Evaluation Service (PDEs), 2010, p. 3: http://www.unhcr.org/4b68042d9.pdf (last accessed 27 April 2012). This definition echoes the original definition of humanitarian space developed by Médecins Sans Frontières in the 1990s and cited by Hubert, Don and Brassard-Boudreau, Cynthia, "Is humanitarian space shrinking?," this volume.

3. Kosovar Albanians claimed that Serb forces killed more than seventy civilians in Drenica in March 1998, and another forty-five Albanian civilians in Racak on 15 January 1999. Demjaha, Agon, "The Kosovo conflict: A perspective from inside," in Schnabel, A. and Thakur, R. (eds), *Kosovo and the Challenge for Humanitarian Intervention*, Tokyo: United Nations University Press, 2000, p. 34.

4. Independent International Commission on Kosovo, "Annex I. Documentation of Human Rights Violations," in *The Kosovo Report: Conflict, International Response, Lesson Learned*, Oxford: Oxford University Press, 2000, pp. 301–18; and Wheeler, Nicholas, *Saving Strangers: Humanitarian Intervention in International Society*, Oxford: Oxford University Press, 2001, pp. 257–84.

5. *UN Security Council Resolution 1244 on the situation relating Kosovo*, S/RES/1244 (1999), 10 June 1999: http://www.unmikonline.org/Documents/Res1244ENG. pdf. (last accessed 27 April 2012).

6. Calic, Marie-Janine, "Kosovo in the twentieth century: a historical account," in Schnabel, A. and Thakur, R. (eds), 2000, 30 and "Federal Republic Of Yugoslavia. Abuses Against Serbs and Roma in the New Kosovo," *Human Rights Watch* vol. 11, no. 10 (August 1999): http://www.hrw.org/reports/1999/kosov2/#_1_10. (last accessed 27 April 2012).

7. Ikenberry, John, "The cost of victory: American power and the use of force in the contemporary order," in Schnabel, A. and Thakur, R. (eds), *Kosovo and the Challenge for Humanitarian Intervention*, Tokyo: United Nations University Press, 2000, p. 87.

8. The Italian prime minister Massimo D'Alema, for example, visited Washington on 5 March and warned President Clinton that if Milosevic did not capitulate immediately the result would be 300,000 to 400,000 refugees passing into Albania and crossing the Adriatic into Italy. Bronner, Ethan and Sciolino, Elaine, "Crisis in the Balkans: the road to war—a special report. How a President, distracted by scandal, entered Balkan war," *The New York Times*, 18 April 1999: http://www. nytimes.com/1999/04/18/world/crisis-balkans-road-war-special-report-presi-dent-distracted-scandal-entered.html?src=pm. On conflict contagion, Buhaug, Halvard and Gleditsch, Kristian S, *The origin of conflict clusters: contagion or bad neighborhoods?*, paper presented at the ECPR general conference, Budapest, 8–10 September 2005: http://www.prio.no/files/file48357_hb_ksg_contagion_sept06. doc, (both last accessed 2 September 2011).

9. On the Italian position, Kostakos, Georgios, "The southern flank: Italy, Greece, Turkey," in Schnabel, A. and Thakur, R. (eds), *Kosovo and the Challenge for*

Humanitarian Intervention, Tokyo: United Nations University Press, 2000, pp. 166–80. Johnstone, Diana, *Fools' Crusade. Yugoslavia, NATO and Western Delusions*, New York: Monthly Review Press, 2002, pp. 259–69; Johnstone reports how for Italy taking part in the Kosovo war was a strategic imperative to "count as a major country" and to acquire membership in the "noble circle of Great Powers."

10. Russia opposed the intervention because of its legacy with Serbia and because of the fear that such a precedent could have triggered future interventions in defence of the many "Kosovo" in its territory (for example, Chechnya). Two days after the beginning of the campaign for example, Russia requested UNSC to condemn the use of force in Kosovo.

11. China insisted that external interventions in a sovereign country should be authorised by UNSC and not by a regional organisation. On China's position see Yunling, Zhang, "China: whither the world order after Kosovo?," Schnabel, A. and Thakur, R. (eds), *Kosovo*, pp. 117–27.

12. Ignatieff, Michael, *Empire Lite*, London: Vintage, 2003, p. 68.

13. *UN Security Council Resolution 1244 on the situation relating Kosovo*, S/RES/1244 (1999).

14. International Court of Justice, *Accordance with international law of the unilateral declaration of independence in respect of Kosovo (Request for Advisory Opinion)—Advisory Opinion*—Advisory Opinion of 22 July 2010: http://www.icj-cij.org/docket/files/141/15987.pdf?PHPSESSID=186bc197c009ad82a187 51bce0275ea2. and UN News Centre, *Kosovo's declaration of independence did not violate international law—UN court*, 22 July 2010: http://www.un.org/apps/news/story.asp?NewsID=35396&Cr=&Cr1=. The text of the Kosovo Declaration of Independence is available at http://www.assembly-kosova.org/?cid=2,128,1635. (last accessed 27 April 2012).

15. For example, Roberts, Adam, "NATO's 'humanitarian war' over Kosovo," *Survival* vol. 41, no. 3 (1999), pp. 102–23.

16. Apthorpe, Raymond, "Was international emergency relief aid in Kosovo 'humanitarian'?," *Humanitarian Exchange* no. 20 (March 2002), p. 21: http://www.odihpn.org/report.asp?id=2417. (last accessed 27 April 2012).

17. Surkhe, A., et al., *The Kosovo Refugee Crisis: an Independent Evaluation of UNHCR's Emergency Preparedness and Response*, UNHCR Evaluation and Policy Analysis Unit, 2000, p. vi.

18. Apthorpe, "Was international emergency relief aid in Kosovo 'humanitarian'?," p. 21.

19. Wiles, Peter, "The Kosovo emergency: the Disasters Emergency Committee Evaluation," *Kosovo and the changing face of humanitarian action*, Uppsala: Uppsala Universitet, 2001, p. 6.

20. Demolli, Gani, "The Mother Teresa Society and the war in Kosovo," *Global*

Policy Forum, 2002: http://www.globalpolicy.org/ngos/credib/2002/1009kosovo. htm. (last accessed 27 April 2012).

21. Surkhe, A., et al., *Kosovo*, p.xi.
22. Ibid. See also Rieff, David, *At the Point of a Gun: Democratic Dreams and Armed Intervention*, New York: Simon & Schuster, 2005, pp. 123–39.
23. According to Wiles, "while donor governments gave US$207 per person through the 1999 UN appeal for Kosovo, those in Sierra Leone received US$16, and those in the Democratic Republic of Congo little over US$8," Wiles, "The Kosovo emergency," p. 13.
24. Tennant, Doyle and Mazou, *Safeguarding humanitarian space: a review of key challenges for UNHCR*, p. 3.
25. Hubert and Brassard-Boudreau, "Is humanitarian space shrinking?," this volume, re-echoing Tennant, Doyle and Mazou, *Safeguarding humanitarian space: a review of key challenges for UNHCR*, p. 3 and the original definition of humanitarian space developed by Médecins Sans Frontières in the 1990s definition
26. Wiles, "The Kosovo emergency," pp. 9–10.
27. Independent International Commission on Kosovo, p. 4. Schnabel, A. and Thakur, R. ask, for example, if the same legitimacy could be assured to a hypothetical military intervention of the Arab League in defence of the human rights of Palestinian citizens in Israel, see Schnabel, A. and Thakur R., "Kosovo, the changing contours of world politics, and the challenge of world order," in Schnabel A. and Thakur, R. (eds), *Kosovo and the Challenge for Humanitarian Intervention*, Tokyo: United Nations University Press, 2000, p. 10.
28. Johnstone, *Fools' Crusade*; and Noam Chomsky, *The New Military Humanism. Lessons from Kosovo*, London: Pluto Press, 1999.
29. International Commission on Intervention and State Sovereignty (ICISS), *The Responsibility to Protect*, Ottawa: International Development Research Centre, 2001.
30. Bellamy, Alex, "The responsibility to protect: opening humanitarian spaces?," this volume.
31. "Responsibility to protect: the lessons of Libya," *The Economist*, 19 May 2011: http://www.economist.com/node/18709571. (last accessed 27 April 2012).
32. Michael Ignatieff, for example, justified the intervention in Kosovo as a member of the Independent International Commission on Kosovo and of the commission who issued the report *The Responsibility to Protect*. Nevertheless, he wrote after few years and in the wake of US intervention in Afghanistan a less positive account of the war in his *Empire Lite*.
33. Ignatieff, *Empire Lite*, p. 59.
34. Fox, Fiona, "New humanitarianism: does it provide a moral banner for the 21st century?," *Disasters* vol. 25, no. 4 (2001), p. 282.
35. Among the exceptions, Médecin Sans Frontières has always been hostile to the

militarisation of humanitarianism and withdrew its US branch from the response committee of InterAction, the umbrella organisation which included all the US-registered NGOs, "on the ground that humanitarian action and military intervention had to be kept separated," Rieff, *A Bed for the Night*, New York: Simon & Schuster, 2002, p. 208.

36. Fox, David, "New humanitarianism," p. 282.

37. Rieff for example argued that "relief workers would leave Kosovo emergency less sure than ever about what their roles were and were not, what they could hope to do, and what they would be allowed to do," Rieff, *A Bed for the Night*, p. 229.

38. Hubert and Brassard-Boudreau, "Is humanitarian space shrinking?," this volume.

39. *Civilian Deaths in the NATO Air Campaign*, Human Rights Watch, 2000: http://www.hrw.org/legacy/reports/2000/nato (last accessed 27 April 2012). NATO lost only two militaries as a consequence of a helicopter crash in Albania.

40. Weiss, Thomas G., "The politics of humanitarian space," this volume.

7. SHIFTING SANDS: HUMANITARIAN RELIEF IN ACEH

1. On the question of vulnerability caused by political breakdown and the "naturalness" of natural disasters see Alexander, D., "The study of natural disasters, 1977–1997: some reflections on a changing field of knowledge," *Disasters* vol. 21, no. 4 (1997), pp. 284–304.

2. The names of some informants and places have been changed to protect their identity.

3. di Tiro, H., *The Price of Freedom (The Unfinished Diary)*, Norsberg: Information Department, Acheh Sumatra National Liberation Front, 1982; Kell, T., *The Roots of Acehnese Rebellion, 1989–1992*, Ithaca, NY: Cornell Modern Indonesia Project, Southeast Asia Program, Cornell University, 1995. Robinson, G., "Rawan is as Rawan does: the origins of disorder in New Order Aceh," *Indonesia* vol. 66 (1998), pp. 127–58. Earlier rebellions in Aceh include the Dutch War, which lasted from 1873–1906, although some isolated fighting did continue until the departure of the Dutch in 1942; the "Cumbok War" (1946–7) between the ruling aristocratic elite—the *Ulee Balang*—and the religious leaders, or *Ulama*; and the *Darul Islam* (House of Islam) Rebellion (1953–62), which was not a secessionist conflict but rather an attempt to establish an Islamic State of Indonesia. Many Acehnese are inspired by these earlier rebellions, but there are few "organisational links" with the GAM rebellion (1976–2005).

4. Aspinall, E., and Crouch H., *The Aceh Peace Process: Why it Failed*, Washington, DC: East-West Center, 2003.

5. Oxfam, *Aceh Background Brief*, Oxford: Oxfam GB, 2003.

6. United Nations News Service "Displaced Indonesians suffer from higher rates of poverty, poor health, WFP reports," 7 May 2002, http://www.un.org/apps/news/printnewsAr.asp?nid=3600 (accessed 8 September 2010).

7. They included the International Catholic Migration Commission (ICMC), the International Rescue Committee (IRC), Oxfam GB, Peace Brigades International (PBI) and Save the Children (US) (SC-US).

8. Aspinall, E., *Peace Without Justice? The Helsinki Peace Process in Aceh*, Geneva: Henry Dunant Centre for Humanitarian Dialogue, 2008, p. 7.

9. Interview with Mahdi, former student leader, 1 September 2007, Amsterdam, Netherlands.

10. Schulze, K.E., *The Free Aceh Movement (GAM): Anatomy of a Separatist Organization*, Washington, DC: East-West Center, 2004.

11. Lindorf-Nielsen, M., *Questioning Aceh's Inevitability: A Story of Failed National Integration?*, 2002: http://www.globalpolitics.net/essays/Lindorf_Nielsen.pdf (accessed 8 September 2010).

12. Interview with international NGO program director, 2 February 2007, Banda Aceh, Indonesia.

13. Human Rights Watch, *Indonesia: the War in Aceh*, Brussels: Human Rights Watch Asia Division, 2001; Frontline, *Frontline Indonesia: Murders, Death Threats and Other Types of Intimidation Against Human Rights Defenders*, Dublin: Frontline, 2002; Amnesty International, *Indonesia: Protecting the Protectors: Human Rights Defenders and Humanitarian Workers in Nanggroe Aceh Darussalam*, London: Amnesty International, 2003.

14. BRR (Badan Rehabilitasi dan Rekonstruksi Aceh dan Nias—Agency for the Rehabilitation and Reconstruction of Aceh and Nias), *Aceh and Nias One Year after the Tsunami: the Recovery Effort and the Way Forward*, A joint report of the BRR and international partners, Banda Aceh: BRR, 2005.

15. Flint, M. and Goyder H., *Funding the Tsunami Response*, London: Tsunami Evaluation Coalition, 2006, pp. 7, 24.

16. Oxfam *Oxfam International Tsunami Fund, Third Annual Report*, Oxford: Oxfam, 2007.

17. Scheper, B., Parakrama, A. and Patel S., *Impact of the Tsunami Response on Local and National Capacities*, London: Tsunami Evaluation Coalition, 2006, p. 9.

18. See also Burke, A. and Afnan, *Aceh: Reconstruction in a Conflict Environment. Views from Civil Society, Donors and NGOs*. Indonesian Social Development Paper, Jakarta: World Bank, 8 October 2005.

19. Telford, J., Cosgrave J. and Houghton R., *Joint Evaluation of the International Response to the Indian Ocean Tsunami: Synthesis Report*. Tsunami Evaluation Coalition, London, 2006, pp. 19–20.

20. Flint and Goyder, *Funding the Tsunami Response*, p. 37.

21. Telephone interview with Mike Novell, Save the Children (US), 30 April 2007, Banda Aceh and Jakarta, Indonesia.

22. Ibid.
23. Interview with David Shields, Catholic Relief Services, 28 April 2007 Banda Aceh, Indonesia.
24. Interviews with Patrick McInnis, Oxfam International, 10 April 2007, Banda Aceh, Indonesia, and with Yanti Lacsana, Oxfam Indonesia, 8 November 2008, Jakarta, Indonesia.
25. While the DEC funding situation frustrated Oxfam staff members, some found that there was still scope for activities relating to policy and research, such as addressing post-tsunami land rights issues, policy on renters and squatters, issues concerning military claims to land, as well as broader gender and land disputes.
26. Despite numerous e-mail and telephone requests for an interview with senior Oxfam GB staff in Oxford in October 2007, this author was told that there was no-one at Oxfam with knowledge of or time to discuss the matter of funding and implementation in different intervention contexts in Aceh. Resources on this subject are thus limited to interviews and discussions with senior country and regional staff.
27. Interview with Lilianne Fan, Oxfam International, 1 February 2007, Banda Aceh, Indonesia.
28. Ibid.
29. Interview with Patrick McInnis, Oxfam International, 10 April 2007, Banda Aceh, Indonesia.
30. Antara News Agency, "Soldiers kill 120 Aceh rebels over past two weeks," 20 January 2005.
31. Interview with a TNI official, 22 January 2005, Lhokseumawe, Indonesia.
32. United Nations News Service, "UN refugee agency ends emergency tsunami relief operations in Indonesia," 24 March 2005, http://www.un.org/apps/news/story.asp?NewsID=13760&Cr=tsunami&Cr1 (accessed 8 September 2010).
33. United Nations News Service, "UN refugee agency invited to return to Aceh for tsunami rebuilding effort," 27 June 2005, http://www.un.org/apps/news/story.asp?NewsID=14778&Cr=tsunami&Cr1= (accessed 8 September 2010).
34. Interview with Patrick McInnis, Oxfam International, 10 April 2007, Banda Aceh, Indonesia.
35. Ibid.
36. Interview with Enayet Madani, UNORC, 3 May 2007, Lhokseumawe, Indonesia.
37. Interview with international NGO director, 2 February 2007, Banda Aceh, Indonesia.
38. At this point I must remind the reader of a conflict of interest since I was hired for the position of protection advisor.
39. The IRC did support a local NGO's (CARE Aceh) media campaign in raising public awareness of the peace process in late 2005.

40. Interview with Margaret Green, International Rescue Committee, 1 November 2007, New York, United States.

41. Interview with Marcel de Brune, International Rescue Committee, 31 January 2007, Banda Aceh, Indonesia.

42. Interview with Jana Mason, International Rescue Committee, 2 November 2007, Washington, DC, US

43. Interview with Marcel de Brune, International Rescue Committee, 31 January 2007, Banda Aceh, Indonesia.

44. Ibid.

45. The GoI and GAM convened five times in Helsinki between January and July 2005. They discussed matters relating to self-government, security arrangements, an amnesty for political prisoners, local political parties, a truth and reconciliation commission, and a human rights court for Aceh. Of these, the most contentious issue was local political parties, which almost derailed the talks during the fifth and final round in mid-July 2005. The MoU, signed on 15 August 2005, contained all of these provisions. See CMI, *Memorandum of Understanding*.

46. The gubernatorial elections led to a rift within GAM's ranks among the "old guard" and the "Young Turks," who supported different GAM gubernatorial candidates. However, this did not result in any serious conflict or splinter groups. Cf. ICG (International Crisis Group) "Indonesia: how GAM won in Aceh," *Asia Briefing* no. 61, Jakarta/Brussels: ICG, 22 March 2007.

47. See BRR, *Aceh and Nias One Year after the Tsunami*.

48. MSF (Médecins Sans Frontières), "One year after the Indian Ocean tsunami disaster," 20 December 2005. http://www.msf.org/msfinternational/invoke.cfm?objectid=4779BD1E-0323–28C7-D4BF508ECF63E0E6&component=toolkit.article&method=full_html (accessed 8 September 2010).

49. Interview with Anne-Marie Loof, MSF-Holland, 12 January 2007, Banda Aceh, Indonesia.

50. It is important to note that the MSF-Holland photographic exhibition was the only public conflict-related advocacy activity conducted by any of the large international NGOs in Aceh.

51. Interview with Anne-Marie Loof, MSF-Holland, 12 January 2007, Banda Aceh, Indonesia.

52. Interview with Dewi Suralaga, Hivos, 31 August 2007, Utrecht, Netherlands.

53. For a complete account on international engagement in the Aceh peace process see Barron, P. and Burke A., "Supporting peace in Aceh: development agencies and international involvement," *Policy Studies* vol. 47 (Southeast Asia, Washington, DC: East-West Center, 2008.

54. The AMM consisted of 240 unarmed personnel for the first six months of the mission who came from EU states and five contributing Association of South-

East Asian Nations (ASEAN) countries (Brunei, Malaysia, Philippines, Singapore and Thailand). Switzerland and Norway also contributed monitors through the EU.

55. Interviews with Mark Knight, International Organization for Migration, 1 May 2007, Banda Aceh, Indonesia, and Renate Korber, European Union, 1 May 2007, Banda Aceh, Indonesia. In a separate paper this author argues that the AMM's focus on technical matters such as disarmament and demobilisation, and its decision not to pursue sensitive issues such as human rights, in fact strengthened the immediate post-conflict process. See Zeccola, P., "Humanitarian action and conflict transformation in Aceh, Indonesia, 1998–2008," Paper presented at the World Conference of Humanitarian Studies, Groningen, Netherlands, 4–8 February 2009.

56. Barron and Burke, "Supporting peace in Aceh," pp. 50–1.

57. Interview with Imogen Wall, United Nations Development Programme, 11 October 2007, London, United Kingdom.

58. Ibid.

59. Ibid.

8. SPOTLIGHTS AND MIRRORS: MEDIA AND THE HUMANITARIAN COMMUNITY IN HAITI'S DISASTER

1. Herz, Ansel, "Wikileaked cables reveal: as U.S. militarized quake response, it worried about international criticism," *Haiti Liberté* and *The Nation*, 15–21 June 2011.

2. Schuller, Mark, "Unstable foundations: impact of NGO aid on human rights for Port-au-Prince's internally displaced people," New York and Port-au-Prince: CUNY and UEH, 4 October 2010.

3. Schuller, Mark, "Mèt Ko Veye Ko: foreign responsibility in the failure to protect against cholera and other man-made disasters," New York and Port-au-Prince: CUNY and UEH, 22 January 2011.

4. See Schuller, Mark, "Haiti's bitter harvest: NGOization of aid," in Donini, Antonio (ed.), *The Golden Fleece: Manipulation and Independence in Humanitarian Action*, Sterling, VA: Kumarian Press, 2012.

5. Lawless, Robert, *Haiti's Bad Press*, Rochester, VT: Schenkman Books, 1992; Trouillot, Michel-Rolph, *Silencing the Past: Power and the Production of History*, Boston: Beacon Press, 1995; Ulysse, Gina Athena, "Why representations of Haiti matter now more than ever," NACLA Report on the Americas vol. 43, no. 5 (2010).

6. For example, Schwartz, Timothy, *Travesty in Haiti: A True Account of Christian Missions, Orphanages, Fraud, Food Aid and Drug Trafficking*, Charleston, SC: Book Surge Publishing, 2008.

9. LEAP OF FAITH: NEGOTIATING HUMANITARIAN ACCESS IN SOMALIA'S 2011 FAMINE

1. UN Security Council, "Report of the Monitoring Group on Somalia and Eritrea pursuant to Security Council Resolution 1916 (2010)," S/2011/433, New York, 18 July 2011, p. 56.
2. Inter-Agency Standing Committee, "IASC Real Time Evaluation of the Somalia Drought Crisis Response," First Draft, Nairobi, March 2012, p. 9.
3. Bradbury, Mark, "Normalising the crisis in Africa," *Disasters* vol. 22, no. 4 (December 1998), pp. 328–38.
4. "IASC," p. 9.
5. UN Security Council, "Report of the Monitoring Group on Somalia and Eritrea pursuant to Security Council Resolution 1853 (2008)," S/2010/91, New York, 10 March 2010, p. 60.
6. Hammond Laura and Vaughan-Lee, Sarah, "Humanitarian Space in Somalia: A Scarce Commodity," Humanitarian Policy Group Working Paper, London: Humanitarian Policy Group, ODI, April 2012, p. 2.
7. UNHCR, "2012 UNHCR Country Operations Profile: Somalia," http://www.unhcr.org/pages/49e483ad6.html (accessed April 2 2012).
8. Hammond and Vaughan-Lee, p. 4.
9. Interview by the author, 2009, Nairobi, Kenya.
10. Stoddard, Abby, et al., "Providing Aid in Insecure Environments: 2009 Update—Trends in Violence against Aid Workers and the Operational Response," Humanitarian Policy Group Policy Brief no. 34, London: ODI, 2009.
11. Hammond and Vaughan-Lee, p. 11.
12. Menkhaus, Ken, "Stabilisation and humanitarian access in a collapsed state: the Somali case," *Disasters* vol. 34, suppl. no. 3 (October 2010), pp. 320–41.
13. Ould-Abdallah, Ahmedou, "Why the world should not let Somalia go to the dogs," *Kenyan Daily Nation*, July 25 2009.
14. See UN Monitoring Group report of July 2011, p. 61.
15. Ibid., pp. 27–30.
16. Gettleman, Jeffrey, "US delays Somalia aid, fearing it is feeding terrorists," *New York Times*, 1 October 2009.
17. For details, see the March 2010 Report of the Monitoring Group, pp. 60–7.
18. Famine Early Warning System, "Special Brief: Marketing Functioning in southern Somalia," 27 July 2011, p. 3.
19. Interviews by the author, September 2011.
20. IASC, pp. 11–16.
21. UN OCHA 2011, "Horn of Africa Crisis, Situation Report no. 19," 21 October 2011.
22. The article in question is Gettlemen, Jeffrey, "Somalis waste away as insurgents

block escape from famine," *New York Times*, 1 August 2012, p. A1. The article and accompanying photograph briefly galvanised international attention on the famine.

23. Hammond and Vaughan-Lee, p. 10.

24. Pflanz, Mike, "Al-Shabaab backtracks on promise to allow foreign aid workers back into the country," *The Telegraph*, 22 July 2011: http://www.telegraph.co.uk/news/worldnews/africaandindianocean/somalia/8655351/Famine-Al-Shabaab-backtracks-on-promise-to-allow-foreign-aid-workers-back-into-the-country.html.

25. Correspondence with author, September 2011.

26. OSAFA, "Fact Finding Committee Conducts Organization Performance Appraisal," 28 November 2011.

27. "Somali islamists ban Red Cross," *The Guardian*, 31 January 2012: http://www.guardian.co.uk/world/2012/jan/31/somali-islamists-ban-red-cross.

28. Most of the observations that follow in this section are based on the author's own episodic involvement in these discussions in Washington DC in July and August 2011, or personal communications with those involved.

29. Eyewitnesses recount one instance in which an inexperienced Turkish relief worker was found weeping in the seaport because the food aid his charity had shipped was stuck for weeks. Somalis negotiated with the port authorities on his behalf until an acceptable cut of the aid was diverted, and the rest was allowed to pass. Interview by the author, April 2012.

30. Bradbury, Mark, "State-building, Counter-Terrorism, and Licensing Humanitarianism in Somalia," Feinstein International Center Briefing Paper, September 2011, p. 9.

10. ETHICAL COMPLEXITY AND PERPLEXITY: HUMANITARIAN ACTORS, DISASTERS AND SPACE

1. Consequentialism is also found in teleological accounts of ethics, such as Aristotelian or neo-Aristotelian arguments for virtue ethics. Hursthouse, Rosalind, *On Virtue Ethics*, Oxford: Oxford University Press, 2001; Foot, Philippa, *Natural Goodness*, Oxford: Oxford University Press, 2003; Crisp, Roger and Slote, Michael (eds), *Virtue Ethics*, Oxford: Oxford University Press, 2002. I do not address virtue ethics specifically here. Instead, I utilise the more often invoked framework of utilitarianism.

2. Kant, Immanuel, *Grounding for the Metaphysics of Morals*, translated by James W. Ellington, Indianapolis: Hackett Publishing Co., 1993. These principles are of course the different formulations of the categorical imperative. Depending upon the Kantian argument one endorses, one may privilege one formulation over another or attempt, like Kant, to hold them of moral equality. For an excel-

lent discussion of weighting the humanity principle, see Donagan, Alan, *The Theory of Common Morality*, Chicago: University of Chicago Press, 1977.

3. Cf. Dunn, Elizabeth, "The Anthropology of Nothing: Humanitarian Voids in the Republic of Georgia," 2011, unpublished essay in file with the author. Terry, Fiona, *Condemned to Repeat: The Paradox of Humanitarian Action*, Ithaca: Cornell University Press, 2002, pp. 51–4. Dufour, Charlotte, Huges, Maury, du Geoffroy, Véronique and Grünewald, François, "Rights, standards and quality in a complex humanitarian space: is sphere the right tool?," *Disasters* vol. 28, no. 2, (2004), pp. 124–41.

4. Fiona Terry notes that humanitarian action can provide legitimacy to individuals, political movements, factions and regimes. She cites the aid given during 1969–1987 to the South African government as providing the government with "some respectability, implying that the regime cooperated with international inspection." Terry, *Condemned to Repeat*, p. 45. This example, of course, presupposes a right to received aid, and that an aid organisation's decision to help one group over another for political reasons would violate such a right.

5. In the aforementioned example, applying the deontologist's framework presupposes that there is a right to receive aid, and that omitting aid from a portion of the population would be considered a moral wrong.

6. Anderson, Mary B., *Do No Harm: How Aid Can Support Peace—or War*, Boulder, CO: Lynne Rienner Press, 1999. A better rule of thumb is more likely to "do no wrong," that is to not incur a rights violation. Harm is an extremely pliable notion and is often too broad a framework. For arguments about the notion of harm see Feinberg, *Harm to Others*, Oxford: Oxford University Press, 1984.

7. While states are one of the primary actors in international relations, and we might argue that they have a type of corporate moral agency, I am not going to delve into these matters here. Soldiers are representative of state policies, and they are the actors on the ground who will find themselves in a myriad of possible ethical dilemmas. Moreover, all other corporate moral agents involved in humanitarian actors are going to be represented by human actors in these disaster zones. Therefore, using the combatant/noncombatant distinction addresses many of the issues at hand without wading into the deeper philosophical waters of corporate moral agency.

8. Walzer, Michael, *Just and Unjust Wars: A Moral Argument with Historical Illustrations*, 4th edn, London: Basic Books, 2006, p. 144.

9. Walzer discusses the fact that soldiers can either voluntarily join an army, or they can be conscripted. In either situation, at some point, soldiers are made to fight, and thus because of this coercive activity they all ought to be considered "morally equal," Walzer, *Just and Unjust Wars*, pp. 34–47. The moral equality of soldiers is important in making the combatant/noncombatant distinction, as all soldiers gain war rights (such as the right not to be killed when surrendering, to

be humanely treated and to retain their property), while all noncombatants retain the right not to be killed or harmed. Cf. The Hague Convention II: Convention with Respect to the Laws and Customs of War on Land (1899) at: http://frank.mtsu.edu/~baustin/hague2.html (last accessed 23 August 2011).

10. The Hague Convention, Annex, Section 1, Article 1, no. 1 at: http://frank. mtsu.edu/~baustin/hague2.html

11. Walzer, *Just and Unjust Wars*, note 7, p. 187.

12. Ibid, p. 145.

13. Ibid, p. 146.

14. The status of munitions workers is explained further in Walzer, *Just and Unjust Wars*, pp. 145–6.

15. There is, of course, the problem of the Doctrine of Double Effect (DDE). DDE is an attempt to reconcile the absolute prohibition on killing noncombatants with the tactical or strategic necessity of fighting war. In other words, DDE permits the lives of civilians to be taken if it is a result of a foreseen but unintended consequence of targeting a legitimate military installation and such "collateral damage" is not the primary aim of the attack. DDE is philosophically quite problematic for both deontologists and consequentialists as its principles are in tensions with one another. To alleviate these tensions, some ethicists follow Walzer in claiming that soldiers must have a "dual intention" when it comes to firing on targets in civilian areas. This means that soldiers must take on more risk to themselves to attempt to save civilian lives, rather than hiding under the umbrella of DDE. Walzer, *Just and Unjust Wars*, p. 155.

16. Albala-Bertrand, J.M., "Responses to complex humanitarian eEmergencies and natural Disasters: an analytical comparison," *Third World Quarterly* vol. 21, no. 2 (2000), p. 218.

17. Ibid, p. 219.

18. Ibid, pp. 219–24.

19. Ibid.

20. Kleinfeld, Margo, "Misreading the post-tsunami political landscape in Sri Lanka: the myth of humanitarian space," *Space and Polity* vol. 11, no. 2 (2007), pp. 169–84. Kleinfeld's excellent account of the 2004 Sri Lankan disaster throws the notion of "humanitarian space" into sharp relief with the politics of aid.

21. Andreas, Peter, *Blue Helmets and Black Markets: The Business of Survival in the Siege of Sarajevo*, Ithaca: Cornell University Press, 2008, p. 39.

22. Smith, David, "UN-backed troops 'murdering and raping villagers' in Congo," *The Guardian*, 15 October 2010.

23. Ibid.

24. United Nations Convention on the Rights of the Child, (A/Res/44/25) at: http://www2.ohchr.org/english/law/crc.htm. Optional Protocol on the Involvement of Children in Armed Conflict (A/Res/54/263) at: http://www2.

ohchr.org/english/law/crc-conflict.htm (last accessed 23 August 2011). The Optional Protocol says nothing about rules of engagement with child soldiers. It roughly requires that states do not recruit child soldiers and will do what is in their power to reintegrate and disarm former child soldiers.

25. Terry, *Condemned to Repeat*, p. 19.

26. Ibid.

27. Ibid.

28. de Torrenté, Nicolas, "Humanitarianism sacrificed: integrations false promise," *Ethics and International Affairs* vol. 18, no. 2 (2004), p. 3. De Torrenté argues that making aid contingent on political gains is illegitimate and aid workers and politicians should depoliticise aid. However, this argument seems to miss the point that politicians giving either do not want to do so, or it may be impossible for them to do so. Furthermore, the integration of aid with political agendas is consequentialist based, and so the claim that making aid contingent upon pursing enduring and just resolutions to conflict is unjust or wrong, does little to undermine the consequentialist argument that peaceful outcomes outweigh short-term withholding of aid.

29. Ibid, pp. 3–7.

30. Rubenstien, Jennifer, "Humanitarian NGOs' duties of justice," *Journal of Social Philosophy* vol. 40, no. 4 (2009), p. 529.

31. Dunn, "The Anthropology of Nothing," p. 8.

32. Ibid., p. 9.

33. Hubert, Don and Brassard-Boudreau, Cynthia, "Is humanitarian space shrinking?," this volume.

34. Interestingly, Hubert and Brassard-Boudreau cite a decline in the "human impact of civil conflict" since the end of the Cold War. As their source for empirical evidence, they cite Melander, Erik, Öberg, Magnus and Hall, Jonathan, "Migration before and after the end of the Cold War," *European Journal of International Relations* vol. 15, no. 3 (2009), pp. 505–36. However, Fearon and Laitin find that civil conflict is the cause of five times the amount of total battle deaths than inter-state conflict since 1945, and such civil conflicts are about seven times as long as inter-state wars. Fearon, James D. and Laitin, David D., "Ethnicity, insurgency and civil war," *Political Science Review* vol. 97, no. 1 (2003), pp. 75–90. We should, therefore, take with caution empirical "evidence" one way or the other.

11. THE RESPONSIBILITY TO PROTECT: OPENING HUMANITARIAN SPACES?

1. Paragraphs 138–40 of the World Summit Outcome document, A/60/L.1, 20 September 2005; UN Security Council Resolution 1674, 28 April 2006; UN Security Council Resolution 1894, 11 November 2009.

2. Ki-moon, Ban, "On responsible sovereignty: international cooperation for a changed world," SG/SM11701, Berlin, 15 July 2008.
3. General Assembly Resolution 63/308, 7 October 2009.
4. Annan, "Two concepts of sovereignty," *The Economist*, 18 September 1999.
5. Cohen, Roberta and Deng, Francis M., *Masses in Flight: The Global Crisis of Internal Displacement*, Washington, DC: The Brookings Institution, 1998, p. 275.
6. Deng, Francis M., Kimaro, Sadikiel, Lyons, Terrence, Rothchild, Donald and Zartman, I. William, *Sovereignty as Responsibility: Conflict Management in Africa*, Washington, DC: The Brookings Institution, 1996, p. 1.
7. See Deng, Francis M., *Guiding Principles on Internal Displacement*, UN doc. E/CN.4/1998/53/Add.2 (1998).
8. UN Commission on Human Rights, *Responses of Governments and Agencies to the Report of the UN Special Representative for Internally Displaced Persons*, E/CN.4/1993/SR.40, 1993.
9. E/CN.4/1993/SR.40, 1993.
10. "World fears for plight of Myanmar cyclone victims," *New York Times*, 13 May 2008.
11. Reported in Bellamy, Alex and Davis, Sarah, *Global Politics and the Responsibility to Protect*, New York: Routledge, p. 57.
12. Borger, Julian and MacKinnon, Ian, "Bypass junta's permission for aid, US and France urge," *The Guardian*, 9 May 2008.
13. For example, Evans, Gareth, *The Responsibility to Protect: Ending Mass Atrocity Crimes Once and for All*, Washington, DC: Brookings Institution Press, 2008, p. 106; and Tutu, Desmond, "Taking the responsibility to protect," *New York Times*, 9 November 2008.
14. Cited in Cohen, Roger, "How Kofi Annan rescued Kenya," *New York Review of Books* vol. 55, no. 13 (2008), pp. 48–9.
15. Statement attributable to the spokesperson for the secretary-general on the situation in Kenya, New York, 2 January 2008.
16. Ban Ki-moon, Address to the Summit of the African Union, Addis Ababa, 31 January 2008.
17. S/PRST/2008/4, 6 February 2008
18. International Crisis Group, "Kenya in crisis," *Africa Report* no. 137, 21 February 2008.
19. Harder, Sean, "How they stopped the killing," The Stanley Foundation, June 2009.
20. Keynote Address by Jean Ping, chairperson of the AU Commission, at the Roundtable High-Level Meeting of Experts on "The responsibility to protect in Africa," Addis Ababa, 23 October 2008.

12. HUMANITARIANISM, INTERVENTION AND THE UN: A WORK IN PROGRESS

1. International Crisis Group, *War Crimes in Sri Lanka*, 17 May 2010.
2. 'Beating the drum', *Economist*, 18 November 2010.
3. Foley, Conor, "What really happened in Sri Lanka," *Guardian*, 16 July 2009.
4. "From our own correspondent," *British Broadcasting Corporation*, 4 February 1996.
5. Hilberg, Raul, *Perpetrators, Victims, Bystanders: The Jewish Catastrophe 1933–1945*, London: HarperCollins, 1992.
6. See LeBor, Adam, *'Complicity with Evil': the United Nations in the Age of Modern Genocide*, New Haven: Yale University Press, 2006.
7. See Brivati, Brian and Spencer, Philip, "Shameful evasions," *Guardian*, 25 October 2006.
8. Slim, Hugo, "Military humanitarianism and the new peace-keeping: an agenda for peace?," *The Journal of Humanitarian Assistance*, 3 June 2000, available at http://www.jha.ac/articles/a003.htm.
9. Roberts, Adam, *Humanitarian issues and agencies as triggers for international military action*, paper presented at the 600th Wilton Park conference, May 2000.
10. Rodley, Nigel (ed.), *To loose the bands of wickedness, international intervention in defence of human rights*, Brassey's, 1992.
11. See the Caroline case 1841–42 for more details see Harris, D. J., *Cases and Materials in International Law*, 5th edn, London: Sweet and Maxwell, 1998, pp. 894–917.
12. Articles 39–42. See also *Certain expenses of the United Nations (Article 17(2) of the Charter) Advisory Opinion*, 20 July 1961, ICJ Rep 1962, p. 151.
13. *Supplement to an Agenda for Peace. Position Paper of the Secretary General*, UN Doc. A/50/60-S/1995/1, 3 January 1995, para 11.
14. Roberts, Adam, "Humanitarian war: military intervention and human rights," *International Affairs* vol. 69, no. 3 (1993), pp. 429–49.
15. Holt, Victoria K. and Berkman, Tobias C., *The Impossible Mandate? Military Preparedness, The Responsibility To Protect, and Modern Peace Operations*, Washington, DC: Henry Stimson Center, 2006.
16. *New York Times*, 31 December 1993.
17. Interview conducted by the author with Christopher Greenwood at a seminar on the use of force under international law, Save the Children UK Offices, London, June 2002.
18. Robertson, Geoffrey, *Crimes Against Humanity: the Struggle for Global Justice*, London: Allen Lane, 1999, p. 72.
19. Ibid.
20. In response to questions about northern Iraq by the Foreign Affairs Committee in 1992. Quoted in Harris, *Cases and Materials in International Law*, p. 921.

21. *UK Foreign Office Policy Document, No. 148*, Quoted in Harris, *Cases and Materials in International Law*, p. 918.
22. Ibid.
23. Hlzgrefe J. L. and Keohane, Robert (eds), *Humanitarian Intervention: Ethical, Legal and Political Dilemmas*, Cambridge: Cambridge University Press, 2003, p. 1.
24. For details see Cooke, Helena, *The Safe Haven in Northern Iraq*, Essex Human Rights Centre and Kurdish Human Rights Project, 1995.
25. Statement by the UK representative to the Security Council, S/PV 3988 (1999).
26. Blair Speech Transcripts, from 1997–2007, Chicago, 24 April 1999, http://keeptonyblairforpm.wordpress.com/blair-speech-transcripts-from-1997-2007.
27. Evans, Gareth, *Hypocrisy, Democracy, War and Peace*, International Crisis Group, 16 June 2007.
28. See, *The Relationship between the Responsibility to Protect and the Protection of Civilians in Armed Conflict*, Global Centre for the Responsibility to Protect, January 2009.
29. Foley, Conor, *The Thin Blue Line: how Humanitarianism went to War*, London and New York: Verso, 2010.
30. Pantuliano, Sara and O'Callaghan Sorcha, '*The protection crisis': a review of field-based strategies for humanitarian protection in Darfur*, London: Overseas Development Institute Humanitarian Policy Group discussion paper, December 2006.
31. DuBois, Marc, "Protection: fig-leaves and other delusions," *Humanitarian Exchange*, March 2010.
32. *MSF Activity Report 2000–2001*, http://www.msf.org (visited 3 September 2002). See also Barry, Jane with Jefferys, Anna, *A bridge too far: aid agencies and the military in humanitarian response*, Humanitarian Practice Discussion Network, January 2002, p. 16.
33. See Holt, Victoria and Taylor, Glyn, *Protecting civilians in the context of UN peacekeeping operation*, New York: United Nations, 2009.
34. UNSC S/RES/1270 of 22 October 1999, para.14, emphasis added.
35. UN-led missions include: UNAMSIL; MONUC; UNMIL; ONUB; MINUSTAH; UNOCI; UNMIS; UNIFIL; UNAMID; and MINURCAT. The Council also used similar language for missions led by others.
36. S/RES/1794 of 21 December 2007, para. 5.
37. Holt and Taylor, *Protecting civilians*, p. 5.
38. Ibid., p. 16.
39. Flint, Julie and de Waal, Alex, "Case closed: a prosecutor without borders," *World Affairs Journal*, Spring 2009.

13. THE DILEMMAS OF PSYCHOSOCIAL INTERVENTIONS

1. Pupavac, Vanessa, "Pathologizing populations and colonizing minds: international psychosocial programs in Kosovo," Working Paper (UNHCR, Geneva), 59, 2002; and Summerfield, Derek, "What exactly is emergency or disaster 'mental health'?," *Bulletin of the World Health Organization* vol. 83, no. 1 (2005), pp. 76–7.

2. Ingleby, David, *Forced Migration and Mental Health: Rethinking the Care of Migrants and Displaced Persons*, New York: Springer, 2005.

3. Summerfield, "What exactly is emergency or disaster 'mental health'?," pp. 76–7.

4. Summerfield, Derek, "Cross cultural perspectives on the medicalisation of human suffering," in Rosen, G. (ed.), *Posttraumatic Stress Disorder: Issues and Controversies*, John Wiley, 2004, pp. 233–45.

5. Furedi, Frank, *Therapy Culture: Cultivating Vulnerability in an Uncertain Age*, London: Routledge, 2004.

6. O'Keefe, Phil and Rose, Joanne, *International Encyclopaedia of Public Health*, London: Elsevier, 2008, pp. 506–13.

7. International Federation of Red Cross and Red Crescent Societies, "Psychosocial Support—Healing Wounded Souls," *Reference Centre for Psychosocial Support*, 2010, Available at: http://psp.drk.dk/sw38265.asp (last accessed 22 February 2011).

8. The Psychosocial Working Group, "Psychosocial Interventions in Complex Emergencies: A Conceptual Framework," Working Paper, 2003, Available at: http://www.forcedmigration.org/psychosocial/papers/Conceptual%20 Framework.pdf (last accessed 23 February 2011).

9. Inter-Agency Standing Committee, "IASC Guidelines on Mental Health and Psychosocial Support in Emergency Settings," *International Guidelines* (2007), Available at: http://www.humanitarianinfo.org/iasc/mentalhealth_psychosocial_support (last accessed 22 December 2011).

10. Summerfield, "What exactly is emergency or disaster 'mental health'?," pp. 76–7.

11. Jayawickrama, Janaka, "Ethics and international mental health programmes," *Fourth World Journal* vol. 8, Washington, 2009, pp 7–18.

12. Ingleby, *Forced Migration and Mental Health: Rethinking the Care of Migrants and Displaced Persons*.

13. Jayawickrama, Janaka, "Rethinking mental health and wellbeing interventions in disaster and conflict-affected communities: case studies from Sri Lanka, Sudan and Malawi," UK: Northumbria University, 2010.

14. Ingleby, *Forced Migration and Mental Health: Rethinking the Care of Migrants and Displaced Persons*.

15. Onyut, Lamaro P., "The Nakivale Camp Mental Health Project: building local competency for psychological assistance to traumatised refugees," *Intervention* vol. 2, no. 2 (2004), pp. 90–107.

16. van Ommeren, M., Saxena, S. and Saraceno B, "Mental and social health during and after acute emergencies: emerging consensus?," *Bulletin of the World Health Organization* vol. 83, no. 1 (2005), pp. 71–5.

17. Jayawickrama, "Ethics and International Mental Health Programmes," pp. 7–18.

18. Ashcroft, Richard, "What's the good of counselling and psychotherapy: developing an ethical framework," *Counselling and Psychotherapy Journal* vol.12, no. 8 (2001), pp. 10–12.

19. Jayawickrama, "Ethics and International Mental Health Programmes," pp. 7–18.

20. Ibid.

21. Summerfield, Derek, "Addressing human response to war and atrocity: major challenges in research and practices and the limitations of Western psychiatric models," in Kleber, R.J., Figley, C.R. and Gersons, B.P.R. (eds), *Beyond Trauma*, New York: Plenum Press, 1995, pp. 17–29.

22. Jayawickrama, "Ethics and International Mental Health Programmes," pp. 7–18.

23. Easterly, William, *White Man's Burden: Why the West's Efforts to Aid the Rest Have Done So Much Ill and So Little Good*, New York: The Penguin Press, 2006, pp. 196–7.

14. THE IMPACT OF CRIMINALISING THE ENEMY ON HUMANITARIANISM

1. The Patriot Act (2001) and the Reform and Terrorism Prevention Act (2004).

2. Cf. Bialostozky, Noah, "Material support of peace? The on-the-ground consequences of U.S. and international material support of terrorism laws and the need for greater legal precision," *The Yale Journal of International Law online* vol. 36 (Spring 2011), pp. 62, 65, available at: http://www.yjil.org/docs/pub/o-36-bialostozky-material-support-of-peace.pdf.

3. CCR website, "Holder v humanitarian law project," http://ccrjustice.org/holder-v-humanitarian-law-project (last accessed 26 August 2011).

4. Cf. for example, "Supreme Court Ruling criminalizes speech in material support law case," CCR, Press Release, 21 June 2010, http://ccrjustice.org/newsroom/press-releases/supreme-court-ruling-criminalizes-speech-material-support-law-case. "The Supreme Court goes too far in the name of fighting terrorism," *The Washington Post*, Editorials, 22 June 2010.

5. Holder v humanitarian law project—Amicus Brief of the Carter Center et al., 23 November 2009, p. 26, available at http://www.aclu.org/files/assets/08–1498_and_09–89_tsac_The_Carter_Center.pdf (last accessed 5 September 2011).

6. United States Court of Appeal for the Ninth Circuit, Appeal No.07–55893, Humanitarian Law Project, et al. v US Dept. of Treasury, et al., Appellant Opening Brief, 7 January 2008, p. 11. Available at http://ccrjustice.org/files/HLP/HLP_4_Ninth-Circuit_Plaintiffs_Opening_Brief.pdf (last accessed 26 August 2011).

7. Appellant Opening, p. 12
8. Appellant Opening, p. 12.
9. Appellant Opening, pp. 12–13.
10. Holder, Attorney General, et al. v Humanitarian law project et al., Certiorari to the United States Court of Appeals for the Ninth Circuit, no.08–1498. Argued February 23 2010—Decided June 21 2010, p. 4. Available at: http://www.supremecourt.gov/opinions/09pdf/08–1498.pdf (last accessed 26 August 2011).
11. Ibid., p. 5.
12. Cf. Weissman, Fabrice, "Silence heals… from the Cold War to war on terror, MSF speaks out: a brief history," in Magone, C., et al. (eds), *Humanitarian Negotiations Revealed. The MSF Experience*, London: Hurst & Co., 2011.
13. See Weissman, Fabrice, (ed.), *In the Shadow of Just Wars. Violence, Politics and Humanitarian Action*, London: Hurst & Co, 2004.
14. Cf. for instance, Weissman, Fabrice, "Sri Lanka: MSF in all-out war," in Magone, C., et al. (eds), *Humanitarian Negotiations Revealed. The MSF Experience*, London: Hurst & Co., 2011.
15. The material support provided by organisations such as the ICRC or MSF to the LTTE is derisory compared with the funds raised from the diaspora and profits generated from arms and drugs smuggling… and the aid provided by the government, which continued to pay the salaries of civil servants (including in health and education) living there as a symbol of its continued sovereignty over rebel areas.

15. FOR HUMANITY OR FOR THE UMMA?: IDEOLOGIES OF HUMANITARIANISM AMONG TRANSNATIONAL ISLAMIC AID NGOS

1. Yaylaci, Ismail "Communitarian humanitarianism? The politics of Islamic humanitarian organisations," Paper presented at the workshop *Religion and Humanitarianism*, Cairo, 3–5 June 2008. Notable exceptions are Benthall, Jonathan and Bellion-Jourdan, Jerome, *The Charitable Crescent. The Politics of Aid in the Muslim World*, London: I.B. Tauris, 2003. See also de Cordier, Bruno, "Faith-based aid, globalization and the humanitarian frontline: an analysis of Western-based Muslim aid organisations," *Disasters* vol. 33, no. 4 (2009), pp. 608–28; Kaag, Mayke, "Transnational Islamic NGOs in Chad: Islamic solidarity in the age of neoliberalism," *Africa Today* vol. 54, no. 3 (2008), pp. 3–18; and Ghandour, Abdel Rahman, "The modern missionaries of Islam," in Weissman, Fabrice (ed.), *In the Shadow of 'Just Wars': Violence, Politics, and Humanitarian Action*, Ithaca: Cornell University Press, 2004.
2. For other examples of this, see Minear, Larry, *The Humanitarian Enterprise*,

Bloomfield: Kumarian Press, 2002, or Weiss, Thomas and Collins, Cindy, *Humanitarian Challenges and Intervention*, Boulder: Westview Press, 1996.

3. Bornstein, Erica and Redfield, Peter, *Forces of Compassion*, Santa Fe: SAR Press, 2011, p. 3.

4. The analysis builds on my PhD project, titled "For humanity or for the umma? Ideologies of aid in transnational Muslim NGOs," University of Copenhagen, 2011. Findings from the study are also published in Petersen, Marie Juul, "Islamizing aid? Transnational Muslim NGOs after 9.11," *Voluntas: International Journal of Voluntary and Non-profit organisations*, 2011.

5. For a historical account of Islamic charity, see Singer, Amy, *Charity in Islamic Societies*, Cambridge: Cambridge University Press, 2008.

6. For a history of Western humanitarianism, see Barnett, Michael and Weiss, Thomas (eds), *Humanitarianism in Question*, New York: Cornell University Press, 2008.

7. Ghandour, "The modern missionaries of Islam," p. 340.

8. Yaylaci, Ismail, "Communitarian humanitarianism: The politics of islamic humanitarian organisations."

9. Hegghammer, Thomas, *Jihad in Saudi Arabia. Violence and Pan-Islamisn since 1979*, Cambridge: Cambridge University Press, 2010, p. 17.

10. Pripp, Charles, *Islam and the Moral Economy*, Cambridge: Cambridge University Press, 2006, p. 104.

11. Benthall and Bellion-Jourdan, *The Charitable Crescent*, p. 72.

12. Ratcliffe, John, "Islamic charities after catastrophes: the Kashmir earthquake and the Indian Ocean tsunami," in Alterman, J. B. and Von Hippel, K. (eds), *Understanding Islamic Charities*, Washington, DC: Center for Strategic and International Studies, 2007, p. 57.

13. Ghandour, "Modern missionaries of Islam," p. 336; Ratcliffe, "Islamic charities after catastrophes," p. 59.

14. Kaag, "Transnational Islamic NGOs in Chad: Islamic solidarity in the age of neoliberalism," p. 10.

15. Ghandour, "Modern missionaries of Islam," p. 328.

16. Bellion-Jourdan, Jerome, "Islamic Relief organisations: between 'Islamism' and 'humanitarianism'," *ISIM Newsletter 5*, 2000, p. 15.

17. Ghandour, "Modern missionaries of Islam," p. 333.

18. Benthall and Bellion-Jourdan, *The Charitable Crescent*, p. 41. See also Ahmed, Chanfi, "Networks of Islamic NGOs in sub-Saharan Africa: Bilal Muslim Mission, African Muslim Agency (Direct Aid) and al-Haramayn," *Journal of Eastern African Studies* vol. 3, no. 3 (2009), p. 427.

19. Cf. Benthall and Bellion-Jourdan, *The Charitable Crescent*, p. 71.

20. Information from Islamic Relief Annual Reports 2003–2009, available at www.islamic-relief.com and Muslim Aid Annual Reviews 2000–2009, available at www.muslimaid.org (both last accessed 14 June 2011).

21. Howell Jude, and Lind, Jeremy, *Counter-terrorism, Aid and Civil Society: Before and After the War on Terror*, Basingstoke: Palgrave Macmillan, 2009, p. 47.

22. At a reception hosted by Muslim Aid at the British Houses of Parliament, MP Martin Horwood praised Muslim Aid: "This fantastic organisation has led the way in the development world in terms of building links within communities and promoting tolerance." Quoted from Muslim Aid website, www.muslimaid. org/index.php/media-centre/25th-anniversary/427-messageprime-minister (last accessed 25 March 2011).

23. For a discussion of research on faith-based organisations see Jones, Ben and Petersen, Marie Juul, "Instrumental, narrow, normative? Reviewing recent work on religion and development," *Third World Quarterly* vol. 32, no. 7 (2011), pp. 1291–1306.

24. Khan, Ajaz Ahmed, "The impulse to give: the motivations of giving to Muslim charities," in Barnett, Michael and Stein, Janice, *Between Heaven and Earth*, Oxford and New York: Oxford University Press, 2011; Muslim Aid, *Annual Review*, 2009, p. 26, available at www.muslimaid.org (last accessed 14 June 2011). Some of this funding stems from Middle Eastern and Muslim organisations; however, the majority comes from Western and international aid agencies.

25. Benedetti, Carlo, "Islamic and Christian inspired relief NGOs: between tactical collaboration and strategic diffidence," *Journal of International Development* vol. 18, no. 6 (2006), p. 855.

26. Smith, Steven R. and Sosin, Michael, "The varieties of faith-related agencies," *Public Administration Review* vol. 61, no. 6 (2001), p. 655.

27. Examples from Muslim Aid, *Annual Review* 1999. Available at www.muslimaid. org (last accessed 15 June 2011).

28. Muslim Aid, *Financial Statement 2008*, p. 11. Available at www.muslimaid.org (last accessed 15 June 2011).

29. However, both organisations still focus primarily on Muslim countries and populations. In 2009, for instance, more than 40 per cent of Islamic Relief's aid went to Pakistan, Palestine and Bangladesh. Islamic Relief, Annual Report 2009. Available at www.islamic-relief.com (last accessed 18 May 2011).

30. Barnett, Michael, "Humanitarianism transformed," *Perspectives on Politics* vol. 3, no. 4 (2005), p. 733.

31. Palmer, Victoria, "Analysing cultural proximity: Islamic relief worldwide and rohingya refugees in Bangladesh," *Development in Practice* vol. 21, no. 1 (2011), p. 103.

16. HUMANITARIANS AND DIPLOMATS: WHAT CONNECTIONS?

1. Junge, Traudl, *Bis zur letzten Stunde: Hitlers Sekretärin erzählt ihr Leben*, Berlin: Claassen, 2005, p. 199.

2. Kershaw, Ian, *Hitler 1936–45: Nemesis*, London: Penguin Books, 2001, p. 819.
3. Gilbert, Martin, *The Holocaust: The Jewish Tragedy*, London: Fontana/Collins, 1986, p. 796.
4. For an overview of different understandings of the term, see Smith, Hazel, "Humanitarian diplomacy: theory and practice," in Minear, Larry and Smith, Hazel (eds), *Humanitarian Diplomacy: Practitioners and their Craft*, Tokyo: United Nations University Press, 2007, pp. 36–62.
5. For a memoir detailing this kind of activity, see Picco, Giandomenico, *Man Without a Gun: One Diplomat's Secret Struggle to Free the Hostages, Fight Terrorism, and End a War*, New York: Times Books, 1999.
6. See Levine, Hillel, *In Search of Sugihara: The Elusive Japanese Diplomat Who Risked His Life to Rescue 10,000 Jews from the Holocaust*, New York: The Free Press, 1996.
7. See Betts, Alexander, *Protection by Persuasion: International Cooperation in the Refugee Regime*, Ithaca: Cornell University Press, 2009.
8. See Axelrod, Robert, *The Evolution of Cooperation*, New York: Basic Books, 1984.
9. See Loescher, Gil, *The UNHCR and World Politics: A Perilous Path*, Oxford: Oxford University Press, 2001, pp. 295–301; *The Humanitarian Decade: Challenges for Humanitarian Assistance in the Last Decade and into the Future*, New York: Office for the Coordination of Humanitarian Affairs, United Nations, 2004, Vols. I–II.
10. See Barnett, Michael, "Humanitarianism transformed," *Perspectives on Politics* vol. 3, no. 4 (2005), pp. 723–40; and Barnett, Michael, *Empire of Humanity: A History of Humanitarianism*, Ithaca: Cornell University Press, 2011.
11. See Heine, Jorge, "On the manner of practising the new diplomacy," in Cooper, Andrew F., Hocking, Brian and Maley, William (eds), *Global Governance and Diplomacy: Worlds Apart?*, London: Palgrave Macmillan, 2008, pp. 271–87.
12. See Weiss, Thomas G., *What's Wrong with the United Nations and How to Fix It*, Cambridge: Polity Press, 2008, pp. 72–106.
13. Jackson, Robert, *A Study of the Capacity of the United Nations Development System*, Geneva: United Nations, 1969, pp. iv–v.
14. Bernadotte, Folke, *Das Ende: Meine Verhandlungen in Deutschland im Frühjahr 1945 und ihre politischen Folgen*, Zürich: Europa Verlag, 1945, p. 22.
15. See Goodhand, Jonathan, *Aiding Peace? The Role of NGOs in Armed Conflict*, Boulder: Lynne Rienner, 2006. This is even more the case with the security companies and private commercial contractors that are increasingly found in conflict zones.
16. Jönsson, Christer and Hall, Martin, *Essence of Diplomacy*, New York: Palgrave Macmillan, 2005, p. 119.
17. Maley, William, *The Foreign Policy of the Taliban*, New York: Council on Foreign Relations, 1999, p. 23.

18. Sharp, Paul, "Mullah Zaeef and Taliban diplomacy: an English School approach," *Review of International Studies* vol. 29, no. 4 (2003), pp. 481–98.

19. Maley, William, "Afghanistan in 2010: continuing governance challenges and faulty security," *Asian Survey* vol. 51, no. 1 (2011), pp. 87–8.

20. Wiseman, Geoffrey, "Engaging the enemy: an essential norm for sustainable US diplomacy," in Constantinou, Costas M. and Der Derian, James (eds), *Sustainable Diplomacies*, New York: Palgrave Macmillan, 2010, pp. 213–34.

21. For a measured discussion, see Favez, Jean-Claude, *Une Mission Impossible? Le CICR, les Deportations et les Camps de Concentration Nazis*, Lausanne: Éditions Payot, 1988.

22. Rieff, David, *A Bed for the Night: Humanitarianism in Crisis*, New York: Simon & Schuster, 2002, p. 137. See also Kennedy, David, *The Dark Sides of Virtue: Reassessing International Humanitarianism*, Princeton: Princeton University Press, 2004.

23. Maley, William, *The Afghanistan Wars*, New York: Palgrave Macmillan, 2009, pp. 206–7.

24. *Agence France Presse*, 2 December 1999. See also Crossette, Barbara, "Gentle negotiations said to soften Taliban's rules for women," *The New York Times*, 23 January 2000.

25. Margalit, Avishai, *On Compromise and Rotten Compromises*, Princeton: Princeton University Press, 2010, p. 54.

26. Terry, Fiona, *Condemned to Repeat? The Paradox of Humanitarian Action*, Ithaca: Cornell University Press, 2002, pp. 195–6.

27. See *The Responsibility to Protect: Report of the International Commission on Intervention and State Sovereignty*, Ottawa: International Development Research Centre, 2001; Evans, Gareth, *The Responsibility to Protect: Ending Mass Atrocity Crimes Once and For All*, Washington, DC: Brookings Institution Press, 2008; Bellamy, Alex J., *Responsibility to Protect: The Global Effort to End Mass Atrocities*, Cambridge: Polity Press, 2009; Bellamy, Alex J., *Global Politics and the Responsibility to Protect: From Words to Deeds*, New York: Routledge, 2011; Thakur, Ramesh, *The Responsibility to Protect: Norms, Laws and the Use of Force in International Politics*, New York: Routledge, 2011.

28. Moorehead, Caroline, *Dunant's Dream: War, Switzerland and the History of the Red Cross*, London: HarperCollins, 1998, p. 549.

29. See Bregman, Ahron, *A History of Israel*, New York: Palgrave Macmillan, 2003, p. 58; Morris, Benny, *1948: A History of the First Arab-Israeli War*, New Haven: Yale University Press, 2008, p. 312. One of the three members of the committee was a future prime minister of Israel, Yitzhak Shamir.

17. FROM ARROW TO PATH: INTERNATIONAL RELATIONS THEORY AND THE HUMANITARIAN SPACE

1. Bellamy, Alex J., "The 'next stage' in peace operations theory?," *International Peacekeeping* vol. 11, no. 1 (2004), pp. 17–38. Michael Pugh, "Peacekeeping and critical theory," *International Peacekeeping* vol. 11, no. 1 (2004), pp. 39–58.

2. Reus-Smit, Christian and Snidal, Duncan (eds), *The Oxford Handbook of International Relations*, New York: Oxford University Press, 2008, p. 7.

3. More specifically on the relations between IR ethics, morals and humanitarianism, see Lechner, Silviya, "Humanitarian intervention: moralism versus realism?," *International Studies Review* vol. 12, no. 3 (2010), pp. 437–43.

4. Weiss, Thomas G., "The politics of humanitarian space," this volume.

5. Stoddard, Abby, "Humanitarian NGOs: challenges and trends," in Macrae, J. and Harmer, A. (eds), Humanitarian action and the 'global war on terror' a review of the trends and issues, *HPG Report 14*, London: Humanitarian Policy Group, 2003, p. 25.

6. Wohlforth, William C., "Realism," in Reus-Smit, C. and Snidal, D. (eds), *The Oxford Handbook of International Relations*, New York: Oxford University Press, 2008, p. 133.

7. Morgenthau, Hans, *Politics Amongst Nations*, 5th edn, New York: Alfred A Knopp Press, 1973, pp. 3–15. Waltz, Kenneth, *Theory of International Politics*, London: Random House, 1979.

8. Cozette, Murielle, "What lies ahead: classical realism on the future of international relations," *International Studies Review* vol. 10, no. 4 (2008), p. 678.

9. Donnelly, Jack, "The ethics of realism," in Reus-Smit, C. and Snidal, D. (eds), *The Oxford Handbook of International Relations*, New York: Oxford University Press, 2008, p. 152.

10. Morgenthau, Hans, *Politics Amongst Nations*, pp. 5–11.

11. Eberwein, Wolf Dieter, "Realism or idealism or both? Security policy and humanitarianism," *Arbeitsgruppe: Internationale Politik*, October 2001, p. 1.

12. Cooley, Alexander and Ron, James, "The NGO scramble: organizational insecurity and the political economy of transnational action," *International Security* vol. 27, no. 1 (2002), p. 6.

13. This was the driving rationale behind Immanuel Kant's Sketch for Perpetual Peace.

14. Moravscik, Andrew, "The new liberalism," in Reus-Smit, C. and Snidal, D. (eds), *The Oxford Handbook of International Relations*, New York: Oxford University Press, 2008, pp. 234–54.

15. Richardson, James L., "The ethics of neoliberal institutionalism," in Reus-Smit, C. and Snidal, D. (eds), *The Oxford Handbook of International Relations*, New York: Oxford University Press, 2008, p. 230.

16. Sørensen, Georg, "Liberalism of restraint and liberalism of imposition: liberal

values and world order in the new millennium," *International Relations* vol. 20, no. 3 (2006), p. 259.

17. Wendt, Alexander, "Constructing international politics," *International Security* vol. 20 (1995).

18. Wendt, Alexander, "narchy is what states make of it: the social construction of power politics," *International Organization* vol. 46, no. 2 (1992), p. 396.

19. Refer to Wendt, Alexander, "Collective identity formation and the international state," *American Political Science Review* vol. 88, no. 2 (June 1994), pp. 384–96.

20. The classic here is Sikkink, Kathryn, *Ideas and Institutions—Developmentalism in Brazil and Argentina*, Ithaca: Cornell University Press, 1991.

21. See Zehfuss, Maja, *Constructivism in International Relations: The Politics of Reality*, New York: Cambridge University Press, 2002.

22. Cf. Price, Richard, "The Ethics of Constructivism," in Reus-Smit, C. and Snidal, D. (eds), *The Oxford Handbook of International Relations*, New York: Oxford University Press, 2008, p. 320.

23. Flockhart, Trine, "Masters and novices: socialization and social learning through the Nato parliamentary assembly," *International Relations* vol. 18, no. 3 (2004), pp. 361–80.

24. See Katzenstein, Peter and Sil, Rudra, "Analytical eclecticism," in Reus-Smit, C. and Snidal, D. (eds), *The Oxford Handbook of International Relations*, New York: Oxford University Press, 2008, pp. 109–30.

18. INTERSECTING DISASTERS: ESCHEWING MODELS, EMBRACING GEOPOLITICS

1. Elsewhere I have critiqued humanitarian responses that focus mostly on the technical aspects of disasters, without assessing the history, geopolitics and cultural politics of the place in question. I critique the use of "gender" specifically in the context of humanitarianism in refugee camps. See: Hyndman, Jennifer, "Refugee camps as conflict zones: the politics of gender," in *Sites of Violence: Gender in Conflict Zones*, 2004, pp. 193–212.

2. Hyndman, Jennifer, *Dual Disasters: Humanitarian Aid after the 2004 Tsunami*, Sterling, VA: Kumarian Press, 2011.

3. Kelman, Ilan and Gaillard, Jean-Christophe, "Disaster diplomacy in Aceh," *Humanitarian Exchange: Practice and Policy Notes* no. 37 (2007), pp. 37–9.

4. Waizenegger, Arno and Hyndman, Jennifer, "Two solitudes: tsunami and conflict landscapes in Aceh," *Disaster* vol. 34, no. 3 (2010), pp. 787–808.

5. Van Kemenade, Luc, "UN: Somalia drought is worst humanitarian crisis," *Huffington Post*, Associated Press, 10 July 2011, available at http://www.huffing-

tonpost.com/2011/07/10/somalia-drought-worst-humanitarian-crisis-_n_894072.html (last accessed 24 August 2011).

6. Newton, Melanie, "The future of the world in Haiti," University of Toronto, 26 January 2010. http://www.news.utoronto.ca/commentary/the-future-of-the-world-in-haiti.html (last accessed 19 June 2011).

7. Simpson, Edward, "Was there discrimination in the distribution of resources after the earthquake in Gujarat? Imagination, epistemology, and the state in western India," Working Paper, London: London School of Economics and Political Science, 2008. http://eprints.soas.ac.uk/5581/ (last accessed 16 July 2011).

8. John Cosgrave, *Synthesis Report: Expanded summary—joint evaluation of the international response to the Indian Ocean tsunami*, London: Tsunami Evaluation Coalition, 2007. http://www.alnap.org/initiatives/tec.aspx (last accessed 19 February 2010).

9. Ibid.

10. Hyndman, *Dual Disasters*.

11. MacKinnon, Paul, "How to fix a broken city," *The Globe and Mail*, 16 January F1, pp. 6–7.

12. Jeganathan, Pradeep, "South paw one." *Lines*, e-journal vol. 3, no. 4 (2005).

13. See the responses of Dr Eric Steig, an earth scientist at the University of Washington in Seattle, at http://news.nationalgeographic.com/news/2006/05/060524-global-warming.html (last accessed 24 August 2011).

14. Cf. MacKinnon, "How to fix a broken city."

15. *New York Times*, 2009. Sichuan earthquake. http://topics.nytimes.com/topics/news/science/topics/earthquakes/sichuan_province_china/index.html (last accessed 24 August 2011).

16. Bajak, Frank, "Why Chile dodged Haiti-style ruin," *Toronto Star*, 28 February 2010.

17. Cited in Ibid.

18. Nesiah, V., Nanthikesan, S. and Kadirgamar, A., "Post-tsunami reconstruction—new challenges, new directions," *Lines*, e-journal vol. 3, no. 4 (2005), at http://www.lines-magazine.org/tsunami/linestsunamivision.htm (last accessed 10 July 2008).

19. Klein, Naomi, *The Shock Doctrine*, New York: Metropolitan, 2007.

20. See Anderson, Mary B., *Do No Harm*, Boulder, CO: Lynne Rienner, 1999; and Culbert, Vance, "Civil society development vs. the peace dividend: International aid in the Wanni," *Disasters* vol. 29, no. 1 (2005), pp. 38–57.

21. Waizenegger and Hyndman, "Two solitudes," p. 787.

22. F. Kelly, Philip, "The geographies and politics of globalization," *Progress in Human Geography* vol. 23, no. 3 (1999), p. 381.

23. Mountz, Alison and Hyndman, Jennifer, "Feminist approaches to the global intimate," *Women's Studies Quarterly* vol. 34, nos 1–2 (2006), pp. 446–63.

19. HUMANITARIANISM, DEVELOPMENT AND THE LIBERAL PEACE

1. Sen, A., *Development as Freedom*, New York: Knopf, 1999, p. xii.
2. Ibid, p. 11.
3. Ibid, p. 262.
4. Ibid, p. 53.
5. See respectively Duffield, Mark, *Development, Security and Unending War: Governing the World of Peoples*, Cambridge: Polity, 2007, pp. 101–5; and Pupavac, Vanessa, "Witnessing the demise of the developing state: problems for humanitarian advocacy," in Hehir, A. and Robinson, N. (eds), *State-Building: Theory and Practice*, London: Routledge, 2007.
6. Pupavac, "Witnessing the demise of the developing state," p. 96.
7. Sen, *Development as Freedom*, p. 174.
8. Cf. Duffield, *Development, Security and Unending War*.
9. Brown, Gordon, "Our final goal must be to offer a global new deal," *The Guardian* 11 January 2006. Available at http://www.guardian.co.uk/politics/2006/jan/11/debtrelief.internationalaidanddevelopment (last accessed 11 September 2011).
10. See for example, Harrison, Graham, "Post-conditionality politics and administrative reform: reflections on the cases of Uganda and Tanzania," *Development and Change* vol. 32, no. 4 (2001), pp. 634–65; Rowden, Rick and Irama, Jane O., *Rethinking Participation: Questions for Civil Society about the Limits of Participation in PRSPs*, Action Aid USA/Action Aid Uganda Discussion Paper, Washington, DC, April 2004. Available at: http://www.actionaidusa.org/pdf/rethinking_participation_april04.pdf; Gould, Jeremy and Ojanen, Julia, "*Merging in the Circle': The Politics of Tanzania's Poverty Reduction Strategy,*, Institute of Development Studies, University of Helsinki Policy Papers, 2003. Available at: http://www.valt.helsinki.fi/kmi/policy/merging.pdf; Craig, David and Porter, Doug, *Poverty Reduction Strategy Papers: A New Convergence*, draft, later published in *World Development* vol. 31, no. 1 (2003), pp. 53–69. Draft available at: http://www1.worldbank.org/wbiep/decentralization/afrlib/craig.pdf 2002 (all last accessed 10 August 2011); Fraser, A., "Poverty reduction strategy papers: now who calls the shots?," *Review of African Political Economy* no. 104/5 (2005), pp. 317–40; Cammack, Paul, "The mother of all governments: the World Bank's matrix for global governance," in Wilkinson, R. and Hughes, S. (eds), *Global Governance: Critical Perspectives*, London: Routledge, 2002; and Chandler, David, *Empire in Denial: The Politics of State-building*, London: Pluto, 2006, (all last accessed 11 September 2011).
11. Cited in Lord Lugard, *The Dual Mandate in British Tropical Africa*, Abingdon, Oxon: Frank Cass, 1923, p. 26.
12. Ibid, p. 201.

13. Ibid, pp. 203–4.
14. Pye, L. W., *Politics, Personality, and Nation Building: Burma's Search for Identity*, New Haven: Yale University Press, 1962, p. 7.
15. Huntington, Samuel, *Political Order in Changing Societies*, New Haven: Yale University Press, 1968, p. 41.
16. Ibid, p. 4.
17. Ibid, p. 137.
18. Cf. NEF (New Economics Foundation), *Africa—Up in Smoke 2: The second report on Africa and global warming from the Working Group on Climate Change and Development*, London: New Economics Foundation, October 2006, p. 12. Available at: http://www.oxfam.org.uk/what_we_do/issues/climate_change/downloads/africa_up_in_smoke_update2006.pdf (last accessed 10 August 2011).
19. See for example UNFCCC (Secretariat of the United Nations Framework Convention on Climate Change), *United Nations Framework Convention on Climate Change*, 21 March 1994. Available at: http://unfccc.int/resource/docs/convkp/conveng.pdf (last accessed 10 August 2011).
20. DFID, UK Department for International Development, *Eliminating World Poverty: Making Governance Work for the Poor*, London: The Stationery Office, 2006. Available at: http://www.dfid.gov.uk/wp2006/default.asp (last accessed 10 August 2011).
21. McCarthy, Michael and Brown, Colin, "Global warming in Africa: the hottest issue of all," *Independent*, 20 June 2005.
22. Quoted in ibid.
23. In Conway, Gordon, "Climate change and development for Africa: the need to work together," speech by Professor Sir Gordon Conway KCMG FRS, Chief Scientific Adviser, Department for International Development, Addis Ababa, Ethiopia, April 2006. Available at: http://www.dfid.gov.uk/news/files/speeches/climate-change-development.asp (last accessed 10 August 2011).
24. Ibid.
25. Simms, Andrew, *Africa—Up in Smoke? The second report from the Working Group on Climate Change and Development*, London: New Economics Foundation, June 2005, p. 2. Available at: http://www.oxfam.org.uk/what_we_do/issues/climate_change/downloads/africa_up_in_smoke.pdf (last accessed 10 August 2011).
26. Ibid., p. 4.
27. NEF, *Africa—Up in Smoke 2*, p. 3.
28. The problems of climate monitoring capabilities, particularly in Africa, are highlighted in UNFCC (Secretariat of the United Nations Framework Convention on Climate Change), Report of the African Regional Workshop on Adaptation, September 2006. Available at: http://unfccc.int/files/adaptation/adverse_effects_

and_response_measures_art_48/application/pdf/advance_unedited_african_
wkshp_report.pdf., pp. 4–5.

29. NEF, *Africa—Up in Smoke 2*, p. 10.

30. Ibid.

31. In Donnelly, Jack, "Drought imperils Horn of Africa," *Boston Globe*, 20 February 2006.

32. Sen, *Development as Freedom*, p. 174.

20. HUMANITARIAN DIPLOMACY: THE ICRC EXPERIENCE

1. I would like to thank Pierre Gentile and Patrick Vial for comments on the draft. Philippe Gaillard, Rwanda 1994: "In situations like that, it is vital not to let on that you are dead scared…" Talk given on 18 October 1994 at the International Museum of the Red Cross and Red Crescent, Geneva, entitled "Rwanda 1994: La vraie vie est absente" (Arthur Rimbaud). Available at http://www.icrc.org/eng/resources/documents/misc/5xkca5.htm (last accessed 4 April 2011).

2. For an excellent account of the work of the ICRC and MSF teams during the genocide, see Melvern, Linda, *A People Betrayed: The Role of the West in Rwanda's Genocide*, London and New York: Zed Books, 2000.

3. Ibid., p. 156.

4. For a more detailed discussion on the rejection of neutrality by all sides in the Afghan conflict, and the ICRC's efforts to reassert it, see Terry, Fiona, "The International Committee of the Red Cross in Afghanistan: reasserting the neutrality of humanitarian action," *International Review of the Red Cross* vol. 93, no. 881 (2011), pp. 173–88.

5. Bangerter, Olivier, "Talking to armed groups," *Forced Migration Review* vol. 37 (2011), pp. 7–9.

6. See *Professional Standards for Protection Work Carried out by Humanitarian and Human Rights Actors in Armed Conflict and Other Situations of Violence*, Geneva: ICRC, 2009, pp. 41–2. This manual, which was produced in consultation with other organisations working on protection, provides some excellent guidance on all aspects of protection work including conducting interviews with victims and raising issues with the authorities responsible. Available at http://www.icrc.org/eng/resources/documents/publication/p0999.htm (last accessed 14 February 2011).

7. *The Wall Street Journal* published extracts of the report on 7 May 2004, and the entire report on 10 May specifying that the leak did not come from the ICRC.

8. "Confidentiality: key to the ICRC's work but not unconditional," Interview with Dominik Stilhart, ICRC deputy director of operations, 20 September 2010, available at http://www.icrc.org/eng/resources/documents/interview/confidentiality-interview-010608.htm (last accessed 14 February 2011).

9. "Myanmar: ICRC denounces major and repeated violations of international humanitarian law," Geneva: ICRC Press Release no. 07/82, 29 June 2007.

21. ON "OPENING" HUMANITARIAN DIPLOMACY: A DIALECTIC SPACE

1. For a critique of dialectics, and the fragility of their truths (or syntheses), see Adorno, Theodor W., *Negative Dialectics*, trans. by Ashton, E.B., London: Routledge, 1973 (the expression here is from p. 33). For a critique of, and defence of, this method also see Sherman, Howard, "Dialectics as a method," *Critical Sociology* vol. 6, no. 4 (1976), pp. 57–64.

2. The idea of "opening black boxes," originated in the sociology of technology, is now commonplace across most political sociology, representing the need to unpack those social structures that become naturalised, if not invisible, into the everyday practices we face. Cf. Berger and Luckmann, *The Social Construction of Reality*, London: Penguin, 1984; and Winner, Langdon, "Upon opening the black box and finding it empty," *Science, Technology and Human Values* vol. 18, no. 3 (1993), pp. 362–78.

3. This albeit the scholarship on humanitarian spaces and diplomacy has to date overlooked it almost in toto.

4. I rely here on the understanding of "social space" as a human geography of social relations that can be found in Bourdieu, Pierre, "Social space and the genesis of groups," *Theory and Society* vol. 14, no. 4 (1985), pp. 723–44.

5. Albala-Bertrand, Jose Miguel, "What is a complex humanitarian emergency? An analytical essay," Department of Economics Working Paper No. 420, London: Queen Mary, University of London, October 2000, p. 6.

6. Cox, Kevin R., "Spaces of dependence, spaces of engagement and the politics of scale, or: looking for local politics," *Political Geography* vol. 17, no. 1 (1998), pp. 1–23.

7. Cox, "Spaces of dependence," p. 2.

8. Ibid, pp. 3–4.

9. Wiseman, Geoffrey, ""Polylateralism' and new modes of global dialogue," in Jönsson, C. and Langhorne, R. (eds), *Diplomacy*, London: Sage, 2004, pp. 36–57.

10. See for example Pettit, Stephen, Beresford, Anthony, Whiting, Michael and Banomyong, Ruth, "The 2004 Thailand tsunami revisited," in Christopher, M. (ed.), *Humanitarian Logistics*, London: Kogan Page, 2011, pp. 103–20; and Stephenson, Max and Schnitzer, Marcy H., "Interorganizational trust, boundary spanning, and humanitarian relief coordination," *Nonprofit Management and Leadership* vol. 17, no. 2 (2006), pp. 211–33.

11. As for instance argued in Vaux, Tony, "Humanitarian trends and dilemmas,"

Development in Practice vol. 16, no. 3/4 (2006), pp. 240–254, and in *Hoffman, P. and Weiss* T., *Sword & Salve: Confronting New Wars and Humanitarian Crises*, Lanham: Rowman & Littlefield, 2005.

12. See for instance Calhoun, Craig, "The imperative to reduce suffering: charity, progress, and emergencies in the field of humanitarian action," in Barnett, Michael and Weiss, Thomas G. (eds), *Humanitarianism in Question*, Ithaca: Cornell University Press, 2008, pp. 73–97. Hammond, Laura, "The power of holding humanitarianism hostage, and the myth of protective principles," in Barnett, Michael and Weiss Thomas G. (eds), *Humanitarianism in Question*, Ithaca: Cornell University Press, 2008, pp. 172–95.

13. Roberts, Adam, "Humanitarian war: military intervention and human rights," *International Affairs* vol. 69, no. 3 (1993), p. 429.

14. As cited in Rieff, David, "Humanitarianism in crisis," *Foreign Affairs* vol. 81, no. 6 (2002), p. 117.

15. This separation of politics and humanitarianism is also cited as the original take on "humanitarian spaces," as presented in Brauman, Rony, *Humanitaire—le Dilemme*, Paris: Les Editions Textuel, 1996, pp. 43–4.

16. A trend highlighted already by Stockton, Nicholas, "The changing nature of humanitarian crises," in OCHA, *The Humanitarian Decade* vol. 2, New York: United Nations, 2004.

17. On the evolution of "aggregate" dimensions see Dimitrov, Radoslav S., "Inside Copenhagen: the state of climate governance," *Global Environmental Politics* vol. 10, no. 2 (2010), pp. 18–24; and more generally Rosenau, James, *Turbulence in World Politics*, Hemel Hempstead: Harvester Wheatsheaf, 1990, p. 14. I have argued this more at length in Acuto, Michele, "Hybridization and global governance," *The Diplomatic Courier* vol. 5, no. 3 (2011), pp. 14–15.

18. These are for instance the cases, respectively, of the Good Humanitarian Donorship initiative, or of the increasing impact of private contractors not just on security, but more broadly on the delivery of aid. See Harmer, Adele, Cotterrell, Lin and Stoddard, Abby, "From Stockholm to Ottawa: a progress review of the Good Humanitarian Donorship initiative," *HPG Policy Briefs no. 18*, London: Overseas Development Institute, October 2004; as well as Spearin, Christopher, "Private security companies and humanitarians: a corporate solution to securing humanitarian spaces?," *International Peacekeeping* vol. 8, no. 1 (2001), pp. 20–43.

19. Rieff, David, "Charity on the rampage," *Foreign Affairs* vol. 76, no. 1 (1997), p. 137.

20. Der Derian, James, *On Diplomacy: A Genealogy of Western Estrangement*, Oxford: Blackwell, 1987, p. 6.

21. Riordan, Shaun, *The New Diplomacy*, Oxford: Polity, p. 20; Ronald Barston had already raised this point in an early (and indeed forward-looking) version

of a core text of diplomatic studies, in the late 1980s. See Barston, Ronald, *Modern Diplomacy*, London: Longman, 1988, p. 250.

22. Sharp, Paul, "Diplomatic theory of international relations," in *Clingendael Diplomacy Papers no. 20*, The Hague: Netherlands Institute of International Relations, Clingendael, 2009, p. 36.

23. Sharp, Paul, "For diplomacy: representation and the study of international relations," *International Studies Review* vol. 1, no. 1 (1999), p. 36.

24. On a similar approach see Hocking, Brian, "Catalytic diplomacy: beyond 'Newness' and 'Decline'," in Melissen, J. (ed.), *Innovation in Diplomatic Practice*, Basingstoke: Macmillan, 1999, pp. 21–42.

25. See Slim, Hugo, *Marketing Humanitarian Space: Argument and Method in Humanitarian Persuasion*, Geneva: Centre for Humanitarian Dialogue (HDC), p. 7.

26. The social dynamics of "spatialisation" are extensively unpacked in Lefebvre, Henri, *The Production of Space*, Oxford: Blackwell.

27. See Thürer, Daniel, "Dunant's pyramid: thoughts on the humanitarian space," *International Review of the Red Cross* vol. 89, no. 865, 2007, p. 54; as well as Wagner, Johanna Grombach, "An IHL/ICRC perspective on 'humanitarian space'," *Humanitarian Exchange Magazine* no 32 (2005).

28. Thürer, "Dunant's pyramid:," p. 55.

INDEX

INDEX

Bangladesh: 194–5; Rohingya refugee population of, 196–7

al-Banna, Hassan: founder of Muslim Brotherhood, 187

Barnett, Michael: 5; concept of 'empire of humanity', xix

Barre, Siad: removed from power (1991), 115

Baruman, Rony: former President of MSF, 14

al-Bashir, Omar: indicted by ICC (2009), 20, 68, 70, 163, 253

Batay Ouvriye (Workers' Struggle): 102

Belgium: Brussels, xxii

Bellerive, Max: Haitian Prime Minister, 106

Benevolence International: 192

Berkman, Tobias: 160

Bernadotte, Count Folke: meeting with Heinrich Himmler (1945), 201–2, 205; murder of (1948), 209; President of International Red Cross Conference, 209

Biafra: 209

Blair, Tony: foreign policy of, 162–3

Bosnia and Herzegovina: xxii, 161, 203, 207; ethnic Serbian population of, 158

Bosnian War (1992–5): 159; Dayton Peace Accords (1995), 74; Siege of Sarajevo (1992–6), 142; Srebrenica Massacre (1995), 76, 158

Brahimi, Lakhdar: 206; Chairperson of Independent Panel on Safety and Security of United Nations Personnel and Premises, xxiv

Brassard-Boudreau, Cynthia: 81; concept of humanitarian space, 3, 48, 64, 72, 144, 268

Brauman, Rony: concept of humanitarian space, 202–3

Brazil: 158, 252

Bri Kouri Nouvèl Gaye (Noise Travels, News Spreads): 102

British Broadcasting Corporation (BBC): 6; personnel of, 158

Briquemont, Francis: Commanding Officer in UNPROFOR, 161

Brown, Gordon: Chancellor of the Exchequer, 236

de Brune, Marcel: IRC Protection Unit Deputy Director for Programs in Aceh, 92

Buddhism: 157

Burundi: 162

Bush, George W.: administration of, 253

Cable News Network (CNN): 6; coverage of Haiti Earthquake (2010), 99–100

Cambodia: government of, 180

Campbell, David: 57

Canetti, Elias: 169

CARE International Foundation: 103, 125; CARE USA, 68; expulsion from Darfur, 68

Caritas: xxiii

Carter, Kevin: Sudan photograph (1993), 50

Carter Center: 178

Catholic Relief Services (CRS): 89, 103

Celestin, Jude: family of, 102

Center for Constitutional Rights (CCR): contesting of Material Support Statute, 177–9

Central African Republic: 162

Chechnya: 20

Chile: 222; Earthquake (2010), 227

China: 75, 152, 158; Beijing, 208; contribution to official humanitarian assistance, xxii–xxiii; govern-

INDEX

ment of, 227; prison system of, 255; Sichuan Earthquake (2008), 226–7; Sichuan Province, 226–7; Tangshan Earthquake (1976), 226
Christianity: xix; conversion to, 114; missionaries, 189–90
Clinton, Bill: UN Special Envoy, 104
Clinton, Hillary: issued directive to US embassies concerning media guidelines (2010), 100–1; US Secretary of State, 100
Cluster for Camp Coordination and Management (CCCM): 102; Displacement Tracking Matrix (DTM), 102, 107; Water, Sanitation and Hygiene (WASH) cluster, 102, 104
Cohen, Roberta: 149
Cold War: xix, 1, 5, 14, 17–18, 75, 168–9, 182, 225, 233, 265; end of, xx, 169; foreign policy frameworks during, 239–41
Colombia: Conflict (1964–), 20
colonialism: 43, 186, 233–4; British, 236–8; French, 223
Commission for the Disappeared and Victims of Violence (KontraS Aceh): 93–4
complex humanitarian emergencies (CHEs): 6–7
consequentialism: concept of, 138
constructivism: 217, 219
Conway, Prof Sir Gordon: Chief Scientific Adviser to DfID, 242
Cox, Kevin: 261–2
crisis photography: 47, 50–1, 57–8; authority of, 49; circulation of, 53–4; emotional content of, 48–9, 51–3; political nature of, 54–7; techniques used in, 53–6
Cuba: 150, 158

Darfur: 8, 18–19, 40, 66, 69, 88, 109, 154, 171, 174, 251–2, 255, 263; Conflict (2003–), xxv, 47, 61, 66, 163, 251; expulsion of aid workers, 20, 68; Janjaweed militias, 66
Democratic Republic of Congo (DRC): 19–20, 34, 47, 154, 162, 164; military of, 142
Denmark: Jewish population of, 202
Deng, Francis: 153; UN Secretary-General's Special Representative on IDPs, 149
development: 241; Africa, 241–3; concepts of, 231–2; discourse periods of, 234–5; economic, 239, 241; humanitarian ideal of, 232, 235, 244–5; policies for, 232; state-building, 233–4, 240; Western frameworks of, 235–6
diplomacy: 3, 75, 82, 118, 130, 149, 152–3, 182, 264–5, 268–9; coordination, 203; disaster, 222; humanitarian, 4, 8–9, 148, 155, 202–9, 247–8, 259–61, 263, 268, 270; use of R2P in, 154–5
Disaster Accountability Project: 103
Disasters Emergency Committee (DEC): 87; donor restriction guidelines, 89
DuBois, Marc: 164
Dunant, Henri: 5
Dunn, Elizabeth: 144
DynCorp International Inc.: 32; DI Development, 32

East Timor (Timor-Leste): 95, 162
Economic Community of West African States (ECOWAS): members of, 150
Egypt: 158, 187
Einstein, Albert: 169
Emergency Committee for Humanitarian Response: xxii

323

INDEX

Holmes, John: UN Under-Secretary-General for Humanitarian Affairs, 152

Holt, Victoria K.: 160

Hooper, Ed: Ugandan portrait (1986), 54–7

Hubert, Don: 81; concept of humanitarian space, 3, 48, 64, 72, 144, 268

Huffington Post: coverage of Haiti Earthquake (2010), 101

Human Rights Watch: 82

Humanitarian Accountability Partnership (HAC): 30

humanitarian actors: 7, 9, 14, 32–3, 38, 63–5, 77, 80, 109, 113, 141–2, 145, 218; analysis of fault lines by, 227–8; concept of, 139–40; legitimacy narratives, 33–4; local, 96; local perceptions of, 28–9, 42–3; non-combatants, 140, 142–3; non-state, 34; role of, 16

humanitarian assistance politics: criminalisation, 179–84; defiance of prohibition, 180–1; legitimacy, 183; political solidarity, 178–9; risks of co-opting, 182–3

humanitarian diplomacy: 4–5, 8–9, 203–4, 247–8, 260, 264–5, 268–9; concept of, 202, 263–4; coordination diplomacy, 203; development of, 208–9

humanitarian operations: 21, 43; budgets for, 19–20; impact of emotion on, 53; management practices used in, 42

humanitarian principles: 33, 41; ill-defined, 38

humanitarian spaces: 3, 8–9, 25, 28, 31, 99, 116, 217, 219–20, 250, 260, 262, 266; concepts of, 3, 21, 23–4, 48, 62, 64–5, 72, 95, 142,

186, 202–3, 215, 221, 268–9; influence of disaster on, 109; narratives of, 37; opening of, 259; politicisation of, 214; rhetoric of, 18–19; role of R2P in, 148; 'shrinking' of, 145; uses of concept, 13–15

humanitarian system: 24–5, 31–2, 266–7; humanitarian establishment, 26–7

humanitarianism: xxv–xxvi, 1–2, 7, 29, 39–40, 44–5, 53, 62–3, 79, 81, 137, 145, 204, 260, 264, 266–8; concept of, 5, 44, 138, 142–4; contemporary, 5–6; ethics of, 9; human geography of, 4, 260; ideal of development, 232, 235, 244–5; Islamic, 186, 188–9, 196–7; opposition to, 218; principled, 37; relationship with IRT, 211–12, 219

Huntington, Samuel: *Political Order in Changing Societies* (1968), 239–40

Hussein, Saddam: regime of, 162

India: 148; contribution to official humanitarian assistance, xxii–xxiii; Gujarat Earthquake (2001), 224

Indian Ocean Earthquake and Tsunami (2004): 3, 83, 92–3, 95, 222, 225, 261; humanitarian aid response to, xxii, 33, 84, 87–8, 90, 93, 95–6; photography depicting, 52; socio-political effect of, 83–4, 89, 92, 94–5, 97, 222, 228–9

Indonesia: 222; Aceh, 8, 20, 83–5, 87–90, 92–4, 96–7, 222, 224, 229, 262–3; Aceh Reintegration Agency (BRA), 94; Banda Aceh, 89; government of (GoI), 83, 85, 87, 90, 92–6; IDPs in 83, 85; Indonesian National Armed Forces (TNI), 90; Jakarta, 84, 86, 95; Law on Governing Aceh (LoGA) (2006),

325

INDEX

Kouchner, Bernard: 152; French Foreign Minister, 151, 163
Kundera, Milan: 169
Kurdistan Workers' Party (PKK): 178–9
Kurds: xxi; territory inhabited by, 162, 165
Kuwait:ʼ186, 188

Lebanon: 128
Lehi: members of, 209
Lemkin, Raphael: xxi
liberalism: 215–16, 219, 238; classical, 215; contemporary, 215
Liberation Tigers of Tamil Eelam (LTTE): 40, 141, 143, 178–9; funding of, 180; territory held by, 228
Liberia: 162
Libya: 255, 266; Benghazi, 250; Civil War (2011), xxi, xxvii, 79, 250; Tripoli, 250
Luciates, John Lewis: 57
Luck, Edward: 153; UN Special Adviser to the Secretary-General on R2P, 152
Lugard, Lord: 234, 240; concept of 'Dual Mandate', 234; strategy of indirect rule, 237–8

Malawi: 168, 174
Malkki, Lisa: 56
Marxism: 217
Médecins Sans Frontières (MSF): xxvi, 15, 34, 41, 100, 180, 186, 267; activity in Aceh, 93; Activity Report (2000–1), 164; expenditures of, xxiii; funding of, 96; personnel of, 14, 164; withdrawal from Afghanistan (2004), xxiv; withdrawal from Zaire refugee camps (1994), 208

mental health delivery: 168–70, 172–3, 175–6; counselling, 172–3; Eye Movement Desensitization and Reprocessing (EMDR) therapy, 173; Post Traumatic Stress Disorder (PTSD) models, 168, 174; scientific knowledge systems, 170; traditional knowledge systems, 170
Mercy Corps: expulsion from Darfur, 68
Milošević, Slobodan: 74
Minear, Larry: *Humanitarian Diplomacy*, 3
Morgentheau, Hans: 'Six Principles of Political Realism' (1948), 213–14
Morris, Eric: Head of UNORC, 92
Mother Teresa Society: 77; food distribution shelters operated by, 261
mujahedeen: 182, 191; territory controlled by, 181
Muhammad, Prophet: 195
Muslim Aid: 186, 193, 195; aims of, 194; budget of, 192–3; establishment of, 190; microfinance projects of, 195–6; offices of, 193–4
Muslim Brotherhood: 188; founding of (1928), 187
Muslim World League: 188
Myanmar (Burma): 34, 148, 151–2, 154, 203, 254; borders of, 180; Civil War (1948–), 20; Cyclone Nargis (2008), 79, 151–2, 163, 203, 226, 254–5; government of, 151; State Peace and Devlopment Council (SDPC), 226

Nasser, Gamal Abdul: 187
National Union for the Total Independence of Angola (UNITA): 181
nationalism: Arabic, 187
Nepal: 42
Netherlands: 84

INDEX

al-Qaradawi, Yusuf: 191; founder of IICO, 190

Radio Mille Collines: broadcasts during Rwandan Genocide (1994), 248

realism: 219; classical, 213; concept of, 213–15; structural, 213

Reflection and Action Force for the Housing Cause (FRAKKA): 102

Republic of Ireland: 233, 245

responsibility to protect (R2P): xxi, xxvi, 69, 152–3, 263–4; application of, 151–5; association with sovereignty as responsibility, 150; concept of, 147; influence of, 64; origins of, 64; role in humanitarian space, 148; support for, 163; weak response, 70

Reus-Smit, Christian: 217; concept of IRT, 212–13

Reuters: AlertNet, 101

Revolutionary United Front (RUF): 181

Roberts, Adam: 17

Roberts Jr., John G.: 179

Roberston QC, Geoffrey: former president of SCSL, 161

Rubenstein, Jennifer: 144

Rugova, Ibrahim: 74

Russian Federation: 75, 148, 152, 255

Rwanda: 162; Genocide (1994), 3, 34, 37, 159, 164, 171, 247–8, 257, 264; Kigali, 247; Tutsi population of, 248, 257

Rwandan Armed Force: 248

Rwandan Patriotic Front: 248

Ryacudu, Ryamizard: Chief of Staff of TNI, 90

Salafism: 117

Saltman, Nicola: 242

Saudi Arabia: 186; contribution to official humanitarian assistance, xxii–xxiii; government of, 190

Sawers, John: British Ambassador to UN, 152

Save the Children: expansion of operations, 20; presence in Aceh, 88–9

Schwartz, Timothy: Haitian IDP report (2011), 105, 107, 109

Second World War (1939–45): xxi, 17, 63, 77, 201–2, 208–9; concentration camps, 202; Holocaust, 207

Sen, Amartya: Nobel Prize for Economic Science recipient (1998), 231

Serbia: Belgrade, 75; military of, 76

al-Shabaab: 114, 117, 124–9, 133; affiliates of, 118; decline in power, 119; designated as terrorist organization by US government (2008), 118; Emergency Relief Committee, 120; expulsion of aid agencies, 122, 125; funding to, 120; members of, 125, 134; Office for the Supervising Foreign Agencies, 126; partnership with Somali Red Crescent, 121; *shura*, 120; territory controlled by, 112, 124, 127, 129–30

Shapiro, Michael: concept of 'personal code', 54

Sharif, Sheikh: Somali TFG President, 119, 184

Sierra Leone: 26, 162, 181

Small Arms Survey: 107

Smith, Hazel: *Humanitarian Diplomacy*, 3

Snidal, Duncan: 217; concept of IRT, 212–13

Somali Red Crescent: 134; partnership with al-Shabaab, 121

Somalia: 8, 16, 18–19, 37, 42,

INDEX

INDEX

Ut, Nick: Kim Phuc photograph (1972), 49–50
utilitarianism: concept of, 138

Voluntary Organisations in Cooperation in Emergencies: xxii
Vieira de Mello, Sergio: death of (2010), xxiv
Vietnam War (1955–75): photography of, 49–50; PTSD diagnoses of veterans following, 171
violent conflict: international responses to, 62

de Waal, Alex: 1–2
Waizenegger, Arno: 228–9
Wall, Imogen: 95
Wallenberg, Raoul: 202
Waltz, Kenneth: 213
War on Terror: 20, 191
Washington Consensus: concept of, 235

Weiss, Thomas: concept of humanitarian space, 144–5
Wendt, Alexander: 217
WikiLeaks: 100, 253
Wirajuda, Hassan: Indonesian Foreign Minister, 152
Wohlforth, William C.: concept of realism, 213
World Bank: xxii; Kecamatan Development Program (KDP), 94
World Vision: xxiii, 103
World Wide Fund for Nature: 242

Yudhoyono, Susilo Bambang: 93
Yugoslavia: 82, 162; Yugoslav People's Army (JNA), 74

Zaire: 162, 181, 208
Zelizer, Barbie: 49
Zimbabwe: 255
Zionism: 209